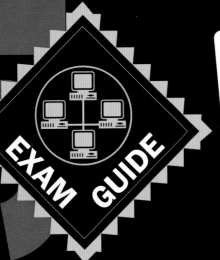

Microsoft®
Windows NT® 4.0
Workstation
Chapter Notes

SECOND EDITION

Quick review of the most important
concepts and terms from the *Exam Guide*

que®

Emmett Dulaney, MCSE

Chapter 2

Key NT 4.0 Features

Microsoft Windows NT is a 32-bit operating system that is designed for power computer users, such as software developers, CAD programmers, and design engineers.

Multiple Platform Support

Microsoft Windows NT is engineered to run on several hardware platforms.

The Hardware Abstraction Layer, or HAL, component of the NT architecture isolates platform-specific information for the operating system.

Preemptive Multitasking

All processes in NT are given at least one thread of operation.

Thread: a piece of code relating to a process.

NT can treat each thread of a process independently of the others, providing a greater degree of control over the overall performance of the system.

Each thread also is given a processing priority based on its function. For example, an operating system process, such as memory allocation, receives a higher priority for its threads than a file-save process.

Expanded Processing Support

Symmetric multiprocessing enables the NT operating system to load-balance process threads across all available processors in the computer, as opposed to asymmetric multiprocessing, in which the operating system takes control of one processor and directs application threads to other available processors.

Expanded Memory Support

Windows NT supports computers with up to 4 gigabytes of RAM and theoretic file or partition sizes of up to 16 exabytes.

Expanded File System Support

Windows NT provides support for the following:

- MS-DOS FAT
- NTFS

NTFS: New Technology File System

Version 4.0 no longer provides support for HPFS.

Enhanced Security

In addition to this mandatory logon, NT offers share-level resource control, security auditing functions, and file- and directory-level permissions (in NTFS partitions).

Network and Communications Support

The NetBEUI, NWLINK (IPX/SPX), TCP/IP, AppleTalk, and DLC protocols are all supported and included.

RAS clients can share folders and printers.

Choosing Windows NT Workstation or Server

Choosing between NT Workstation and NT Server really comes down to the features specific to each product and the type of network model that will be implemented.

Microsoft Windows NT Workstation

NT Workstation offers the following specific characteristics:

- Workstation has unlimited outbound peer-to-peer connections.
- It has 10 inbound client connections for resource access.
- It can be either a RAS client or server, but it supports only one remote dial-in session.
- The retail installation supports two processors for symmetric multiprocessing.
- It acts as an import server for Directory Replication Services.

Microsoft Windows NT Server

NT Server offers the following capabilities:

- NT Server allows as many inbound connections to resources as there are valid client licenses (virtually unlimited).

- It supports as many as 256 remote dial-in RAS sessions.

- The retail installation supports as many as four processors for symmetric multiprocessing.

- It provides a full set of services for application and network support, such as the following:

    - Services for Macintosh that enable client support for Macintosh computers.

    - Gateway Service for NetWare that enables NT clients to access Novell NetWare file and print resources.

    - Directory Replication Service for copying of directory structures and files from a source NT Server computer to a target NT Server or Workstation computer.

- It provides full integration into the Microsoft BackOffice suite, including System Management Server, SNA Server, SQL Server, and Microsoft Exchange Server.

Features and Functions in Windows NT 4.0

- Windows 95-like user interface.
- Windows Explorer.
- Hardware profiles.
- Enhanced dial-up networking support.
- NDS-aware client services for Novell NetWare 4.x.
- Integrated Windows Messaging engine.
- Internet Explorer 2.0—Although Internet Explorer 5.0 is available, version 2.0 ships with NT 4.0 and therefore is the version with which you should be familiar when prepping

for the test. Internet Explorer requires that the TCP/IP protocol be installed and a connection made to the Internet.

- Web services.

Though the Windows Explorer replaces the File Manager Utility by default, the File Manager is still available and can be launched.

Plug and Play is a feature of Windows 95 and Windows 98 that is much appreciated. Note that, although the Plug and Play service has been included with Windows NT 4.0, "hot" Plug and Play (the capability for the operating system to recognize a configuration change on-the-fly and implement it) will not be fully supported until the next major release of Windows NT. Windows NT 4.0 does, however, recognize some hardware changes when it restarts.

As of this writing, Internet Explorer 5.0 has been released. It was not available at the time the exam was written, and the exam has not been updated for 5.0. Internet Explorer 2.0 was included with NT 4.0, and you are expected to be familiar with this version for the certification exam.

Internet Explorer requires that the TCP/IP protocol be installed and a connection made to the Internet.

Distinguishing a Workgroup from a Domain

Two distinct types of networking are supported by Windows NT:

- Workgroup
- Domain

Workgroup Model

The workgroup model of networking is more commonly referred to as the peer-to-peer model.

Computers using Windows NT, Windows 95, and Windows for Workgroups can participate in a workgroup network model.

Windows 95 can provide user-level network resource security by using an NT (Server or Workstation) or Novell Server. However, providing such security requires that one or the other be present on the network.

The workgroup model works well with smaller networks where the number of users requiring access to workgroup resources is small—between 10 and 20 computers/users.

Domain Model

Enterprise: a network of servers and workstations. Also known as a domain.

The domain model of networking, also known as the enterprise model, was introduced by Microsoft as a response to the management challenges presented by the growing workgroup model.

Resource access is provided by permitting access to users and groups that are members of the domain, and thus appear in the domain's account database.

Organizing an Enterprise Network

When you're planning a large wide area network for an organization—hereafter referred to as the enterprise—Microsoft advocates implementing a structure that answers the following challenges:

- A single network logon account for the user, regardless of the user's location or domain affiliation
- Centralized account administration
- Easy user access to network resources, regardless of the location of the user or the resource in the enterprise
- Network resource administration focused in the hands of the resource owner or administrator
- Synchronization of account and security information across the enterprise

Chapter 3

Preparing to Install

Windows NT Workstation 4.0 System Requirements:

Component	Description
CPU	32-bit Intel 486/33 or higher
Disk	120MB free disk space
Memory	12MB RAM minimum
Video	VGA resolution or higher
Drives	CD-ROM drive and 3.5-inch disk drive if installing locally
Network	One or more supported adapter cards if member of a network and/or if installing over the network
File System	A FAT or NTFS partition

Choosing NT or 95

- Windows NT Workstation 4.0 has higher hardware requirements than Windows 95.
- Windows 95 can be installed on a computer with a minimum 386DX processor, 4MB of memory (although having 8MB is recommended), a VGA or higher monitor, and 35 to 40MB of disk space.
- Windows NT Workstation 4.0 requires a minimum 486/33 processor, 12MB of memory (16MB recommended), 120MB or more of disk space, and a CD-ROM drive or some other access to source files.
- Windows NT Workstation 4.0 offers a greater number of security options, multiple platform support, symmetric multiprocessing, and full 32-bit processing. Windows 95 does not provide these features but does offer a wider scope of device driver support, and it fully supports Plug and Play (PnP).

NT Setup Basics

The setup process is essentially the same for Intel-based and RISC-based computers.

Although a computer name can contain spaces, using spaces is not recommended. Passwords in Windows NT are case sensitive.

If you choose not to create an Emergency Repair Disk during installation, you can always create one later using the utility RDISK.EXE.

Beginning Setup

The first phase of the setup process, by default, requires the creation of three startup disks.

The Windows NT Setup executable on the Intel platform is named WINNT.EXE.

If you already have a copy of Windows NT installed on the computer and intend to upgrade to Windows NT 4.0 or install a new copy of Windows NT 4.0, you can use an alternative executable called WINNT32.EXE.

WINNT.EXE and WINNT32.EXE Option Switches:

/B	/O
/OX	/S
/U	/T
/I	/C
/F	/R
/RX	

The DOS/text mode phase of setup has six basic events:

- A menu of startup options
- Detection and configuration of storage devices such as SCSI drives
- Initial hardware verification
- Choice of the installation disk partition
- Choice of file system for the installation partition
- Installation directory name

On all setup screens, you can access a useful help dialog box by pressing F1. You can exit setup at any time by pressing F3.

Formatting the Partition

- NTFS supports Windows NT file and directory permissions security and access auditing; FAT supports only the Read Only, System, Hidden, and Archive attributes.
- NTFS supports transaction tracking and sector sparing for data recovery; FAT does not.
- NTFS supports partition sizes of up to 16EB and file sizes of 4 to 64GB depending on cluster sizes; FAT supports a maximum file size of 4GB and is inefficient for partition sizes greater than 400MB.
- NTFS provides file and directory compression implemented as a property; FAT does not.
- NTFS is recognized by Windows NT only on that computer; FAT is recognized by NTFS, MS-DOS, or OS/2.

Dual-Booting NT and OS/2

Windows NT and OS/2 can coexist on the same computer if you jump through some hoops first (using OS/2 Boot Manager). Otherwise, NT will disable the OS/2 partition.

Because Windows NT 4.0 no longer supports HPFS, if you intend to keep OS/2 on HPFS, you must install Windows NT in another partition.

Dual-Booting Workstation and Server

You may choose to have both Windows NT Workstation 4.0 and Server installed on your computer. Press N for "New Directory" as offered on the installation screen, and install this version of Windows NT in a different directory.

Installation Directory

If you choose to upgrade Windows, setup migrates most INI settings, such as those contained in the win.ini, system.ini, and application .ini files from the previous installation over to Windows NT 4.0.

You cannot install Windows NT Workstation 4.0 in the same directory as Windows 95.

Installing NT Networking

If you chose Wired to the Network and do not have a card installed in the machine, you can choose the MS Loopback Adapter to enable all network functionality within the machine without the card.

Unattended Setup

The five basic steps involved in implementing an unattended setup of Windows NT Workstation 4.0 are as follows:

- Create a distribution server by placing the Windows NT Workstation 4.0 installation files for the appropriate computer platform in a shared directory on a file server.
- Create an answer file that supplies information common to all the computers being installed.
- Create a uniqueness data file that supplies information specific to each computer's installation.
- Provide access to the installation files on the distribution server for the computers that are being installed.
- Run Windows NT setup, referencing the location of the setup files, answer files, and uniqueness data files.

SYSDIFF

You can use the SYSDIFF utility to automate the installation of applications as well as configure Windows NT. SYSDIFF must be run with the /snap mode to create a snapshot first.

After the applications are installed and the configuration changed, you use the /diff mode to create a differences file from the snapshot that can be applied to multiple computers (via the /apply mode).

NT Boot Process

The Windows NT boot process has two primary phases: Boot and Load.

Along with NTLDR, the following boot files are read during the Boot Phase:

BOOT.INI	NTDETECT.COM
NTOSKRNL.EXE	NTBOOTDD.SYS
NTOSKRNL.EXE	HAL.DLL

BOOT.INI

The BOOT.INI file is a read-only, system, ASCII text file created by Windows NT during installation.

It is stored in the root directory of the primary boot partition of the computer and contains the information that Windows NT uses to display the boot menu when the computer is booted using ARC paths.

ARC path: Advanced RISC Computer

Boot Menu

Each ARC path has a text menu selection associated with it enclosed in quotation marks.

Windows NT provides a variety of switches that can be added to these or additional Windows NT boot entries to modify the way Windows NT boots.

Control Sets and the Last Known Good Option

The HKEY_LOCAL_MACHINE\System hive contains several control set subkeys. Windows NT uses them to boot the system, keep track of configuration changes, and provide an audit trail of failed boot attempts.

In general, the four control sets are as follows:

- Clone
- ControlSet001
- ControlSet002
- CurrentControlSet

Troubleshooting the Boot Process

The most common errors that you are likely to encounter during the boot process are the result of corrupt or missing boot files.

The ARC path indicated in the Default parameter in the Boot Loader section of the BOOT.INI must match an ARC path for a parameter under the Operating Systems section. If it does not, the menu displays a phantom selection option called "NT (default)," which may result in the same error message described for a missing BOOT.INI file.

Emergency Repair Disk

To use the Emergency Repair Disk, you must first boot the computer using the Windows NT Startup disk set.

If you do not have a set of startup disks but have access to the original installation files, you can create a set by typing the command **WINNT /OX**. Be sure to have three disks available.

The files on the Emergency Repair Disk overwrite the files in the Registry.

NT Boot Disk

When you format a diskette under Windows NT, Windows NT creates a boot sector on that disk that references NTLDR. Simply copy the five boot files to this disk, and you have a Windows NT boot disk.

You can format a disk from My Computer. To do so, right-click the A: Drive icon, and select Format. Make the appropriate selections and choose OK.

Uninstalling NT

The steps required to remove Windows NT Workstation 4.0 from your computer depend on the file system your computer uses when booting.

Upgrading to NT Workstation

When you're upgrading from earlier versions of Windows NT Workstation, setup migrates all account information, network settings, and most other Registry settings.

Upgrading to Windows 95

The Windows NT Workstation 4.0 setup program does not allow you to upgrade over Windows 95.

Upgrading to Windows 3.1 and Windows for Workgroups

NT automatically migrates existing program groups other than those that have a Windows NT counterpart, such as Main, Accessories, and Games.

The program groups appear under Programs on the Start menu.

Chapter 4

Logging On

After you press Ctrl+Alt+Del, Windows NT displays the Logon Information dialog box.

After the Windows NT Security Subsystem authenticates your account, the Windows NT 4.0 desktop appears.

Windows NT Security Dialog Box

From the Windows NT Security dialog box, you can shut down the system, log off, change your password, access the Task Manager, and lock the workstation.

NT 4.0 Desktop

The desktop consists of two basic elements: objects and the taskbar.

Objects

Objects provide you with a unified way of dealing with icons on the screen.

Objects include files, folders, programs, printers, and modems.

All objects have properties, settings, and parameters that you can access by right-clicking.

Taskbar

The Windows NT taskbar appears, by default, on the bottom of the desktop screen.

It consists of the Start button at the far left and the clock at the far right.

Starting Programs

All programs can be accessed through the Start menu on the taskbar.

Programs

Choosing Programs from the Start menu displays a list of programs and program folders including Accessories, the Startup folder, the Command Prompt, and the Windows NT Explorer.

Any new program groups created as a result of installing an application or migrating from previous Windows versions are also displayed here.

Documents

Choosing Documents from the Start menu displays the last 15 documents that were opened.

Settings

Settings offers access to configuration utilities through Control Panel and Printers, as well as another way to change the properties of the taskbar.

Find

Using the Find utility, you can search the computer for files and folders, as well as the network for shared computers.

Help

Windows NT 4.0 Help provides quick interface information.

Run

Selecting Run displays a box in which you can enter the path and name of the program you want to execute.

Shut Down

Shut Down provides the appropriate way to shut down the computer or log off.

Shortcuts

A shortcut is a pointer to the file.

My Computer

Selecting the My Computer icon displays all resources that are available on your computer.

Network Neighborhood

The Network Neighborhood icon represents access to the network in which your computer participates.

Recycle Bin

When a file is deleted through the interface, it is placed in the Recycle Bin, where it can be recovered.

My Briefcase

My Briefcase is a utility designed primarily for laptop use.

It allows you to take copies of files with you on the laptop or on disk and work on them in another location or while on the road.

When you return to your office computer or dock your laptop, My Briefcase can synchronize the files you worked on while you were away with the files located on the desktop by overwriting the original files with the changes you made to the copies. You must synchronize the Briefcase before you leave also.

Other Icons

Depending on the additional Windows NT 4.0 services or programs that you install, additional icons may be displayed on the desktop.

NT 4.0 Explorer

Windows NT Explorer is the primary navigation tool for your system.

Open Window

Windows Explorer lets you drill down through drives, folders, and so on.

The left pane of the window displays the object's folders and files; the right pane displays the contents of the folder.

Chapter 5

Desktop Environment

Windows NT Workstation 4.0 offers several ways to customize your desktop environment, chiefly through Display Properties and the Control Panel.

Display Properties

access the Display Properties sheet by right-clicking anywhere on the desktop background and then choosing Properties.

Exploring Control Panel

Control Panel offers a variety of applets that modify your system configuration:

- Accessibility Options
- Network
- Add\Remove Programs
- PC Card
- DOS Console
- Ports
- Printers
- Regional Settings
- Date\Time
- SCSI Adapters
- Devices
- Server
- Display
- Services
- Fonts
- Sounds
- Internet
- System
- Keyboard
- Tape Devices
- Modems
- Telephony
- Mouse
- UPS
- Multimedia

Administrative Tools

The Administrative Tools group contains utilities that are specific to your installation of either Windows NT Workstation 4.0 or Windows NT Server 4.0.

These seven tools are installed on Windows NT Workstation 4.0:

- Backup
- Disk Administrator
- Event Viewer
- Performance Monitor
- Remote Access Administrator
- User Manager
- Windows NT Diagnostics

Hardware Profiles

Hardware profiles offer a way for you to create and maintain different hardware configurations—including which services and devices are initialized—for different computing scenarios.

The most common use for hardware profiles is with laptop computers that are sometimes placed in a docking station.

Creating Profiles

To create a hardware profile, you must first access the System Properties dialog box.

The Services and Devices applets in Control Panel allow you to identify which services and devices to enable and disable for each profile.

NT Registry

The Registry is central to the operation of Windows NT 4.0. User environment settings are stored here. Driver information, services, hardware profile information, security objects and their permissions, and account information are all stored in the Registry.

A good rule of thumb for modifying the Registry: If a utility can do the modification, use the utility!

Registry Editor

the Registry by starting the Registry Editor utility, and you can access this utility in several ways:

- Open the Windows Explorer and select the SYSTEM32 folder under the Windows NT system folder (usually called WINNT or WINNT40). Double-click the file REGEDT32.EXE.
- Choose Run from the Start menu, and type **REGEDT32.EXE**. Then click OK.

Windows NT Workstation 4.0 includes two Registry editors: REGEDT32.EXE and REGEDIT.EXE. The former is the original editor that has been with Windows NT since version 3.1. The latter is a Windows 95 tool new to NT with version 4.0. REGEDT32 can show all five value types (REGEDIT shows only three) and includes features for security, auditing, and so on (none of which are available with REGEDIT).

The subtrees/hives are as follows:

- HKEY_LOCAL_MACHINE
- HKEY_CURRENT_CONFIG
- HKEY_USERS
- HKEY_CURRENT_USER
- HKEY_CLASSES_ROOT

By default, only users with Administrator access can make modifications to the Registry. Other users can only view the information contained there.

Beneath HKEY_LOCAL_MACHINE are five keys:

- HARDWARE
- SOFTWARE
- SYSTEM
- SAM
- SECURITY

The HARDWARE key is built during the startup process. This information is not written down anywhere or stored permanently on the system. Instead, Windows NT "detects" this information each time it boots. Thus, it is referred to as a "volatile" hive or key because it is created during the boot process, can change as hardware changes, and is not written to disk.

All the entries you see under the SID subkey represent changes that can be made to the user's environment, primarily through Control Panel. If the user changes his or her color scheme, cursor pointers, wallpaper, and so on, the values can be found in the respective keys here. If you need to modify a user's entries, perhaps remotely, you can do so here as well. The values stored here correspond to an actual file like the HKEY_LOCAL_MACHINE hives do. Windows NT creates a subfolder in WINNT40/Profile for each user who logs on and changes his or her profile. This subfolder contains two files that correspond to the Registry entries for that user's profile: NTUSER.DAT.LOG and NTUSER.DAT.

Windows 95 and Windows 98 operating systems employ user profiles as well. They serve the same purpose and function as NTUSER.DAT but are saved as USER.DAT on those operating systems.

Configuring with the Registry

Rule of thumb: If the Registry does not display parameter values when you select a subkey, you can assume that Windows NT is using the defaults for that subkey, realizing that a default can be to have no values loaded at all.

Finding Subkey Names in the Registry

You can use the Registry's FIND KEY function to look up entries.

These five types of values appear in Registry:

- REG_SZ
- REG_DWORD
- REG_BINARY
- REG_EXPAND_SZ
- REG_MULTI_SZ

Rule of thumb: If you're making a user environment change, the user has to log off and log back on before the change takes effect. If you're making a system change, you have to shut down and restart the computer before the change takes effect.

Parameter names are not case sensitive. However, because they can be quite lengthy, Microsoft uses proper case when displaying these values to make them easier to read.

System Policy Editor

A system policy can be established by workstation name, thus regulating a user's environment and access by workstation.

The workstation and user policies are saved in a file called NTCONFIG.POL and stored in the WINNT40\SYSTEM32\REPL\IMPORT\ SCRIPTS subdirectory of each domain controller—also known by the share name NETLOGON.

Windows 95 and Windows 98 operating systems employ system policies as well. They serve the same purpose and function as NTCONFIG.POL but must be named CONFIG.POL for those operating systems.

The Registry Editor provides a facility for accessing the computer's Registry remotely. You must have an Administrator account on your computer that matches one on the other machine.

Chapter 6

User and Group Accounts

The user account is the first and foremost security object for access to local and network resources.

SID: Each user and group account that is created is unique to Windows NT and as such has a unique security identifier associated with it.

If you delete the user account and re-create it using exactly the same information, Windows NT will create a new SID for that user, and all security access and permissions will have to be reestablished.

The account information is stored in the Security Accounts Manager database (SAM), part of the Windows NT 4.0 Registry.

A local account, in general, has to have access only to resources on the local workstation. A network or global account has access as provided to network resources such as shared printers, files, and folders.

Default User Accounts

When you first install Windows NT Workstation 4.0, two default accounts are created for you: Administrator and Guest.

Neither of these accounts can be deleted.

Default Group Accounts

When you first install Windows NT Workstation 4.0, six default groups are created:

- Administrators
- Power Users
- Users
- Guests
- Backup Operators
- Replicator

These groups are considered local groups.

Windows NT also creates and manages four groups, called internal or system groups, to "place" a user for accessing resources. These groups are as follows:

- Everyone
- Interactive
- Network
- Creator Owner

Group Management in Domains

Two types of group accounts can be created in a domain: local and global groups.

The Power Users group is not created for a domain controller.

Planning for New User Accounts

You should consider these four basic areas before creating new accounts:

- Account naming conventions
- How to deal with passwords
- Group membership
- Profile information

Naming Conventions

Usernames must be unique both locally and to the enterprise.

Usernames are not case sensitive and can contain up to 20 characters, including spaces, except the following:

"" / \ { } : ; | = , + * ? < >

Passwords

When you create a new user account, you have three password-related options to determine:

- User Must Change Password at Next Logon
- User Cannot Change Password
- Password Never Expires

It is important to set company policy and educate the users in the importance of protecting the integrity of their accounts by using unique and "unguessable" passwords. Among the most common choices for passwords are children's names, pets' names, favorite sports teams, or team members. Your users should try to avoid the obvious associations when choosing passwords.

Passwords are case sensitive and can be up to 14 characters in length.

Group Membership

The easiest way to manage large numbers of users is to group them together logically, functionally, and departmentally.

User Profile Information

In a larger workgroup or enterprise, the user profile might be a file of environment settings stored on a specific computer and downloaded to whatever Windows NT-based computer the user is logging in from.

The User Manager

User and group accounts are created and managed through an administrative tool called the User Manager.

On a domain controller, the User Manager utility is called the User Manager for Domains.

New Local Groups

Before you create a group, select all the usernames you want in the group from the User Manager Username screen by Ctrl-clicking the additional accounts. Then create the group. The Members list box displays any user account that has been highlighted before the group was created.

Managing Accounts

If you choose to delete an account, remember that the account's SID is also deleted, and all resource access and user rights are lost. This means that if you re-create the account even exactly as it was before, the SAM database generates a new SID for the account, and you have to reestablish resource access and user rights for that account.

You cannot delete built-in user or group accounts.

When you copy a user account, the following settings are maintained:

- Description
- Password options that have been checked off
- Group membership
- Profile information

Policies, System Rights, and Auditing

Account policy information includes password-specific information, such as password age and minimum length, and account lockout options.

User rights represent the functional rights that a user acquires for a given workstation when logging in.

Auditing for file and directory access, print access, and so forth is accomplished by specifying the users or groups whose access you want to audit and is done at the file, directory, and print level.

Creating and Managing User Profiles

The user profile in Windows NT 4.0 is the user's working environment.

Home Directory

The home directory simply represents a place where the user can routinely save data files.

UNC: Universal Naming Convention—a method of specifying the path to a resource. The UNC identifies the name of the server that contains a share with the syntax *servername\sharename*.

Logon Scripts

Logon scripts are files that contain a set of network commands that need to be executed in a particular order.

The name of the logon script is arbitrary.

User Profiles

The user profile itself represents the user's environment settings, such as screen colors, wallpaper, persistent network and printer connections, mouse settings and cursors, shortcuts, personal groups, and Startup programs.

Settings are normally saved as part of the Windows NT Registry (NTUSER.DAT) and loaded when the user logs on to the system.

Server-Based User Profiles

Windows NT Workstation and Server 4.0 computers support two types of server-based profiles:

- Roaming user
- Mandatory user

The user can change environment settings while in a particular session, but those settings are not saved back to the mandatory profile. Also, if the mandatory profile is not available to the user when trying to log on, the user cannot log on.

Creating Server-Based Profiles

If you permit several users or a group of users to use the same roaming profile, remember that the profile can be modified by the users. Multiple users may make multiple changes to the profile. Mandatory profiles are better used for groups of users. Individual roaming users should each have their own roaming "changeable" profiles.

Profile Alternative

On a server or domain controller in an enterprise domain, the System Policy Editor can alternatively be used to control user profile settings.

The policy file is saved as NTCONFIG.POL in the WINNT40\SYSTEM32\REPL\IMPORT\SCRIPTS subdirectory on all validating domain controllers.

Troubleshooting Accounts, Policies, and Profiles

Most of the problems that you will encounter regarding user and group accounts have to do with permissions to use resources rather than with the account setup itself.

User Cannot Logon

When a user cannot log on, usually the user incorrectly typed his or her username, or more likely, his or her password.

Cannot Access Controllers or Servers

If the user is logging on locally, he or she is being validated on the local computer for access to resources on that computer. Unless the computer suddenly turns itself off, the user should be able to log on successfully.

If the user is validating on an enterprise network domain controller, the domain controller must be accessible to the user, or the user might not be able to log on.

Other Logon Problems

Other problems may be related to settings made through the User Manager for Domains.

Chapter 7

NT Security Model

All security provided by Windows NT 4.0 is handled through an executive service known as the Security Reference Monitor.

Two types of permissions can be applied in Windows NT: share-level and resource-level.

Share-level permissions: Define how a user can access a resource that has been made available (shared) on the network.

Resource-level permissions: Define a user's access to a resource, but at the resource itself.

If you do not have a partition formatted for NTFS, you can use only the FAT-level properties—Ready Only, Archive, System, and Hidden:

Under NTFS, you get a more robust set of properties, including Read, Write, Delete, Execute, and Change permissions.

Any resource for which access can be determined is considered to be a security object.

NT Logon Process

When a user logs on to Windows NT, the username, password, and point of authentication must be provided. This is part of the Winlogon service that monitors the logon process.

The Winlogon service passes this information to the CSR (client/server) subsystem, which in turn passes it to the Security Reference Monitor.

The Security Reference Monitor checks the information entered against the Security Accounts Manager (SAM) database.

Account Access Token

The account access token contains important security information about the user, including the user's SID.

SID: The unique security identifier that Windows NT assigned to the user's account when the account was created.

Local Versus Domain Access Tokens

- When a user logs on to a local Windows NT workstation participating in a workgroup model, the user's account resides in a component of the local Windows NT workstation's Registry (the SAM database portion).

- When a user logs on to a Windows NT workstation that is a member of a domain, the user's account resides in the domain SAM database on the domain controller.

- In a domain, the user and group accounts are global and can be used in the ACL of any resource in the domain.

- In a workgroup model, a user's access token is only good on the local Windows NT workstation.

Access Control Lists

An access control list (ACL) is a list of users and groups that have some level of access to the resource.

ACE: Access Control Entries, entries in the ACL.

Determining Access

The Security Reference Monitor checks the SID entries in the access token against the SID entries in the ACL.

As long as the user maintains access to the object, the same security handle is in effect, even if the owner or administrator of the resource changes the user's access. The changed permissions do not take effect for the user until the user releases control of the object and tries to access it again.

Sharing and Network Access

- Only a Power User or Administrator can share a resource on a workstation or server.
- The Server service must be running, and the network card must be operational to share resources.
- You share a folder by selecting the file or folder through Windows Explorer or My Computer, right-clicking it, and choosing Sharing, or through the object's Properties sheet.
- The maximum number of connections allowed on Windows NT workstation is 10.
- On a server, the number of connections is effectively unlimited.
- Windows NT's philosophy of sharing resources is to make information readily and easily available. Therefore, the default is to give every network user access to the resource. Hence, the default permission is always Everyone with Full Control.
- It is recommended that you either remove the Everyone group and explicitly assign permissions to specific users and groups, or give Everyone the least level of access (Read) to provide a greater level of security. Do not give the Everyone group No Access. Because every network user is automatically a member of Everyone, giving this group No Access results in locking every user—even the owner and administrator—out of that shared resource.
- You can assign four share-level permissions in your ACL: Read, Change, Full Control, and No Access.

- Share permissions take effect for a user accessing the resource remotely over the network. If the user sits down at a computer that has the folder, and no other permissions have been assigned, the user still has complete access to the folder and its files.

Effective Permissions

- Effective share permissions are cumulative.
- No Access always supersedes any other permission.

Administrative and Hidden Shares

When Windows NT is installed, it creates several shares, called administrative shares, all of which are hidden—except for NETLOGON.

You can create hidden shares yourself by adding the $ to the end of the share name.

Accessing a Shared Folder

You can access shares by doing the following:

- Connecting directly to the resource through Network Neighborhood or the Find command
- By mapping a drive letter to a shared folder through My Computer or Windows Explorer

Network Neighborhood

The easiest way to connect to a shared folder is to use Network Neighborhood.

Find Command

The Find command on the Start menu can be used effectively to search for computers that do not show up right away in a browse list like Network Neighborhood displays, or for a specific file or folder in a shared folder whose name you cannot recall.

My Computer and Windows Explorer

- My Computer can be used to map a network drive to a shared folder on a computer.

- Mapped drives can be disconnected when no longer needed.

NTFS Permissions

You set permissions for a file or folder by right-clicking the file or folder, displaying its Properties sheet, and selecting the Security tab.

File and Folder Permissions

Effective file or folder permissions are cumulative.

Assigning File and Folder Permissions

These six individual permissions can be applied to files and folders:

- Read (R)
- Write (W)
- Execute (E)
- Delete (D)
- Change Permission (P)
- Take Ownership (O)

The Folder permission Full Control provides the user an inherent ability to delete files in a folder even if the user is given No Access permission to a specific file. This is done to preserve Posix application support on UNIX systems, for which Write permission on a folder allows the user to delete files in the folder. This permission can be superseded by choosing the Special Directory Access standard permission and checking all the individual permissions.

The effect of Replace Permissions on Existing Files is to change any and all permissions that you set on individual files with the permissions that you set at the folder level. Because this option is selected by default, you can easily forget it when setting permissions at the folder level, and you can accidentally change permissions on files that you do not want to change.

Share and NTFS Permissions

When a user accesses a file or folder protected by NTFS permissions across the network through a share, the Security Reference Monitor determines the cumulative permissions at the share and the cumulative permissions at the file or folder.

Whichever permission is most restrictive becomes the effective permission for the user.

Ownership

The user who creates a file or folder is noted by Windows NT to be the owner of that file or folder, and is placed in the Creator Owner internal group for that file or folder.

A user cannot give someone else ownership of his or her files or folders. However, a user can give someone the permission to take ownership of his or her files and folders.

Taking Ownership

If any member of the Administrators group takes ownership of a file or folder or creates a file or folder, the owner becomes the Administrators group.

Copying and Moving Permissions

When you copy a file from one folder to another, the file assumes the permissions of the target folder.

When you move a file from one folder to another, the file maintains its current permissions.

A move is only a move where permissions are involved when you move a file from a folder in one partition to another folder in the same partition.

Troubleshooting Security

The most likely problem that you will have with security is a user who is unable to access a resource.

Be sure to check the share permissions and file and folder permissions.

When using NTFS permissions, the most common problem is that the user might have access through one group but is restricted through another.

Chapter 8

Partitions

- Before an operating system can be installed, the computer's hard disk or disks must be partitioned into the storage space required by the OS and the user, and formatted with a file system supported by the OS.
- The primary partition usually holds the operating system files.
- Four primary partitions are supported per physical disk device under NT. MS-DOS can recognize only one primary partition per physical disk device.
- Extended partitions offer a way to partition a drive into more than four logical drives.
- The ARC path specifies the physical location of the partition that contains the NT OS files.

File System Support

NT supports FAT, NTFS, and CDFS file systems.

NTFS: New Technology File System

CDFS: CD-ROM file system

Previous versions of NT provided support for IBM OS/2's HPFS.

FAT

- FAT is required for the system partition if you intend to dual-boot between NT and MS-DOS or Windows 95.
- FAT supports filenames of up to 255 characters.
- The filename can have multiple sections, separated by periods and can be considered multi-qualified.
- Filenames must begin with an alphanumeric character and can contain any characters, including spaces, but excluding the following:
  " / \ [ ] : ; | = , ^ * ?
- FAT offers the traditional file attributes—Read, Archive, System, and Hidden. As such, it does not provide the range of security that NTFS permissions can.
- Folders in a FAT partition can be shared.
- FAT supports a maximum partition (file) size of 4GB.
- FAT is considered most efficient for file access on partitions of less than 400MB in size.
- FAT requires less than 1MB of overhead for the file system.
- The system partition of RISC-based systems must be at least 2MB, formatted as FAT.

NTFS

- NTFS supports 255-character names, including extensions.
- Filenames preserve case but are not case sensitive, except when using Posix-based applications.
- File and folder names can contain any characters, including spaces, but excluding the following:
  " / \ < > : | * ?

- NTFS supports a theoretical partition (file) size of up to 16 exabytes.
- NTFS is considered more efficient on partitions larger than 400MB.
- Formatting a partition as NTFS requires between 4MB and 5MB of system overhead, making it impossible to format a floppy disk with NTFS.
- NTFS provides support for built-in file compression.
- NTFS offers automatic Transaction Tracking, which logs all disk activity and provides a means of recovery in the event of a power failure or system crash.
- NTFS offers automatic Sector Sparing, also called hot fixing, in which so-called bad clusters are determined and marked, and the data contained therein is moved to a new good cluster.
- NTFS provides support for Macintosh files.
- NTFS provides the highest level of security for files and folders through its permission set.
- NTFS maintains a separate Recycle Bin for each user.

FAT to NTFS

No data is lost during the conversion process with CONVERT.EXE because this is not a reformatting operation.

Long Filenames

Both FAT and NTFS under NT 4.0 support long filenames for files and folders.

8.3 Naming

NT takes the first six characters of the name, minus spaces, and adds a ~ (tilde character) followed by a number increment. After the fifth iteration, NT's algorithm performs a name hash, retaining the first

two characters of the long filename and generating the remaining characters randomly.

Using Long Filenames

- When you refer to long names at a DOS prompt, most DOS commands require that you place the name in quotation marks.
- Some DOS and Windows 16-bit applications save files by creating a temporary file, deleting the original file, and renaming the temporary file to the original name. This process deletes the long filename and NTFS permissions associated with the file.
- Third-party DOS-based disk utilities that manipulate the FAT can also destroy long filenames contained in FAT because they do not recognize those entries as valid DOS files.
- You can display the 8.3 version of the long filename at a DOS prompt by typing **DIR /X** at the prompt.
- Every long filename utilizes one FAT directory entry for the 8.3 name (called the alias) and a hidden secondary entry for up to every 13 characters of the long filename. The FAT root directory has a hard-coded limit of 512 directory entries. Therefore, you can run out of directory entries if you use very long filenames consistently.

NTFS File Compression

- Compression is treated as another attribute of the file and folder.
- Compression is handled on-the-fly and results in greater disk capacity.
- Compression can result in a performance decrease especially across heavy traffic networks.

Enabling Compression

If a folder's Compress attribute is set, any new files placed in the folder also have their Compress attribute set.

Managing Compression

COMPACT.EXE can enable and disable file and folder compression on NTFS partitions.

Managing Disks with the Disk Administrator

If a primary partition already exists, when you create the next two to four primary partitions, NT displays a message to the effect that the partition scheme may not be compatible with MS-DOS. You must confirm any partition changes to NT (by choosing Partition, Commit Changes Now) before being allowed to format. Deleting a partition is as simple as choosing Partition, Delete. The Disk Administrator gives you the ability to assign a specific drive letter to a logical drive or primary partition.

System, Boot, and Active Partitions

NT refers to the partition that contains the NT boot files (NTLDR, NTDETECT.COM, NTBOOTDD.SYS, BOOT.INI, and BOOTSECT.DOS) as the system partition. NT refers to the partition that contains the installation directory as the boot partition.

Volume Sets

In NT, a volume can be a single contiguous area of disk space or a collection of noncontiguous areas of disk space. The latter is called a volume set. A volume set can consist of from 2 to 32 areas of free disk space on one or more physical disk drives. A volume can be formatted as either FAT or NTFS.

- Volume sets can contain areas of free space from different drive types such as SCSI, ESDI, and IDE.
- Data is written to each member of a volume set in turn. Therefore, a volume set really does not improve disk I/O performance.

- NT system and boot partitions cannot participate in a volume set.
- Like NTFS, on workstations that dual-boot between NT and MS-DOS or Windows 95, volume sets cannot be accessed by MS-DOS or Windows 95.
- If any member of a volume set fails, or the disk that a member resides on fails, the entire volume set is corrupted.

Extending a Volume Set

NTFS volume sets can be extended. FAT volume sets must be deleted and re-created to change the size.

Stripe Sets

A stripe set consists of free space from at least 2 and up to 32 different physical drives. Data is written uniformly in 64KB blocks across all members of the stripe set. Because data can be written concurrently across the physical disks, a stripe set can result in an overall disk I/O performance increase.

- NT system and boot partitions cannot participate in a stripe set.
- Like NTFS, on workstations that dual-boot between NT and MS-DOS or Windows 95, stripe sets cannot be accessed by MS-DOS or Window 95.
- If any member of a stripe set fails, or the disk that a member resides on fails, the entire stripe set is corrupted.

System Partition and RISC

The system partition on a RISC-based computer must be formatted as FAT because these computers can boot only from FAT.

Backing Up and Restoring

Backups can be performed by the Administrator, local Backup Operators group, local Server Operators group, users with proper rights, and users who have Read permission to files and folders. The backup drive must be NT-compatible. You cannot back up the Registry from a remote computer. The Registry cannot be restored to a remote computer.

Troubleshooting

If you have chosen to log the backup and restore operations, any exceptions to the process, such as open files that couldn't be backed up, are recorded in the log file.

Scheduling

NT provides a command-line backup utility that you can use in combination with NT's AT command to schedule a tape backup operation.

Chapter 9

NT Print Process

Windows NT follows the concept of one driver that can be used by all applications running under Windows NT.

Printer: The print driver

Print device: The actual hardware box that does the printing

The printer interacts with the print device to ensure that the print device receives a print job that has been formatted appropriately for that device.

- When an application makes a print request, the print process begins.
- Although clients need a print driver to process print requests, these clients do not require that a print driver be installed locally.
- Windows NT 4.0 supports MS-DOS-based applications and Windows-based applications.

Components

The four basic components of the print process are as follows:

- Print driver
- Spooler
- Print processor
- Print monitor

Print spooler: The spooler service running in Windows NT 4.0. It is responsible for making a connection to the spooler on a remote print server.

By default, print job files are spooled to the WINNT40\SYSTEM32\SPOOL\PRINTERS directory.

Print processor: The feature responsible for carrying out any formatting or rendering of the print job required for the specific printer to understand it

The default print processor for Windows NT 4.0 is WINPRINT.DLL.

Print monitor: The feature responsible for tracking the status of the print job

LPD Devices

The Line Printer Port print monitor (LPRMON.DLL) is loaded when the TCP/IP Printing Support is installed on the print server.

To direct a print job to a UNIX host print device, open a command prompt window, and enter the following command:

LPR -S *IP address of UNIX host* -P *Printer Name filename*

To receive queue information on the print server, enter the following command:

LPQ -S *IP address of UNIX host* -P *Printer Name* -l

Print Process

■ You can create and connect printers by using the Add Printer Wizard, which you can access through the Printers folder in My Computer or by choosing Start, Settings, Printers.

■ If you choose not to share the printer while you are installing it, you can do so later.

■ Printer share names must remain within the eight-character range in order for non-Windows NT and non-Windows 95 clients to be able to see the names.

■ You cannot set any permissions directly on a printer share. Instead, you set permissions on the printer itself.

Four permissions can be used to secure a printer in Windows NT 4.0: No Access, Print, Manage Documents, and Full Control.

Printer Access

As with files and folders, access to a printer can be audited, provided auditing has been enabled in the User Manager.

Auditing places additional strain on resources and the processor. It is designed as a troubleshooting technique rather than as a reporting tool.

Members of the Administrators, Print Operators, Server Operators, and Power Users groups have the ability to take ownership of a printer. Also, any other user or group that has been given Full Control permission for the printer can take ownership of that printer.

Printer Properties

The General tab of the printer's Properties sheet gives you the option of entering a descriptive comment about the printer. You also can identify a

Separator Page, choose an alternate Print Processor, and print a Test Page.

A separator page is a text file and can be created and saved with an .SEP extension in the WINNT40\ SYSTEM32 directory using any text editor.

You use the Ports tab of the Properties sheet to see which port the printer and print device is associated with and what kind of print device it is.

Print Pools

A print pool represents one printer associated with two or more print devices.

The Scheduling tab of the Properties sheet, besides allowing you to define when the printer can service jobs, lets you set a priority for the printer and define additional spool settings.

Priority

When you set a priority for a printer, you are really setting a priority for all print jobs received by that printer. In the Priority section of the Scheduling tab, you can set the printer priority from 1 (lowest) to 99 (highest).

Management

Double-clicking a printer icon in the Printers folder displays its print management window. You can choose from four menu options: Printer, Document, View, and Help.

■ Check to see whether the print device is turned on and online.

■ Check to see whether the print device connection is good. Swap out cables; then check the network card, IP address, and so on.

■ Verify that the printer driver installed is compatible with the print device.

- Confirm that the printer is available and has been selected. Verify that sharing has been enabled and that the permissions allow printing to take place for the users affected.
- Verify that the appropriate printer port has been selected and configured by printing a test page.
- Monitor network traffic in the case of remote printing to verify that print jobs are being routed correctly and not being dropped.
- Check the amount of disk space available for spooling.
- Determine whether the printing problem is the result of a specific application error, or it occurs with all applications.
- Resubmit the print job to print to a file and then copy the file to a printer port.

Chapter 10

Subsystem Architecture

Windows NT 4.0 architecture consists of two primary processing areas: User (or Application) mode and Kernel (or Privileged Processor) mode.

User (or Application) mode: A mode of the operating system that provides application processing and logon support. Four subsystems run in User mode: OS/2, POSIX, Security, and CSR.

CSR: The Client/Server subsystem. It supports both 32-bit Windows and Windows 95 applications, as well as 16-bit DOS and Windows applications.

The OS/2 subsystem supports only 1.x-based applications on Intel-based computers.

The OS/2 subsystem is not loaded at Windows NT boot time.

POSIX is an application standard created for UNIX-based operating systems that meet United States Federal Information Processing Standard 151.

NTFS provides compliance with the POSIX.1 Library of function calls.

The POSIX subsystem is loaded only when a POSIX application is started.

Kernel (or Privileged Processor) mode: A mode that provides support for all major operating system functions. The Kernel mode consists of these three main parts:

- The Executive Services, the largest part of Kernel mode, provides support for window management and graphics device interaction, processes, threads, memory management, I/O, IPC, and security.
- The Windows NT Kernel provides support for thread scheduling and context switching, synchronization among services and processes in the Executive Services, multiprocessor load balancing, and exception and interrupt handling.
- The Hardware Abstraction Layer (HAL) provides hardware platform support.

WIN32-Based Application Support

- Each application written to the WIN32 API is offered the full benefit of OpenGL graphics support, OLE (across both WIN32 and WIN16 applications), DirectX, multithreading, and multiprocessing.
- Every WIN32-based application has one or more threads of execution associated with it.

- Windows NT 4.0 generates a virtual DOS machine (NTVDM) within which the MS-DOS–based application will load and run.

- Every NTVDM that is created is given one thread of execution.

Configuring the NTVDM

The NTVDM is configured through the PIF created for each MS-DOS application.

The MS-DOS application's Properties sheet consists of six tabs: General, Program, Font, Memory, Screen, and Misc.

- General settings include an informational display of the application path and size; created, modified, and last accessed dates; and DOS attributes (Read, Archive, Hidden, and System).

- On the Program tab, you can modify the icon and name associated with the application; path and executable; working directory; and whether to run it maximized, minimized, or in a normal window.

- On the Misc tab, you can set background operation options, idle processing time, termination warnings, and reserved shortcut keys.

Any MS-DOS–based application that interacts directly with hardware, such as modem dial-out programs or disk management utilities, cannot run under Windows NT because those functions are isolated from the application through the HAL.

WIN16 Application Support

Windows-based 16-bit applications are also supported under the Windows NT 4.0 Win32 API.

WOW: WIN16 on WIN32

Thunking: Converting 16-bit calls into 32-bit calls, and vice versa

WOWEXEC.EXE and WOW32.DLL provide Windows 3.1 environment emulation. KRNL386.EXE, GDI.EXE, and USER.EXE correspond to the same files in Windows 3.1 and manage the thunking process for each one's specific function set.

Managing WIN16 Applications with Multiple NTVDMs

Under Windows NT 4.0, each WIN16 application can be run in its own NTVDM, and thus in its own memory space.

You can start a 16-bit Windows application in its own memory space in one of the following three ways:

- Issue a command-line command to execute it in its own memory space.

- Make the selection through the Start, Run dialog box for that application or its properties.

- Modify the application's run association through Windows Explorer.

Although each WIN16 application can be run in its own memory space, only one NTVDM can have multiple WIN16 applications running in it. Each WIN16 application that is run in its own memory space creates a new NTVDM.

Troubleshooting Applications

- MS-DOS or Windows-based applications that interact directly with hardware through interrupt calls or virtual device drivers, such as disk utilities or memory managers, do not function successfully or at all under Windows NT 4.0.

- WIN32 and POSIX applications run only on the platform for which they have been compiled.

- OS/2 applications that can be forced to run in an NTVDM (bound applications) can be run on other hardware platforms.
- A new NTVDM is created for each MS-DOS-based application that you run under Windows NT 4.0.
- By default, all WIN16 applications run in the same WOW NTVDM.

Thread Priority

The Windows NT kernel assigns thread priorities based on the type of activity associated with the thread. Priority levels range from 0 (lowest) to 31 (highest).

Performance

The Performance tab on the System applet's Properties sheet provides three settings that affect foreground application responsiveness:

- Maximum gives the application a two-level priority boost when the application is running in the foreground.
- The middle setting boosts the priority level of a foreground application by one level, leaving the background applications at the normal level.
- None leaves the foreground and background settings both at the normal level.

Task Manager

You can access the Task Manager by right-clicking the taskbar and selecting Task Manager or by pressing Ctrl+Alt+Del and choosing it from the pop-up menu.

The Task Manager offers three tabs of information: Applications, Processes, and Performance.

Chapter 11

Networking Model

The NT 4.0 network architecture is positioned as part of the Executive Services running in Kernel mode. The three layers are the File System (or Redirector) Layer, the Protocol Layer, and the NIC (or Adapter) Layer.

Each layer is separated but bound by a boundary or transmission interface through which the request must pass to get to each layer.

OSI Model Versus NT's Network Model

The seven layers of the OSI model are as follows:

- Application—Corresponding to the File System layer in NT's model
- Presentation—Corresponding to the File System layer in NT's model
- Session—Corresponding to the File System layer in NT's model
- Transport—Corresponding to the Protocol layer in NT's model
- Network—Corresponding to the Protocol layer in NT's model
- Data Link—Corresponding to the NIC layer in NT's model
- Physical—Corresponding to the NIC layer in NT's model

File System Layer

The File System layer is also known as the Redirector layer because the NT I/O Manager determines where to "redirect" the request for the resource in this layer.

If the request is for a local resource, a file on an NTFS partition, the request is kept local and directed to the appropriate file system—in this case, to NTFS on the partition.

If the request is for a resource on another computer in the network, the request must be "redirected" to that remote location.

Protocol Layer

NT supports five protocols: TCP/IP, NWLink IPX/SPX, NetBEUI, Data Link Control (DLC), and AppleTalk (Server only).

NIC Layer

NT supports the installation of one or more network interface cards in each NT computer, provided that the card is compatible with NT and has an NDIS 4.0-compatible driver available to support it.

TDI: Transport Device Interface, a boundary interface between the Redirector layer and protocols. It provides a common programming interface that any redirector can use to build a path (bind) to any and all appropriate installed protocols.

NDIS 4.0: A boundary interface that provides a common programming interface between the protocols and the NICs.

NetBEUI

NetBEUI is a fast, efficient networking protocol used mostly for small, single subnet LANs rather than large, multiple subnet WANs because NetBEUI is not a routable protocol. This protocol relies heavily on network broadcast messages. NetBEUI has no configuration parameters in NT.

NWLink IPX/SPX Compatible Transport

NWLink IPX/SPX Compatible Transport is Microsoft's 32-bit NDIS-compatible implementation of the IPX/SPX protocol; it enables NT computers to establish connections with other computers or networks running IPX/SPX (NetWare).

NWLink is configurable on NT with three options: frame type, network number, and Routing Information Protocol (RIP).

NWLink supports Ethernet II, 802.2, 802.3, and SNAP for Ethernet topologies; 802.5 and SNAP for Token Ring; and 802.2 and SNAP for FDDI (Fiber Distributed Data Interface).

NetWare networks default to 802.3 frames for versions 3.11 and older and 802.2 for versions 3.12 and later.

TCP/IP

TCP/IP is the communications protocol of the Internet and the default protocol selected during installation of NT Workstation and Server. TCP/IP comes with these utilities:

Utility	Description
PING	Tests and verifies communications between IP addresses
IPCONFIG	Displays current TCP/IP settings associated with the computer
FTP	Provides a bidirectional file transfer mechanism between two TCP/IP configured computers
Telnet	Provides a terminal emulation mechanism to another TCP/IP host computer
Finger	Retrieves configuration information from another computer running TCP/IP

The IP address is the address of your computer (called a host) on the network. It is a 32-bit address more commonly displayed as a four-part decimal address separated by dots.

Each host address must be unique in the network, and each host must have an address.

The subnet mask is used to identify the IP addresses of one network from those of other networks. The default gateway address is the specific router to which these "nonsubnet" packets are sent for further address resolution.

Network Options

The Workstation service is your "outgoing" pipe to the NT network. The "incoming" pipe is the Server service.

Computer Browser Service

The Computer Browser's primary mission is to provide lists of network servers and their resources to waiting clients. Browser lists are maintained on specific computers called browsers. There are various types of browsers, each with a specific role to play in the process:

- Master Browser—Maintains browser list
- Domain Master Browser—Maintains browser list and must be a PDC
- Backup Browser—Holds backup copies of browser list
- Potential Browser—Does not fulfill any role but may
- Non-Browser—Cannot participate in list maintenance

Browser Elections

Computers assume their browser roles through an election process. Criteria that decide browser roles include the operating system type and version; current browser role—master browser, backup browser, or potential browser; the server type—primary domain controller, secondary domain controller, or member server; and length of time it has been a browser.

Configuring Browsers

The Registry key for configuration is HKEY_LOCAL_MACHINE\ System\ CurrentControlSet\Services\Browser\Parameters\ MaintainServerList.

- When computers boot or share a resource, they announce themselves to the master browser.
- Computers announce themselves once a minute for the first 5 minutes after booting and then every 12 minutes thereafter.
- The master browser compiles a list of computers and their available resources and sends a copy of the list to the backup browser(s) approximately once every 15 minutes.

Joining a Domain

You can switch your computer's participation from workgroup computing to a domain through the Identification tab in the Network applet accessible through the Control Panel.

For your NT computer to join a domain, it must have a computer account created for it on the domain controller.

Only NT Workstation computers require a computer account in an NT domain. Other NT network clients do not.

Dial-Up Networking and RAS

Remote Access Service services on an NT workstation support 1 inbound dial-in connection and, on an NT server, support up to 256 inbound dial-in connections. RAS provides the NT network with standardized WAN-based remote access support.

Dial-Up Networking is the service a client computer uses to connect to remote network resources through a RAS server.

Both SLIP and PPP can be used to establish connections to RAS servers.

SLIP: Serial Line Internet Protocol

PPP: Point-to-Point Protocol

Multilink: A protocol that enables modems to be combined into logical groups, thus increasing the bandwidth for transmissions

Point-to-Point Tunneling Protocol

PPTP: Point-to-Point Tunneling Protocol

Clients using PPTP on their NT workstations can connect securely to a RAS server in their company network either directly through the Internet—if they are themselves directly connected—or through their local Internet provider. Connecting this way is known as Virtual Private Networking

VPN: Virtual Private Network

A VPN provides the ability to "tunnel" through the Internet or other public network to connect to a remote corporate network without sacrificing security.

RAS Security

RAS supports NT's domain security, requiring dial-in users to authenticate using the domain account database before resource access can take place. The RAS server also maintains an ACL that identifies which domain users have permission to dial in. Dial-Up Networking is a TAPI-compliant application in NT.

TAPI: Telephony Application Programming Interface, a set of standards for communications programs to manage and control data, voice, and fax dial-up functions

The Dial-Up Networking program (DUN) is accessed through the Accessories group. The first time you access DUN, a dial-up wizard will prompt you for the first phone book entry.

Windows Messaging

Windows Messaging client (Microsoft Exchange 4.0): A universal inbox client that can create, send, receive, and organize electronic mail

To install Messaging, double-click the Inbox icon on the desktop to initiate the installation wizard.

Peer Web Services

- For NT 4.0 Server, Microsoft has included the Internet Information Server (IIS).
- For NT Workstation, it has included Peer Web Services (PWS).

Internet Service Manager (ISM) is used to configure the PWS services. Through ISM, you can manage remote servers, specify user connections, log on and authenticate parameters, specify home directories, log server activity, and secure access through keys for each component service.

NetWare Server Connections

The following are options for connecting NT network clients to a NetWare network:

Service	Description
Gateway Service for NetWare (GSNW)	This service connects the NT server to a NetWare server via a service account established on the NetWare server.
File and Print Service (FPNW)	This add-on service effectively makes an NT server look like a NetWare server to NetWare client computers.
Directory Service Manager (DSMN)	This add-on service enables NetWare accounts to be copied to and managed by a single NT domain controller with changes propagated back out to the NetWare servers as required.
Migration Tool for NetWare	This utility lets you merge NetWare account and group information into the NT account database.

Client Services for NetWare (CSNW)and NWLink IPX/SPX Compatible Protocol provide basic file and print access to NetWare 3.x and 4.x servers on your NT workstation.

Network Troubleshooting

If you experience a network problem after the first installation of NT Workstation or after the installation of an adapter card, double-check the adapter settings.

Check the Services applet in the Control Panel and the Event Viewer to see whether any network-related services failed to start and why.

If the Workstation service is not running, you cannot connect to network resources.

If the Server service is not running, you cannot share resources or service network requests.

Chapter 12

Virtual Memory Management

The memory architecture of Windows NT 4.0 is a 32-bit, demand-based, flat, linear model. This model allows the Virtual Memory Manager to provide each process running in Windows NT up to 4GB of memory.

The Windows NT pagefile (PAGEFILE.SYS) is created when Windows NT is installed. It defaults in size to 12-plus physical RAM.

This process of assigning virtual addresses to the application effectively hides the organization of physical RAM from the application.

Pagefile Usage

The maximum size the pagefile can be is 3×physical RAM.

In Windows NT Server, the paging file's initial size is equal to RAM only.

During installation, Windows NT looks for a disk partition large enough to hold the pagefile it creates. It is often the same as the installation (boot) partition, but it may be another formatted partition.

An optimization suggestion for the pagefile, which will also improve overall disk performance, is to move the pagefile to a partition on a separate disk drive.

Moving the Pagefile to Another Disk—All pagefile configuration takes place through the Virtual Memory dialog box.

Right-Sizing the Pagefile—The pagefile grows and shrinks within the range specified, but it is important to note that it is not cleaned up in any way.

Creating Multiple Pagefiles—Another optimization technique is to create multiple pagefiles—for example, one on each physical disk drive.

The performance of the pagefile and accompanying disk I/O is directly related to the performance of your applications and any other system processes as a result of the way virtual memory maps physical addresses to virtual addresses.

Troubleshooting NT with Event Viewer

Any events generated by the Windows NT operating system—missing an application or security auditing—are collected in log files that can be viewed with the Event Viewer utility.

Each entry records the following:

- The icon type of the event
- The date and time it occurred
- The source of the event
- A category or classification
- An event number
- The name of the user involved
- The computer on which the event occurred

NT Diagnostics Utility

Windows NT Diagnostics gives detailed information culled directly from the Windows NT Registry relating to system configuration.

The Services tab of Windows NT Diagnostics shows a list of Windows NT services and devices available and their current status.

Performance Monitor

Counters: Performance Monitor treats system resources as objects with characteristics, or counters.

Instances: Multiple occurrences of an object and counter, or variations on them, are called instances.

With Performance Monitor, you can also create and view log files, view summary statistics, and create system alerts based on monitored values.

Performance Monitor is used primarily for two purposes:

- Creating baselines of performance
- Monitoring aberrations from the baseline— that is, troubleshooting

Performance Monitor, by default, displays a line chart that charts activity for every second in time.

You can modify defaults by selecting Options, Chart to display the Chart Options dialog box.

Object counter values can be collected and saved in a log file. The Performance Monitor does not have a facility to print charts.

Objects to Monitor

The four basic objects to monitor—especially when you're creating a baseline of "normal" system activity—are the processor, process, logical disk, and memory.

You can enable disk monitoring by typing the following command at a DOS command prompt

DISKPERF -Y *computername*

where *computername* optionally references a remote computer whose disk activity you want to monitor.

To disable monitoring, type

DISKPERF -N *computername*

Emergency Repair

You can create (and update) the Emergency Repair Disk at any time by running the Windows NT utility RDISK.EXE at the Windows NT command prompt.

If you do not have a Windows NT Startup disk but have access to the original installation files, you can create one by accessing the installation file directory and typing **WINNT /OX** at a command prompt.

The security files on the Emergency Repair Disk overwrite the security files in the Registry.

If you know of a file that is missing or corrupt, you can replace the file directly from the source files by using the NT EXPAND utility.

Windows NT Boot Disk

When you format a disk under Windows NT, Windows NT creates a boot sector on that disk that references NTLDR.

The boot files to copy to the Windows NT boot disk include:

- NTLDR
- NTDETECT.COM
- BOOT.INI
- BOOTSECT.DOS
- NTBOOTDD.SYS

Reviewing System Recovery Options

Windows NT provides a recovery utility in which you can specify how Windows NT should handle such an error. You can set its options through the Startup/Shutdown tab of the System applet in the Control Panel.

You can set four recovery options:

- Write an Event to the System Log
- Send an Administrative Alert
- Write Debugging Information
- Automatically Reboot

MCSE
Windows® NT®
4.0 Workstation
Exam Guide
Second Edition

Written by Emmett Dulaney

Contents
at a Glance

A Division of Macmillan USA
201 W. 103rd Street
Indianapolis, Indiana 46290

MCSE Windows® NT® 4.0 Workstation Exam Guide, Second Edition

Copyright© 2000 by Que Corporation

International Standard Book Number: 0-7897-2262-3

Library of Congress Catalog Card Number: 99-65931

Printed in the United States of America

First Printing: November 1999

01   00   99   4   3   2   1

Use of the Microsoft Approved Study Guide Logo on this product signifies that it has been independently reviewed and approved in complying with the following standards:

- Acceptable coverage of all content related to Microsoft exam number 70-073, entitled Implementing and Supporting Microsoft Windows NT Workstation 4.0.

- Sufficient performance-based exercises that relate closely to all required content; and

- Technically accurate content, based on sampling of text.

Trademarks

Warning and Disclaimer

Credits

Publisher
Paul Boger

Associate Publisher
Jim Minatel

Acquisitions Editor
Tracy Williams

Series Editor
Jill Hayden

Senior Development Editor
Rick Kughen

Managing Editor
Lisa Wilson

Senior Editor
Susan Ross Moore

Copy Editor
Chuck Hutchinson

Indexer
Kevin Kent

Proofreader
D&G, Limited

Technical Editor
Jim Cooper

Team Coordinator
Vicki Harding

Media Developer
Michael Hunter

Interior Design
Anne Jones

Cover Design
Karen Ruggles

Copy Writer
Eric Borgert

Layout Technician
Eric S. Miller

To Karen, Kristin, Evan, and Spencer for making every day wonderful.

Acknowledgements

First and foremost, all credit should be given to Steve Kaczmarek, the author of the first edition of this book. Were it not for his expertise and prose in the beginning, the book you hold in your hands would never have come to pass.

At Que, Jim Minatel, Tracy Williams, and Jill Hayden are owed an enormous amount of gratitude for making this edition possible. Rick Kughen is to be thanked for his skillful development edit, and Jim Cooper for overseeing the technical accuracy.

Last, thanks are due to Jeff Durham for helping manage the project from conception to submission.

About the Author

Emmett Dulaney, MCSE, MCP+I, CNA, A+, Network+ is the Certification Corner columnist for *Windows NT Systems Magazine* and cofounder of D S Technical Solutions. A Windows NT/certification instructor for Indiana University/ Purdue University of Fort Wayne, he is also the author of more than a dozen titles on certification and Windows NT integration.

Tell Us What You Think!

As the reader of this book, *you* are our most important critic and commentator. We value your opinion and want to know what we're doing right, what we could do better, what areas you'd like to see us publish in, and any other words of wisdom you're willing to pass our way.

As a Publisher for Que, I welcome your comments. You can fax, email, or write me directly to let me know what you did or didn't like about this book—as well as what we can do to make our books stronger.

Please note that I cannot help you with technical problems related to the topic of this book, and that due to the high volume of mail I receive, I might not be able to reply to every message.

When you write, please be sure to include this book's title and author as well as your name and phone or fax number. I will carefully review your comments and share them with the author and editors who worked on the book.

Fax: 317-581-4666

Email: certification@macmillanusa.com

Mail: Publisher
       Que Corporation
       201 West 103rd Street
       Indianapolis, IN 46290 USA

Table of Contents

This book was written by Microsoft Certified Professionals, for Microsoft Certified Professionals and MCP candidates. It is designed, in combination with your real-world experience, to prepare you to pass the Implementing and Supporting Windows NT Workstation 4.0 Exam (70-073), as well as give you a background in performance monitoring, optimizing, system management, and troubleshooting in a Windows NT environment.

You should already have a strong working knowledge of the following subjects before beginning a study of this product:

- Windows 95. It is strongly suggested that you be well acquainted with the look and feel of Windows 95 because it is also the interface used by Windows NT 4.0. Although Windows 98 is available as a product and a certification exam, the NT exams were written and released when Windows 95 was the newest non-NT client available. As a result, you must know certain elements of Windows 95 for questions that can appear on this exam, but you need no knowledge of Windows 98.

- Windows NT Workstation 4.0. It is not the intention of this book to teach you Windows NT Workstation 4.0. Rather, it is designed to build on your existing knowledge of the product. Wherever doing so is appropriate, however, functions and procedures will be reviewed.

- Basic networking concepts. Again, it is not the intention of this book to teach you how to network or what networking is all about. Rather, this book is designed to explain how Windows NT Workstation 4.0 can be used as a client in a network environment.

As of this writing, the exams cost $100 each. The exam format changes regularly, and Microsoft need not announce a change. The most popular formats used are a 15-question "adaptive" exam, a 30-question "shortened standard" exam, and a 51-question "standard" exam. Each of these formats is described in the appendix section, but regardless of the format, you are expected to know the product well, which is the purpose of this book.

Depending on the certification you are pursuing (MCP, MCSE, and so on), you may have to take as many as seven exams, covering Microsoft operating systems, application programs, networking, and software development. Each test involves preparation, study, and for some, heavy doses of test anxiety. Is certification worth the trouble?

Microsoft has cosponsored research that provides some answers.

Benefits for Your Organization

At companies participating in a 1994 Dataquest survey, a majority of corporate managers stated that certification is an important factor to the overall success of their companies because of the following reasons:

- Certification increases customer satisfaction. Customers look for indications that their suppliers understand the industry and have the ability to respond to their technical problems. Having Microsoft Certified Professionals on staff reassures customers; it tells them that your employees have used and mastered Microsoft products.

- Certification maximizes training investment. The certification process specifically identifies skills that an employee is lacking or areas where additional training is needed. By so doing, it validates training and eliminates the costs and loss of productivity associated with unnecessary training. In addition, certification records enable a company to verify an employee's technical knowledge and track retention of skills over time.

Although the Dataquest survey was one of the most conclusive done, Microsoft maintains current case studies on the benefits of certification, and they can be found at **http://www.microsoft.com/train_cert**.

Benefits Up Close and Personal

Microsoft also cites a number of benefits for the certified individual:

- Industry recognition of expertise, enhanced by Microsoft's promotion of the Certified Professional community to the industry and potential clients.

- Access to technical information directly from Microsoft.

- A complimentary one-year subscription to *Microsoft Certified Professional Magazine*.

- Microsoft Certified Professional logos and other materials to publicize MCP status to colleagues and clients.
- Invitations to Microsoft conferences and technical training sessions, plus a special events program newsletter from the MCP program.

Additional benefits, depending on the certification, include the following:

- Microsoft TechNet or Microsoft Developer Network membership or discounts.
- Eligibility to join the Network Professional Association, a worldwide independent association of computer professionals.

Some intangible benefits of certification are as follows:

- Enhanced marketability with current or potential employers and customers, along with an increase in earnings potential.
- Methodology for objectively assessing current skills, individual strengths, and specific areas where training is required.

Exam Objectives

The Implementing and Supporting Microsoft Windows NT Workstation 4.0 certification exam measures your ability to implement, administer, and troubleshoot Windows NT Workstation 4.0 computer systems in a networked environment. It focuses on determining your skill in these seven major categories:

- Planning
- Installation and Configuration
- Managing Resources
- Connectivity
- Running Applications
- Monitoring and Optimization
- Troubleshooting

The Implementing and Supporting Microsoft Windows NT Workstation 4.0 certification exam uses these categories to measure your ability. Before taking this exam, you should be proficient in the job skills described in the following sections.

Planning

The Planning section is designed to make sure that you understand the hardware requirements of Windows NT Workstation 4.0. The knowledge needed here also requires understanding of general networking concepts.

Objectives for Planning

- Create unattended installation files.
- Plan strategies for sharing and securing resources.
- Choose the appropriate file system to use in a given situation. File systems and situations include the following:
    - NTFS
    - FAT
    - HPFS
    - Security
    - Dual-boot systems

Installation and Configuration

The Installation and Configuration part of the Workstation exam tests you on virtually every possible component of the product.

Objectives for Installation and Configuration

- Install Windows NT Workstation on an Intel platform in a given situation.
- Set up a dual-boot system in a given situation.
- Remove Windows NT Workstation in a given situation.
- Install, configure, and remove hardware components for a given situation. Hardware components include the following:
    - Network adapter drivers
    - SCSI device drivers
    - Tape device drivers
    - UPS
    - Multimedia devices
    - Display drivers
    - Keyboard drivers
    - Mouse drivers
- Use Control Panel applications to configure a Windows NT Workstation computer in a given situation.
- Upgrade to Windows NT Workstation 4.0 in a given situation.
- Configure server-based installation for wide-scale deployment in a given situation.

Managing Resources

The Managing Resources component concentrates on daily administration issues.

Objectives for Managing Resources

- Create and manage local user accounts and local group accounts to meet given requirements.
- Set up and modify user profiles.
- Set up shared folders and permissions.
- Set permissions on NTFS partitions, folders, and files.
- Install and configure printers in a given environment.

Connectivity

The Connectivity component of the Workstation certification exam concentrates on how to use the various interconnecting components of the TCP/IP protocol, PWS, and NetWare, among others.

Objectives for Connectivity

- Add and configure the network components of Windows NT Workstation.
- Use various methods to access network resources.
- Implement Windows NT Workstation as a client in a NetWare environment.
- User various configurations to install Windows NT Workstation as a TCP/IP client.
- Configure and install Dial-Up Networking in a given situation.
- Configure Microsoft Peer Web Services in a given situation.

Running Applications

The Running Applications component of the Workstation certification exam makes it stand apart from the two server exams and focuses on issues surrounding executables.

Objectives for Running Applications

- Start applications on Intel and RISC platforms in various operating system environments.
- Start applications at various priorities.

Monitoring and Optimization

The Monitoring and Optimization component of the NT Workstation 4.0 certification exam focuses on performance issues.

Objectives for Monitoring and Optimization

- Monitor system performance by using various tools.
- Identify and resolve a given performance problem.
- Optimize system performance in various areas.

Troubleshooting

The Troubleshooting component of the certification exam has a number of components running the entire gamut of troubleshooting.

Objectives for Troubleshooting

- Choose the appropriate course of action to take to when the boot process fails.
- Choose the appropriate course of action to take when a print job fails.
- Choose the appropriate course of action to take when the installation process fails.
- Choose the appropriate course of action to take when an application fails.
- Choose the appropriate course of action to take when a user cannot access a resource.
- Modify the Registry using the appropriate tool in a given situation.
- Implement advanced techniques to resolve various problems.

How Does This Book Fit In?

One of the challenges that has always faced the would-be Microsoft Certified Professional is to decide how to best prepare for an examination. In doing so, you always face conflicting goals, such as how to prepare for the exam as quickly as possible and yet still learn how to do the work that passing the exam qualifies you to do.

The goal for this book is to make your studying job easier by filtering through the reams of Windows NT 4.0 technical material. Through the chapters and lab exercises, this book presents only the information that you actually need to know to pass the Windows NT 4.0 certification exam (plus a little bit extra). Other information that we think is important for you to have available while you're working has been relegated to the appendixes, sidebars, and notes.

How to Study with This Book

This book is designed to be used in a variety of ways. Rather than lock you into one particular method of studying, force you to read through sections you're already intimately familiar with, or tie you to your computer, we've made it possible for you to read the chapters at one time and do the labs at another. We've also made it easy for you to decide whether you need to read a chapter by giving you a pre-chapter quiz, providing a list of the topics and skills covered at the beginning of each chapter, and describing how the chapter relates to previous material.

Labs are arranged topically so that you can use them to explore the areas and concepts of Windows NT 4.0 that are new to you or that you need reinforcement in. We've also decided not to intermix them with the text of the chapter; we know that nothing is more frustrating than not being able to continue reading a chapter because your child is doing his homework on the computer, and you can't use it until the weekend.

The chapters are written in a modular fashion so that you don't necessarily have to read all the chapters preceding a certain chapter to be able to follow a particular chapter's discussion. The prerequisites for each chapter specify what knowledge you need to have to successfully comprehend the current chapter's contents. Frequently, subsequent chapters build on material presented in previous chapters. For example, Chapter 2, "Understanding Microsoft Windows NT 4.0," explains the features and functions offered by the network operating system. If you don't have a thorough understanding of the implications of this concept, the rest of the material presented in the book will be less than satisfying for you.

Don't skip the lab exercises, either. You certainly can practice what you read on your PC while you are reading. Some of the knowledge and skills you need to pass the Windows NT 4.0 MCP exam can be acquired only by working with Windows NT 4.0. Lots of practice and the lab exercises help you acquire these skills.

The Chapter Notes companion booklet accompanies this book and condenses the information within each chapter into bullets and lists. Use the Chapter Notes to

- Review pertinent facts before reading each chapter
- Study key concepts after reading each chapter
- Review right before taking the actual exam

Note that the Chapter Notes booklet is a companion to this text and is not intended to be a standalone entity. Only the Exam Guide gives you all the information you need to pass the exam.

How This Book Is Organized

The book is broken up into 12 chapters. Each chapter contains information relating to a common subject or theme that is an important piece of the overall picture.

- Chapter 1, "Microsoft Certified Professional Program," gives you an overview of the Microsoft Certified Professional program, what certifications are available to you, and where Windows NT 4.0 and this book fit in.
- Chapter 2, "Understanding Microsoft Windows NT 4.0," provides an overview of the network operating system and the features it includes.
- Chapter 3, "Installing Windows NT Workstation 4.0," explores how Windows NT is installed in the Intel environment.
- Chapter 4, "An Overview of the Windows NT 4.0 Interface," explores the Explorer shell.
- Chapter 5, "Configuration and the Registry," describes how changes are made to the desktop and working environment.
- Chapter 6, "Managing Users and Accounts," delves into system policies and user profiles.
- Chapter 7, "Windows NT 4.0 Security Model," covers the logon process as well as sharing resources and permissions.
- Chapter 8, "Managing Disk Resources," describes FAT versus NTFS and the different partitioning options that NT supports.
- Chapter 9, "Managing Printers," examines the printing process and how to add a printer, including information on printer spooling and setting priorities.
- Chapter 10, "Running Applications Under Windows NT 4.0," dives into the functional side of NT, describing the subsystem, priorities, and normal operation.
- Chapter 11, "Network Connectivity and Remote Support," provides a brief review of the basics of networks, how they affect Windows NT, and how implementation is done.
- Chapter 12, "Tuning, Optimizing, and Other Troubleshooting Tips," examines Performance Monitor, boot disks, and the Emergency Repair Disk.

A glossary, lab exercises, and references to other resources can be found in the appendix section. As mentioned earlier, you can do the lab exercises at your own pace, when you want to; you're not tied down to the computer for every chapter. However, any dependencies among the labs will be noted at the beginning of each lab. Also, most of the labs will assume that the very first lab has been completed; this lab configures the computers initially.

All the Windows NT Workstation 4.0 exam objectives are covered in the material contained in the text of the chapters and the lab exercises. Information contained in sidebars is provided to give history, extend the topic, expound on a related procedure, or provide other details. It is useful information, but not primary exam material.

Finally, every appendix in this book is designed to provide you with additional advice, resources, and information that can be helpful to you as you prepare and take the Implementing and Supporting NT Server 4.0 Certified Professional exam, and later as you work as a Windows NT 4.0 Certified Professional:

- Appendix A, "Glossary," provides you with definitions of terms that you need to be familiar with as a Windows NT 4.0 MCP.
- Appendix B, "Certification Process," provides an overview of the certification process.
- Appendix C, "Testing Tips," gives you tips and pointers for maximizing your performance when you take the certification exam.
- Appendix D, "Objectives Index," presents a list of reading resources, Web sites, and other items that can help you prepare for the certification exam.
- Appendix E, "Using the CD-ROM," gives you the basics of how to install and use the CD-ROM included with this book.
- Appendix F, "Lab Exercises," leads you through hands-on application for practice and review.
- Appendix G, "Suggested Reading," provides information on other resources you might want to review.

Special Features of This Book

The following features are used in this book.

Chapter Prerequisites

Chapter prerequisites help you determine what you need to know before you read a chapter. You meet the prerequisites either by reading other chapters in this book or through your prior work experiences.

Key Concept

A Key Concept points out those concepts that are vital to your success as a network professional. You will be tested on these concepts on the exam. Pay close attention to them, and make sure you understand all the Key Concepts. The following is an example.

Key Concept

For communication to occur between two computers on an Ethernet network, they both must use the identical frame type.

In addition to these special features, several conventions are used in this book to make it easier to read and understand. These conventions include underlined hotkeys (mnemonics), shortcut key combinations, menu commands, and typeface enhancements.

Underlined Hotkeys, or Mnemonics

Hotkeys in this book appear underlined, like they appear onscreen. In Windows, many menus, commands, buttons, and other options have these hotkeys. To use a hotkey shortcut, press Alt and the key for the underlined character. For instance, to choose the Properties button, press Alt and then R. In general, when you're studying for MCP exams, you should be aware that most environments are mouse-centric, and you will be expected to know how to navigate them by clicking, right-clicking, and using drag and drop.

Shortcut Key Combinations

In this book, shortcut key combinations are joined with plus signs (+). For example, Ctrl+V means that you hold down the Ctrl key while you press the V key.

Menu Commands

In the text, instructions for choosing menu commands follow this form:

Choose File, New.

This example means that you should open the File menu and select New, which in this case opens a new file.

Typeface Enhancements

This book also has special typeface enhancements to indicate special text, as indicated in the following table:

Typeface	Description
Italic	Along with adding emphasis to text, italic is used to indicate terms and variables in commands or addresses.
Boldface	Bold is used to indicate text you type, and Internet addresses and other locators in the online world.
`Computer type`	This typeface is used for onscreen messages and commands (such as DOS copy or UNIX commands).

Microsoft Certified Professional Program

WHILE YOU READ

1. An MCP is any individual who has passed a current exam in any Microsoft Professional track, with one exception. What is the exception?

2. True or False: The MCSE is a widely respected certification because it focuses on one aspect of computing.

3. Which certification instructionally and technically qualifies you to deliver Microsoft Official Curriculum through Microsoft authorized education sites?

4. To maintain certification, a Microsoft Certified Trainer is required to pass the exam for a new product within how many months of the exam's release?

5. An MCP+I is an MCP who has specialized in _____ technologies.

As Microsoft products take an increasing share of the marketplace, the demand for trained personnel grows, and the number of certifications follows suit. As of July 1999, the team of Microsoft Certified Professionals increased in number to more than 376,000 product specialists, more than 159,000 engineers, and more than 23,000 solution developers. There were also more than 20,000 certified trainers of Microsoft products.

There is every indication that these numbers will continue to grow, given Microsoft's commitment to its products and to the certification program, as well as the continued market interest in these products and in those certified to administer them. The best place to look for changes would be Microsoft's Web site at **www.microsoft.com/train_cert**.

This chapter covers the Microsoft Certified Professional Program and describes each certification in more detail. Microsoft certifications include the following:

- Microsoft Certified Professional (MCP)
- Microsoft Certified Professional + Internet (MCP+I)
- Microsoft Certified Professional + Site Builder
- Microsoft Certified Systems Engineer (MCSE)
- Microsoft Certified System Engineer + Internet (MCSE+I)
- Microsoft Certified Database Administrator (MCDBA)
- Microsoft Certified Solutions Developer (MCSD)
- Microsoft Certified Trainer (MCT)

Exploring Available Certifications

When Microsoft started certifying people to install and support its products, only one certification was available, the Microsoft Certified Professional (MCP). As time went on, employers and prospective customers of consulting firms demanded more specialized certifications. Now a number of certifications are available from Microsoft, as described in the following sections.

Microsoft Certified Professional (MCP)

As of October 1998, an MCP is any individual who has passed a current exam in any Microsoft Professional track, with one exception: Networking Essentials (exam 70-058). Passing only the Networking Essentials exam does not qualify you as an MCP.

If you take only the exam for which this book is written, you will become an MCP in Windows NT.

Microsoft Certified Professional + Internet (MCP+I)

An MCP+I is an MCP who has specialized in Internet-related technologies. To become certified as such, you must take three exams:

- Implementing and Supporting Microsoft Windows NT Server 4.0 (exam 70-067)
- Internetworking with Microsoft TCP/IP on Microsoft Windows NT 4.0 (exam 70-059)
- Implementing and Supporting Microsoft Internet Information Server 4.0 (exam 70-087)

As of this writing, exam 70-087 can be replaced by exam 70-077 (Implementing and Supporting Internet Information Server 3.0 and Microsoft Index Server 1.1), but the latter exam is scheduled to retire.

Microsoft Certified Professional + Site Builder

One of the newest certifications, Microsoft Certified Professional + Site Builder requires passing two of the following three exams:

- Designing and Implementing Web Sites with Microsoft FrontPage 98 (exam 70-055)
- Designing and Implementing Commerce Solutions with Microsoft Site Server 3.0, Commerce Edition (exam 70-057)
- Designing and Implementing Web Solutions with Microsoft Visual InterDev 6.0 (exam 70-152)

Microsoft Certified Systems Engineers (MCSE)

Microsoft Certified Systems Engineers are qualified to plan, implement, maintain, and support information systems based on Microsoft Windows NT and the BackOffice family of client/server software. The MCSE is a widely respected certification because it does not focus on just one aspect of computing, such as networking. Instead, the MCSE has demonstrated skills and abilities on the full range of software, from client operating systems to server operating systems to client/server applications. Currently, you can choose from two tracks to MCSE certification, both requiring that you pass six exams. Within the NT 4.0 track, the exams required are as follows:

- Implementing and Supporting Microsoft Windows NT Server 4.0 (exam 70-067)
- Implementing and Supporting Microsoft Windows NT Server 4.0 in the Enterprise (exam 70-068)
- Networking Essentials (exam 70-058)

- The choice of a client exam; choices include Windows NT Workstation 4.0 (exam 70-073), Windows 95 (exam 70-064), and Windows 98 (exam 70-098)
- Two electives of your choice from a large list of valid options

The Networking Essentials exam requirement is waived for those candidates who are also Novell Certified NetWare Engineers (CNE) or Certified Banyan Engineers (CBE).

Microsoft Certified Systems Engineer + Internet (MCSE+I)

An expansion of the MCSE certification, with a specialty in Internet technology, the Microsoft Certified Systems Engineer + Internet certification has the following requirements:

- Implementing and Supporting Microsoft Windows NT Server 4.0 (exam 70-067)
- Implementing and Supporting Microsoft Windows NT Server 4.0 in the Enterprise (exam 70-068)
- Networking Essentials (exam 70-058)
- Internetworking with Microsoft TCP/IP on Microsoft Windows NT 4.0 (exam 70-059)
- The choice of a client exam; choices include Windows NT Workstation 4.0 (exam 70-073), Windows 95 (exam 70-064), and Windows 98 (exam 70-098)
- Implementing and Supporting Microsoft Internet Information Server 4.0 (exam 70-087) or Implementing and Supporting Microsoft Internet Information Server 3.0 and Microsoft Index Server 1.1 (exam 70-077)
- Either Implementing and Supporting Microsoft Internet Explorer 4.0 by Using the Internet Explorer Administration Kit (exam 70-079) or Implementing and Supporting Microsoft Internet Explorer 5.0 by Using the Microsoft Internet Explorer Administration Kit (exam 70-080)
- Two electives of your choice from a list that has now been narrowed to include only SQL, Site Server, Exchange, Proxy Server, and SNA

Microsoft Certified Database Administrator (MCDBA)

To become certified as a Database Administrator, you must pass five exams:

- Implementing and Supporting Microsoft Windows NT Server 4.0 (exam 70-067)
- Implementing and Supporting Microsoft Windows NT Server 4.0 in the Enterprise (exam 70-068)
- Administering Microsoft SQL Server 7.0 (exam 70-028)
- Designing and Implementing Databases with Microsoft SQL Server 7.0 (exam 70-029)
- An elective in a number of categories, including more SQL, Visual C++, TCP/IP, IIS, Visual Basic, or Visual FoxPro

Microsoft Certified Solution Developers (MCSD)

Microsoft Certified Solution Developers are qualified to design and develop custom business solutions with Microsoft development tools, platforms, and technologies such as Microsoft BackOffice and Microsoft Office. MCSD candidates are required to demonstrate a full understanding of 32-bit architecture, DCOM, Visual Studio, and other related topics. Requirements include passing four exams:

- Analyzing Requirements and Defining Solution Architectures (exam 70-100)
- An exam in designing desktop applications in either Visual C++, Visual FoxPro, or Visual Basic
- An exam in designing distributed applications in either Visual C++, Visual FoxPro, or Visual Basic
- An elective from a number of programming categories

Microsoft Certified Trainers (MCT)

Microsoft Certified Trainers are instructionally and technically qualified to deliver Microsoft Official Curriculum through Microsoft authorized education sites. These sites are made up of Microsoft Certified Technical Education Centers (CTECs), including companies such as Productivity Point International, which specializes in offering technical and application training to corporate clients; and Authorized Academic Training Partners (AATPs), which represent educational institutions that offer certified classes for continuing education. For a trainer to be certified as an MCT by Microsoft, that trainer must also have attended and completed, or in some cases studied, each certified class that he or she expects to teach.

Understanding the Exam Requirements

The exams are computer-administered tests that measure your ability to implement and administer Microsoft products or systems; troubleshoot problems with installation, operation, or customization; and provide technical support to users. The exams do more than test your ability to define terminology and/or recite facts. Product knowledge is an important foundation for superior job performance, but definitions and feature lists are just the beginning. In the real world, you need hands-on skills and the ability to apply your knowledge—to understand confusing situations, solve thorny problems, optimize solutions to minimize downtime, and maximize current and future productivity.

To develop exams that test for the right competence factors, Microsoft follows an eight-phase exam development process:

- In the first phase, experts analyze the tasks that make up the job being tested. This job-analysis phase identifies the knowledge, skills, and abilities relating specifically to the performance area to be certified.

- The next phase develops objectives by building on the framework provided by the job analysis. The job function tasks are translated into specific and measurable units of knowledge, skills, and abilities. The resulting list of objectives (the objective domain) is the basis for developing certification exams and training materials.

- Selected contributors rate the objectives developed in the preceding phase. The reviewers are technology professionals who are currently performing the applicable job function. After the objectives are prioritized and weighted based on the contributors' input, they become the blueprint for the exam items.

- During the fourth phase, exam items are reviewed and revised to ensure that they are technically accurate, clear, unambiguous, plausible, free of cultural bias, and not misleading or tricky. Items are also evaluated to confirm that they test for high-level, useful knowledge, rather than obscure or trivial facts.

- During alpha review, technical and job function experts review each item for technical accuracy, reach consensus on all technical issues, and edit the reviewed items for clarity of expression.

- The next step is the beta exam. Beta exam participants take the test to gauge its effectiveness. Microsoft performs a statistical analysis based on the responses of the beta participants, including information about difficulty and relevance, to verify the validity of the exam items and to determine which items are used in the final certification exam.

- When the statistical analysis is complete, the items are distributed into multiple parallel forms, or versions, of the final certification exam, usually within six to eight weeks of the beta exam.

Key Concept

If you participate in a beta exam, you can take it at a cost that is lower than the cost of the final certification exam (typically by half), but you should not approach the beta exam lightly. Beta exams actually contain the entire pool of possible questions, about 30 percent of which are dropped after the beta. The remaining questions are divided into the different forms of the final exam. If you decide to take a beta exam, you should review and study as seriously as you would for a final certification exam. Passing a beta exam counts as passing the final exam; you receive full credit for passing a beta exam.

Also, because you will be taking all the questions that will be used for the exam, you can expect a beta to take significantly longer than the final exam.

Also during this phase, a group of job function experts determine the cut, or minimum passing score, for the exam. (The cut score differs from exam to exam because it is based on an item-by-item determination of the percentage of candidates who answered the item correctly.)

- The final phase—Exam Live!—is administered by Sylvan Prometric or Virtual University Enterprise (VUE), which are independent testing companies. The exams are always available at Sylvan Prometric testing centers worldwide; you can schedule them by calling 800-755-exam or by going to **www.2test.com**. To register with VUE worldwide, visit its Web site at **www.vue.com**, or call 888-837-8616.

Microsoft posts beta exam notices on the Internet (**http://www.microsoft.com/mcp** or **http://www.microsoft.com/train_cert**) and mails notices to certification development volunteers, past certification candidates, and product beta participants.

Windows NT 3.51 Track to the MCSE Certification

As of this writing, the NT 3.51 track is still valid for MCSE certification but is scheduled to retire with the release of the Windows 2000 exams. The following exams are required:

- Implementing and Supporting Microsoft Windows NT Server 3.51 (exam 70-043)
- Implementing and Supporting Microsoft Windows NT Workstation 3.51 (exam 70-042)
- Networking Essentials (exam 70-058)
- A valid client exam
- Two electives of your choice from a large list

As with the MCSE track under 4.0, exam 70-058 (Networking Essentials) is waived for those who are similarly certified by another vendor.

Continuing Certification Requirements

After you gain an MCP certification, such as the Microsoft Certified Systems Engineer certification, your work isn't over. Microsoft requires you to maintain your certification by updating your exam credits as new products are released and old ones are retired.

A Microsoft Certified Trainer is required to pass the exam for a new product within three months of the exam's release. For example, the Windows NT Server 4.0 exam (70-67) and Enterprise Exam (70-68) were released in December 1996. All MCTs were required to pass these exams by March 31, 1997, or lose certification to teach the Windows NT 4.0 Core Technologies course.

Holders of the other MCP certifications (MCSD and MCSE) are required to replace an exam that gives them qualifying credit within six months to a year of the withdrawal of that exam. For example, the Windows for Workgroups exam was one of the original electives for the MCSE certification. When it was withdrawn, MCSEs had six months to replace it with another elective exam, such as the TCP/IP exam.

After you become a certified trainer, you begin receiving monthly updates regarding the tests and courses that have become obsolete, as well as the introduction of new courses and tests and certification requirements via Microsoft's Education Forum newsletter. You also can find updates by browsing Microsoft's Web site at **www.microsoft.com/train_cert**.

QUESTIONS AND ANSWERS

1. An MCP is any individual who has passed a current exam in any Microsoft Professional track, with one exception. What is the exception?

   A. Networking Essentials (exam 70-058)

2. True or False: The MCSE is a widely respected certification because it focuses on one aspect of computing.

   A. False. The MCSE has demonstrated skills and abilities on the full range of software, from client operating systems to server operating systems to client/server applications.

3. Which certification instructionally and technically qualifies you to deliver Microsoft Official Curriculum through Microsoft authorized education sites?

   A. Microsoft Certified Trainers (MCT).

4. To maintain certification, a Microsoft Certified Trainer is required to pass the exam for a new product within how many months of the exam's release?

   A. Three.

5. An MCP+I is an MCP who has specialized in _____ technologies.

   A. Internet-related.

CHAPTER PREREQUISITE

You should already be familiar with the basic operation of either Windows 3.x or Windows 95. Although a brief overview of the new Windows NT 4.0 user interface is provided in this book, it is essential that you have a strong working knowledge of basic networking concepts and terms.

Understanding Microsoft Windows NT 4.0

WHILE YOU READ

1. The type of multitasking employed by Windows NT Workstation 4.0 is _____ .

2. True or False: NT supported HPFS through all versions until 4.0.

3. The maximum number of remote dial-in sessions supported by NT Workstation is _____ .

4. The number of NT Servers needed to implement the workgroup model is _____ .

5. Web publishing is accomplished with Windows NT Workstation through what service?

Before beginning a detailed discussion of Microsoft Windows NT 4.0 Workstation, an overview of the NT product line is provided so that you'll have a clearer understanding of what is included in the product line and how it can be used within an organization. This chapter then covers the features and functionality of Microsoft Windows NT 4.0 Server.

Exploring Windows NT 4.0's Features

Microsoft Windows NT is a 32-bit operating system that is designed to provide fast and efficient performance for power computer users, such as software developers, CAD programmers, and design engineers. Figure 2.1 displays a glimpse of the features common to both Windows NT Workstation and Windows NT Server (versions 3.51 and 4.0, respectively). Because NT provides better performance for existing 16-bit applications (both MS-DOS and Windows), as well as 32-bit applications developed specifically for the operating system, it is increasingly found on the desks of business users. The performance enhancements include the following:

- Multiple platform support
- Preemptive multitasking
- Expanded processing support
- Expanded memory support
- Expanded file system support
- Enhanced security
- Network and communications support

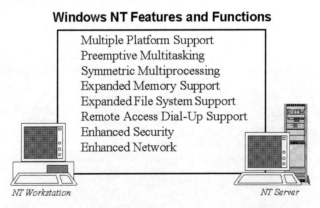

Windows NT Features and Functions

Multiple Platform Support
Preemptive Multitasking
Symmetric Multiprocessing
Expanded Memory Support
Expanded File System Support
Remote Access Dial-Up Support
Enhanced Security
Enhanced Network

NT Workstation   *NT Server*

Figure 2.1
These features are common to both Windows NT Workstation and Windows NT Server.

Multiple Platform Support

Microsoft Windows NT is engineered to run on several hardware platforms. The Hardware Abstraction Layer, or HAL, component of the NT architecture isolates platform-specific information for the operating system—for example, how to interact with a RISC-based processor as opposed to an Intel x86 processor. This architecture makes NT a highly portable system. Only a few pieces of code, such as the HAL, need to be recompiled. NT supports Intel x86 and Pentium-based computers, as well as RISC-based computers, such as MIPS R4000, DEC Alpha AXP, and PowerPC. Future support will be limited to Intel machines.

Preemptive Multitasking

All processes in NT are given at least one thread of operation. A thread represents a piece of code relating to a process. For example, loading a file may require several "threads" to carry out the process—in other words, locating the file on disk, allocating RAM for the file, moving it into that allocated memory space, and so forth. Many processes and applications written for Windows and NT have multiple threads associated with them.

NT can treat each thread of a process independently of the others, providing a greater degree of control over the overall performance of the system. Each thread also is given a processing priority based on its function. For example, an operating system process, such as memory allocation, receives a higher priority for its threads than a file-save process.

Each thread is given a specific amount of time with the processor. This process sometimes is called time-slicing. Higher priority threads are processed ahead of lower priority threads. All the threads of one priority are processed first before those of the next priority, and so on. This process is called preemptive multitasking. In addition, certain threads, primarily those that are system related, are processed in the protected mode of the processor (known as ring 0) and, thus, are protected from other processes and crashes.

Other threads, those relating to application functions such as file printing, run in the unprotected mode of the processor. This means that, although they may be given their own memory space, other "poorly written" applications (and their threads) might try to "butt in" and cause what is generally referred to as a General Protection, or GP, fault. Microsoft has taken several precautions to ensure that this situation does not happen in NT. These threads, and the precautions Microsoft has installed in NT, are discussed in more detail later in this book. Supporting both multitasking and multithreading gives applications excellent processing support and protection against system hang-ups and crashes.

Expanded Processing Support

Microsoft Windows NT provides symmetric multiprocessing with support for OEM implementations of up to 32 processors in Server and 2 processors in Workstation. Every process that runs under NT has at least one thread of operation or programming code associated with it. A process might be either user-generated, such as the writing of a file to disk or printing a document, or system-generated, such as validating a user logon or providing read access to a file.

Symmetric multiprocessing enables the NT operating system to load-balance process threads across all available processors in the computer, as opposed to asymmetric multi-processing, in which the operating system takes control of one processor and directs application threads to other available processors.

Expanded Memory Support

Windows NT supports computers with up to 4 gigabytes of RAM and theoretic file or partition sizes of up to 16 exabytes (though this number will vary depending on the type of hardware you have). An exabyte is one billion gigabytes. You might consider that number to be theoretical, and to a certain extent it is. However, it was not very ago that MIS departments debated the wisdom of purchasing 10-megabyte disk drives for their users' computers because they felt that the drives would never be filled up.

Expanded File System Support

Windows NT provides support for the MS-DOS File Allocation Table (FAT) file system, as well as its own New Technology File System (NTFS). Previous versions of NT also supported OS/2's High Performance File System (HPFS) though that support was dropped in NT 4.0.

Key Concept

Version 4.0 no longer provides support for HPFS.

NTFS provides a high level of security in the form of file- and directory-level permissions similar to those found in other network operating systems, such as trustee rights that are used in Novell's NetWare. NTFS also provides transaction tracking, which helps recover data in the event of system failure, and sector sparing, which identifies potentially bad disk storage space and moves data to good storage. NTFS also provides data compression implemented as a file or directory property.

Enhanced Security

Security begins with NT's WINLOGON and NETLOGON processes, which authenticate a user's access to a computer, workgroup, or enterprise by validating his or her username and password, and assigning each with his or her own security identifier. In addition to this mandatory logon, NT offers share-level resource control, security auditing functions, and file- and directory-level permissions (in NTFS partitions).

Network and Communications Support

Windows NT is designed to provide several internetworking options. The NetBEUI, NWLINK (IPX/SPX), TCP/IP, AppleTalk, and DLC protocols are all supported and included. NT is also supported on Novell NetWare networks, Microsoft LAN Manager, IBM LAN Server and SNA networks, Banyan VINES, and DEC PATHWORKS.

NT Server offers a secure dial-up option for clients and servers. RAS clients can remotely access any shared network resource to which they have been given access through RAS's gateway functions, such as shared folders and printers.

In an NT network, valid workstation clients include Microsoft Windows NT Workstations and Servers, Windows 3.x, MS-DOS, Windows for Workgroups, Windows 95, OS/2, Novell NetWare (client/server), and Macintosh.

Choosing Windows NT Workstation or Server

The difference in choosing when to use NT Workstation or NT Server is not necessarily the difference between desktop and enterprise computing. Both NT Workstation and NT Server provide the capability to make resources available on the network and thus act as a "server." For that matter, an NT Server can be made part of a workgroup of NT Workstations to act as the resource server for that workgroup. Choosing between NT Workstation and NT Server really comes down to the features specific to each product and the type of network model that will be implemented. The following sections describe the differences between NT Workstation and NT Server.

Microsoft Windows NT Workstation

Microsoft Windows NT Workstation is designed for the so-called power user, such as developers or CAD designers, but increasingly is becoming the desktop operating system of choice for end-user business computing because of its robust feature set, as described previously. In addition to those features and functions that are common to both NT Workstation and NT Server, NT Workstation offers the following specific characteristics (see Figure 2.2):

- Workstation has unlimited outbound peer-to-peer connections.
- It has 10 inbound client connections for resource access.

- It can be either a RAS client or server, but it supports only one remote dial-in session.
- The retail installation supports two processors for symmetric multiprocessing.
- It acts as an import server for Directory Replication Services.

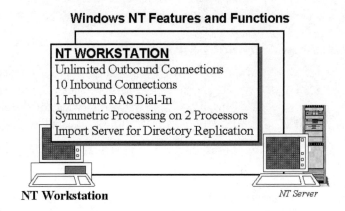

Windows NT Features and Functions

> **NT WORKSTATION**
> Unlimited Outbound Connections
> 10 Inbound Connections
> 1 Inbound RAS Dial-In
> Symmetric Processing on 2 Processors
> Import Server for Directory Replication

NT Workstation   *NT Server*

Figure 2.2
Windows NT Workstation features and functions.

Microsoft Windows NT Server

Windows NT Server is designed to provide file, print, and application service support within a given network model. Figure 2.3 illustrates specific characteristics of NT Server. Although it also can be used as a desktop system, it is engineered to provide optimum performance when providing network services—for example, by optimizing memory differently for application servers than it does for domain controllers. In addition to the features and functions described previously, NT Server offers the following capabilities:

- NT Server allows as many inbound connections to resources as there are valid client licenses (virtually unlimited).
- It supports as many as 256 remote dial-in RAS sessions.
- The retail installation supports as many as four processors for symmetric multiprocessing.
- It provides a full set of services for application and network support, such as the following:
  - Services for Macintosh that enable client support for Macintosh computers.
  - Gateway Service for NetWare that enables NT clients to access Novell NetWare file and print resources.

- Directory Replication Service for copying of directory structures and files from a source NT Server computer to a target NT Server or Workstation computer.

- It provides full integration into the Microsoft BackOffice suite, including System Management Server, SNA Server, SQL Server, and Microsoft Exchange Server.

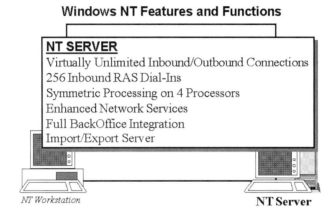

Figure 2.3
Windows NT Server features and functions.

The Microsoft Windows NT Server product can be installed either as a server that provides only network-accessible resources or as a domain controller that additionally provides centralized administration of user accounts and resource access. These concepts are reviewed later in this chapter.

Features and Functions in Windows NT 4.0

Windows NT 4.0 continues Microsoft's commitment to reliable, performance-driven, network-ready operating systems by incorporating the power, features, and functions of the NT operating system with the object-oriented Windows 95 user interface. Enhanced features and functions common to both NT Workstation and Server 4.0 include the following:

- Windows 95-like user interface
- Windows Explorer
- Hardware profiles
- Enhanced dial-up networking support

- NDS-aware client services for Novell NetWare 4.x
- Integrated Windows Messaging engine
- Internet Explorer 2.0
- Web services

Windows 95 User Interface

All the basic features of Microsoft's Windows 95 interface have been integrated into Windows NT 4.0. These features include updated or enhanced system utilities, as well as additional utilities, such as the Windows Explorer, Network Neighborhood, Briefcase, Desktop shortcuts, Microsoft Network support, and the Recycle Bin.

Windows Explorer

The Explorer feature of the interface replaces the File Manager utility. It provides excellent browsing capabilities for management of drives, directories, files, and network connections. The Explorer presents the user's data-access information as a hierarchy of drives, desktop, network connections, folders, and files. The browsing capabilities of the Explorer offer not only browsing of file and directory names, but also of data strings within files. Throughout this book and its labs, you will use Windows Explorer to access files and folders, set permissions, create and manage shared folders, and so on.

Key Concept

Although the Windows Explorer replaces the File Manager utility by default, the File Manager is still available and can be launched.

You can run the File Manager by following these simple steps:

1. Choose Start from the taskbar.

2. Choose Run from the Start menu.

3. Enter the File Manager filename as follows: **winfile.exe**.

4. Click OK.

Microsoft recommends using File Manager only until you become comfortable with Windows Explorer. File Manager is made available only for transitional purposes.

Hardware Profiles

Perhaps one of the most useful features in Windows NT 4.0 is the support for multiple hardware profiles. First introduced in Windows 95, this feature enables you to create hardware profiles to fit various computing needs. The most common example of using hardware profiles is with portable computers. You can create separate profiles to support the portable computer when it is in use by itself and for use when it is positioned in a docking station.

Key Concept

Plug and Play is a feature of Windows 95 and Windows 98 that is much appreciated. Note that, although the Plug and Play service has been included with Windows NT 4.0, "hot" Plug and Play (the capability for the operating system to recognize a configuration change on-the-fly and implement it) will not be fully supported until the next major release of Windows NT. Windows NT 4.0 does, however, recognize some hardware changes when it restarts. For example, additional memory or a new hard disk will be automatically detected by NT the next time you boot up.

CH

2

Enhanced Dial-Up Networking Support

The RAS client service now is installed as Dial-Up Networking. In addition, NT 4.0 provides the Dial-Up Networking Monitor for monitoring user connections and devices, as well as Remote Access Admin for monitoring remote user access to a RAS Server.

NT 4.0 also offers Telephony API version 2.0 (TAPI) and universal modem driver (Unimodem) support, which provides communications technology for FAX applications, the Microsoft Exchange client, the Microsoft Network (MSN), and Internet Explorer.

API provides access to the signaling for setting up calls and managing them, as well as preserving existing media stream functionality to manipulate the information carried over the connection that TAPI establishes. This capability allows applications not only to dial and transfer calls, but also to support fax, desktop conferencing, or applications that use the telephone set dial pad to access voice-prompted menus.

NDS-Aware Client Service for Novell NetWare 4.x

Microsoft provides an enhanced version of its Client Services for NetWare (CSNW) with NT 4.0, which supplies compatibility with Novell NetWare servers (versions 3.x and later) running NetWare Directory Services (NDS). This capability enables users to view NetWare-shared resources that are organized in a hierarchical tree format.

Integrated Microsoft Windows Messaging

Microsoft Windows Messaging is Microsoft's newest electronic mail product. Windows Messaging, which has been included with NT 4.0, enables users to send and receive mail, embed objects in mail messages, and integrate mail functionality into Microsoft applications.

Internet Explorer 2.0

 Key Concept

As of this writing, Internet Explorer 5.0 has been released. It was not available at the time the exam was written, and the exam has not been updated for 5.0. Internet Explorer 2.0 was included with NT 4.0, and you are expected to be familiar with this version for the certification exam.

Microsoft's Internet Explorer 2.0 is included with NT 4.0 to provide users access to the Internet. However, Microsoft now has made Internet Explorer 5.0 available through its various Internet sites (**www.microsoft.com**, for example). Watch for Microsoft to continue to enhance this product and make upgrades widely (and cheaply) available.

Internet Explorer requires that the TCP/IP protocol be installed and a connection made to the Internet.

Web Publishing

Microsoft includes Web publishing services in NT 4.0 that enable you to develop, publish, and manage Web pages, as well as FTP and Gopher services for your company's intranet or for smaller peer-to-peer networks. With NT 4.0 Server, Microsoft provides Internet Information Services (IIS) designed for heavy intranet and Internet usage. With NT Workstation 4.0, Microsoft provides Peer Web Services (PWS) for smaller workgroup–based Web publishing.

Integrated Network Monitor Agent

NT 4.0 includes a version of the Network Monitor utility, which is included with Microsoft's System Management Server BackOffice product. Network Monitor provides a full range of network-analysis tools for tracking and interpreting network traffic, frames, and so forth.

Distinguishing a Workgroup from a Domain

Two distinct types of networking are supported by Windows NT: workgroup computing and the domain model. As you plan your network, you need to distinguish between these two and decide which model best meets your networking needs. The following sections compare these two models.

Workgroup Model

The workgroup model of networking is more commonly referred to as the peer-to-peer model. In this model, all computers participate in a networking group. They all can make resources available to members of the workgroup and can access one another's resources. In other words, each computer acts as both a workstation and a server.

CH
2

Computers using Windows NT, Windows 95, and Windows for Workgroups can participate in a workgroup network model, as shown in Figure 2.4. In fact, both Windows NT Workstations and Windows NT Servers can be members of a workgroup. However, only Windows NT Server offers the added capability of providing user-level security for network resources.

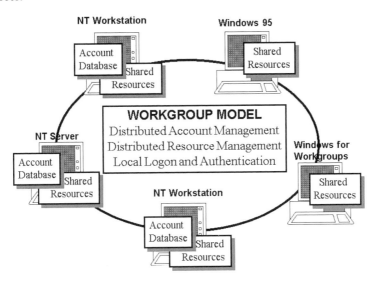

Figure 2.4
An example of the workgroup network model.

Key Concept

Windows 95 can provide user-level network resource security by using an NT (Server or Workstation) or Novell Server. However, providing such security requires that one or the other be present on the network.

On computers using Windows NT, access to resources is provided by authenticating the inbound user at the resource computer. Each Windows NT computer participating in a workgroup must maintain a list of users who will be accessing the resources on that computer.

Potentially, each computer will have at least as many user accounts as there are participating members in the workgroup. Account administration in a workgroup thus is considered to be distributed, as is resource administration. In other words, the responsibility for maintaining the integrity of user accounts and resource access generally falls to the owner of the computer. A workgroup model, then, might be construed to have limited security potential.

The workgroup model works quite well within smaller networks where the number of users requiring access to workgroup resources is small and easily managed. This number has been suggested to be between 10 and 20 computers/users. As mentioned before, a Windows NT Server can participate in a workgroup. If a larger number of computers or users is required within a workgroup model (more than 10), the more heavily used resources might be located in a Windows NT Server participating in the workgroup. Using the NT Server this way can help simplify the management of large groups of users accessing resources. Nevertheless, the main characteristics of this network model are distributed account management, distributed resource management, and limited security.

Domain Model

The domain model of networking, also known as the enterprise model, was introduced by Microsoft as a response to the management challenges presented by the growing workgroup model.

Unlike the workgroup model, the domain model (see Figure 2.5) maintains a centralized database of user and group account information. Resource access is provided by permitting access to users and groups that are members of the domain, and thus appear in the domain's account database. Recall that, in the workgroup model, each computer maintains its own account database, which is used for managing resource access at that computer. In the domain model, by virtue of their participation in the domain, the resources utilize the same central account database for managing user access. Resource managers also enjoy a higher level of security for their resources.

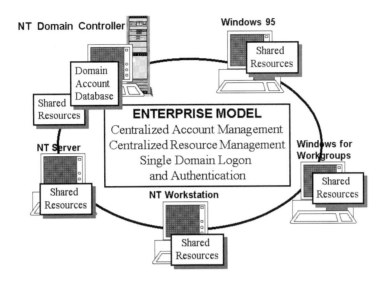

Figure 2.5
An example of the domain network model. The domain model answers what Microsoft refers to as the "enterprise challenge."

Organizing an Enterprise Network

When you're planning a large wide area network for an organization—hereafter referred to as the enterprise—Microsoft advocates implementing a structure that answers the following challenges:

- A single network logon account for the user, regardless of the user's location or domain affiliation
- Centralized account administration
- Easy user access to network resources, regardless of the location of the user or the resource in the enterprise
- Network resource administration focused in the hands of the resource owner or administrator
- Synchronization of account and security information across the enterprise

The structure should be capable of supporting enterprise networks of varying sizes, with servers, computers, and users in a variety of geographic locations. It also should support, and in some cases utilize, a variety of network architectures, protocols, and platforms to provide a completely flexible and open architecture.

CH 2

Microsoft responds to this challenge with its Directory Services solution. Windows NT's Directory Services provides a domain model of enterprise computing that centralizes account information and management into a single domain account database, while focusing network resource management with the owner/administrator of the resource.

You can think of a domain as a logical grouping of computers in a Microsoft network. A domain controller establishes the domain's identity and is used to maintain the database of user, group, and computer accounts for that domain. Besides the domain controller, a Windows NT domain can include member servers and workstation computers. A member server might be a Windows NT Server 4.0 configured as an application server, a database server, a RAS server, a print server, or a file server. Workstation computers might run Windows NT Workstation 4.0, Windows 95, Windows for Workgroups 3.11, MS-DOS, Apple Macintosh System 7, or LanMan 2.2c for DOS or OS/2.

All the computers that identify themselves as belonging to a particular domain are part of the same logical grouping. As such, they have access to the account database on the domain's domain controller for authenticating users as they log on and for creating access control lists (ACLs) for securing network resources stored on those computers. An enterprise can consist of one domain or several domains, following one of the domain models suggested by Microsoft.

For example, a domain might be centered around the organizational hierarchy and reflect its departmental structure. Perhaps the MIS department has assumed all responsibility for maintaining user and group accounts, while placing resource management within each department. Possibly, the enterprise is organized according to regional areas, such as the West, Midwest, and East domains. The domain structure might even be global in nature, reflecting the enterprise's international presence. Windows NT's Directory Services provides a fit for each of these structures because Windows NT domains are logical groupings of computers; therefore, they are extremely flexible. Although the physical layout of your network may affect the type of domain model that you choose to establish, domains simply don't care what the network topology looks like.

Single Network Logon

The concept of a single network logon is really quite simple: Provide the user with a single logon account that can be used to access the network from anywhere within the enterprise. An account executive based in Chicago should be able to fly to her company's office in London, use her same account to log on to the network at any computer in the London office, and access the same resources she has access to when in Chicago.

Windows NT 4.0 Directory Services is designed to provide just that capability by combining the domain model of networking with a security relationship called a trust. Briefly, a trust relationship enables users from one Windows NT domain to be granted access permissions to the network resources in a second Windows NT domain.

Assume that a trust exists between the London and Chicago domains. If the account executive's account is maintained in the Chicago domain, she can still log on to the company network at any computer in the London domain. Directory Services enables the account executive's logon request to be passed through the trust, back to the Chicago domain for authentication (see Figure 2.6). This process of passing the logon request back through the trust to the account domain is called pass-through authentication. After the executive's account has been validated, she can access any resource in the enterprise to which she has been given permission. Note that she needs only one logon account and password to access the network and its resources. Her physical location is not important, nor is the location of the resources.

CH
2

TRUST RELATIONSHIPS

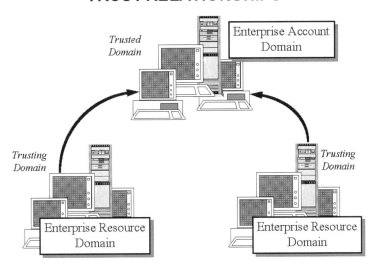

Figure 2.6
A user's logon information is passed through the trust relationship to be authenticated in the appropriate domain, as depicted here.

Centralized Account Administration

Recall that in a workgroup model, account administration tends to be decentralized to the desktop of each member of the workgroup. Each user might maintain his or her own workstation's account database, making it difficult to establish or maintain consistency or security.

By contrast, in a domain model, accounts are centralized on a specific domain server called the domain controller. The domain controller for the domain establishes the domain's identity in the enterprise. In fact, a domain is established by the installation of a primary domain controller (PDC). The PDC maintains the master account database for the domain. The PDC can also authenticate users on the network (or log on users), but its primary function is to maintain the domain's account database.

Although a domain can contain only one primary domain controller for managing accounts and authenticating users, the domain can include one or more backup domain controllers, or BDCs. The BDC receives a copy of the master account database maintained on the PDC. Its primary function is to authenticate users who are trying to log on to the network.

Network Resource Access

Through a combination of single logon accounts, centralized administration, and trust relationships, a user can easily access any resource that he or she has been given permission to use from anywhere in the enterprise.

Windows NT Directory Services provides a flexible set of options for resource management that can fit the needs of most enterprise models.

Summary

This chapter provided an overview of Windows NT 4.0. It was an introduction to concepts that are expanded upon in greater detail in forthcoming chapters.

The next chapter describes the system requirements for Windows NT 4.0 and the installation procedures.

QUESTIONS AND ANSWERS

1. The type of multitasking employed by Windows NT Workstation 4.0 is _____ .

    A. Preemptive. The processor is preemptively kept from being hogged by a runaway process. The older form of multitasking is cooperative.

2. True or False: NT has supported HPFS through all versions until 4.0.

    A. True. NT 3.51 and all earlier versions supported HPFS. With NT 4.0, only FAT and NTFS file systems are supported.

...continues

> **3.** The maximum number of remote dial-in sessions supported by NT Workstation is
>
> _____ .
>
> A. NT Workstation supports a maximum of 1 remote dial-in session, whereas Server supports 256.
>
> **4.** The number of NT Servers needed to implement the workgroup model is
>
> _____ .
>
> A. None. No NT Servers are needed to implement the workgroup model, although they can participate in such if they are configured as member servers. At least one NT Server is needed to create an enterprise/domain model.
>
> **5.** Web publishing is accomplished with Windows NT Workstation through what service?
>
> A. Peer Web Services (PWS) enables NT Workstation to publish Web pages.

CH 2

PRACTICE TEST

1. Which of the following are characteristics of NTFS? Choose three.

- **a.** Transaction tracking
- **b.** File- and directory-level permissions
- **c.** Auto-defragmentation of files
- **d.** Data compression

Answers a, b, and d are correct because NTFS supports transaction tracking, file- and directory-level permissions, as well as data compression. Answer c is not correct because NT does not include a defragmentation utility.

2. Choose two features of Windows NT Server 4.0.

- **a.** Windows 95 Interface
- **b.** Peer Web Services
- **c.** Plug and Play
- **d.** Hardware Profiles

Answer a is correct because the Explorer.exe shell that is used in Windows 95 is also used in Windows NT Server. Answer b is incorrect because Peer Web Services (PWS) runs on NT Workstation, whereas IIS (Internet Information Server) runs on NT Server. Answer c is incorrect because NT Server 4.0 does not include Plug and Play. **Answer d is correct because hardware profiles and user profiles are employed.**

3. Which of the following characteristics best apply to a workgroup network model? Choose two.

 a. A workgroup network model provides a high level of security for resource access.

 b. The workgroup model is best applied to smaller (fewer than 20) workstation groups.

 c. A workgroup model is identified by its domain controller.

 d. Each Windows NT computer participating in a workgroup must maintain a list of users who will be accessing the resources on that computer.

Answer a is incorrect because only share-level security is possible, and it is inferior to user-level security (which cannot be present in a workgroup). **Answer b is correct because the workgroup model is suitable only for small networks.** Answer c is incorrect because the presence of a domain controller creates a domain (enterprise) and not a workgroup. **Answer d is correct because each Windows NT computer participating in a workgroup must maintain a list of users who will be accessing the resources on that computer.**

4. Which of the following characteristics best apply to a domain network model? Choose two.

 a. Resource access is provided by permitting access to users and groups that are members of the domain.

 b. User and group accounts are maintained on each workstation that is a member of the domain.

 c. A domain network model provides a relatively low level of resource security.

 d. Resource and account management is centralized.

Answer a is correct because resource access is provided by permitting access to users and groups that are members of the domain. Answer b is incorrect because user and group accounts are maintained on the domain controller. Answer c is incorrect because the domain offers user-level security, which is superior to the share-level security offered in workgroups. **Answer d is correct because both resource and account management are centralized.**

5. When you're planning a large wide area network for an enterprise, Microsoft advocates implementing a structure that supports which of the following characteristics? Choose all that apply.

 a. Single network logon regardless of location or domain affiliation

 b. Easy user access to network resources regardless of the location of the user or the resource in the enterprise

 c. Decentralized account and resource administration

 d. Synchronization of account and security information across the enterprise

Answers a, b, and d are correct because single logon should be a goal for every network; users should have access to resources they need regardless of where they log on from; and account information—as well as security—must be synchronized. Answer c is incorrect because Microsoft encourages centralized administration.

6. Which of the following are common to Windows NT Server and Windows NT Workstation? Choose all that apply.
   a. Multiple platform support
   b. Preemptive multitasking
   c. Expanded processing support
   d. Expanded memory support

CH 2

All the above. All these answers are correct because both Windows NT Server and NT Workstation offer multiple platform support, preemptive multitasking, expanded processing, and memory support.

7. As a minimum, processes in Windows NT require how many threads of operation?
   a. 0
   b. 1
   c. 2
   d. More than 2

Answer b is correct. All processes in NT are given at least one thread of operation.

8. Windows NT supports file/partition sizes up to how large?
   a. 4GB
   b. 16GB
   c. 16TB
   d. 16EB

Answer d is correct because Windows NT supports file and partition sizes up to a theoretical 16EB.

9. What is the number of dial-in RAS sessions supported in Windows NT Workstation?
   a. 256
   b. 16
   c. 1
   d. 0

Answer c is correct because Windows NT Workstation supports only one RAS dial-in session versus the 256 available in Windows NT Server.

10. IIS is included with Windows NT Server, and PWS is included with Windows NT Workstation. The version of each respective product included with Windows NT offers which services? Choose all that apply.

   a. Web

   b. Gopher

   c. FTP

   d. Archie

Answers a, b, and c are correct because Web, Gopher, and FTP services are included, whereas Archie service is not.

CHAPTER PREREQUISITE

You should already be familiar with the basic workings of your computer system, particularly how to boot it; its current operating system; and the basics of BIOS, memory, hard disks, CPU types, serial and parallel ports, network adapters, video adapters, and the mouse.

Installing Windows NT Workstation 4.0

WHILE YOU READ

1. What is the minimum hardware requirement to install Windows NT Workstation 4.0?

2. What is the minimum amount of RAM needed to install Windows 95?

3. The default directory into which the NT Workstation operating system is installed is _____ .

4. True or False: Windows NT Workstation 4.0 supports NTFS, CDFS, FAT, and HPFS.

5. True or False: Dual-booting with Windows 95 always requires operating systems to be in separate directories.

This chapter explores the Windows NT Workstation 4.0 installation process. We will concentrate on three primary components of the installation process: preparation, execution, and completion.

Preparing to Install Windows NT Workstation 4.0

The installation of Windows NT Workstation 4.0 is actually pretty straightforward and relatively painless. However, you should collect some information ahead of time to make installation even smoother. Before you begin your installation of Windows NT Workstation 4.0, do some detective work. You basically need to ask yourself two questions:

1. What is the system configuration of the computer on which I am installing Windows NT Workstation 4.0?
2. What kind of installation am I implementing?

System configuration includes such information as the make and model of the computer, the BIOS type and date, bus architecture, video card and monitor, network adapter, modem, memory, processor type, disk controller and drive, sound card, and so on. It also includes the current operating system, installed applications, available disk space, and so on.

Beyond deciding from among the Typical, Custom, Portable, and Compact options, you also need to know what kind of network model, if any, the computer will be participating in, the location of the installation files, the number of blank formatted disks you need to have ready, and so on. A more exhaustive checklist will follow later in this chapter.

Finding this information sounds like a lot of detective work. But if you think about it, you probably know the answers to most of these questions right off the top of your head. Windows NT does an excellent job of detecting most of this information for itself. What we are most concerned with here is discovering the nuances of a specific configuration that can throw a speed bump into the installation process. For example, if you have MS-DOS 5.0 or higher installed on your system, you might use the Microsoft Diagnostics utility to provide some of the more subtle details such as interrupt and DMA settings. After you have installed Windows NT Workstation a few times within your own organization, you will begin to understand and appreciate the nuances that your particular computer and network configurations bring to the installation process.

Windows NT Workstation 4.0 System Requirements

Table 3.1 outlines the basic hardware requirements for a successful installation of Windows NT Workstation 4.0.

Table 3.1   Windows NT Workstation 4.0 Hardware Requirements

Component	Description
CPU	32-bit Intel 486/33 or higher, Intel Pentium, Pentium Pro, or supported RISC-based processors such as MIPS, Digital Alpha AXP, Power PC
Disk	120MB free disk space required for Windows NT System file partition (149MB for RISC-based computers)
Memory	12MB RAM minimum required; 16MB suggested (16MB for RISC-based computers)
Video	Display adapter with VGA resolution or higher
Drives	CD-ROM drive and 3.5-inch disk drive if installing locally
Network	One or more supported adapter cards if member of a network and/or if installing over the network
File System	A FAT or NTFS partition on Intel-based computers; a minimum 2MB required FAT partition on RISC-based computers

CH
3

The most important characteristic of the computer's configuration, and the one that you will pay the closest attention to, is the hardware's compatibility with Windows NT Workstation 4.0. For most organizations, the compatibility of the hardware is probably not a big issue. However, if one piece of hardware is incompatible, expect your installation to have problems. In fact, if you have a hardware failure during installation, your first thought should be "incompatible hardware," probably followed by some sort of stress-reducing phraseology.

Microsoft works very closely with most major hardware manufacturers to ensure the compatibility of its products with Windows NT. To this end, Microsoft regularly publishes and updates a Hardware Compatibility List (HCL). If you have any doubt at all about the compatibility of the hardware, consult this list. Pay particularly close attention to network adapters; SCSI adapters and drives, especially CD-ROM drives; video drivers; and sound and game cards. For example, video driver support has changed significantly with Windows NT 4.0, thus rendering earlier version drivers inoperative. Also, do not take for granted that, just because your computer model is BrandName TurboX and it appears on the HCL, all the internal components (especially those mentioned earlier) are also supported. It is reasonable to assume that all internal components are supported. However, if your installation fails because of a hardware problem, check the failed component against the HCL as your first troubleshooting step.

You can access the HCL in several ways. If you subscribe to Microsoft TechNet, you can find a copy of the HCL there by searching for "Hardware Compatibility List." You can also find the most up-to-date versions by accessing Microsoft's Web site.

The second most important consideration regards third-party devices and drivers. Once again, Microsoft provides a tremendous list of support drivers for most major third-party products. Even though Microsoft provides most of the drivers you will need, if you have any doubt, be sure to have a Windows NT-compatible driver available just in case. You can generally obtain one relatively easily from the device manufacturer.

If you are installing Windows NT Workstation 4.0 as part of a major roll-out within your organization, you should consider performing a test installation on sample computer configurations from within your organization.

Choosing Windows NT Workstation 4.0 or Windows 95

When you're deciding between installing Windows NT Workstation 4.0 or Windows 95 on your computer, you should take into account some special considerations. Windows NT Workstation 4.0 has higher hardware requirements than Windows 95. Windows 95 can be installed on a computer with a minimum 386DX processor, 4MB of memory (although having 8MB is recommended), a VGA or higher monitor, and 35 to 40MB of disk space. By contrast, Windows NT Workstation 4.0 requires a minimum 486/33 processor, 12MB of memory (16MB recommended), 120MB or more of disk space, and a CD-ROM drive or some other access to source files.

Other considerations include the feature set of each product. Windows NT Workstation 4.0 offers a greater number of security options, multiple platform support, symmetric multiprocessing, and full 32-bit processing. Windows 95 does not provide these features but does offer a wider scope of device driver support, and it fully supports Plug and Play (PnP).

Your choice of operating system ultimately will depend on the hardware configuration of your computers, the features you desire in an operating system, the role your computer will play (does it contain data that needs a higher level of security, for example), and, of course, your budget.

Preparation Checklist

After you collect the computer's hardware information, ensuring its compatibility with Windows NT Workstation 4.0 and that it meets the minimum installation requirements, you need to know some additional information before executing the setup process. As we explore the setup process itself, we will expound on each of these points in more detail. For future reference, however, use the following checklist as a guide for preparation. With the exception of the first four items, this checklist represents the information that will be requested during the setup process.

- Read all Windows NT documentation files.
- Assess system requirements. See Table 3.1.
- Assess hardware compatibility. Verify by consulting the Hardware Compatibility List.
- Gather device driver and configuration data:
    - Video—Display type, adapter and chipset type
    - Network—Card type, IRQ, I/O Address, DMA, Connector, and so on
    - SCSI Controller—Adapter and chipset type, IRQ, bus type
    - Sound/Media—IRQ, I/O Address, DMA
    - I/O Ports—IRQ, I/O Address, DMA
    - Modems—Port, IRQ, I/O Address, modem type
- Back up your current configuration and data files.
- Determine which type of initial setup will be performed. (You may need three blank formatted disks before running setup.)
- Determine the location of the source files for performing this installation. (Are they on CD-ROM, on a shared network location?)
- Determine on which partition the Windows NT system files will be installed.
- Determine which file system you will install.
- Determine whether you will create an Emergency Repair Disk. (If so, you need one blank disk available before running setup.)
- Identify your installation CD Key.
- Decide on a unique name for your computer.
- Determine which workgroup or domain name the computer will join.
- Identify network connection data—IP addresses, IPX card numbers, and so on.
- Identify in which time zone the computer is located.

CH
3

Key Concept

Well over 90 text files contain additional information specific to individual devices such as network cards and video drivers. You can find them by browsing for .TXT files in the subdirectories for your specific platform. For example, on an Intel computer, look in the I386 platform directory on your Windows NT Workstation 4.0 installation CD-ROM under the DRVLIB.NIC subdirectory for a subdirectory with your network card's name. In that directory, look for and read the files with a .TXT extension.

Certain other files bear close examination. In the platform directory—for example, I386—look for SETUP.TXT. It contains general information regarding devices and drivers used and required during installation. Three compressed files contain release-specific information: readme.wr_, printer.wr_, and network.wr_. You can expand and read them by using the Windows Write program or the Windows 95 WordPad program. From a DOS prompt, switch to the platform directory, and enter the command using the following syntax: **expand file.wr_ c:\target directory\file.wri**. For example, if you've created a directory called readme on the C: drive, you can expand the network.wr_ file there by typing **expand network.wr_ c:\readme\network.wri**.

Executing the Windows NT Workstation 4.0 Startup Process

So far, we have concentrated on preinstallation detective work and preparation. Let's now turn our attention to the actual setup process and begin by examining the five major phases that occur during this process.

1. The setup begins in what is referred to as DOS or text mode. If you have installed Windows before, this blue text screen format will look familiar to you. During this mode, several screens appear, asking for various pieces of information about the computer configuration for Windows NT Workstation 4.0. The screens include the following:

   - A menu of startup options
   - Detection and configuration of storage devices such as SCSI drives
   - Initial hardware verification
   - Choice of the installation disk partition
   - Choice of file system for the installation partition
   - Installation directory name

2. This information is used to reboot the computer and load a mini-version of Windows NT 4.0. It is a 32-bit multithreaded kernel that enhances and supports the setup process.

3. As the computer reboots, Windows NT hardware detection takes place. This event discovers and initializes hardware devices for use by Windows NT. These devices include the following:

   - SCSI adapter
   - Video adapter

- Mouse and keyboard
- Disk drives
- CD-ROM drive(s)
- COM and parallel ports
- Memory configuration
- Bus adapter

4. A GUI interface is installed, and the Windows NT 4.0 Setup Wizard is displayed. The wizard walks you through the rest of the installation process asking for information such as the following:

- Personal information
- Unique computer name
- Network card information
- Network configuration information such as protocols
- Workgroup or domain membership
- First user account and administration information
- Whether to create an Emergency Repair Disk
- Time zone
- Video display setup

5. Any additional support files are copied to the Windows NT system directory, configuration information is saved in the Windows NT Registry, and the setup process completes and restarts the computer.

The following sections describe each of these phases in more detail by walking through an actual installation of Windows NT Workstation 4.0. Read through the process carefully, and then try it yourself in the lab.

The setup process is essentially the same for Intel-based and RISC-based computers. The process described here applies to Intel-based computers. Any variation that applies to RISC-based computers is noted as it occurs in the process.

Beginning Setup

The setup process begins by locating the installation files. If you intend to install Windows NT locally, you need at the very minimum a compatible CD-ROM drive and optionally a 3.5-inch disk drive. If you are installing Windows NT over the network, which is largely the case in most organizations, you need to have an active network connection and at least read access to the location of the installation files.

CH
3

It is interesting to note that the installation files do not need to be on an existing Windows NT computer or that the network you are running need not necessarily be Microsoft-based. Indeed, the installation files could be loaded on a Novell NetWare server, and the computer that is to have Windows NT installed could be running the NetWare client software. As long as the Windows NT computer-to-be can access a network drive, the setup process can be initiated.

The first phase of the setup process, by default, requires the creation of three startup disks. Windows NT copies all the basic boot configuration information as well as the mini-Windows NT kernel to these disks and uses them to start the process. If you are installing Windows NT locally and have the original setup disks and CD-ROM, you probably have a set of startup disks in the Windows NT box. You can use them or let Windows NT create a new set for you. If your computer does not have a compatible CD-ROM drive, you need to use these disks to begin the setup process.

According to Microsoft's technical documentation for Windows NT Workstation 4.0, if the BIOS of your computer supports the El Torito Bootable CD-ROM (no emulation mode) format, you can begin setup from the Windows NT CD-ROM directly and let Windows NT prompt you to create the startup disks. However, problems have been reported with various compatible CD-ROM drives that may require you to use the packaged setup disks to begin setup.

Generally, if you are installing Windows NT over the network, you will not have access to the disks that come in the box and will want Windows NT to create them for you.

Another purpose of the startup disks is to provide a means of starting Windows NT for repair or recovery purposes if you cannot later boot. If you intend to create and keep current an Emergency Repair Disk, you can use this disk only if you first boot using the startup disks.

However, creating these disks during the startup process is not essential. You can save some time by performing a diskless installation of Windows NT. This type of installation is particularly useful when you're performing an over-the-network installation or rolling out Windows NT on a large scale.

The Windows NT Setup executable on the Intel platform is named WINNT.EXE. If you are installing Windows NT for the first time on a computer, you use this executable. If you already have a copy of Windows NT installed on the computer—for example, Windows NT Workstation 3.51—and intend to upgrade to Windows NT 4.0 or install a new copy of Windows NT 4.0, you can use an alternative executable called WINNT32.EXE. This 32-bit version of the setup program runs with increased performance.

Setting Up Windows NT Workstation 4.0 on RISC-Based Systems

On RISC-based systems, the setup process begins a little differently. Remember that on RISC-based computers, you must have a minimum 2MB FAT partition created before proceeding with Windows NT setup. This partition holds the two hardware-specific Windows NT boot files: OSLOADER.EXE and HAL.DLL. If you do not have a FAT partition, you must run the ARCINST.EXE utility located in the \MIPS subdirectory on the Windows NT Installation CD-ROM. When you boot your computer, choose RUN A PROGRAM from the ARC menu, and enter the path to the ARCINSTALL.EXE utility. After the utility starts, choose Configure System Partition and follow the screens. The rest of the setup will proceed generally as described in this book.

WINNT.EXE and WINNT32.EXE offer a variety of setup option switches that give you more control over how the installation proceeds. The syntax for using either executable is as follows:

```
[WINNT¦WINNT32] [/S:sourcepath] [/T:tempdrive] [/I:inffile]
[/O or /OX] [/F] [/C] [/B] [/U[:scriptfile]] [/R or /RX:directory]
```

Table 3.2 outlines these switches.

CH
3

Table 3.2   WINNT.EXE Option Switches

Switch	Explanation
/B	Performs setup without creating startup disks. Instead, it creates a temporary directory called WIN_NT on the hard disk with the most free space. This directory requires an additional 4 to 5MB of free disk space above the 120MB installation minimum.
/O	Creates the three installation startup disks. Note that with this switch, these disks can be created at any time. This switch is used for the network installations of Windows NT.
/OX	Performs the same action as /O, but for local CD-ROM installation.
/S:	Specifies the full drive or network path of the Windows NT *sourcepath* installation files.
/U[:script]	Used with /S, provides an unattended installation by skipping the screen that asks for the installation file location. With an optional script file, this switch does not prompt the installer for any information during setup.
/T:tempdrive	Allows you to specify the location of the temporary files. If the location is not specified, Windows NT chooses a drive for you.
/I:inffile	Specifies the filename of the setup information file. The default file is DOSNET.INF.

...continues

Table 3.2 continued	
Switch	Explanation
/C	Skips the free-space check on the startup disks. Skipping this check can save a little time.
/F	Skips file verifications as they are copied to the startup disks. Skipping the verifications can save a little more time.
/R	Specifies an optional directory to be installed.
/RX	Specifies an optional directory to be copied.

You are now ready to start the setup process. As stated at the beginning of this section, setup begins by locating the installation files.

1. If you have access to the CD-ROM drive on your computer, switch to the CD-ROM drive now and locate the directory that pertains to your system type (I386, MIPS, Alpha, PPC), or connect to the network location of the installation files using your DOS client connection software.

   If you do not have access to your CD-ROM drive, try booting from the startup disk provided in the Windows NT Workstation 4.0 box.

2. Type **WINNT** with any desired option switches. The text mode phase of the setup process is then initiated.

   If you are installing Windows NT Workstation 4.0 from an existing installation of Windows NT, simply choose File, Run in the Program Manager or File Manager, and enter **WINNT32** followed by any desired option switches.

Text Mode Phase

Recall that the DOS or text mode phase of setup has six basic events:

- A menu of startup options
- Detection and configuration of storage devices such as SCSI drives
- Initial hardware verification
- Choice of the installation disk partition
- Choice of file system for the installation partition
- Installation directory name

We will explore each now in more detail.

Startup Menu

The first screen that appears welcomes you to the setup process and presents four different ways to proceed.

Key Concept

On all setup screens, you can access a useful help dialog box by pressing F1. You can exit setup at any time by pressing F3.

1. To learn more about Windows NT Setup before continuing, press F1.

2. To set up Windows NT now, press Enter.

3. To repair a damaged Windows NT version 4.0 installation, press R.

4. To quit Setup without installing Windows NT, press F3.

These options are fairly straightforward and are mirrored with their keyboard shortcuts in the white status bar at the bottom of the screen.

Of these four options, the one that may raise a question is the third, repairing a damaged installation of Windows NT. You use this option with the Emergency Repair Disk to restore configuration information. The Emergency Repair Disk contains data from the Windows NT Registry; you'll learn more details about that later.

Mass Storage Device Configuration

The next step in the setup process is the detection of mass storage devices such as CD-ROMs, SCSI adapters, and so on. The detected devices are displayed on the screen. Integrated Device Electronics (IDE) and Enhanced Small Device Interface (ESDI) drives are also detected but generally not displayed in the list.

If you have a device installed that is not shown on the screen, you can choose to add it by pressing S. Otherwise, press Enter to continue with setup. Of course, you can always add the additional devices after setup has completed by using the Windows NT Control Panel. If you do press S, be sure to have your drivers disk available. (Refer to the Preparation Checklist.)

License Agreement

Setup presents you with a multipage license agreement. It is the standard type of software agreement that Microsoft presents warning you to install a valid copy of Windows NT and not a borrowed copy from somebody else. You need to page down through the license screens to accept the agreement and get to the next step in installation.

CH

3

Verifying Hardware

The setup process next displays the basic list of hardware and software components that it detected, including the following:

- Computer
- Display
- Keyboard
- Keyboard layout
- Pointing device

If the list matches what you have in the computer, press Enter. If you need to make a change, use the up- or down-arrow key to highlight the component that needs to be changed, press Enter, and choose the appropriate item from the list.

Partition Configuration

The next screen involves choosing the disk partition on which the Windows NT system files will be installed. It is referred to as the system partition. The system partition can be an existing formatted or unformatted partition, or it can be an area of free space on the hard disk. Setup displays the partitions and free space that it detects on all physical disks. Use your up- and down-arrow keys to select the partition or free space where you want to install Windows NT.

If you select an area of free space, you need to press C to create the partition. A new screen appears, telling you how large the partition can be and prompting you to enter the desired size. After you enter the desired size of the partition, press Enter. Windows NT creates the partition for you, returns you to the Partition Configuration screen, and displays the new partition in the list. Now select the new partition, and press Enter to continue.

If you are using an existing partition as the Windows NT system partition, select it and press Enter.

You can also select and delete partitions from this screen. This capability can be useful if you need to free up some space and then create a larger partition for Windows NT.

In either case, be sure that you have at least 120MB of free space available on the selected partition. This value is a minimum; more free space will help performance. For example, you need space for a pagefile for virtual memory management. Recall that the default initial size for a pagefile is 12MB + the amount of physical RAM installed in your computer.

Do not install Windows NT on a compressed partition. Disable compression before setup begins.

If the partition is mirrored, disable mirroring before setup begins.

If any partitions are labeled as Windows NT Fault Tolerance, do not delete them because they represent stripe sets, volume sets, and mirrors that could result in significant loss of data.

Formatting the Partition

The system partition contains all the Windows NT system drivers, hardware configuration, security information, the Registry, and so on. There is also a primary or boot partition into which Windows NT copies its boot files. The next screen allows you to choose which file system—FAT or NTFS—you would like to format the proposed system partition with. If you select the wrong partition, just press Escape to return to the previous screen.

Your choice of file system depends on several factors. The following is a list of considerations for choosing NTFS:

CH

3

- NTFS supports Windows NT file and directory permissions security and access auditing; FAT supports only the Read Only, System, Hidden, and Archive attributes.
- NTFS supports transaction tracking and sector sparing for data recovery; FAT does not.
- NTFS supports partition sizes of up to 16EB and file sizes of 4 to 64GB, depending on cluster sizes; FAT supports a maximum file size of 4GB and is inefficient for partition sizes greater than 400MB.
- NTFS provides file and directory compression implemented as a property; FAT does not.
- NTFS is recognized by Windows NT only on that computer; FAT is recognized by NTFS, MS-DOS, or OS/2.

If you are installing Windows NT on a new computer and do not intend to also run MS-DOS or Windows 95 on that computer (called dual-booting), then you can simply create the partition and format it as NTFS or FAT.

If you do intend to dual-boot with MS-DOS or Windows 95, be sure that the boot partition is already formatted as FAT and that Windows 95 is already installed. If you install Windows NT on the boot partition, Windows NT will modify the master boot record (MBR) with its boot information and maintain a boot pointer to the MS-DOS system files. If you install NT first, format the partition as FAT, and then install MS-DOS, the MBR will be altered, and you will not be able to boot Windows NT successfully.

RISC Partition Formats

NTFS can be used on RISC-based computers. However, Windows NT requires at least one FAT system partition of 2MB minimum size for its boot file information. You can create this partition, as well as another system partition of appropriate size, for NTFS following your RISC-based computer's documentation.

Dual-Booting Windows NT Workstation 4.0 and OS/2

Windows NT and OS/2 can coexist on the same computer. If you have installed OS/2 and MS-DOS on the computer and use the OS/2 boot command to switch between operating systems, Windows NT configures its bootup to dual-boot between itself and whichever of the two operating systems you had running when you installed Windows NT.

Because Windows NT 4.0 no longer supports HPFS, if you intend to keep OS/2 on HPFS, you must install Windows NT in another partition. Similarly, if you are using the OS/2 Boot Manager, the Windows NT installation process will disable it upon completion. You must reenable it by marking the Boot Manager partition as the active partition using Windows NT's Disk Administrator utility. If, after working in OS/2, you choose to boot to Windows NT, you can use OS/2's Boot Manager to mark the Windows NT partition as active and then reboot the computer.

Dual-Booting Windows NT Workstation 4.0 and Windows NT Server 4.0

For testing, instruction, or development purposes, you may choose to have both Windows NT Workstation 4.0 and Server installed on your computer, or perhaps even different versions of Windows NT. The setup program detects the existence of another installation of Windows NT, Windows 95, Windows for Workgroups, or Windows 3.1 and displays that installation's system directory as an upgrade directory for your current installation. Simply press N for "New Directory" as offered on the screen, and install this version of Windows NT in a different directory. The setup program keeps the other version or versions intact and installs this version in its own directory. Setup also modifies the boot menu to display this new version at the top of the boot menu and as the default bootup operating system.

Installation Directory

Setup next asks for the name and location of the Windows NT system files. Windows NT displays the path and default name of the directory for you on the selected partition. The default directory name is WINNT. You can change the name to whatever you want, but it is recommended that you keep the name recognizable, such as WINNT40, especially if you have other versions of Windows or Windows NT on the computer.

If you do have an existing version of Windows, Windows 95, or Windows NT on the selected partition, setup detects that version and displays that directory as the installation choice. Setup assumes that you will want to upgrade the existing operating system.

If you choose to upgrade Windows, setup migrates most INI settings, such as those contained in the win.ini, system.ini, and application .ini files from the previous installation over to Windows NT 4.0. When you boot, you still can choose MS-DOS and start Windows.

If you choose to upgrade an existing installation of Windows NT, setup migrates all Registry settings to Windows NT 4.0. However, you lose the ability to boot to the older installation.

You cannot install Windows NT Workstation 4.0 in the same directory as Windows 95. You must choose a new directory for installation. Consequently, no migration of settings will take place, and you will need to reinstall your Windows 95 applications under Windows NT.

Final Screens

The next screen of the text mode phase informs you that setup will examine the disk for corruption. It offers two types of exams: basic and exhaustive. The basic exam, initiated by pressing Escape, is best used on new partitions that do not already have data stored. The exhaustive exam, initiated by pressing Enter, runs slightly longer depending on the size of the partition and the amount of data stored. Even though the exhaustive exam does take a little extra time, it is highly recommended if you are installing Windows NT Workstation 4.0 on an existing partition with existing data.

After you make your selection, setup displays a dialog showing the status of the process as it copies files to the new Windows NT system directory.

After the files have been copied and the directory structure created, setup informs you that the text mode portion has completed and that you should press Enter to restart the computer. At this point, you can press Enter, or if it is getting late, you could just turn off your computer. Actually, it is often suggested that you do power off the computer and then power back on to reset all the hardware devices, particularly network cards, for Windows NT.

Restart, Lock, and Load!

When the computer reboots, if you watch very closely, you will see the Windows NT boot menu appear briefly with a choice for Windows NT installation. This event is the default and starts automatically. If you are quick with your fingers, you can press the up- or down-arrow keys to disable the default time and boot to MS-DOS or Windows 95. You then see a menu entry for either MS-DOS or Windows 95, depending on which operating system has been installed. Otherwise, you can just let Windows NT take over.

During this phase, Windows NT loads its 32-bit multithreaded kernel that enhances and supports the setup process. As the computer reboots, Windows NT hardware detection takes place. This event discovers and initializes hardware devices for use by Windows NT, such as SCSI adapters, a video adapter, mouse and keyboard drivers, CD-ROM drives, COM and parallel ports, memory configuration, and a bus adapter.

You see what will become a familiar set of bootup screens. The first is a black screen that loads system drivers (white consecutive dots), followed by the infamous blue screen— infamous because it is here that you see screen dumps related to unsuccessful boots of Windows NT. Most of the time, however, this screen simply outlines the progress of various boot tasks. If you have chosen to format or convert a partition to NTFS, you see messages to that effect as conversion takes place. Also, Windows NT reboots the system once again for the file system to be recognized and take effect.

After this process is complete, Windows NT loads the GUI portion of setup called the Windows NT Setup Wizard.

Windows NT Setup Wizard

The Setup Wizard is a much streamlined and intuitive interface for gathering information pertinent to the configuration of Windows NT on the computer. Essentially, the wizard asks you configuration option questions during the display of several Windows GUI dialog boxes. After you make your selections and provide the appropriate information, the wizard loads the necessary drivers, updates the Registry, and completes the installation.

The very first screen that you see outlines the standard Microsoft client license agreement. You must click OK to accept this agreement before continuing with setup.

The next dialog box outlines how the wizard will proceed. The three parts to the wizard setup are as follows:

1. Gathering information about your computer
2. Installing Windows NT Networking
3. Finishing setup

Gathering Information About Your Computer

The Setup Options dialog box offers four installation options: Typical, Portable, Compact, and Custom. Table 3.3 highlights which components are installed by default for each setup option.

Table 3.3 Default Components Installed by Each Setup Option

Component	Typical	Portable	Compact	Custom
Accessibility	Yes	Yes	No	Selectable Options
Accessories	Yes	Yes	No	Selectable
Communication	Yes	Yes	No	Selectable Options
Games	No	No	No	Selectable
Windows	No	No	No	Selectable Messaging
Multimedia	Yes	Yes	No	Selectable

The different installation options are described here:

- Typical and Custom are very much the same as the Express and Custom options that most of us have encountered when installing Windows and most Windows applications. The two setup options new to Windows NT 4.0 are Portable and Compact.

- Typical Setup is the default as well as the recommended option. It installs all optional Windows components, including Microsoft Exchange and, of course, the games. It asks few questions and automatically configures component settings.

- Custom, on the other hand, gives the most control over the installation and configuration of options.

- Portable is designed to accommodate the increasing number of users running Windows NT Workstation on their portable computers. This installation offers options that are geared toward portable use, including support for PCCARD (previously referred to as PCMCIA).

- Compact is designed for computer systems that have limited disk space available and does not install any optional components. Only the minimum components necessary are installed. Installing only the minimum components can reduce the space required by 10 to 20MB.

The next two dialog boxes prompt you for a username and company name for registration purposes, as well as a Product Identification number or CD Key. The number is usually included on the CD case or in your Windows NT installation manual. In some

CH
3

organizations, depending on the type of installation being performed, you might not need this number because your organization has negotiated a company-wide license for distributing the software. You must enter something in both these dialogs to proceed to the next dialog box. Contact your MIS department for the appropriate number.

The next dialog box asks for the computer name. It is the name that Windows NT will use to identify this computer internally and for network and remote communication. The name must be unique if the computer will be a member of a workgroup or domain. This name can be up to 15 characters long.

Key Concept

Although a computer name can contain spaces, using spaces is not recommended. In a large network, users connecting to computers can become confused as to the presence or absence of spaces in a name. In fact, in a large corporate network, using a standard naming convention for computer, workgroup, and domain names will greatly simplify the configuration and maintenance of your network.

The next screen references the Administrator account and asks for a password for that account. The Administrator account is a built-in account that Windows NT creates for managing the configuration of the computer, including security and account information. The name of the Administrator account is ADMINISTRATOR, and the password can be up to 14 characters (or you can simply press Enter). You need to enter the password twice, once to confirm it.

Key Concept

Passwords in Windows NT are case sensitive, so be sure that you type your password correctly and then remember it. If you forget your password during the course of installation, you cannnot access Windows NT.

You may have read that certain Pentium-based computers have a faulty floating-point module. In very specific circumstances, having this module can sometimes produce inaccurate results when you're dividing certain values. If setup has detected that your computer has such a problem, the next screen gives you the option to disable the module and let Windows NT perform the math. Taking this approach results in a decrease in performance for floating-point operations. However, if your applications rely heavily on floating-point arithmetic, such as complex Excel macros and SQL database queries and sorts, then you might prefer to choose Yes for this option.

The next screen involves the option of creating an Emergency Repair Disk. The Emergency Repair Disk contains setup information relevant to this installation of Windows NT, including the location of source files and computer configuration and security information from the Registry. You can use it to replace corrupted or missing boot files, recover account information, and restore Windows NT to the master boot record of the computer boot partition if it has been modified. To use this disk, you must have a startup disk to boot with and then press R for repair from the startup menu.

If you choose to create an Emergency Repair Disk, be sure to have a blank disk handy, and choose Yes.

Key Concept

If you choose not to create an Emergency Repair Disk at this time, you can always create one later. Windows NT provides a command prompt command called RDISK.EXE, which is used to create a new Emergency Repair Disk and to update an existing disk.

**CH
3**

Depending on the type of installation you choose at the start of the wizard, you might see a dialog box that lets you choose which optional components to install. You can choose one of two options: Most Common or Show a List.

If you choose Most Common, setup proceeds to the next portion of the Setup Wizard process. If you choose Show a List, you see a new dialog box with a list of options. You see this same dialog box when selecting optional components in Windows 95.

The truly fine thing about this dialog box is the way it presents you with component information. You see a list of five or six main components. Most of them are actually component areas that are composed of a list of component items from which you can choose. As you select each main component, a description box to the right explains what functionality each provides, as well as how many of the component items have been selected for installation. If you select the Details button, another dialog box displays the checklist of component items. You can select or deselect them as you like and then return to the main dialog box. As you select items, the description screen notes how many items you selected, such as "12 of 14 items selected." You also see just how much additional disk space will be required for the items in question.

When you select Next, the wizard takes you to part two of its setup process: installing Windows NT networking.

Installing Windows NT Networking

The next few dialog boxes reference information regarding the configuration of network-related functions and components. Your first choice is to indicate whether you are implementing network features at all, and if so, whether you will be wired to the network through a local interface such as a network card, or if you have remote access to the network through a modem connection, or both.

If you choose Wired to the Network, the next dialog box prompts you to detect and install the network card. You can choose Start Search to begin setup's detection process. The resulting dialog box displays a list of all detected network cards. You can choose to configure any combination of cards by selecting or deselecting their check boxes. If you do not have a card installed in the machine, you can choose the MS Loopback Adapter to enable all network functionality within the machine without the card.

If setup cannot detect the card, or you have a driver disk available, you can install the card from your disk by choosing Select from List and then selecting the Have Disk button.

Remember to check the Hardware Compatibility List to be sure that your network card is supported by Windows NT. (See the Preparation Checklist earlier in this chapter.)

You can install additional cards or change card settings later from Windows NT's Control Panel.

The Setup Wizard most likely next displays a configuration option dialog box for the specific card or cards you selected. This dialog box or series of dialog boxes prompts you to enter the correct IRQ, I/O base port address, and memory buffer address settings, as well as any other card-specific settings such as on-board transceivers, thin versus thick coax, and so on.

Note that Windows NT displays the manufacturer's proposed or factory settings in these dialog boxes. Because some cards are software-configurable, the actual settings on the cards may not match the manufacturer's settings. To avoid conflicts, especially the failure of Windows NT to initialize the card and network settings on your computer, you should be sure to know your card settings ahead of time. (See the Preparation Checklist in the section "Preparing to Install Windows NT Workstation 4.0.")

The next dialog box asks for Network Protocol choices. By default, Windows NT selects TCP/IP and NWLink IPX/SPX as your protocol. However, you can select any combination of TCP/IP, NWLink (Windows NT's 32-bit implementation of IPX/SPX), and NETBEUI. You can add additional protocols by choosing Select from List. Other protocols that you can install include AppleTalk, DLC, and Point-to-Point Tunneling (PPTP), or if you have a protocol disk, you can select Have Disk.

The next step is to select the Network Services that are appropriate for your computer. By default, five services are installed with Windows NT networking and cannot be deselected. They are Computer Browser, RPC Configuration, NetBIOS Interface, Workstation, and Server. Again, you can install additional services such as Client Service for NetWare, Microsoft Peer Web Services, Remote Access Services, and so on by selecting Select from Disk or from disk by choosing Have Disk. Network services will be discussed in Chapter 11, "Network Connectivity and Remote Support."

At this point, you have made all appropriate choices, and the wizard gives you a choice to continue and install the network components, or go back and alter your selections. Choose Back to make changes, and choose Next, of course, to continue.

The next dialog box displays the Network Bindings. Think of bindings as being the network "paths" that determine how services, protocols, and adapters interact to effect network communications. You can adjust the bindings by changing their order, enabling, or disabling them. Windows NT has selected the optimum bindings based on your network component settings. If you need to adjust them later, you can do so from Windows NT's Control Panel.

CH
3

The final piece of information required for you to complete the network portion of the wizard setup is the Network Model. The dialog box displays the computer name that you entered earlier (giving you a last chance during setup to change it) and asks whether you will be joining a workgroup or domain. If you are joining a workgroup or creating a new workgroup, enter the workgroup's name (up to 15 characters).

If you are joining an existing domain, enter the name of the domain that you are joining. Before you join a domain, you must have a computer account created for your computer name in the domain that you are joining. The domain administrator must set up this account for you ahead of time. Do not wait until you get to this point in the installation to ask your domain administrator for a computer account. He or she will probably not be amused. If you are the domain administrator or have been given appropriate administrative privileges in the domain, you can create this account during installation by specifying the computer name and the account name and password that have the appropriate privileges.

You cannot create a new domain during the installation of Windows NT Workstation 4.0. Domains are created from Domain Controller servers. Also, before you can log on to the domain after installation, you need a valid user account for that domain as well.

Each card that you install may require protocol-specific information. For example, if you choose TCP/IP, you need to specify a local address, router information, WINS address information, and so on, or specify DCHP configuration. These dialog boxes are displayed at this time as the wizard completes the setup of network components.

If you began your installation as an over-the-network type, and you did not power off your computer after the text mode, you may see a message to the effect that Windows NT cannot verify the card settings and asking whether it should use them anyway. The answer is Yes, use the settings. You might get this message because, in a warm boot such as Windows NT performs after the text mode setup, all device settings, particularly network card settings, are not reset. Thus, Windows NT detects that those settings are already in use. A cold boot, on the other hand, involves powering off the computer. Cold booting, of course, resets all device settings, including the network card settings that triggered the message in the first place.

If Windows NT is unable to initiate network communication, you have the option to go back and check your settings, or continue without configuring the network.

When you select Next, the wizard takes you to part three of its setup process: finishing setup.

Finishing Setup

You have just two more dialog boxes to consider before the Setup Wizard can complete the installation. The first dialog box displays the Date and Time utility. There, you can adjust the settings to reflect the time zone of the computer, as well as to ensure that the system time is correct.

Several interprocess mechanisms as well as certain applications and Microsoft BackOffice products rely on time stamps and time synchronization among computers. Inaccurate time zones or time values can result in process failures and, in some cases, an incomplete processing of data.

Finally, the Display Properties dialog box pops up. In this dialog, you can configure your video display by changing settings such as pixel resolution, color palette, refresh frequency, and font size, as well as changing your video driver information. Before you complete this screen, choose Test to see whether you can actually read your display with the settings you chose. After testing, you can click OK.

A status dialog box then appears, showing the progress of files copied from the temporary directory (WIN_NT.˜LS). When this process is complete, the wizard asks you to remove any floppy disks and press the Restart button to reboot the computer. As mentioned before, at this point you can safely turn off your computer.

If you let the computer restart and have chosen a dual-boot configuration for your installation, you see the Windows NT boot loader menu. Your new installation of Windows NT Workstation 4.0 is first in the list, and it is the default operating system unless you choose the other operating system option within 30 seconds. If you choose Windows NT, it loads with all the options you chose and presents you with the Welcome screen.

Troubleshooting Installation and Setup

If you carefully read this chapter, you will have relatively few, if any, problems with your installation of Windows NT Workstation 4.0. In fact, installing Windows NT 4.0 is rarely troublesome if you have done your detective work. NT is designed to detect and configure as much on its own as possible. Nevertheless, let's run through a couple of tips, suggestions, and reminders, beginning with the Preparation Checklist.

- Read all Windows NT documentation files.
- Assess system requirements. See Table 3.1.
- Assess hardware compatibility. Verify by consulting the Hardware Compatibility List.
- Gather device driver and configuration data:
    - Video—Display type, adapter and chipset type
    - Network—Card type, IRQ, I/O Address, DMA, Connector, and so on
    - SCSI Controller—Adapter and chipset type, IRQ, bus type
    - Sound/Media—IRQ, I/O Address, DMA
    - I/O Ports—IRQ, I/O Address, DMA
    - Modems—Port, IRQ, I/O Address, modem type
- Back up your current configuration and data files.
- Determine which type of initial setup will be performed. (You may need three blank formatted disks before running setup.)
- Determine the location of the source files for performing this installation. (Are they on CD-ROM, on a shared network location?)
- Determine on which partition the Windows NT system files will be installed.
- Determine which file system you will install.
- Determine whether you will create an Emergency Repair Disk. (If so, you need one blank disk available before running setup.)
- Identify your installation CD Key.
- Decide on a unique name for your computer.
- Determine which workgroup or domain name the computer will join.
- Identify network connection data—IP addresses, IPX card numbers, and so on.
- Identify in which time zone the computer is located.

CH

3

Perhaps most critical to a successful installation of Windows NT Workstation 4.0 is the compatibility of your computer's hardware. We offer two reminders here:

1. Be sure that your computer meets the minimum requirements necessary for installing and running Windows NT Workstation 4.0.

2. Be sure that you have checked all hardware components in your computer against the Hardware Compatibility List for Windows NT Workstation 4.0.

These two actions alone will significantly increase your success rate.

Next, become familiar with the hardware settings for installed devices, particularly network cards. These settings include not only IRQ, DMA, I/O address, and connector data, but also network protocol settings such as IP address, DNS location, router address, DHCP information, IPX card address, and so on.

Finally, follow a naming convention for your computers and workgroups that ensures uniqueness, recognizability, and ease of maintenance. If you're becoming a member of a domain, be sure that your computer already has a computer account in the domain you are joining (as well as a user account for you).

Occasionally, you might encounter unusual errors relating to your hard disk. If installation should fail because of disk-related problems, the following are a few areas to explore:

1. Is the hard disk supported (on the HCL)?

2. Do you have a valid boot sector available on the disk? Recall that, especially for RISC-based systems, Windows NT requires a minimum 2MB FAT system partition.

3. Are your SCSI drives being detected correctly by Windows NT? You might need to check physical settings such as termination.

4. Have you checked for viruses in the master boot record (MBR)? If a virus alters the MBR either before, during, or after installation, Windows NT cannot boot successfully. You are likely to receive this message: Bad or missing NTLDR.

5. If Windows NT fails to start the GUI Setup Wizard when it reboots, usually with the message Bad or missing NTOSKRNL, this problem could be the result of a misdetection of the SCSI drive. In this case, boot to DOS and use the DOS Editor to modify the BOOT.INI file. This read-only system file is created by Windows NT during installation and is used to display the boot menu. It is stored in the root directory of the system partition. Use the DOS ATTRIB command to turn off the Read Only (R) and System (S) attributes before editing the file. Change all references of SCSI for this installation to MULTI. Also, check that the partition numbers listed in the BOOT.INI file for Windows NT match the partition number of the

Windows NT system file directory. Be sure to save your changes and set the attributes back.

The syntax for using the DOS ATTRIB command to turn off attributes is as follows:

```
C:>ATTRIB -S -R BOOT.INI
```

You can set the attributes back by typing

C:>ATTRIB +S +R BOOT.INI

Windows NT counts partitions starting with 0 as follows:

1. Hidden system partitions
2. The first primary partition on each drive
3. Additional primary partitions on each drive
4. Logical partitions on each drive

So, if the physical disk has a hidden system partition (like a COMPAQ BIOS partition), a C: drive primary partition, and a D: drive logical partition, and you are installing Windows NT on drive D:, you are installing Windows NT on partition 2 (hidden–0, C:–1, D:–2).

Using NTHQ to Troubleshoot

Windows NT also supplies a troubleshooting utility that may be of use for both Windows NT Workstation 4.0 and Server in discovering how Windows NT is detecting your hardware configuration. It is called NTHQ and can be found in the \SUPPORT\HQTOOL directory on the installation CD.

To use this utility, boot to DOS, place a blank disk in the A: drive, switch to the directory on the CD, and run MAKEDISK.BAT. By doing so, you create a bootable disk that you can use to run NTHQ. Reboot the computer with this disk, and follow the directions.

NTHQ creates an onscreen report that can be saved to a log file on disk, as well as printed out. It performs a hardware detection on the computer similar to that performed by Windows NT during setup and can be used to determine your hardware settings and specifically which ones are causing setup to fail. It includes data about the motherboard such as I/O, DMA, and IRQ settings for CMOS, Memory Access Controller, COM and printer ports, Plug and Play BIOS; data about the Network Card, Video, Storage Devices; and a summary of all device configuration settings. It also shows what is questionable regarding the Hardware Compatibility List.

CH
3

NTHQ Sample Report

NTHQ captures and reports the following kinds of data:

- Hardware Detection Tool For Windows NT 4.0

    Master Boot Sector Virus Protection Check

    Hard Disk Boot Sector Protection: Off.

    No problem to write to MBR

- ISA Plug and Play Add-in cards detection Summary Report

    No ISA Plug and Play cards found in the system

    ISA PnP Detection: Complete

    EISA Add-in card detection Summary Report

    Scan Range: Slot 0 - 16

    Slot 0: EISA System Board

    EISA Bus Detected: No

    EISA Detection: Complete

- Legacy Detection Summary Report

    System Information

    Device: System board

    Can't locate Computername

    Machine Type: IBM PC/AT

    Machine Model: fc

    Machine Revision: 00

    Microprocessor: Pentium

    Conventional memory: 655360

    Available memory: 32 MB

    BIOS Name: Phoenix

    BIOS Version:

    BIOS Date: 06/12/96

    Bus Type: ISA

- Enumerate all IDE devices

    IDE Devices Detection Summary Report

    Primary Channel: master drive detected

    Model Number: TOSHIBA MK2720FC

Firmware Revision: S1.16 J

Serial Number: 66D70208

Type of Drive: Fixed Drive

Disk Transfer Rate: >10Mbs

Number of Cylinders: 2633

Number of Heads: 16

Number of Sectors Per Track: 63

Number of unformatted bytes per sector Per Track: 639

LBA Support: Yes

DMA Support: Yes

PIO Transfer Cycle Time Mode 2

DMA Transfer Cycle Time Mode 2

- IDE/ATAPI: Complete

Adapter Description: Cirrus Logic VGA

Listed in Hardware Compatibility List: Yes

Adapter Description: Creative Labs Sound Blaster 16 or AWE-32

Adapter Device ID: *PNPB003

Listed in Hardware Compatibility List: Not found—check the latest HCL

Adapter Description: Gameport Joystick

Adapter Device ID: *PNPB02F

Listed in Hardware Compatibility List: Not found—check the latest HCL

Adapter Description: Unknown Cirrus Logic chipset, report!

Adapter Device ID: 12021013

Listed in Hardware Compatibility List: Not found—check the latest HCL

Performing an Unattended Setup of Windows NT Workstation 4.0

The setup process can be automated to provide some or all of the information needed during setup and thus allow for little or no additional user input. Using an automated setup can be especially helpful when you're installing a large number of computers with similar configurations, such as having the same domain name, monitor settings, network card drivers and settings, and so on.

The five basic steps involved in implementing an unattended setup of Windows NT Workstation 4.0 are as follows:

- Create a distribution server by placing the Windows NT Workstation 4.0 installation files for the appropriate computer platform in a shared directory on a file server.
- Create an answer file that supplies information common to all the computers being installed.
- Create a uniqueness data file that supplies information specific to each computer's installation.
- Provide access to the installation files on the distribution server for the computers that are being installed.
- Run Windows NT setup, referencing the location of the setup files, answer files, and uniqueness data files.

The following sections describe each of these steps in more detail.

Create a Distribution Server

Copying the installation files to a shared directory on a file server is a relatively simple task. You can simply identify which Windows NT server you want to use. It should be a server that the target computers will be able to access easily, preferably a server on the same subnet, and one that is not already being used to capacity by other applications or processes. It also should have its own CD-ROM or be able to access a CD-ROM drive.

Next, you create an installation folder on that server. Into that folder, copy the installation files for the target computers' hardware platform from the appropriate platform directory on the Windows NT Workstation 4.0 installation CD-ROM (i386, MIPS, Alpha, or PPc). You can use the MS-DOS xcopy command with the /s switch (to copy all subdirectories) from a command prompt, or you can use Windows Explorer.

Finally, you can share the newly created directory. (See Chapter 7, "Windows NT 4.0 Security Model," for information about sharing folders in Windows NT.)

Create an Answer File

Answer files (unattend.txt) are used to supply setup information that is common to all the computers using those files. The kind of information that would be common to the computers includes network settings such as card driver, interrupts, DMA, protocols to be installed, and services to be installed, which workgroup or domain the computers are joining, modem types, and organization name. The following is a copy of the sample unattend.txt file for an Intel-based computer that can be found on the Windows NT Workstation 4.0 CD-ROM. Each platform directory contains its own version of this file.

```
; Microsoft Windows NT Workstation Version 4.0 and
; Windows NT Server Version 4.0
; (c) 1994 - 1996 Microsoft Corporation. All rights reserved.
;
; Sample Unattended Setup Answer File
;
; This file contains information about how to automate the installation
; or upgrade of Windows NT Workstation and Windows NT Server so the
; Setup program runs without requiring user input.
;
; For information on how to use this file, read the appropriate sections
; of the Windows NT 4.0 Resource Kit.

[Unattended]
OemPreinstall = no
ConfirmHardware = no
NtUpgrade = no
Win31Upgrade = no
TargetPath = WINNT
OverwriteOemFilesOnUpgrade = no

[UserData]
FullName = "Your User Name"
OrgName = "Your Organization Name"
ComputerName = COMPUTER_NAME

[GuiUnattended]
TimeZone = "(GMT-08:00) Pacific Time (US & Canada); Tijuana"

[Display]
ConfigureAtLogon = 0
BitsPerPel = 16
XResolution = 640
YResolution = 480
VRefresh = 70
AutoConfirm = 1

[Network]
Attend = yes
DetectAdapters = "
InstallProtocols = ProtocolsSection
JoinDomain = Domain_To_Join
```

CH

3

```
[ProtocolsSection]
TC = TCParameters

[TCParameters]
DHCP = yes
```

As you can see, this text file looks very much like a Windows .ini file. You can create it by simply copying and modifying the sample file, creating your own using any text editor, or by running the Setup Manager utility, also found on the Windows NT 4.0 installation CD-ROM. Although it is usually called unattend.txt, you can give it any legal filename as long as you refer to it correctly when running setup. The Setup Manager utility provides a graphical interface for creating and modifying the unattend.txt file or files. You can find a complete treatment of the unattend.txt file and using Setup Manager in the Windows NT Workstation Resource Kit Version 4.0.

After you create this file, you should place it in the same location as the Windows NT 4.0 installation source files on the distribution server.

Create a Uniqueness Data File

The unattend.txt file creates a setup data file that contains information that is common to all the computers being installed. However, creating this file does not completely automate the process when you're installing more than one computer. Recall that each computer's computer name, for example, must be unique. That sort of information cannot be supplied in the unattend.txt file alone.

A uniqueness data file (UDF) can be created to supply the more detailed and machine-specific information required to more fully automate the setup process. The UDF identifies specific sections that should be merged into the answer file. The following is a sample UDF:

```
; This section lists all unique ids that are supported by this database.
; The left hand side is a unique id, which can be any string but
; must not contain the asterisk (*), space, comma, or equals character.
; The right hand side is a list of sections, each of which should match the name
; of a section in unattend.txt. See below.
;
id1 = section1,section2
id2 = section1,section3,section4

[section1]
; This is a section whose name should match the name of a section in unattend.txt.
; Each line in this section is written into the same section in unattend.txt,
; via the profile APIs. A line here thus replaces a line in unattend.txt with the
; same left hand side. (If a matching line does not exist in unattend.txt, the line will
```

```
; be added.) A line that just has a left hand side and does not have a value will delete
; the same line in unattend.txt.
;
; To make this section specific to a particular unique id, precede its name with id:.
; This allows specification of different sections in this file that map to the same
; section in unattend.txt. See below.
;
key1 = value
key2 = value

[id2:section2]
; This section is merged into [section2] in unattend.txt for unique id2.
;
key5 = value
```

The sections contained in the UDF are the same sections used in the unattend.txt file. A
section's entries in the UDF are merged into the corresponding section in the
unattend.txt file. The unique ID referred to in the sample represents an ID that you
assign for each computer you are installing. By assigning a unique ID to each section, you
can create copies of the same section, each of which modifies the installation slightly from
computer to computer. For example, the [UserData] section can provide a different username and computer name for each subsequent computer installation if you create multiple copies of the [UserData] section, modify each accordingly, and assign each a unique ID
corresponding to that computer.

Let's say that you're installing three computers. Each should have a unique computer
name: ComputerA, ComputerB, and ComputerC. You assign each computer a unique
ID: ID1, ID2, and ID3. The attend.txt section that modifies the computer name is
[UserData]. The UDF would then look like this:

```
ID1=[UserData]
ID2=[UserData]
ID3=[UserData]
[ID1:UserData]
Computername=ComputerA
[ID2:UserData]
Computername=ComputerB
[ID3:UserData]
Computername=ComputerC
```

Connect to the Distribution Server

The computers on which Windows NT Workstation 4.0 will be installed must be able to
connect to and access the shared folder containing the installation files, answer files, and
UDFs. This is generally accomplished by installing the DOS Network Client 3.0 software

on the computer if no other means of connecting to the distribution server is possible, such as through Windows for Workgroups network connectivity options, Windows 95, or an existing installation of Windows NT Workstation. Chapter 16, "MS Network Client Version 3.0 for MS-DOS," of the MS Windows NT Server 4.0 Resource Kit, provides the steps for creating a network setup disk for your MS-DOS computers.

After you've established a network connection, you can use a simple net command at a command prompt to access the installation source files using the command syntax; for example, you can enter **net use d: \\distribution_server\ shared_folder**. This net command maps a logical drive letter on your computer to the shared folder on the distribution server. Switching to that drive letter at a command prompt or through File Manager or Windows Explorer effectively points you to the files in the shared folder. For example, if the Windows NT Workstation 4.0 installation files have been installed in a shared folder called INSTALL on a distribution server called SOURCE1, you can connect to the folder by typing the following command at a command prompt: **net use E: \\SOURCE1\ INSTALL**. The E: drive is now mapped to the Windows NT 4.0 source file directory on the distribution server.

Run Setup

The final step is to run Windows NT setup by referring to the source directory, answer files, and UDFs that you created. You do so by using several of the boot switches that were outlined in Table 3.2 earlier in this chapter. After you map a drive to the shared folder containing the Windows NT Workstation 4.0 installation files on the distribution server, switch to that drive. At a command prompt, enter the following command syntax: **winnt /u:***answer_filename* **/s:***source_drive* **/UDF:ID**[,*UDF_filename*].

For example, let's say you have created an answer file called unattend.txt that contains common setup information for your computers, as well as a uniqueness data file called unique.txt that contains specific setup instructions for each computer. Each computer is identified by a unique ID following the convention ID1, ID2, and so on. At the first computer, corresponding to ID1, you would map a drive (E:, for example) to the distribution server. At a command prompt, you would enter the following command: **winnt /u:unattend.txt /s:e: /UDF:ID1[,unique.txt]**. At the next computer, you would do the same thing, changing the ID reference to one appropriate to that computer, and so on until you have completed your installation.

Key Concept

The command to map the drive and the setup command can be placed together in a batch file along with any other batch commands you might want to include, such as disconnecting from the mapped drive. The batch file could be sent to users to run on their computers through email or through a package delivery system such as Microsoft's System Management Server, a BackOffice product.

Working with SYSDIFF

You can use the SYSDIFF utility to automate the installation of applications as well as configure Windows NT. SYSDIFF must be run with the /snap mode to create a snapshot first.

After the applications are installed and the configuration changed, you use the /diff mode to create a differences file from the snapshot that can be applied to multiple computers (via the /apply mode).

Understanding the Windows NT Boot Process

CH
3

The Windows NT 4.0 boot process, although a bit more complicated during the operating system load phase, is still pretty much like booting most any other operating system. The five basic steps are as follows:

1. The Power On Self Test (POST) occurs with every computer when you first power it on. It is the BIOS check of installed hardware, interrupts, I/O, memory, and so on.
2. The master boot record (MBR) is read to determine which operating system (OS) will govern the boot process.
3. The OS system file recorded in the MBR is loaded, and the operating system is initialized, the hardware is initialized, and the drivers and configuration files are loaded.
4. The OS kernel is loaded.
5. Environment settings are initialized.

Windows NT 4.0 follows these same basic steps with some variation for steps 3, 4, and 5.

The Windows NT boot process has two primary phases: Boot and Load.

The Boot Phase consists of the preboot sequence during which the operating system is initialized, hardware is detected, and the Executive Services are loaded. When Windows NT is installed, it replaces the MS-DOS entries in the master boot record with its own system file NTLDR. Along with NTLDR, the following boot files are read during the Boot Phase: BOOT.INI, NTDETECT.COM, NTOSKRNL.EXE, and NTBOOTDD.SYS (all some combination of the Hidden, Read Only, and System file attributes and stored in the root directory of the boot partition); NTOSKRNL.EXE and HAL.DLL (stored in the Windows NT system directory); and the HKEY_LOCAL_MACHINE\ SYSTEM hive.

1. NTLDR loads a mini-OS and changes memory to a flat 32-bit model.

2. NTLDR next reads the BOOT.INI file to display the Operating System Menu on the screen.

3. If the user chooses NT or that is the default, NTLDR loads NTDETECT.COM. NTDETECT.COM determines what hardware is installed in the computer and uses this information to build the HKEY_LOCAL_MACHINE\HARDWARE hive.

   If the system boots Windows NT from a SCSI drive whose SCSI adapter BIOS is disabled, NTLDR loads NTBOOTDD.SYS to initialize and access that device.

   If the user chooses MS-DOS or Microsoft Windows (for Windows 95), NTLDR loads BOOTSECT.DOS, which records the boot sector location of the alternative OS system files and loads them. OS initialization then proceeds as normal for that OS.

4. NTLDR next loads NTOSKRNL.EXE, which initializes the Executive Services of the operating system. Think of this file as Windows NT's COMMAND.COM.

5. NTLDR then loads the HAL.DLL and the SYSTEM hive and any drivers that need to initialize at boot time to continue the building of the Executive Services.

6. At this point, the screen displays progress dots across the top, indicating the loading and initialization of drivers. At this time, the user is also prompted to press the spacebar to invoke the Last Known Good boot configuration. Control is passed to NTOSKRNL.EXE, and the Load Phase begins.

   During the Load Phase, the rest of the kernel and user modes of the operating system are set up. The kernel is initialized, control sets information, Windows NT services are loaded, and the WIN32 subsystem starts.

7. The blue screen is displayed, indicating the kernel is initializing, drivers are initialized, and the CurrentControlSet is created and copied to the CLONE control set.

8. The Services Load Phase begins with the starting of SMSS.EXE, the session manager. The session manager runs the programs listed in HKEY_LOCAL_MACHINE\SYSTEM\CURRENTCONTROLSET\ CONTROL\SESSION MANAGER\BootExecute—usually AUTOCHK.EXE, which performs a CHKDSK of each partition. If a drive has been flagged to be converted to NTFS, it also is added to BootExecute, and conversion takes place at this time as well. Next, the pagefile is configured as defined in

KEY_LOCAL_ MACHINE\SYSTEM\CURRENT CONTROLSET\ CONTROL\SESSIONMANAGER\MEMORY MANAGEMENT parameters.

Finally, the required subsystem defined in HKEY_LOCAL_MACHINE\ SYSTEM\CURRENT CONTROLSET\CONTROL\SESSIONMANAGER\ SUBSYSTEMS\REQUIRED is loaded. The only required subsystem at this time is WIN32.

9. With the loading of the WIN32 subsystem, WINLOGON.EXE, the service that governs the logon process, is loaded and started. WINLOGON, in turn, starts the Local Security Authority (LSASS.EXE), which displays the Ctrl+Alt+Del screen, and the Service Controller (SCREG.EXE), which starts services that are configured to start automatically, such as Computer Browser, Workstation, and Server.

10. Finally, the user enters the username and password and logs in to the computer or domain. If the logon is successful, the CLONE control set is copied to Last Known Good. If the boot is not successful, the user can power off or shut down and choose Last Known Good to load the last values that resulted in a successful logon.

CH
3

The Boot Process for RISC-Based Computers

The boot process for RISC-based computers is essentially the same. During the Boot Phase, the resident ROM firmware of the system selects the boot device from a preference table stored in RAM and controls the selection of the boot partition and the appropriate OS file. In this case, the firmware finds and loads OSLOADER.EXE, which is Windows NT's operating system file for RISC-based computers.

OSLOADER, in turn, finds and loads NTOSKRNL.EXE, HAL.DLL, .RAL files (for Alpha systems), and the system hive, and the Load Phase continues as usual.

Note that because the computer's firmware controls the initialization of hardware and the selection of the boot partition, the NTLDR, NTDETECT.COM, BOOT.INI, or BOOTSECT.DOS files are not needed on a RISC-based computer.

BOOT.INI

The BOOT.INI file is a read-only, system, ASCII text file created by Windows NT during installation. It is stored in the root directory of the primary boot partition of the computer. It contains the information that Windows NT uses to display the boot menu when the computer is booted (see step 2 in "Understanding the Windows NT Boot Process"). This file is divided into two sections: Boot Loader and Operating System. The Boot Loader section contains the default operating system and timeout values, and the

Operating System section displays operating system choices and the location of the system files. You can modify it by using any ASCII text editor after first turning off the system and read-only properties.

You can locate the BOOT.INI file by using Windows Explorer, Windows Find, or My Computer. To change its properties, right-click on the file, and choose Properties. Deselect Read Only and System. Be sure to reselect these attributes again after you have finished modifying the file.

In the following example, the default timeout value is 30 seconds. If the user does not make a selection during that time, the default operating system will be loaded. Notice that the unusual looking path to the WINNT40 directory matches a line under the Operating Systems section.

```
[Boot Loader]
Timeout=30
Default=multi(0)disk(0)rdisk(0)partition(4)\WINNT40
[Operating Systems]
multi(0)disk(0)rdisk(0)partition(4)\WINNT40="Windows NT Workstation Version 4.00"
multi(0)disk(0)rdisk(0)partition(4)\WINNT40="Windows NT Workstation Version 4.00
➡[VGA mode]"
   /basevideo /sos
C:\="Microsoft Windows"
```

That unusual looking path is called an ARC path (Advanced RISC Computer). The best way to think of an ARC path is as a hardware path. By now, everyone has used a DOS path. It indicates the drive and directory location of a specific file. An ARC path indicates the physical disk location of the Windows NT system files—the specific partition on a specific physical disk connected to a specific physical controller.

Referring to the example, the ARC path `multi(0)disk(0)rdisk(0)partition(4)\WINNT40` can be interpreted as follows:

> The first value can be either `multi` or `scsi`. It really has no direct relation as to whether the controller is a SCSI controller. Windows NT chooses SCSI if the controller does not have its card BIOS enabled. Otherwise, the choice is MULTI. The number that appears in parentheses is the ordinal number of the controller.

> The next two values are `disk` and `rdisk`. If the first value choice was SCSI, then the disk number represents the SCSI bus number and is incremented accordingly (the physical disk attached to the card), and the `rdisk` value is ignored. If the first value is `multi`, then the disk value is ignored, and the `rdisk` value representing the physical disk on the adapter is incremented accordingly.

> Next, the `partition` value indicates on which partition on the disk the directory \WINNT40 can be found. Recall that this is the Windows NT system directory that you selected during installation.

So, putting it all together for our example, during boot, if the user lets the timeout value expire or specifically selects Windows NT from the menu, Windows NT can find the Windows NT system files (specifically the location of the NTOSKRNL.EXE file) in the WINNT40 directory on the fourth partition of the first disk attached to the first controller in this computer. If the user selects Microsoft Windows from the menu, then NTLDR loads BOOTSECT.DOS and proceeds to boot (in this case) Windows 95.

The Boot Menu

The Operating Systems section values are what build the boot menu that you see during startup. Each ARC path has a text menu selection associated with it enclosed in quotation marks. By default, this section always has two entries for Windows NT and one for the other operating system, usually MS-DOS (C:\=M "MS-DOS") or Windows 95 (C:\="Microsoft Windows"). The second entry for Windows NT represents a fall-back entry that loads Windows NT with a generic VGA driver. If you make changes to the display settings that make it difficult or impossible to read the screen, selecting this choice during startup ignores those settings and loads a generic VGA driver so that you can see the screen and rectify the problem. This is accomplishedthrough the \basevideo switch that you see at the end of that line in the sample BOOT.INI file displayed in the last section.

Windows NT provides a variety of switches that can be added to these or additional Windows NT boot entries to modify the way Windows NT boots. For example, to create another entry in the boot menu that displays all the driver files that are loaded during boot, you can copy the first line in the Operating Systems section to a new line, modify the text to read Windows NT Workstation 4.0 Driver Load, and add the /SOS switch to the end of the line.

Table 3.4 lists the more practical boot switches that can be used in the BOOT.INI file.

Table 3.4   Windows NT Boot Switches for BOOT.INI

Switch	Description
/Basevideo	Boots Windows NT with the standard VGA display driver in 640×480 resolution.
/SOS	Displays driver filenames instead of progress dots during the Load Phase.
/Crashdebug	Used for troubleshooting, enables Automatic Recovery and Restart mode for the Windows NT boot process, and displays a system memory dump during the blue screen portion of the Load Phase.
/Maxmem:n	Specifies the maximum amount of RAM in megabytes that Windows NT will recognize and work with. Using this switch is helpful when you suspect a bad SIMM or memory chip and you are trying to pinpoint its location.

CH
3

Understanding Control Sets and the Last Known Good Option

The HKEY_LOCAL_MACHINE\System hive contains several control set subkeys. Windows NT uses them to boot the system, keep track of configuration changes, and provide an audit trail of failed boot attempts. In general, the four control sets are Clone, ControlSet001, ControlSet002, and CurrentControlSet. A subkey called Select has parameter values that point out which control set is being used for the current settings, default settings, failed settings, and Last Known Good settings. For example, if the value for Current is 0x1, the 1 indicates that CurrentControlSet is being derived from or mapped to ControlSet001.

Clone is used by Windows NT during the boot process (step 7 in "Understanding the Windows NT Boot Process") as a temporary storage area for the boot configuration. Settings from CurrentControlSet are copied into Clone during the Load Phase. When a user logon results in a successful boot, the configuration settings in Clone are copied to another control set such as ControlSet002 and are referred to as the Last Known Good. If the boot attempt is unsuccessful, these values are copied to a different control set number.

ControlSet001ControlSet001ControlSet001, which is generally the default control set, produces the CurrentControlSet. As such, it also, by default, contains the Windows NT boot configuration.

ControlSet00xControlSet00xControlSet00x represents other control sets. The control set with the highest number increment is usually pointed to in the Select subkey as the Last Known Good configuration. Other control set numbers invariably refer to failed boot configurations.

CurrentControlSetCurrentControlSet CurrentControlSet is mapped back to ControlSet001. These settings are copied to Clone during the Load Phase of the boot process. Whenever an administrator makes a change to the configuration of the computer, such as modifying the virtual memory parameters, adding a new driver, or creating a hardware profile, those changes are saved to CurrentControlSet (and thus to ControlSet001 if that control set is set as the Default in the Select subkey).

 Key Concept

During the Load Phase, the settings in CurrentControlSet (derived from ControlSet001) are copied to Clone and used to determine service order, driver files to load, startup configurations, hardware profiles, and so on. If the boot is successful (for example, the user logs in to Windows NT successfully), Clone is copied to the control set designated as the Last Known Good—say ControlSet002. If changes made by the administrator result in a failed boot attempt, the failed configuration in Clone is copied to ControlSet002, what used to be the Last Known Good control set becomes ControlSet003, and the user has the option of selecting to boot with the Last Known Good control set.

The Last Known Good control set contains the last boot configuration that resulted in a successful logon to the computer. The user is given the option to use Last Known Good when the Load Phase begins and the progress dots are displayed on the screen. The user has five seconds within which to press the spacebar to invoke the Last Known Good.

Key Concept

If the system itself detects a severe or critical device initialization or load error, it displays a message asking the user whether choosing Last Known Good might not be a good option. Users can choose to bypass this message, but do so at their own risk.

Key Concept

The Last Known Good helps to recover in the event of a failed boot. But remember that a failed boot is one in which a user cannot successfully log on to Windows NT. The user may be able to log on successfully and still have a system that fails to run correctly because of a configuration error. The Last Known Good is not helpful in this situation because it is created as soon as the boot is successful (for example, the user logs on successfully).

Troubleshooting the Boot Process

The most common errors that you are likely to encounter during the boot process are the result of corrupt or missing boot files. Recall the boot files needed by Windows NT:

NTLDR

BOOT.INI

BOOTSECT.DOS

NTDETECT.COM

NTOSKRNL.EXE

If the NTLDR file is missing or corrupt, the following message is displayed after the POST:

```
BOOT: Couldn't find NTLDR
Please insert another disk.
```

Although this file can become missing or corrupt for a variety of reasons, the most common are viruses that attack the MBR (master boot record) and a user inadvertently reinstalling MS-DOS onto the computer. If the problem involves a virus, you can use a virus protection program to restore the MBR. If this technique is unsuccessful, you can use the Emergency Repair Disk to reestablish NTLDR in the MBR. The worst case is having to reinstall Windows NT from scratch—which you should try to avoid.

If the problem involves a user reinstalling MS-DOS, or "sys-ing" the hard drive, again, you can use the Emergency Repair Disk to reestablish the NTLDR. The worst case is having to reinstall Windows NT.

If BOOT.INI is missing or corrupt, Windows NT looks for the default Windows NT system directory name (usually WINNT) on the boot partition. If Windows NT is installed in a directory other than the default name, or if Windows NT cannot locate it, the following message is displayed after the prompt for Last Known Good:

```
Windows NT could not start because the following file is missing or corrupt:
\winnt root\system32\ntoskrnl.exe
Please reinstall a copy of the above file.
```

If the ARC path to the Windows NT system file directory is incorrect in the BOOT.INI file, NTLDR may display this message:

```
Windows NT could not start because of a computer disk hardware
configuration problem. Could not read from the selected boot disk.
Check boot path and disk hardware. Please check Windows NT (TM)
documentation about hardware disk configuration and your hardware
reference manuals for additional information.
```

Incorrect paths are relatively easy to fix. Because BOOT.INI is a text file, you can turn off its System and Read Only attributes and edit the ARC path using your favorite text editor.

 Key Concept

The ARC path indicated in the Default parameter in the Boot Loader section of the BOOT.INI must match an ARC path for a parameter under the Operating Systems section. If it does not, the menu displays a phantom selection option called "NT (default)," which may result in the same error message described for a missing BOOT.INI file.

If BOOTSECT.DOS is missing, NTLDR displays this error message when the user tries to select the other operating system from the boot menu:

```
I/O Error accessing boot sector file
multi(0)disk(0)rdisk(0)partition(1):\bootsect.dos
```

Because this file is unique to each computer, the best way to recover it would be to restore it from that backup you create regularly or use the Emergency Repair Disk.

If NTDETECT.COM is missing or corrupt, expect the following message after the user selects Windows NT from the boot menu or the menu times out to Windows NT:

```
NTDETECT v1.0 Checking Hardware...
NTDETECT v1.0 Checking Hardware...
```

Again, you can recover using the Emergency Repair Disk or from a backup.

If NTOSKRNL.EXE is missing or corrupt, NTLDR displays this message after the prompt for Last Known Good:

```
Windows NT could not start because the following file is missing or corrupt:
\winnt root\system32\ntoskrnl.exe
Please reinstall a copy of the above file.
```

As before, this file can be recovered using the Emergency Repair Disk or a file backup.

The Emergency Repair Disk

The Emergency Repair Disk is usually created during the Windows NT installation process. However, you can create (and update) it at any time by running the Windows NT command RDISK.EXE at a Windows NT DOS prompt.

To use the Emergency Repair disk, you must first boot the computer using the Windows NT Startup disk set.

Key Concept

If you do not have a set of startup disks but have access to the original installation files, you can create a set by typing the command **WINNT /OX**. Be sure to have three disks available.

From the Startup menu, choose Repair. The repair process offers four options:

- Inspect Registry Files. This option prompts the user for replacement of each Registry file, including System and SAM.

Key Concept

The files on the Emergency Repair Disk overwrite the files in the Registry. For this reason, using this disk is not the best way to recover damaged security or account information. A backup is much more useful in maintaining the integrity of existing account entries.

- Inspect Startup Environment. This option checks the BOOT.INI file for an entry for Windows NT. If it doesn't find one, it adds one for the next boot attempt.
- Verify Windows NT System Files. This option verifies whether the Windows NT system files match those of the original installation files. For this option, you need to have access to the original installation files. This option also looks for and verifies the integrity of the boot files.
- Inspect Boot Sector. This option checks the MBR for NTLDR. If this file is missing or corrupt, this option restores the boot sector.

If you know specifically which file is missing or corrupt, you can replace the file directly from the source files by using the Windows NT EXPAND utility. At a Windows NT prompt, type **EXPAND -R** followed by the compressed filename. If Windows NT is inoperable on your system, you can use another Windows NT system to expand the file and then copy it to your computer.

Windows NT Boot Disk

Another useful tool to have in your toolkit is a Windows NT boot disk. It is not a diskette formatted with NTFS; rather, it is a disk that has been formatted under Windows NT that has copies of the boot files on it.

When you format a diskette under Windows NT, Windows NT creates a boot sector on that disk that references NTLDR. Simply copy the five boot files to this disk, and voila, you have a Windows NT boot disk. This disk can be used in a variety of Windows NT computers because it is not unique to each installation. The only file you might need to modify—for obvious reasons—is the BOOT.INI file. This makes it much easier to replace missing or corrupt boot files.

Key Concept

You can format a disk from My Computer. To do so, right-click the A: Drive icon, and select Format. Make the appropriate selections and click OK.

Uninstalling Windows NT Workstation 4.0

You might need to uninstall Windows NT Workstation 4.0 from your computer—for example, if you were testing it and the evaluation period is over, if you want to install a different operating system entirely, or if you want to change the computer from a Windows NT Workstation 4.0 to a Windows NT Server 4.0. The steps required to remove Windows NT Workstation 4.0 from your computer depend on the file system your computer uses when booting.

FAT Partition

If you dual-boot between MS-DOS or Windows 95 and Windows NT Workstation 4.0, then your system partition is using the FAT file system. You can remove Windows NT Workstation 4.0 and restore the bootup operating system to what it was before (MS-DOS or Windows 95). To do so, follow these steps:

1. Boot your computer to start either MS-DOS or Windows 95.
2. Create a boot disk, also called a system disk.

Key Concept

To create a boot disk, place an unformatted disk in the A: drive of your computer. At a DOS prompt, enter the command **FORMAT A: /S**. This command transfers the MS-DOS or Windows 95 system files used for booting to the disk. Choose Yes at the prompt and proceed.

3. Copy the SYS.COM file from the DOS directory on your computer to the disk you just formatted.
4. Reboot your computer from the system disk you just created by leaving it in the A: drive and restarting your computer.
5. At the A: prompt, enter the command **SYS C:**. This command transfers the MS-DOS or Windows 95 system files from the system disk to the master boot record of the computer.
6. Remove the system disk from the A: drive, and restart the computer. The computer should now boot directly to MS-DOS or Windows 95 and no longer display the Windows NT boot menu.
7. Remove the Windows NT-related files from the hard disk. The following files and folders should be removed:
   - C:\pagefile.sys—This file may be located on a different partition if Windows NT was installed in a different partition.

- C:\boot.ini—This file is marked with the attributes System and Read Only.
- C:\nt*.*—These files are marked with the attributes Hidden, System, and Read Only; they include NTLDR, ntdetect.com, and possibly ntbootdd.sys.
- C:\bootsect.dos—This file is marked with the attributes Hidden and System.
- \winnt system file folder—This folder is found on whichever partition you installed Windows NT Workstation 4.0.
- \program files\Windows NT—This folder is found on whichever partition you installed Windows NT Workstation 4.0.

NTFS Partition

If you chose to install Windows NT in the system partition and formatted the partition to use NTFS, you do not have a dual-boot system. Subsequently, you cannot boot to either MS-DOS or Windows 95 because they require a FAT partition to boot. In this case, you must essentially remove the partition to remove Windows NT Workstation 4.0. You can use the MS-DOS FDISK utility from MS-DOS versions 6.0 and higher to remove the partition and repartition it for MS-DOS, or you can use the Windows NT Setup program to remove the NTFS partition.

Using FDISK

To use the FDISK utility to uninstall, follow these steps:

1. Create a system disk from an MS-DOS or Windows 95-based computer. (See the steps outlined in the preceding section, "FAT Partition.")
2. Copy the file fdisk.exe from the DOS directory on that computer to the system disk.
3. Boot Windows NT Workstation 4.0 from the system disk by placing it in the A: drive and then restarting the computer.
4. At the A: prompt, enter the command **FDISK**.
5. Choose option 3—Delete Partition or Logical DOS Drive from the FDISK menu.
6. Choose option 4—Delete Non-DOS Partition from the Delete Partition menu.
7. Select the partition number of the partition you want to delete. It is likely partition number 1.
8. Confirm your intent to delete the partition.

Using Windows NT 4.0 Setup

To use the Windows NT 4.0 Setup to uninstall, follow these steps:

1. Restart the computer with the Windows NT startup disk in the A: drive. (Refer to the section "Executing the Windows NT Workstation 4.0 Startup Process," as well as Table 3.2 for information about using and creating a startup disk.)

2. Proceed through setup to the screen prompting you to choose or create a partition.

3. Select the NTFS partition that you want to delete.

4. Press D on the keyboard to delete the partition.

5. Press F3 to exit Windows NT setup, and the partition is deleted.

You also can use other utilities to delete the NTFS partition. The Windows NT and Windows Resource Kits include a utility called DELPART that can be used to remove partitions. Partition Magic, manufactured by PowerQuest, and Norton Utilities for Windows NT, manufactured by Symantec, also provide partition management utilities with options for deleting NTFS partitions.

CH
3

Upgrading to Windows NT Workstation 4.0

The following sections describe some of the considerations for upgrading existing versions of Windows and Windows NT Workstation to Windows NT Workstation 4.0.

Windows NT Workstation

When you're upgrading from earlier versions of Windows NT Workstation, setup migrates all account information, network settings, and most other Registry settings. It migrates environment settings to the extent that the new interface supports them; color sets, cursors schemes, and the like are migrated. Program Manager settings are not because Program Manager does not exist in the new interface. Program Groups appear under the Programs selection on the Start menu.

If you choose to install Windows NT Workstation 4.0 in a new directory, you are in effect installing a new version of Windows NT on your computer. Consequently, previous settings, account information, and so on are not migrated. Also, if this installation of Windows NT will participate in the same workgroup or domain as the current installation, and you plan to switch between them, you must assign a new, unique computer name for this installation and create a separate computer account for the installation in the domain.

Windows 95

Recall that the Windows NT Workstation 4.0 setup program does not allow you to upgrade over Windows 95. Therefore, settings do not automatically migrate from Windows 95 to Windows NT Workstation 4.0. You must reinstall applications and reset environment settings after installation is complete.

Windows 3.1 and Windows for Workgroups 3.11

Just as we saw with Windows NT Workstation, during the installation process, the Windows NT 4.0 setup program detects an earlier version of Windows and offers to upgrade it by installing it in the existing Windows directory. If you choose to do so, you can boot to DOS and run Windows, or boot to Windows NT and run Windows NT with most of the same settings.

When Windows NT boots and displays the Welcome screen for the first time after installation, it automatically migrates existing program groups other than those that have a Windows NT counterpart, such as Main, Accessories, and Games. The program groups appear under Programs on the Start menu. In addition, Windows NT migrates Startup Group programs; file associations and OLE information from the Windows Registry (REG.DAT); application settings; and any WIN.INI, SYSTEM.INI, and CONTROL.INI parameter values that do not conflict with similar or changed settings contained in the Windows NT Workstation 4.0 Registry.

When a user (not the Administrator account) logs on to Windows NT Workstation for the first time, Windows NT automatically migrates those user environment settings that do not conflict with the new Windows NT 4.0 interface. For example, the user's color schemes, wallpaper, and mouse setup are migrated; however, the desktop arrangement of program groups is not.

Persistent network connections are not migrated. Persistent connections are network mappings that the user created through File Manager or at the command prompt that, by default, are saved in the WIN.INI file. Windows NT 4.0 creates and saves these connections differently. If you do have existing drive connections that you want to preserve, you should note them and reestablish them under Windows NT. Default domain names and usernames from Windows for Workgroups are also not migrated.

If you choose to install Windows NT 4.0 in its own directory, no Windows settings are migrated. However, you can manually cause Windows NT to migrate the Windows settings as described previously. To do so, simply copy the .INI and .GRP files from the Windows root directory into the Windows NT root directory (by default called \WINNT). When Windows NT is next booted and a user logs on, the migration process will occur as outlined earlier.

If, for some reason, migration does not take place, or you need to execute the migration process again, you need to make a modification to the Windows NT Registry. Working with the Registry is covered in Chapter 5, "Configuration and the Registry." Briefly, you need to find the Registry key \HKEY_CURRENT_USER\Windows Migration Status and remove it. Then restart Windows NT, and migration should proceed as before.

Summary

This chapter described in some detail the installation and setup process for Windows NT Workstation 4.0. Now that you have it installed, you need to become familiar with the Windows 95 interface. If you are already Windows 95 literate, you will have no trouble adjusting to Windows NT Workstation 4.0. If you are coming from a Program Manager background, you will want to spend a little more time playing with the new interface to find all your favorite utilities and explore the enhancements that the new interface brings to the desktop.

The next two chapters, "An Overview of the Windows NT 4.0 Interface" and "Configuration and the Registry," are designed to help you become familiar with the new interface and explore how to modify the configuration.

**CH
3**

QUESTIONS AND ANSWERS

1. What is the minimum hardware requirement to install Windows NT Workstation 4.0?

   A. 486/33 with 12MB of RAM.

2. What is the minimum amount of RAM needed to install Windows 95?

   A. 4MB.

3. The default directory into which the NT Workstation operating system is installed is _____.

   A. WINNT.

4. True or False: Windows NT Workstation 4.0 supports NTFS, CDFS, FAT, and HPFS.

   A. False. Previous versions of Windows NT Workstation supported NTFS, CDFS, FAT, and HPFS, but 4.0 has stopped the HPFS support.

5. True or False: Dual-booting with Windows 95 always requires operating systems to be in separate directories.

   A. True. Dual-booting with Windows 95 always requires operating systems to be in separate directories. This action is the default (WINDOWS and WINNT); if you place both in the same directory, you are overwriting one with the other.

PRACTICE TEST

1. You are planning to roll out Windows NT Workstation 4.0 to a workgroup that has the following computer configurations. On which computers can you install Windows NT Workstation 4.0 successfully?

   a. 3 386/25, 150MB free space, 8MB RAM, VGA, Windows 3.1

   b. 2 386/33, 120MB free space, 16MB RAM, VGA, Windows for Workgroups

   c. 5 486/66DX, 200MB free space, 16MB RAM, Super VGA, Windows for Workgroups

   d. 2 Pentium/120, 100MB free space, 16MB RAM, Super VGA, Windows NT 3.51

Answer a is incorrect because NT cannot be installed on less than a 486/33 with 12MB of RAM. Answer b is incorrect because NT cannot be installed on a 386. **Answer c is correct because Windows NT requires a 486/33 with 12MB RAM and 120MB free disk space.** Answer d is incorrect because 120MB of free space is needed.

2. Which of the following dialogs take place during the text mode of the Setup process? Choose three.

   a. Detection and configuration of storage devices

   b. Initial hardware verification

   c. Request for network card settings

   d. Choice of file system for the system partition

Answers a, b, and d are correct because all three actions take place during the text mode portion of the setup process. Answer c is incorrect because the NIC card is configured during the wizard portion of setup.

3. Which of the following dialogs take place as part of the Setup Wizard? Choose three.

   a. Personal information

   b. Detection and configuration of storage devices

   c. Request for network card settings

   d. Video display setup

Answers a, c, and d are correct because all three dialogs transpire during the wizard portion of setup. Answer b is incorrect because the detection and configuration of storage devices take place as part of the text mode setup.

4. Which of the following switches allow you to install Windows NT without creating the three startup disks? Choose only one.

    a. WINNT /B

    b. WINNT /F

    c. WINNT /OX

    d. WINNT /S

Answer a is correct because the /B switch is used to install NT without the startup disks. Answer b is incorrect because the /F switch skips the file verification phase. Answer c is incorrect because it creates the three startup disks. Answer d is incorrect because it specifies a source for the installation files.

5. On a RISC-based computer, which of the following statements is true regarding Windows NT installation?

    a. You can execute setup from either the CD-ROM or over the network by typing **WINNT32** and any optional switches.

    b. You must have a 2MB FAT minimum system partition before starting setup.

    c. You can execute setup only from a CD-ROM by running WINNT /ARC.

    d. You can run SETUPLDR from the I386 subdirectory on the CD-ROM.

Answer a is incorrect because WINNT32 cannot be used. **Answer b is correct because a FAT partition must be used to boot NT.** Answer c is incorrect because /ARC is not a valid switch. Answer d is incorrect because the I386 directory is only for Intel installations.

6. You have begun the setup process and have been queried for mass storage devices. Setup presents you with a blank list of devices, but you know that you have a 1.2GB IDE drive installed.

    a. IDE devices are detected but generally not displayed in the list.

    b. Windows NT has incorrectly identified your devices. Press F3 to exit setup, and double-check your drive configuration.

    c. Press S to add the drive configuration to the list.

    d. Exit setup and run NTHQ to verify hardware detection.

Answer a is correct because, under normal circumstances, the IDE devices do not show up in the list even though they are detected. Answer b is incorrect because IDE devices typically do not show up at detection. Answer c is incorrect because the S does not search for IDE. Answer d is incorrect because IDE devices typically do not show up at detection.

7. You are installing Windows NT on a RISC-based computer and want to format the Windows NT system partition as NTFS.

a. Create a 2MB FAT partition for the Windows NT boot files and a second partition large enough for the Windows NT system files before starting setup. Select the partition during setup, and format it as NTFS.

b. Create a 2MB FAT partition for the Windows NT boot files before starting setup. During setup, choose free space, create a partition, and format it as NTFS, just as in an Intel installation.

c. Windows NT requires a FAT partition for its system files. You can format only nonsystem partitions with NTFS.

d. Windows NT does not support NTFS on RISC-based systems.

Answer a is correct because you must have a partition present before you begin. Answer b is incorrect because you must make the second partition prior to starting setup. Answer c is incorrect because NT can run in either FAT or NTFS. Answer d is incorrect because NT does support FAT and NTFS.

8. During the text mode phase, Windows NT displays a dialog box that shows you two drive partitions and 600MB free space on one drive. You would like to install Windows NT on the free space but want to use only 200MB.

a. You must preconfigure the free space before starting setup.

b. You can select the free space during setup, but you cannot change its size.

c. Select the free space, and press Enter.

d. Select the free space, and choose C to create the new partition. Then select the new partition and continue with installation.

Answer a is wrong because you need not preconfigure the partition. Answer b is incorrect because you can change the size. Answer c is wrong because this approach does not allow you to change the size. **Answer d is correct because you can choose to create a new partition within the free space during the installation.**

9. Which of the following statements regarding NTFS is true? More than one could be correct.

a. NTFS supports file and directory permissions security and access auditing.

b. NTFS supports transaction tracking and sector sparing for data recovery.

c. NTFS supports file and partition sizes of up to 4GB.

d. NTFS provides file and directory compression.

Answers a, b, and d are true statements. Answer c is false because partition sizes to 16EB are supported.

10. You are installing Windows NT Workstation 4.0 on a computer with a previous installation of Windows for Workgroups. You would like to retain that installation and boot to either Windows or Windows NT. You keep the partitions as FAT. What else must you do?

    a. You must install Windows NT in a new directory to preserve the original installation.

    b. Do nothing. Windows NT automatically installs as dual-boot in this installation.

    c. Create a new partition using FDISK, and install Windows NT in that partition.

    d. You cannot dual-boot between Windows and Windows NT.

Answer a is incorrect because this operation is the default. **Answer b is correct because Windows NT automatically sets up a dual-boot environment.** The only method of overriding this is to install Windows NT in the same directory that Windows for Workgroups is installed in, thus overwriting key files. Answer c is incorrect because you need not change the partition. Answer d is incorrect because you can dual-boot between Windows and Windows NT.

CH

3

CHAPTER PREREQUISITE

You should be familiar with the feature set of Windows NT Workstation 4.0 as described in Chapter 2. This chapter is an overview of the Explorer shell. If you have been working with NT Workstation for some time or with Explorer in the Windows 9x platform, you should jump ahead to Chapter 5.

CHAPTER

4

An Overview of the Windows NT 4.0 Interface

WHILE YOU READ

1. True or False: The default option for the taskbar is Auto Hide.

2. What is the extension assigned to a shortcut file?

3. The Control Panel can be found on the Start menu under what option?

4. Files deleted through the graphical interface go into the _____.

5. True or False: The Help index *always* shows items alphabetized.

In this chapter, we will review the Windows NT 4.0 user interface. This interface incorporates the Windows 95 object-oriented look and feel into Windows NT 4.0's 32-bit architecture. This chapter is not designed to detail the Windows NT look and feel. It does, however, provide an overview of the interface, particularly as it applies to Windows NT 4.0 utilities, configuration, and so on, which will be more than sufficient knowledge to pass the exam.

Logging On to Windows NT Workstation 4.0

Before beginning a discussion of the new Windows NT 4.0 user interface, you need to log on to Windows NT 4.0. The logon process really hasn't changed from previous versions of Windows NT. When Windows NT is booted, you are presented with an animated Begin Logon dialog box encouraging you to press Ctrl+Alt+Del to log on.

Pressing Ctrl+Alt+Del is really the first Windows NT security function. Traditionally, this sequence terminated all open applications and rebooted your MS-DOS computer. Similarly, the same sequence at this point of the logon process sends a terminate interrupt to the processor. It is designed, however, to terminate any "stealth" program that might record your username and password and otherwise breach logon security.

After you press Ctrl+Alt+Del, Windows NT displays the Logon Information dialog box. You are prompted to enter a valid username and password and then click OK. This dialog box also features a Shutdown button, which allows you to shut down your computer at this point without logging on.

At this point, you can log on either with the Administrator account that you created or with the user account created during installation. After the Windows NT Security Subsystem authenticates your account, the Windows NT 4.0 desktop appears. On top of the desktop, Windows NT displays its Welcome dialog box (see Figure 4.1).

From the Welcome dialog box, you can choose to get a quick overview of the new features of the desktop and how to get around, open the Windows NT Help program, or display a Windows NT working tip. The Welcome dialog box is displayed each time you log on. You can configure this dialog so that it is not displayed by deselecting the check box in its lower-left corner. You can always reopen the dialog through the Help program by using the following steps:

1. Select Start, Help from the taskbar.
2. Select the Contents tab in the Help dialog box.
3. Open the topic Tips and Tricks.
4. Open the subtopic Tips of the Day.
5. Open the document Viewing the Welcome Screen.
6. Follow the instructions to reopen the Welcome screen.

Figure 4.1
You see this Welcome screen when you first start Windows NT Workstation 4.0.

CH

4

Among the first things you will notice about the desktop is the Start button on the taskbar in the lower-left corner of the screen. This button is the point of origin for all your installed applications and utilities. Also, notice some default objects along the left side of your screen. We will describe them in more detail in just a moment. First, now that you have logged on to Windows NT, you also need to know how to log off properly.

As in previous versions of Windows NT, as well as Windows 95 and Windows, it is very important that you exit the operating system in the appropriate manner. This means performing a proper shutdown of your system before powering off the computer. A proper shutdown closes all open applications, writes cached information to the disk, closes all system files, stops all services, and notifies the network that you are going offline. Unfortunately, many users have developed the bad habit of simply powering off the computer when they are finished. Powering off this way may have had minimal consequences on the Windows-based systems but is far more serious on a Windows NT-based computer. Improperly shutting down your Windows NT workstation may result in a mildly annoying loss of data files to a more serious corruption of system files, resulting in a failed attempt to reboot Windows NT.

The proper steps for shutting down your Windows NT Workstation 4.0 are as follows:

1. Click the Start button on the taskbar.

2. From the Start menu that appears, choose the last menu option, Shut Down. A dialog box appears with three options:

   ■ Choose Shut Down the Computer to prepare Windows NT for being powered off. In this case, an orderly shutdown occurs, and Windows NT displays a message asking whether you want to restart your computer when shutdown is complete. If your computer supports power management, Windows NT may also be enabled to power off the computer when the shutdown is complete.

   ■ Choose Restart the Computer to reboot the computer after the shutdown is complete. This option performs a warm boot of the computer.

   ■ Choose Close All Programs and Log On as a Different User to close down open applications and save data, log off the current user, and display the Begin Logon dialog box for the next user.

3. Choose the appropriate option from the list, and click Yes or press Enter on the keyboard.

Windows NT Security Dialog Box

Another option for shutting down or logging off your system is the Windows NT Security dialog box. You can access it by pressing Ctrl+Alt+Del on your keyboard. From this dialog box, you can shut down the system, log off, change your password (provided you know the original), access the Task Manager, and lock the workstation. Locking the workstation password protects the screen so that only the user who locked it or an administrator can unlock the desktop.

Exploring the Windows NT 4.0 Desktop

Responding to the suggestions and needs of its Windows NT clients, Microsoft has incorporated the Windows 95 interface into the default desktop of Windows NT 4.0. As a result, the desktop is easier to use, customize, and manage than the Program Manager interface. The desktop consists of two basic elements: objects and the taskbar.

Objects

Objects provide you with a unified way of dealing with icons on the screen. Objects include files, folders, programs, printers, modems, and so on. All objects have properties, settings, and parameters that you can access by right-clicking. These settings and parameters are displayed in a Properties sheet and vary depending on the type of object and the program it is accessing.

The sample Properties sheet in Figure 4.2 was displayed by selecting a folder, right-clicking, and choosing <u>P</u>roperties from the menu. This one shows the name of the folder (read: directory), its location, its size and contents, when it was created, and any attributes that have been assigned to it. The Sharing tab displays a second page that lets you share the folder with other members of the workgroup or domain that your computer might participate in. The concept and process of sharing is covered in detail in Chapter 7, "Windows NT 4.0 Security Model."

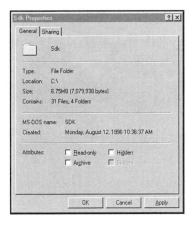

Figure 4.2
Sample Properties sheet.

Taskbar

The Windows NT taskbar appears, by default, on the bottom of the desktop screen. It consists of the Start button at the far left and the clock at the far right. The taskbar also acts as your task manager by maintaining a row of open program titles. Moving from one window to another is as easy as a click of the mouse on the taskbar, so you don't need to resize, tile, or cascade your open applications into a confusing array of windows. Being able to see all the open programs also minimizes the possibility of your opening multiple versions of the same application. A quick scan of the taskbar can confirm that a program is already running, and a quick mouse click can take you there. Alt+Tab is still available to task-switch between programs as well. Also, a right-click on the taskbar displays a pop-up from which you can select Task Manager and switch between programs.

The taskbar is also an object and as such has properties. Right-clicking the taskbar displays a menu that looks a lot like the Program Manager menu option <u>W</u>indow. From here, you can cascade, tile (horizontally or vertically), and minimize all windows, as well as access the new Windows NT Task Manager and the Properties sheet.

Taskbar Properties

The Taskbar Properties sheet has two tabs (see Figure 4.3). The first, Taskbar Options, allows control over how the taskbar appears on the screen.

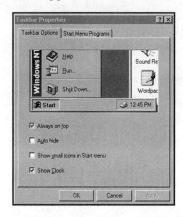

Figure 4.3
You right-click the taskbar and choose Properties to display its Properties sheet.

Option choices are outlined in Table 4.1.

Table 4.1 Taskbar Options	
Selection	Description
Always on Top	Default. Always displays the taskbar on the desktop, regardless of whether a window is maximized.
Auto Hide	Hides the taskbar so as not to detract from the desktop real estate. The taskbar reappears when the cursor is moved over last location of taskbar.
Show Small Icons in Start Menu	Displays a smaller version of Smart menu icons useful for lower resolution screens.
Show Clock	Default. Toggles the taskbar clock on and off.

The second tab of the taskbar Properties dialog box, called Start Menu Programs, offers a means of customizing the Start menu itself (see Figure 4.4). For example, you could place your favorite program directly on the Start menu so that you would not have to browse through several other folders to find it.

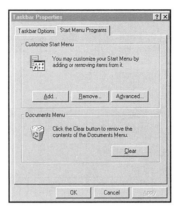

Figure 4.4
You can customize the Start menu from the Taskbar Properties sheet by selecting the Start Menu Programs tab.

Follow these steps to customize the Start menu:

1. From the Start Menu Programs tab, choose <u>A</u>dd to open a wizard for changing the Start menu.

2. Either type in the path and filename of the application you want to add, or browse for it by clicking the B<u>r</u>owse button (see Figure 4.5). The filename here is called a shortcut because it is a pointer to the file, and not the actual file itself. Then click <u>N</u>ext.

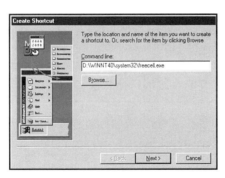

Figure 4.5
The wizard makes it easy to add a program to the Start menu. First, tell it what you want to add.

CH

4

3. The next screen of the wizard prompts you to select the folder in which you'll add the shortcut (see Figure 4.6). You can click the Start menu itself or any folder within the Start menu, create a new folder for the shortcut with the New Folder button, or even choose to place the shortcut on the desktop. Make your choice and click Next.

Figure 4.6
Next, tell the wizard where you want to add the shortcut.

4. Enter a name for the shortcut (see Figure 4.7).

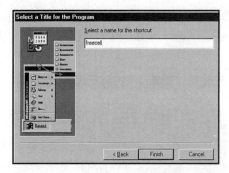

Figure 4.7
Tell the wizard what you want to call the program (called a shortcut).

5. Choose Finish and then OK. Click Start, Menu on the taskbar to see your new shortcut.

You can drag the taskbar itself to any side of the screen. Just click and drag it to the sides, top, or bottom of the screen to change its position.

Starting Programs

All programs can be accessed through the Start menu on the taskbar. The Start menu effectively replaces the Program Manager for application access.

When you click the Start menu, Windows NT displays a menu of choices for finding and running programs (see Figure 4.8).

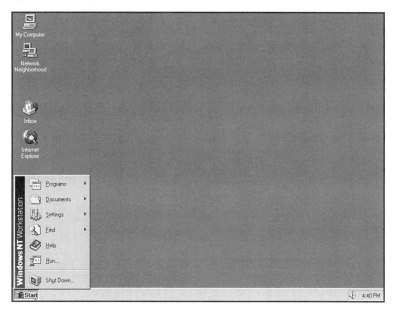

Figure 4.8
The Start menu substitutes for Program Manager and is used for launching your Windows NT applications.

Programs

Choosing Programs from the Start menu displays a list of programs and program folders, including Accessories, the Startup folder, the Command Prompt, and the Windows NT Explorer (see Figure 4.9). Any new program groups created as a result of installing an application or migrating from previous Windows versions are also displayed here. (The Games folder can be found under Accessories.) On the lower portion of the Programs menu, you will find the Windows NT Administrative Tools group.

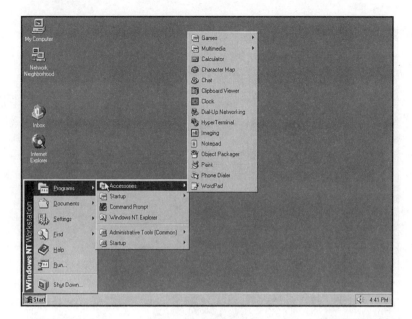

Figure 4.9
Select Programs on the Start menu to open the majority of your Windows NT applications.

Documents

Choosing Documents from the Start menu displays the last 15 documents that were opened. This feature provides an efficient and productive way to get started quickly.

Settings

Settings offers access to configuration utilities through Control Panel and Printers, as well as another way to change the properties of the taskbar (see Figure 4.10).

Find

Using the Find utility, you can search the computer for files and folders, as well as the network for shared computers. This Find utility also searches for text contained within documents, providing a truly robust search utility for Windows NT 4.0. We will discuss this utility in more detail later in this chapter.

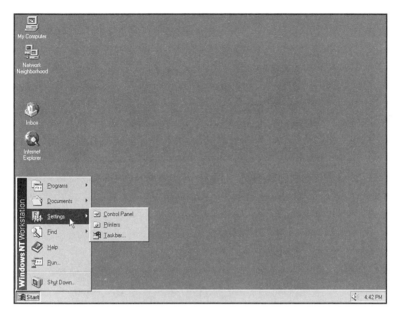

Figure 4.10
Select Settings from the Start menu to access Control Panel, Printers, and Taskbar.

Help

The Help menu choice starts the Windows NT Help program. Windows NT 4.0 Help has been greatly enhanced, making an already helpful program even better. You can always access Help by pressing F1 on the keyboard or by clicking the numerous Help buttons that now show up in almost every dialog box. Help is now also linked directly to many dialog boxes so that when you find help on a certain topic, you can click a button and have Windows NT display the appropriate dialog box for you to fill in while you are reading the Help information. A thorough discussion of how to use this program will follow later in this chapter.

Run

Run takes the place of the Program Manager and the File Manager's File, Run menu option. When you select Run, Windows NT displays a box in which you can enter the path and name of the program you want to execute (see Figure 4.11). You also can use a Browse button to look for the program.

Figure 4.11
In the Run box, you can enter the path and name of a program you want to execute.

Shut Down

Shut Down, as you saw earlier, provides the appropriate way to shut down the computer or log off.

Shortcuts

Another way to customize your desktop is to create a shortcut to an application or file and place it on your desktop to facilitate access and loading. Moving a file actually changes its location and file pointer in Windows NT. Copying a file creates another file object—taking up twice the space. A shortcut is simply a pointer to the file. The shortcut is given a filename of Shortc˜x.lnk, where x represents the number of this shortcut—for example, 1, 2, and so on. It is stored in the WINNT40\Profiles*Username*\Desktop folder, where *Username* is the login name of the user who created the shortcut.

To create a shortcut, follow these steps:

1. Find the application or file by using My Computer or the Windows Explorer.
2. Right-click its icon, and drag it to the desktop. Windows NT responds with a menu of choices:

    <u>M</u>ove Here

    <u>C</u>opy Here

    Create <u>S</u>hortcut(s) Here

3. Choose Create <u>S</u>hortcut(s) Here. Windows NT then creates a shortcut object on the desktop that you can use to access the file or application directly.

My Computer

Selecting the My Computer icon displays all resources that are available on your computer (see Figure 4.12). My Computer resembles the File Manager in the way you can drill down through folders to find what you want. You can also switch to a directory, as shown in the figure. Note that in addition to directories, folders can also represent printers, Control Panel, network members, and so on.

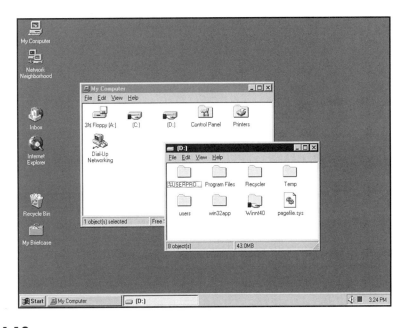

Figure 4.12
Selecting My Computer opens a window that shows three drives: A:, C:, D:, and icons
to open Dial-Up Networking, Control Panel, and Printers.

You can see at a glance each drive (including CD-ROM) and any network drive mappings; you also can access Control Panel and Printers for configuring Windows NT.

The window that is opened through My Computer also features a menu bar. On this menu bar, you'll find File (from which you can create new folders and shortcuts), Edit (for copy, paste, and undo operations), View (to modify the window display, arrange icons, and refresh the screen), and Help options.

Network Neighborhood

The Network Neighborhood icon represents access to the network in which your computer participates. This network might include members of a workgroup, domain, or enterprise (see Figure 4.13). As with My Computer, clicking the various icons in each window takes you further into the network relationship that your computer is a part of. This way, you can relatively easily navigate through the enterprise. In addition to the usual File, Edit, View, and Help menu options, right-clicking a computer's shared resource gives you the option either to map a network drive to that resource or create a shortcut for that resource on the desktop.

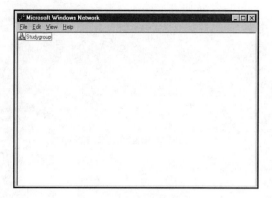

Figure 4.13
Selecting Network Neighborhood opens a window that displays your network at a glance. In this example, you can see that this computer is using Microsoft's networking and is a member of a workgroup called Studygroup.

Opening the properties screen of Network Neighborhood actually displays the Network dialog box from Control Panel. We will explore that utility program in more detail in Chapter 11, "Network Connectivity and Remote Support." You will find that there are often multiple ways of viewing properties screens.

Recycle Bin

The Recycle Bin provides a handy way of dealing with deleted files. When a file is deleted through the interface—for example, through Windows Explorer—it is placed in the Recycle Bin (see Figure 4.14). If you need to recover the file for any reason, you can open the Recycle Bin, select the file to recover, choose File from the menu, and then choose Recover.

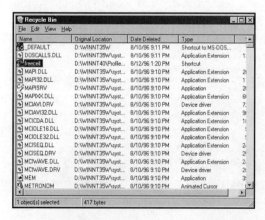

Figure 4.14
In this Recycle Bin, many files have been deleted but not yet purged from the computer's hard disk.

The File menu choice also offers an option to clear out the Recycle Bin or delete selected files. Doing so, in effect, purges the files and makes the disk space formerly occupied by the files immediately available to the system.

A quick look at the properties of the Recycle Bin (see Figure 4.15) shows that, by default, Windows NT reserves 10 percent of the hard disk space on all or selected drives for storage of deleted files. When this space fills up, the oldest files are automatically purged to make room for newer files. Although this purging happens automatically, you might want more control over how much disk storage is reserved and just when the files are purged. Modifying these properties and regularly maintaining the Recycle Bin provide that control.

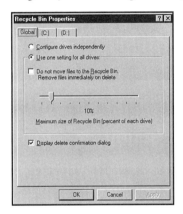

Figure 4.15
The Recycle Bin's Properties sheet on this computer shows that it is using the default 10% of the hard disk for storing deleted files.

CH
4

My Briefcase

My Briefcase is a unique utility designed primarily for laptop use but adaptable for the desktop computer as well. It allows you to take copies of files with you on the laptop or on disk and work on them in another location or while on the road. When you return to your office computer or dock your laptop, My Briefcase can synchronize the files you worked on while you were away with the files located on the desktop computer (or on the office network and so on) by overwriting the original files with the changes you made to the copies. Thus, you need not concern yourself with which copy is the most recent because My Briefcase keeps track of versions by modification date.

As you can see from Figure 4.16, you can set up and use My Briefcase relatively easily.

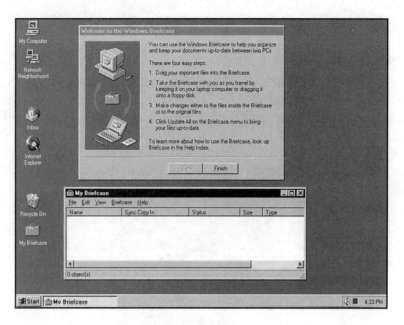

Figure 4.16
This example shows both the Welcome screen and the contents window that appears when opening My Briefcase.

Follow these steps to use My Briefcase:

1. Drag the files you want into the briefcase.

2. Keep it on your laptop, or drag the entire briefcase to a disk.

3. Work with either set of files.

4. Update all or selected files by opening My Briefcase, choosing Briefcase from the menu, and then Update All or Update Selection.

When you copy a file into My Briefcase, you are creating a separate file rather than a shortcut. A 2MB file requires 2MB storage space. Consequently, all files might not fit on a floppy disk. Check your storage space before using My Briefcase.

Other Icons

Depending on the additional Windows NT 4.0 services or programs that you install, additional icons may be displayed on the desktop. For example, if the Microsoft Exchange client is installed, Windows NT adds Inbox and Exchange icons to your screen. If you have added the Internet Explorer, an icon for that utility is also installed. If you choose to set up The Microsoft Network, you see an icon for that program also.

Of course, you can add your own shortcut icons to the screen to more effectively customize your environment and keep you most productive. For example, you could create a shortcut for your printer and shortcuts for the documents you work on frequently. When you need to print a document, you need only drag the document shortcut onto the printer shortcut to start the print process.

Using Windows NT 4.0 Explorer

The Windows NT Explorer is the closest utility in look and function to the Windows File Manager. The Explorer is the primary navigation tool for your system. When you open an object such as My Computer, Windows NT displays a window with the contents of My Computer. As you open an icon in this window, another window opens, and then another, and…well, it can get messy, not to mention confusing, to have all those windows open on the desktop and then have to close them all. With My Computer and Network Neighborhood, you do have the option of replacing each previous window with the succeeding window. However, then you lose the path back from where you came.

Changing the Open Window Option for My Computer and Network Neighborhood

When you open My Computer and Network Neighborhood, Windows NT displays a window with the contents of the object. When you open one of the content's objects, another window opens, and so on. Having multiple windows open can fill your desktop quickly and make it harder to find your way around.

CH
4

These two objects have a view option that will replace each open window with a new window as you open each icon. You can set this option as follows:

1. Open My Computer (or Network Neighborhood).
2. Choose <u>V</u>iew, <u>O</u>ptions.
3. On the folder tab, select the radio button option labeled Browse Folders by Using a S<u>in</u>gle Window That Changes as You Open Each Folder.
4. Click OK.

If you set this option for either object, it takes effect for both.

Other View options include the ability to hide certain file types; display file extensions; display compressed files; and add, remove, or modify the settings of file types.

Windows Explorer, like the File Manager, lets you drill down through drives, folders, and so on. The left pane of the window displays the object's folders and files. As each folder is selected here, the right pane displays the contents of the folder.

You can use Windows Explorer to browse your desktop, drives, CD-ROM, Recycle Bin, and Network Neighborhood, as shown in Figure 4.17. In addition, Windows Explorer includes all your network connections and shared resources. You can browse them as well, all from the same interface. So, you can think of Windows Explorer not as a replacement for the File Manager, but more like File Manager Deluxe!

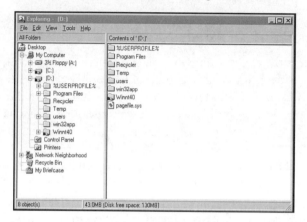

Figure 4.17
When Windows NT Explorer was started on this computer, the default directory focus was on the D: drive, so that drive is expanded. Note that besides files and directories, you can also see desktop objects such as Network Neighborhood and disk drives.

You can start Windows Explorer by clicking Start, selecting Programs, and then choosing Windows Explorer. This technique opens Explorer for the entire desktop. However, you can also right-click a desktop object such as Network Neighborhood or My Computer and choose Explore. This technique opens Windows Explorer and sets the focus on that particular object.

Quick Tour of the Windows Explorer Menu

You can easily use and configure Windows Explorer by selecting the appropriate option from its menu.

File

You can use options from the Windows Explorer File menu to create new folders or shortcuts (and other objects), delete or rename folders and files, and to look at or modify the properties of an object.

Edit

You can use Edit menu options to cut, copy, or paste folders and files and to make selections.

View

The Yiew menu provides most of the configuration options for Windows Explorer. Use View to display a toolbar to help you navigate Explorer and facilitate its use. You can also display a status bar that gives a one-line description of your selection. Choose whether to display items listed with large or small icons, and with or without showing all file details. Arrange the icons by name, type, size, or date, or automatically by Explorer. Select Options to display a Properties sheet that lets you further refine how the file items are displayed, and add, modify, or delete file types. Use Refresh to refresh the panes to be sure you are seeing the most current information.

For example, to display files with their file extensions, choose Yiew, Options to display the Options dialog box. In the Options dialog box, deselect the Hide File Extensions for Known File Types option.

Tools

From the Tools menu, you can use the Windows Find program to search for files, folders, or computers on your system. From this menu choice, you can also map and disconnect network drives to shared resources. It also features a Go To option that lets you type in the name of the folder you would like to open and takes you there directly.

Help

Choosing Help in Windows Explorer, of course, opens the Windows NT 4.0 Help program.

Viewing Documents

Another convenient feature that Microsoft has brought over to Windows NT 4.0 from Windows 95 is the capability to display most documents with a document viewer utility called Quick View. Quick View works off the program association that a document may have. For example, if a document is a bitmap with a .BMP extension, it is already associated with the Paint program. If you right-click it from within Windows Explorer (or from any other window), you can choose the Quick View option to open Paint and display the bitmap. If a file has no program association, then you can right-click the file and choose Open With. This option displays a dialog box asking you to choose a program to use to view the file. You can also associate all files of the same type with the specified viewer.

Searching Your Computer with the Windows NT 4.0 Find Program

Microsoft has added a new search function called Find to Windows NT 4.0. Using this utility, you can search for files, folders, and computers on the network (see Figure 4.18).

CH
4

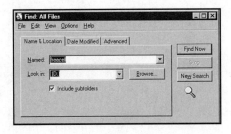

Figure 4.18
Here, Find was asked to locate the file Freecell in all the directories (folders) on the D: drive.

This utility is quite intuitive to use. A quick look at the Properties sheet for Find shows that you can search by name and location of the file, or you can search based on specific date and time modification parameters, such as between a range of dates or in the last specified number of days. You can even specify the kinds of file types within which to narrow your search, their size, and perhaps most useful, by files that contain a specified string of text.

Your search criteria can be saved and reused or modified later. From the Options menu, you can make your search case sensitive.

When the search is completed, Find displays an expanded results pane showing all the files that matched the criteria specified (see Figure 4.19). From here, you can copy files, open files, create shortcuts, delete files, and so on.

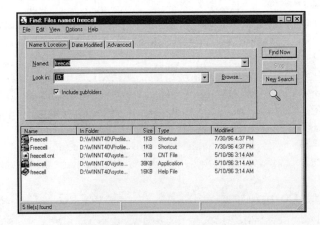

Figure 4.19
Find completed the search for Freecell and displays five related files in its results window.

Exploring Windows NT 4.0 Help

Microsoft has greatly enhanced the Help program available in Windows NT. Windows NT Help is now both context-sensitive and task-based. Context-sensitive, of course, means that if you choose the Help button in a dialog box or Properties sheet, or press F1 with a particular item selected, Windows NT will display a help window for that item. It might be a pop-up description box, or it might be the Help program itself with more detailed directions. Windows NT Help also features a What's This? button. At the top-right corner of most dialog boxes and Properties sheets is a ? (question mark) button. Click it and then click an item in the screen; Windows NT then displays a pop-up about that item.

Task-based help follows a "how to" approach. Task-based help screens include button links back to the appropriate dialog boxes for accomplishing a specific task. By clicking the button, you can stay in Help and read the step-by-step directions for completing a task, while actually working in the dialog box.

For example, if you want to know how to change the computer's date and time, you can look up that information in Help. When you open the corresponding help document (see Figure 4.20), you can click the link (arrow) button, and Windows NT will open the Date/Time Properties dialog box for you to work in.

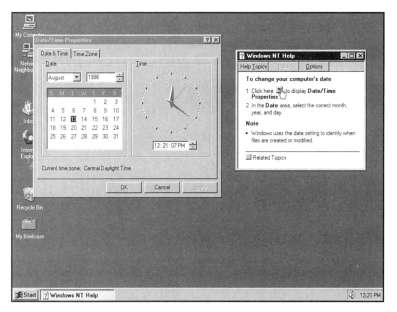

CH

4

Figure 4.20
Here, you see both the NT Help screen and the NT dialog box it opens when clicking the arrow button for task-based help.

Using Windows NT Help

You can start Windows NT Help from most menu bars or from the Start menu. The Help screen consists of three tabs: Contents, Index, and Find. Each lets you navigate Help a little differently, depending on your needs and what you want to look up.

Contents

The Contents tab, as shown in Figure 4.21, focuses on subjects or topics such as Tips and Tricks and How To. It also contains a complete list of Windows NT Command Prompt commands, their syntax, and suggested usage.

Figure 4.21
Windows NT Help: Contents tab.

Index

The Index tab, shown in Figure 4.22, displays certain selected topics alphabetically. You can scroll through to find the topic you are looking for, or you can type the first few letters in the text box. Optionally, if you do not find what you have typed, you can enter a synonym to see related topics.

Find

The Find tab, shown in Figure 4.23, contains a search engine that lets you enter a word or phrase. Windows NT Help displays a list of matching words to help you narrow the search; then you can select the appropriate topic from the third list.

Figure 4.22
Windows NT Help: Index tab.

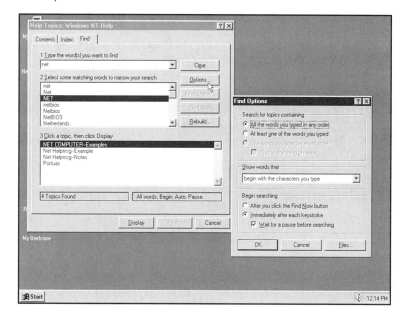

Figure 4.23
Windows Help: Find tab.

The Options button (shown in Figure 4.23) lets you further refine the search by specifying how Windows NT should make the match against what you typed.

Help Topics

After you have determined which topic to open, simply double-click the topic, or click Display at the bottom of the Help screen.

Windows NT Help displays the topic for you. Each topic screen is a little different. For example, the sample screen in Figure 4.24 presents three buttons, each of which will display additional information. Selecting Command List opens another window with a choice of Windows NT commands listed alphabetically. You can further explore each of these commands by clicking its button.

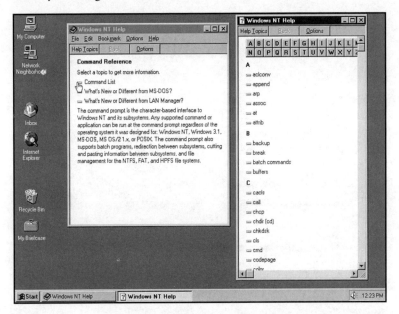

Figure 4.24
This Help screen was displayed by selecting Windows NT Commands from the Contents tab of Windows NT Help.

At the top of the Help screen are buttons to take you back to the main Help screen or, if you have drilled through several subtopics and related topics, to take you to the previous topic, or to select various options such as printing the topic, annotating it, copying it, changing the font, and so on. Annotate is particularly useful because it allows you to add your own comments and notes to the help topic for future reference.

On the menu bar is the Bookmark menu choice. As in Windows, Bookmark lets you mark this selection for easy and direct access in the future.

Summary

So far, you have installed Windows NT Workstation 4.0 and become familiar with some of the more significant features of its new interface. There is certainly a lot more to the interface, so we encourage you to explore these features on your own.

The next step is to learn how to configure Windows NT—changing settings, adding drivers, modifying the Registry and so on.

QUESTIONS AND ANSWERS

1. True or False: The default option for the taskbar is Auto Hide.

    A. False. The default option for the taskbar is Always on Top.

2. What is the extension assigned to a shortcut file?

    A. .LNK

3. The Control Panel can be found on the Start menu under what option?

    A. On the Start menu under the Settings option.

4. Files deleted through the graphical interface go into the _____.

    A. Files deleted through the graphical interface go into the Recycle Bin and can be removed or restored from there.

5. True or False: The Help index *always* shows items alphabetized.

    A. True. The Help index always shows items in alphabetical order.

CH
4

PRACTICE TEST

1. You need to log on to a workstation with Windows NT Workstation 4.0 that another person is using to administer a shared resource. What does the other person need to do? Choose two.

    a. From the Start menu, choose Shutdown, select Close All Programs, and log on as a different person.

    b. From the Start menu, choose Shutdown, and then select Restart the Computer.

    c. Press Ctrl+Alt+Del on the keyboard to display the Windows NT Security dialog box, and then click Shutdown.

    d. Press Ctrl+Alt+Del on the keyboard to display the Windows NT Security dialog box, and then click Logoff.

Answer a is correct because this choice allows you to log off the system and log on again. Answer b involves the much-unneeded step of shutting down the computer when all you want to do is log off the user. Answer c involves the much-unneeded step of shutting down the computer when all you want to do is log off the user. **Answer d is correct because this choice allows you to log off the system and log on again.**

2. What is the correct way to shut down Windows NT? Choose two.
   a. Press Ctrl+Alt+Del on the keyboard, and then choose Shutdown in the Windows NT Security dialog box.
   b. Choose Shutdown from the Start menu, and select the Exit choice.
   c. Choose Shutdown from the Start menu, and then shut down the computer.
   d. Press Ctrl+Alt+Del on the keyboard, and then power off the computer.

Answers a and c are correct because they close all open files and update the Registry before shutting down the system. Answer b is incorrect because no Exit choice is available. Answer d is incorrect because it does not properly shut down the operating system.

3. Which of the following Windows NT 4.0 options lets you switch between open windows? Choose three.
   a. Click the window title in the taskbar.
   b. Press Alt+Tab on the keyboard to select the desired window.
   c. Press Ctrl+Esc to display the Windows NT Task Switcher.
   d. Right-click the taskbar to display the Windows NT Task Manager.

Answers a, b, and d are correct because they enable you to move from one window to another. Answer c is incorrect because NT does not have a Task Switcher.

4. What is the best way to navigate among my files and directories?
   a. From the Start menu, choose Programs, Accessories, File Manager.
   b. From the Start menu, choose Run and then type **WINFILE.EXE** to start the File Manager.
   c. From the Start menu, choose Programs, Windows Explorer.
   d. From the Start menu, choose Run and then type **PROGMAN.EXE**.

Answer a is a possibility but not the best way. This method was used in older versions and is listed in Accessories only if you have upgraded. If you have not done so, you must run winfile.exe. Answer b brings up the File Manager, an older method of navigation. **Answer c is correct because it allows for the most convenient navigation of the choices listed.** Answer d is not a valid option.

5. Randy works with a particular budget file almost every day and would like to be able to open it quickly without having to browse through several directories to find it. What is the best solution you can recommend?

  a. Tell Randy that a quick open feature is coming in the next release of Windows NT.

  b. Create a shortcut to the file, and place it on Randy's desktop.

  c. Use the File Manager to browse for the file so that not as many windows are opened.

  d. Use My Computer with the Replace Window option to minimize the number of open windows on the screen.

Answer a does not solve the problem. **Answer b is correct because it erases all time in locating the file.** Neither answer c nor d reduces the time in finding the file.

6. Which of the following objects lets you browse through your files, folders, drives, and shared network resources?

  a. Network Neighborhood

  b. My Computer

  c. Windows NT Explorer

  d. Task Manager

Answer a does not show network resources and is not intended to display them on your system per se. **Answers b and c are correct because they display files, folders, and drives (shared and unshared on all).** Answer d shows processes running, not files and folders.

7. Beth frequently travels for your company. She takes several files with her that she works on while making client calls. When she returns, she docks her laptop and then needs to update the copies she keeps on the network. She thinks there must be a better way to keep the files updated. What can you suggest?

  a. Create shortcuts to the network files on the laptop's desktop. This way, Beth can access the files while she is away and just update them when she gets back.

  b. Copy the files into the briefcase on Beth's laptop. She will have copies of the files that she can work on while away and can synchronize them with her work copies when she returns.

  c. Use Windows Explorer to copy the laptop copies on top of the network copies.

  d. Windows NT automatically updates laptop copies of network files when you dock the laptop. It is called autosynch.

Answer a is incorrect because the shortcuts do not perform the function desired. **Answer b is correct because the files can be synchronized as Beth moves from one platform to another.** Answer c does not keep the files updated. Answer d is incorrect because there is no such thing as autosynch.

CH
4

8. Bill has created an important legal document but cannot remember where he saved it or exactly what he called it. However, he knows he created it yesterday. How can you help him?

   a. Use Windows Explorer to display all files by their date. Then browse each directory until you find the missing file.

   b. From the Start menu, choose Documents. Bill should be able to find his document listed there.

   c. From the Start menu, choose Find Files or Folders. On the Date\Time tab, enter yesterday's date. Bill should be able to find his file in the Find results window.

   d. Suggest Bill re-create the file.

Answer a would take days to complete and frustrate Bill. **Answers b and c are correct because both methods allow Bill to search for his file in an efficient manner.** Answer d does not address the problem.

9. Linda cannot remember how to connect to shared resources on her network. You cannot go to her desk right now because you are currently assisting Bill with his lost file. What quick self-help advice can you give Linda now?

   a. Use the Contents tab of Windows Help to find the topic relating to connecting to network shared resources. Click the task-based Help button to open the appropriate dialog box and connect to the resource following the directions in the Help screen.

   b. Use the Properties screen of Network Neighborhood to connect to the shared resource.

   c. You can help her only while at her desk.

   d. Suggest that Linda only work locally.

Answer a is correct because it brings up the tool to allow Linda to work through the problem herself. Answer b does not offer help that she can refer to, and the properties that appear for Network Neighborhood have to do with configuration, not connections. Answer c is incorrect because help can be offered and used from anywhere. Answer d is incorrect because it does not address the problem.

10. You frequent a particular Help topic. Is there a way to quickly access it when you open Help?

    a. Annotate the topic, and then browse annotations when you start Help.

    b. Annotate the topic, and then use Find to find all help documents with your annotation.

    c. Create a bookmark. When you start Help, access the page by selecting the bookmark.

    d. You cannot mark a page in Help.

Answer a does not allow you to quickly access the topic. The better solution is to create a bookmark and reference it. Answer b is convoluted and involves a number of steps. The better solution is to utilize bookmarks. **Answer c is correct because bookmarks allow you to perform this operation.** Answer d is a fallacy; you can create bookmarks and use them to perform the action.

CHAPTER PREREQUISITE

Before reading this chapter, you
should be familiar with the
Windows NT Workstation 4.0
interface (introduced in Chapter 4,
"An Overview of the Windows NT
4.0 Interface").

Configuration and the Registry

WHILE YOU READ

1. What are the two Registry editors available with Windows NT?

2. The System Policy file for Windows NT Workstation clients should be stored on the domain in _____ .

3. The System Policy file for Windows 95 clients must be named
   _____.

4. The System Policy file for Windows NT Workstation clients must be
   named _____ .

5. True or False: All changes made to the Registry are immediate.

This chapter explores various means of configuring and customizing Windows NT Workstation 4.0. Customization includes tasks as simple as changing the color of the desktop. Configuration includes tasks such as installing new device drivers. The Registry maintains the configuration information for Windows NT and provides Windows NT with the data it needs to boot successfully.

Windows NT provides several utilities for accomplishing these tasks. This chapter introduces you to these utilities and the Registry.

Personalizing Your Desktop Environment

One of the first things most users want to do when they get Windows, Windows 95, or now Windows NT 4.0 is change the desktop. Usually, the first to go is the default color set, or the desktop background becomes a picture of the grandkids. Everyone likes to have control over his or her working space.

Windows NT Workstation 4.0 offers several ways to customize your desktop environment. The first that we discuss here is the Display Properties sheet.

Display Properties

access the Display Properties sheet by right-clicking anywhere on the desktop background and then choosing Properties.

The Display Properties sheet, as shown in Figure 5.1, has five tabs, each corresponding to one of the more popular changes users like to make: Background, Screen Saver, Appearance, Plus!, and Settings. A nice addition to this and many other Properties sheets is the Apply button. Using this button, you can apply a change without closing the dialog box.

Using the Background tab, you can change the desktop wallpaper and pattern. You may have made these same types of changes in Windows when using the Desktop applet in Control Panel. A wallpaper can be any bitmap image and can be stored anywhere on your computer. The Browse button lets you easily find the bitmap you like.

Screen savers, of course, are designed to protect your monitor from "burning in" an image of what's on the screen by displaying a moving image on the screen after a predetermined time period of inactivity on the keyboard or mouse. They can also be fun to look at. Most new monitors today are designed to prevent burn in.

Because Windows NT 4.0 conforms to the OpenGL standard (direct draw to the screen, 3D graphics support, and so on), it supports some pretty cool screen savers. Among the new screen savers included in Windows NT Workstation is the 3D Maze. This one displays a three-dimensional maze (à la Doom) and proceeds to maneuver you through it.

Figure 5.1
In this sample Display Properties sheet, a new wallpaper bitmap has been chosen to replace the default background.

Most of the screen savers have additional customization options that can be accessed through the Settings button on the Screen Saver tab. You can also determine the period of inactivity before it kicks in, preview it in full screen, and password-protect it. Password-protecting is a good idea, especially if you are in the habit of walking away from your workstation with important stuff on your screen. You have to know the password before you can release the screen saver and return to your screen. However, screen savers can use a lot of processor time. If you have an application that requires extensive calculations or other processor-intensive processes, you might want to disable the screen saver while the application performs. If you walk away, and the screen saver engages, it can actually "steal" processor time away from the application.

Through the Appearance tab, you can change your color schemes or set color, size, and sometimes font settings for individual items, including icons.

The Plus! tab gives you the option of using different icons for some of your desktop objects, as well as refining visual settings. For example, a visually impaired person might use large icons. If you have a high-resolution monitor, you can have Windows NT smooth the edges of screen fonts and display icons using the full color range available.

On the Settings tab, you can make changes to the monitor settings. From this tab, you can modify the display type, screen resolution, refresh frequency, color palette, and font size. Before you apply a change, Microsoft suggests that you click the Test button and preview the screen to be sure that it is viewable.

CH

5

Exploring Control Panel

If you have worked with previous versions of Windows, you have spent some time in Control Panel. Control Panel offers a variety of applets that modify your system configuration. Microsoft has reworked most of the Control Panel applets in Windows NT 4.0 to provide you with a much greater degree of granularity when making your selections.

Control Panel, shown in Figure 5.2, can be opened in a variety of ways. You will most commonly open it by choosing the <u>S</u>ettings option from the Start menu. However, you can also access it through My Computer or Windows Explorer; alternatively, you can create a shortcut to it or any of its 25 applets on your desktop.

Figure 5.2
Windows NT Workstation 4.0 Control Panel.

As you add applications or Windows NT services to your computer, additional applets are likely added to Control Panel. For example, when you add Client Services for NetWare, which allows your Windows NT workstation to connect to a NetWare server, an additional Client Services icon is added to Control Panel, from which you can select your preferred NetWare logon server.

Whenever you need to change a system parameter, your first stop should be Control Panel. The following is a list of the applets provided in Control Panel:

- Accessibility Options
- Network
- Add\Remove Programs
- PC Card
- DOS Console
- Ports

- Printers
- Regional Settings
- Date\Time
- SCSI Adapters
- Devices
- Server

- Display
- Services
- Fonts
- Sounds
- Internet
- System

- Keyboard
- Tape Devices
- Modems
- Telephony
- Mouse
- UPS
- Multimedia

Let's briefly review what functions each applet provides.

Accessibility Options

The Accessibility Options applet is new to Windows NT 4.0. It is designed for individuals with visual, hearing, or movement challenges. It offers several modifications, including making the keyboard easier to use, visualizing computer sounds, and using the keyboard to control the mouse.

In this applet, you change settings to control whether keys need to be held down, to ignore some repeated keystrokes, or even if you want to be notified with a sound when toggle keys such as Caps Lock are pressed. You can also choose to have Windows show you each time a sound is made or allow you to use the keyboard as if it were a mouse.

Add/Remove Programs

The Add/Remove Programs applet lets you install and remove Windows NT components, such as games and accessories. It also provides a built-in procedure for automatically installing or uninstalling applications from disk or CD-ROM. If the application that is being installed is set up using either a Setup.exe or Install.exe file, Add/Remove Programs records the setup process, displays the application in its list of installed applications, and lets you remove the application using its Uninstall Wizard.

MS-DOS Console

The MS-DOS Console applet is often confused with the MS-DOS Prompt accessed through the Start menu. MS-DOS Console provides a means of modifying the way a DOS window appears on the desktop. You can alter screen colors, window size, font style and size, cursor size, and command history buffer.

Date/Time

The Date/Time applet, of course, modifies the computer's internal date and time values. Nothing is really remarkable here except that the screens are far more graphic and easy to use than ever before. This applet even shows you what part of the world your time zone is in.

Devices

The Devices applet shows you all the device drivers detected and installed by Windows NT and which devices are currently running. It enables you to start, stop, and configure startup types for device drivers.

CH
5

Display

The Display applet produces exactly the same Display Properties sheet described earlier. This applet is just another place to access it.

Fonts

The Fonts applet lets you view fonts installed on your system, add new fonts, and remove fonts that are no longer needed. You can also find the option to display only TrueType fonts in applications.

Internet

The Internet applet is installed in Control Panel if you have installed Internet Explorer. It lets you set the proxy server on your network through which you access the Internet. The proxy server is usually the firewall filtering which users from your network can access the Internet and which users from the Internet can access your network.

Keyboard

The Keyboard applet allows adjustment of the delay and repeat rates of your keyboard and lets you change the keyboard type. It also lets you specify alternative language keyboards to include foreign language symbol sets.

Modems

The Modems applet displays the properties of any modems installed on your computer. From here, you can add and remove modems and modify modem settings. Choosing Add starts the Install Modem Wizard. This wizard walks you through detecting, selecting, and setting up your system's modem.

Mouse

The Mouse applet lets you customize many characteristics of your mouse device. You can switch button usage for left-handed persons, modify the double-click speed (test it on the jack-in-the-box), and change the pointer speed. It also has a tab for changing the various mouse pointers. In this applet, you'll find more interesting visual representations for the select, wait, working, and other pointers (see Figure 5.3). Clicking Browse displays all the pointer files that Windows NT supplies, including the infamous animated cursors. Look for the files with an .ANI extension. You can preview them before applying.

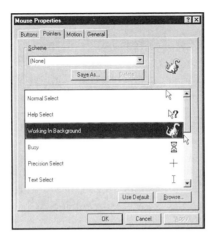

Figure 5.3
The Browse button displays a list of mouse pointer files that can be used to customize
the pointers. You can change the mouse pointer for Working in Background from the
default hourglass with arrow to a dinosaur.

Multimedia

The Multimedia applet provides configuration options for audio, video, MIDI, CD
music, and any other multimedia-related devices.

Network

The Network applet identifies the computer, its relationship to the rest of the network,
and all service, protocol, adapter, and bindings settings. By selecting the properties for
Network Neighborhood, you can also access this applet. The majority of your network
configuration takes place here.

PC Card (PCMCIA)

The PC Card (PCMCIA) applet displays whether you have PC Card support on your
computer, which cards are currently in use, and which resources they are using.

Ports

Using the Ports applet, you can add, modify, or delete parameters for your computer's
COM ports. For example, if you add a new COM port adapter card to your computer or
connect a serial printer to an existing port, you might want to configure it for a certain
speed and parity.

Printers

The Printers applet replaces Print Manager and displays icons related to each printer installed on your computer or connected through the network. From these icons, you can manage the printing devices and print jobs. An Add Printer Wizard walks you through the process of installing, configuring, and sharing your printing device. You can also access this applet from the taskbar by choosing Start, Settings, Printers.

Regional Settings

The Regional Settings applet displays current settings for number symbols, currency format, date and time values, and input locales based on world regions. This applet, which used to be called International, has been greatly enhanced.

SCSI Adapters

The SCSI Adapters applet displays SCSI adapters and drivers that have been installed on your computer and their resource settings (I/O, interrupt, and so on).

Server

The Server applet opens a dialog box that offers statistics relating to the server-based activities of your computer. It shows which network users are currently connected to your Windows NT workstation, which shared resources are being used and by whom, and any replication settings that may have been configured. It also lets you set administrative alerts, delivering system message pop-ups to a specified user or computer.

Services

The Services applet displays a list of all services that have been installed on your computer and their current running status. Windows NT services are functions or applications that are loaded as part of the Windows NT Executive. Thus, they run as part of the operating system rather than as a background or resident program (TSR).

As you can see in Figure 5.4, this applet also enables you to start and stop services and to modify their startup configuration.

You can also set services based on hardware profiles so that only certain services run given a specific hardware installation. For example, a laptop that is not connected remotely to a network while the user is on the road may have certain network-related services turned off. Turning off services makes additional resources available to other applications. When the laptop is docked at the user's desk at a station that is wired to the network, those network services would be turned back on.

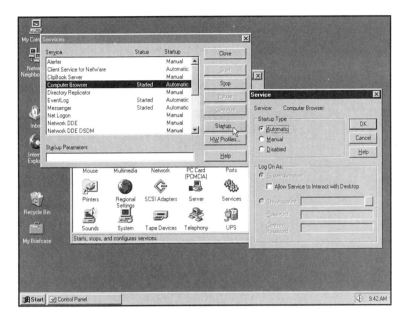

Figure 5.4
This Services dialog box shows the status of several Windows NT services running on
this computer. The startup options box for one of the services is displayed by selecting
Startup.

Sounds

The Sounds applet lets you assign different types of sounds to system and application
events, such as opening a program, doing what you shouldn't, and so on.

System

The System applet displays the System Properties sheet through which you can define the
default operating system at boot time, set recovery options for Stop errors, determine
which hardware profiles to use during startup, view and delete user profiles stored on
your computer, view and define environment variables, modify application performance,
and configure and customize pagefile parameters.

Tape Devices

The Tape Devices applet displays a dialog box in which you can view, add, or delete tape
devices and their driver settings that are installed on your computer.

CH
5

Telephony

The Telephony applet opens the Dialing Properties dialog box; in this dialog, you can view, add, or remove telephony drivers and modify dialing parameters such as pressing 9 to get an outside line or disabling call waiting. You can create a different set of dialing parameters for different situations or locations. For example, dialing out through your modem at work may require no additional settings, whereas dialing out from a hotel room may require dialing one or more numbers in sequence to access a local or long-distance line.

UPS

Using the UPS applet, you can set configuration parameters for your uninterruptible power supply connected to the computer. Parameters include setting interface voltages for power failure and low battery signals, specifying a command file to be executed when the UPS is activated, and setting other UPS-specific characteristics, such as expected battery life.

Exploring the Administrative Tools

The Administrative Tools group contains utilities that are specific to your installation of either Windows NT Workstation 4.0 or Windows NT Server 4.0.

Seven tools are installed on Windows NT Workstation 4.0, as shown in Figure 5.5: Backup, Disk Administrator, Event Viewer, Performance Monitor, Remote Access Administrator, User Manager, and Windows NT Diagnostics. These tools are described in more detail in later chapters.

Backup

The Backup utility gives you considerable control over what data you want to back up and where you are backing it up to. It also controls the restore process. You can back up entire disks or directories or specific files, including the Registry. This utility keeps summary logs indicating what was backed up or restored and when, as well as any files that it determined were corrupted.

Disk Administrator

The Disk Administrator can best be described as a much improved and GUI FDISK utility. From here, you can easily create and format disk partitions, create volume sets and extended volumes, and create stripe sets. On the Server version, you can also enable software fault tolerance (also known as RAID, or Redundant Array of Inexpensive Disks) such as striping with parity and mirrored disk partitions.

Event Viewer

The Event Viewer is a great troubleshooting utility. It records system events such as services that failed to start or devices that could not be initialized. When various audit functions are enabled in Windows NT, Event Viewer provides logs that record the audit information and display it for your review.

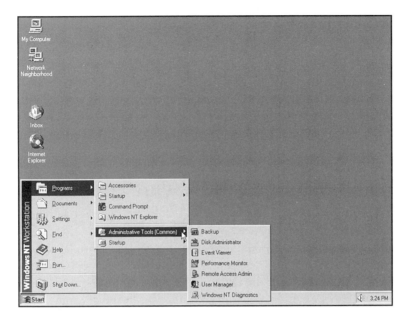

Figure 5.5
You can find the Administrative Tools by selecting Programs from the Start menu.

Performance Monitor

Performance Monitor is still receiving rave reviews from Windows NT administrators for the sheer amount of system performance data that can be charted, saved, and reviewed. This utility is used to help determine performance bottlenecks on your system, processor utilization, server access, and so on. It is covered in more detail, along with Event Viewer, in Chapter 12, "Tuning, Optimizing, and Other Troubleshooting Tips."

CH
5

Remote Access Service

After Remote Access Service (RAS) has been installed and configured on your computer, the Remote Access Administrator utility offers you management functions for your RAS client, such as defining which network users can access your computer through a dial-in connection, who is currently connected, which ports are in use, and whether the service is running. This utility is reviewed again in Chapter 11, "Network Connectivity and Remote Support."

User Manager

You can create and manage user and group accounts through User Manager. Password policy information, location of user profiles and login scripts, users' functional rights, and user access auditing are all configured through User Manager. This utility is examined thoroughly in the next chapter, "Managing Users and Accounts."

Windows NT Diagnostics

Windows NT Diagnostics is an enhanced and GUI version of Microsoft's MS-DOS–based MSD (Microsoft Diagnostics). This cool utility gives detailed information culled directly from the Windows NT Registry relating to the system, display, disk drives, memory and pagefile usage, network statistics, environment variable values, resources in use and their settings, and services installed and their state. This version actually provides a far greater level of detail than previous Windows NT versions. You can even print the information screens.

Creating and Managing Hardware Profiles

Hardware profiles offer a way for you to create and maintain different hardware configurations—including which services and devices are initialized—for different computing scenarios. The most common use for hardware profiles is with laptop computers that are sometimes placed in a docking station. While elsewhere, the user can use the laptop's modem to dial in to the company network. When the laptop is docked, that user can access the network through the network card installed in the docking station.

These two different methods of connecting to the network are used in two different scenarios and require different hardware. You can certainly maintain the same profile for both scenarios. However, when your computer is portable, you are likely to receive event or system messages relating to the "missing" network card. Likewise, if the docking station disables the laptop's modem, you can receive similar messages when the computer is docked. If you maintain two hardware profiles, you can customize which device is activated during which scenario.

Creating a Hardware Profile

To create a hardware profile, you must first access the System Properties dialog box, as shown in Figure 5.6. You can open the System Properties dialog box in one of two ways:

- Right-click My Computer on the desktop, and then choose Properties.
- Open Control Panel, and start the System applet.

After the System Properties dialog box is displayed, follow these steps to create a new hardware profile:

1. Select the Hardware Profiles tab.
2. Choose an existing or original profile from the Available Hardware Profiles list box, and choose Copy.
3. Enter the name of the new profile, and click OK.

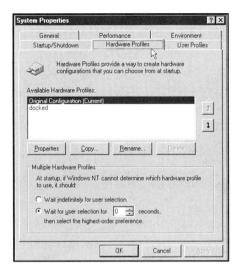

Figure 5.6
The System Properties dialog box with the Hardware Profiles tab selected.

4. Use the arrow buttons to the right of the profile list to determine the order preference of the profiles. This order determines which order Windows NT uses to load
the profiles during system startup.

5. Use the Properties button to open the Properties sheet, where you can indicate
whether the computer is a portable and indicate its docking state, and also indicate
whether this profile should disable all network functions (see Figure 5.7).

CH

5

Figure 5.7
This hardware profile has been designated as a portable computer that is undocked.

6. Specify what Windows NT should do during startup. If you want Windows NT to display a list of profiles at startup, choose Wait Indefinitely for Use Selection. Windows NT does not continue with the startup operation until a profile selection is made. Profiles are displayed after you are prompted to press the spacebar for the Last Known Good Configuration.

If you want to set a timeout value for selecting a profile before Windows NT selects the first profile in the list, choose Wait for User Selection for xx Seconds, Then Select the Highest-Order Preference. If you set the timeout value to 0, Windows NT simply boots with the highest order profile on startup. Pressing the spacebar when you're prompted for the Last Known Good Configuration redisplays the profile list.

Now that you've created the hardware profile, you need to identify which services and devices to enable and disable for each profile. You do so through the Services and Devices applets, respectively, in Control Panel.

To define a specific service or device to the hardware profile, follow these steps:

1. Select the service or device from the list.

2. Click the HW Profiles button. A new dialog box appears, as shown in Figure 5.8.

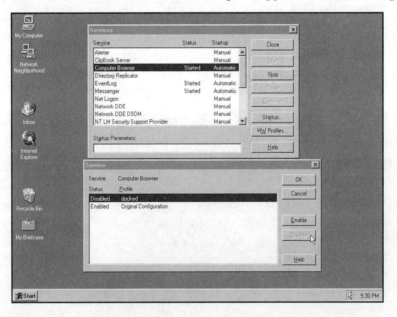

Figure 5.8
The Computer Browser service, while enabled normally, has been set to disabled for the profile called docked.

3. Select the profile that you are modifying from the list.

4. Choose <u>E</u>nable or <u>D</u>isable to turn the service or device on or off, respectively, for that profile.

5. Click OK, and close the Services or Devices applet.

When you start Windows NT and choose your hardware profile, the services and devices start as you configured them.

Examining the Windows NT Workstation 4.0 Registry

The Windows NT 4.0 Registry is perhaps the single most important element of the Windows NT operating system architecture. The Registry is an encrypted database of configuration and environment information relating to the successful booting of Windows NT 4.0. Think of this file as being the DOS AUTOEXEC.BAT and CONFIG.SYS files rolled into one—and then some.

The Registry is central to the operation of Windows NT 4.0. User environment settings are stored here. Driver information, services, hardware profile information, security objects and their permissions, and account information are all stored in the Registry. Microsoft considers the Registry so integral a part of Windows NT that it strongly discourages you from making changes to the Registry.

In fact, the Control Panel, Administrative Tools group, and various Properties sheets give you all the utilities you need to modify and customize your installation of Windows NT 4.0 for normal maintenance. All these utilities modify one or more Registry entries. Therefore, there are only limited and specific reasons for you to make changes to the Registry directly.

Key Concept

A good rule of thumb for modifying the Registry: If a utility can do the modification, use the utility! If you make substantial changes to the Registry that result in problems during bootup or execution, Microsoft disallows your support call.

That said, in specific instances, you have to modify the Registry directly. They usually have to do with the absence of a utility to make a necessary change or troubleshooting purposes. Some of the more common are described later in this chapter in the section "Using the Registry to Configure Windows NT Workstation 4.0."

CH

5

Navigating with the Registry Editor

You can access the Registry by starting the Registry Editor utility, and you can access this utility in several ways. Here are two:

- Open the Windows Explorer, and select the SYSTEM32 folder under the Windows NT system folder (usually called WINNT or WINNT40). Double-click the file REGEDT32.EXE.

- Choose Run from the Start menu, and type **REGEDT32.EXE**. Then click OK.

If you access the Registry often, you can also create a shortcut to REGEDT32.EXE on your desktop.

Throughout the remainder of this book, we'll refer to the Windows NT system directory as WINNT40.

 ### Key Concept

Windows NT Workstation 4.0 includes two Registry editors: REGEDT32.EXE and REGEDIT.EXE. The former is the original editor that has been with Windows NT since version 3.1. The latter is a Windows 95 tool new to NT with version 4.0. REGEDT32 can show all five value types (REGEDIT shows only three) and includes features for security, auditing, and so on (none of which are available with REGEDIT). Due to these differences and the great quantity of additional features available with REGEDT32, that editor is used throughout this chapter. For the exam, you should know that both exist and are included with the product.

The Registry Editor displays the five main windows, called subtrees, of the Windows NT 4.0 Registry for the local computer, as shown in Figure 5.9.

The subtrees are as follows:

- HKEY_LOCAL_MACHINE
- HKEY_CURRENT_CONFIG
- HKEY_USERS
- HKEY_CURRENT_USER
- HKEY_CLASSES_ROOT

By default, only users with Administrator access can make modifications to the Registry. Other users can only view the information contained there.

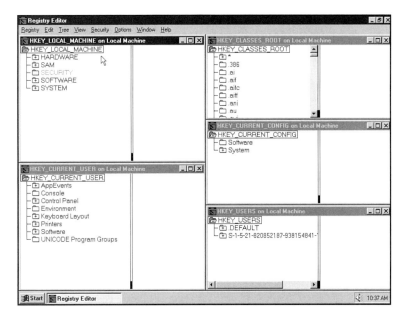

Figure 5.9
This screen shows the five subtrees of the Windows NT Registry, tiled for better viewing.

It is highly recommended that you set the View option to Read Only to guard against any accidental modifications that can lead to serious boot and operation problems. You enable it by selecting Read Only Mode from the Options menu in Registry Editor.

From Options, choose Font to change the font style and size to facilitate viewing, and choose Confirm on Delete to guard against accidental deletions.

At first glance, these windows look a lot like File Manager or Windows Explorer, and in fact, you can navigate them in much the same way. The left pane of each subtree window displays the keys pertinent to that subtree. As each key is selected, the parameters and values assigned to that key are displayed in the right pane. You can think of a key as being a more sophisticated .INI file.

You may recall that an .INI file consists of section headings, each section containing one or more parameters unique to that section, and each parameter having an appropriate value or values assigned to it. The values can be text strings, filenames, or simple yes or no or 1 or 0 values.

A Registry key is quite similar. Think of it as a "nested" .INI file (see Figure 5.10). A key can consist of parameters with assigned values, or it can consist of one or more subkeys, each with its own parameters.

CH
5

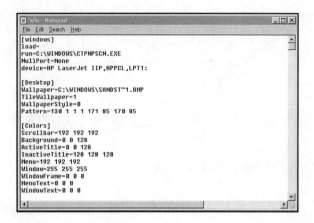

```
Win - Notepad                                          _ □ ×
File  Edit  Search  Help
[windows]
load=
run=C:\WINDOWS\CTPNPSCN.EXE
NullPort=None
device=HP LaserJet IIP,HPPCL,LPT1:

[Desktop]
Wallpaper=C:\WINDOWS\SANDST~1.BMP
TileWallpaper=1
WallpaperStyle=0
Pattern=130 1 1 1 171 85 170 85

[Colors]
Scrollbar=192 192 192
Background=0 0 128
ActiveTitle=0 0 128
InactiveTitle=128 128 128
Menu=192 192 192
Window=255 255 255
WindowFrame=0 0 0
MenuText=0 0 0
WindowText=0 0 0
```

Figure 5.10
In this Windows .INI file, notice the section headings in square brackets. Each section has at least one parameter. The values assigned to each parameter represent what the parameter "expects."

HKEY_LOCAL_MACHINE contains all the system configuration data needed to boot and run the operating system successfully. This information includes services that need to be run, device drivers, hardware profiles (including what is currently loaded), login parameters, and so on. This Registry key is composed of five primary keys called hives, each of which can contain subtrees several folders deep (see Figure 5.11). Each of the hives relates to a corresponding Registry file saved in the WINNT40\SYSTEM32\CONFIG directory, except for the HARDWARE hive, which is built when the computer is booted.

The five hives are as follows:

- HARDWARE (properly called a "key")
- SOFTWARE
- SYSTEM
- SAM
- SECURITY

The HARDWARE hive, or key, contains data related to detected hardware devices installed on your computer.

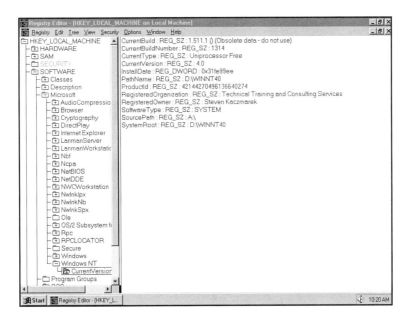

Figure 5.11
A Windows NT Registry key can go several levels deep before finally displaying parameter values.

Key Concept

The HARDWARE key is built during the startup process. This information is not written down anywhere or stored permanently on the system. Instead, Windows NT "detects" this information each time it boots. Thus, it is referred to as a "volatile" hive or key because it is created during the boot process, can change as hardware changes, and is not written to disk.

It includes information such as processor type and power, keyboard class, port information, SCSI adapter information, drive data, video, and memory. This information is primarily stored as binary data and, because it is built during startup, is useless to modify. The Windows NT Diagnostics utility is the best tool to use to view this data.

SAM SECURITY The SAM and SECURITY hives contain security-related information. SAM stands for Security Account Manager and, as you may suspect, contains user and group account information as well as workgroup or domain membership information. The SECURITY hive contains Local Security Account (LSA) policy information, such as specific user rights assigned to user and group accounts.

Neither of these hives nor their subtrees are viewable. It is part of Microsoft's security policy to hide this information even from the system administrator. Even if you could look at it, it probably would not make a lot of sense or give you any insight into violating account information.

Unlike the HARDWARE key, SAM and SECURITY are written to files on the hard disk. Each has a Registry and log file associated with it—SAM and SAM.LOG, and SECURITY and SECURITY.LOG, respectively. You can find them in the WINNT40\SYSTEM32\ CONFIG subdirectory on the Windows NT system partition.

The SOFTWARE hive consists of computer-specific software installed on your computer, as opposed to user-specific settings. It includes manufacturer and version; installed driver files; descriptive and default information for Windows NT-specific services and functions such as the Browser, NetDDE, and Windows NT version information; and the WINLOGON service. This hive also has two files associated with it: SOFTWARE and SOFTWARE.LOG. They can be found in the WINNT40\SYSTEM32\CONFIG subdirectory.

Although the SOFTWARE hive contains more descriptive information regarding the installation of applications, drivers, and so forth on your computer, the SYSTEM hive provides configuration and parameter settings necessary for Windows NT to boot successfully and correctly maintain your computer's configuration. A quick look at the subtrees below SYSTEM shows at least three control set entries, as shown in Figure 5.12.

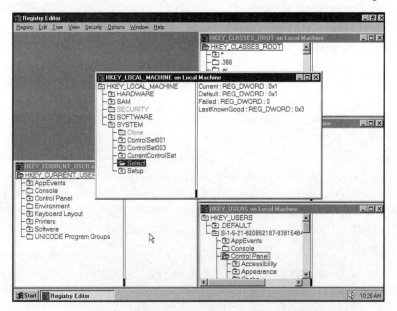

Figure 5.12
HKEY_LOCAL_MACHINE with the SYSTEM hive expanded to show the boot control sets.

These control set entries are used to control the startup process, indicating which services should load, which drivers to load and initialize, and so on. Any changes you make to existing driver settings or any new drivers you install and configure are added to a control set in the SYSTEM hive. Its corresponding files in the WINNT40\SYSTEM32\ CONFIG subdirectory are SYSTEM and SYSTEM.ALT.

HKEY_CURRENT_CONFIG is a new subtree added to Windows NT 4.0. It is a subset of HKEY_LOCAL_MACHINE and reflects only the current software and system modifications made during the current session, as well as the current startup settings. This information is useful for isolating data specific to a hardware profile from other data stored in the Registry.

HKEY_CLASSES_ROOT will look familiar to administrators of previous versions of Windows. It represents OLE and file association data specific to file extensions. This information was stored in the Windows REG.DAT file. This subtree is also a subset of HKEY_LOCAL_MACHINE and can be found there under the SOFTWARE hive.

HKEY_USERS consists of two subkeys relating to user settings. DEFAULT contains system default settings used when the LOGON screen is first displayed. The second entry represents the user who is currently logged on to the system. The long alphanumeric value you see is the user's Security Identifier, hereafter called the SID of the user.

Key Concept

All the entries you see under the SID subkey represent changes that can be made to the user's environment, primarily through Control Panel. If the user changes his or her color scheme, cursor pointers, wallpaper, and so on, the values can be found in the respective keys here. If you need to modify a user's entries, perhaps remotely, you can do so here as well. The values stored here correspond to an actual file like the HKEY_LOCAL_MACHINE hives do. Windows NT creates a subfolder in WINNT40/Profile for each user who logs on and changes his or her profile. This subfolder contains two files that correspond to the Registry entries for that user's profile: NTUSER.DAT.LOG and NTUSER.DAT.

Key Concept

Windows 95 and Windows 98 operating systems employ user profiles as well. They serve the same purpose and function as NTUSER.DAT but are saved as USER.DAT on those operating systems.

HKEY_CURRENT_USER represents a subset of HKEY_USERS and points back to the settings of the current user (the SID entry in HKEY_USERS).

Using the Registry to Configure Windows NT Workstation 4.0

This section is designed with two purposes in mind. The first is to introduce you to the method for looking up keys and making changes to them. The second is to point out some specific modifications that you can accomplish only by changing the Registry.

Let's begin by examining the not-so-obvious. As you navigate through the Registry and select various keys, you may or may not see parameter values displayed in the windows. That does not necessarily mean that no values are present. It may simply mean that Windows NT is using the default values for that entry.

For example, if you select the HKEY_CURRENT_USER\CONTROL PANEL\ CURSORS subkey, and you have made no changes to your mouse pointers, you see no entries here. However, it is obvious that you do, in fact, have default mouse pointers displayed on your screen. In this case, Windows NT does use parameter values—the default values.

Key Concept

Rule of thumb: If the Registry does not display parameter values when you select a subkey, you can assume that Windows NT is using the defaults for that subkey, realizing that a default can be to have no values loaded at all.

Let's use the example of changing the cursor pointer. A user has selected the peeling banana to replace the hourglass "wait" cursor and wants to change it to the running horse. Also, this user wants to change the application starting cursor (the hourglass with an arrow) to the lumbering dinosaur. You can simply and easily do so through the Mouse applet in Control Panel, but you feel particularly bold today.

You need to know basically three pieces of information before modifying this particular entry and in general for changing any Registry entry. These three pieces of information are as follows:

- Know which Registry entry you are going to change, what subkey or subkeys are involved (yes, more than one might be involved), and where they are located.
- Know which parameter needs to be added, modified, or deleted to bring about your change.
- Know what value needs to be assigned to the parameter and its type.

Now let's look at this process step-by-step.

First, it is not always easy to determine what the subkey is and where it is. If the change you are making modifies the way the system operates (using a new device driver, changing the video display, adding a new hardware profile), those subkeys are most likely found under HKEY_LOCAL_MACHINE in the SYSTEM hive under one of the control set entries. If the change you are making affects the working environment of a particular user (desktop wallpaper, cursors, colors, window properties), those subkeys are most likely found under HKEY_USERS in the current user's subkey identified by the user's SID.

Also, sometimes the subkeys that need to be modified are easy to identify, like "cursors." Sometimes they are not. Who knew that the HKEY_LOCAL_MACHINE\SYSTEM\ CURRENTCONTROLSET\SERVICES\CE2NDIS31 entry refers to the driver settings for the Credit Card Ethernet Adapter installed in a laptop? So how do you find out? Sometimes your documentation tells you. Most times, you find the subkeys by exploration, trial, and error. But remember, Microsoft recommends that you not make configuration changes through the Registry directly, especially when a utility can do the job for you. In the case of that network adapter, we don't really need to know where its configuration values are stored in the Registry because we can configure it through the Network applet in Control Panel or through the Properties sheet of the Network Neighborhood.

Finding Subkey Names in the Registry

If you are not sure of the subkey name you are looking for but know what it might be called or a category that it might fall into, you can use the Registry's FIND KEY function to look it up. Follow these steps:

1. Place your cursor at the top (root) of the directory structure in the subtree where you think the key is located.
2. Choose View, Find Key.
3. Type in the key name you are looking for.
4. Choose Match Whole Word Only or Match Case if you are relatively sure of the key entry; otherwise, deselect these options.
5. Choose Find Next.

FIND KEY places a box around the first subkey entry that matches the text string you entered. You can move the Find window out of the way if it blocks your view. Choose FIND NEXT again until you locate the appropriate subkey.

FIND KEY works only with key entries. It does not work on parameter entries.

Getting back to the example, because you want to make a user environment change, you know you can find the subkey in the HKEY_USERS subtree, under the user's SID entry.

You can also select the HKEY_CURRENT_USER subtree because it points to the same location in the Registry.

From there, because you are modifying cursors, you can look for a subkey called Cursors. Because you modify cursors through Control Panel, it is a pretty safe bet that you will find a Cursors subkey under the Control Panel subkey. You now know the location and the subkey to modify: HKEY_CURRENT_USER\CONTROL PANEL\CURSORS.

The second thing you should know is which parameter needs to be added, modified, or deleted to bring about your change.

Once again, finding out which parameter value is difficult unless someone gives you the parameter and value to enter. In this example, the parameter corresponding to the working hourglass is called WAIT, and the parameter corresponding to the application start hourglass with the arrow is called APPSTARTING.

Finally, you need to know what value needs to be assigned to the parameter and its type.

By now, you get the idea. Again, in this example, the filenames that correspond to the various cursors either have a .CUR or .ANI extension. You can find them listed in the WINNT40\SYSTEM32 subdirectory. Recall that the WAIT cursor needs to change from the banana (BANANA.ANI) to the running horse (HORSE.ANI), and that the APPSTARTING cursor needs to be the lumbering dinosaur (DINOSAUR.ANI).

Five data types can be applied to a parameter value. Again, you usually know which one to use, either because it is obvious or because someone has told you. Table 5.1 lists the value types and a brief description of each.

Table 5.1   Parameter Value Data Types

Data Type	Description
REG_SZ	Expects one text string data value
REG_DWORD	Expects one hexadecimal string of one to eight digits
REG_BINARY	Expects one string of hexadecimal digits, each pair of which is considered a byte value
REG_EXPAND_SZ	Expects one text string value that contains a replaceable parameter such as %USERNAME% or %SYSTEMROOT%
REG_MULTI_SZ	Expects multiple string values separated by a NULL character

In the example, cursors can be associated with only one filename (a text string). Therefore, the parameter value will have a data type of REG_SZ, and its value will be the filename. Now you can modify the Registry. Just follow these steps:

1. Open the Registry Editor. From <u>O</u>ptions, deselect <u>R</u>ead Only Mode if it is selected.

2. Maximize the HKEY_CURRENT_USER subtree window to make it easier to work with.

3. Expand the Control Panel key.

4. Highlight the Cursors key. In the right pane, because the WAIT cursor has already been modified once, you'll see an entry called WAIT, of data type REG_SZ and value BANANA.ANI.

5. Double-click the parameter entry (WAIT) to display the String Editor (see Figure 5.13).

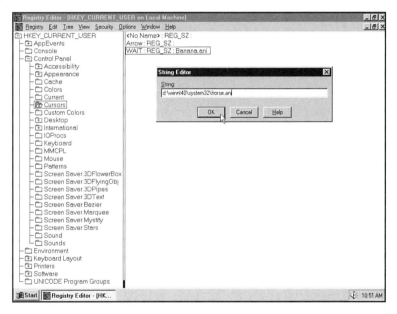

Figure 5.13
The WAIT cursor currently has the value BANANA.ANI. Double-click it to display the String Editor and change the value to HORSE.ANI.

6. Enter the new parameter value; in this case, enter **D:\WINNT40\SYSTEM32\HORSE.ANI**.

7. To add a new parameter and value, choose <u>E</u>dit from the Registry Editor menu bar, and then choose Add <u>V</u>alue.

8. In the Add Value dialog box, enter the Value Name (in this case, enter **APPSTARTING**), and choose the appropriate Data Type (REG_SZ), as shown in Figure 5.14. Then click OK.

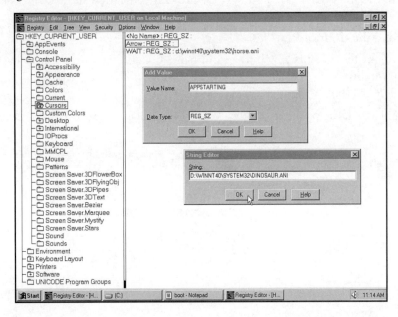

Figure 5.14
Choose Edit, Add Value to add the new cursor parameter APPSTARTING with a data type of REG_SZ, and click OK. In the String Editor, type **DINOSAUR.ANI**.

9. In the String Editor dialog box, enter the appropriate parameter value (for this example, enter **D:\WINNT40\SYSTEM32\DINOSAUR.ANI**), and click OK.

10. Select Read Only Mode from the Options menu again; then close the Registry Editor.

The change does not take effect immediately.

Key Concept

Rule of thumb: If you're making a user environment change, the user has to log off and log back on before the change takes effect. If you're making a system change, you have to shut down and restart the computer before the change takes effect.

Key Concept

Parameter names are not case sensitive. However, because they can be quite lengthy, Microsoft uses proper case when displaying these values to make them easier to read.

If you misspell a parameter name, the result may simply be that Windows NT ignores it, or a service may stop altogether. This case is also true with parameter values. If you're in doubt, look it up in the Windows NT Resource Kit, or test it first. Before testing, back up your original Registry or, at the least, save the original subkey.

The following sections describe some other modifications that you can make to the Registry for which a utility does not exist.

Legal Notices

Legal notices are dialog boxes that pop up before a user can log on; they usually indicate who is authorized to access that computer. You generally see these notices while logging in to enterprise networks. You can change them in the Registry by modifying the following subkey and parameter values:

```
HKEY_LOCAL_MACHINE\SOFTWARE\MICROSOFT\WINDOWS NT\CURRENTVERSION\WINLOGON\
LegalNoticeCaption and LegalNoticeText
```

LegalNoticeCaption modifies the title bar of the dialog box that appears during logon, and LegalNoticeText is the text that is displayed in the dialog box.

For example, you can modify LegalNoticeCaption to display Legal Notice for Computer SDK. Or you can modify LegalNoticeText to display Unauthorized users will be shot on sight!

To see this change, log off and log back on.

Shutdown Options

You may notice that the logon dialog box displays an option button to shut down the computer. On Windows NT Workstation 4.0, you are allowed, by default, to shut down the computer without logging on to the system. This capability is a convenience for the user so that he or she does not have to wait for Windows NT to load (two or more minutes on lower performance computers) before he or she can effect a shutdown. You want to avoid having users just power off at all costs. So this capability is a good thing.

It is interesting to note, however, that for installations of Windows NT Server 4.0, the Shutdown button does not appear in the logon dialog box. Therefore, a user, preferably an administrator, must log on to the server computer before effecting a shutdown. Again,

CH

5

because you don't necessarily want just anybody to be able to walk up to a server and shut it down, this restriction is also a good thing.

The display or hiding of the Shutdown button is controlled through a Registry entry. If you want to modify this value to hide the Shutdown button on your workstation (or display it on a server), you can modify the following entry:

```
HKEY_LOCAL_MACHINE\SOFTWARE\MICROSOFT\WINDOWS NT\CURRENTVERSION\WINLOGON\
ShutdownWithoutLogon
```

A "1" for the value means "Yes, display the Shutdown button," whereas a "0" means "No, do not display the Shutdown button."

If your computer's BIOS supports a powering off of the computer when the operating system shuts down, you can modify the following entry from "0" (not supported) to "1" (supported):

```
HKEY_LOCAL_MACHINE\SOFTWARE\MICROSOFT\WINDOWS NT\CURRENT VERSION\WINLOGON\
PowerdownAfterShutdown
```

Logon Usernames

By default, Windows NT remembers the last user who logged on to a system and records this information (along with the workgroup or domain that the user logged in to) in the Registry. You can view this information in the following entries:

```
HKEY_LOCAL_MACHINE\SOFTWARE\MICROSOFT\WINDOWS NT\CURRENT VERSION\WINLOGON\
DefaultUserName and DefaultDomainName
```

For added security, you can hide the display of the last user who logged on so that no one can try guessing the password to get on to the system. As we all know, users tend to use passwords that are easily guessed. If a potential hacker must also guess at the username, that makes the computer less desirable to hack (kind of like putting an anti-theft device on your car's steering wheel). If you would rather not display the name of the last user who logged on to a computer, you need to add the following parameter name and value:

```
HKEY_LOCAL_MACHINE\SOFTWARE\MICROSOFT\WINDOWS NT\CURRENT VERSION\WINLOGON\
DontDisplayLastUserName
```

DontDisplayLastUserName expects a data type of REG_SZ and a value of either "1" (Yes, don't display the last username) or "0" (No, do display the last username). This sample parameter does not appear in the right pane, but its default value is loaded by the Registry.

The System Policy Editor

Windows NT Server 4.0 includes a configuration management utility called the System Policy Editor. This utility is not included with the Workstation version. It is intended for managing server-based workstation and user policies—that is, configuration information that is stored on a login server (domain controller) and downloaded to the user's workstation when the user logs on to the network. Most of the Registry changes that have been described in this chapter so far can be made more safely through the System Policy Editor. Also, the configuration is assured to "follow" the user and, thus, be consistent and standard.

In Figure 5.15, for example, a system policy has been created for user SDKACZ. Note that simply by pointing and clicking through a variety of intuitive screens, you can fix the user's access and environment. In this example, the user's ability to modify the screen is reduced, a wallpaper has been selected, and the RUN and Settings Folders have been removed. This policy affects the user wherever SDKACZ logs on.

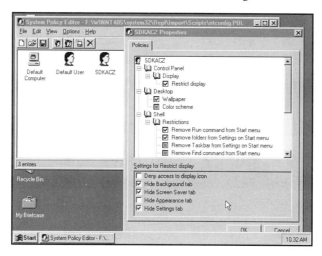

Figure 5.15
Sample System Policy Editor screen from Windows NT Server 4.0.

Similarly, a system policy can be established by workstation name, thus regulating a user's environment and access by workstation. For example, you could disable the last username from being displayed, or you could modify the legal notice dialog box again by simply pointing and clicking the appropriate check box. These settings then would affect every user who logged on to this specific workstation.

The workstation and user policies are saved in a file called NTCONFIG.POL and stored in the WINNT40\SYSTEM32\REPL\IMPORT\SCRIPTS subdirectory of each domain controller. This directory is also known by the share name NETLOGON.

CH
5

Key Concept

Windows 95 and Windows 98 operating systems employ system policies as well. They serve the same purpose and function as NTCONFIG.POL but must be named CONFIG.POL for those operating systems.

Changing the Default Startup Screen

The default startup screen is the Ctrl+Alt+Del screen that is displayed when you log off or boot Windows NT. You can modify how this screen looks by modifying entries in the DEFAULT subkey of HKEY_USERS. For example, if you have created a company logo called XYZ.BMP that you want all your computers to display during startup, you need to modify the default desktop wallpaper. Access the following Registry entry:

```
HKEY_USERS\DEFAULT\DESKTOP\Wallpaper
```

Change the Wallpaper entry from (DEFAULT) to XYZ.BMP. The change takes effect when you log off, and the logo appears centered on the desktop.

If you want your bitmap to be tiled, change the TileWallpaper value in the same subkey from "0" to "1."

Through a little experimentation, you will find other changes you can make here. For example, try changing the cursor pointers!

Accessing the Registry Remotely

A computer's Registry might be modified either through a utility or directly so that the computer is not quite functioning as it should. The Registry Editor provides a facility for accessing the computer's Registry remotely. If you have an Administrator account on your computer that matches one on the other machine (including the password), you can access the other computer's Registry. Just follow these steps:

1. Open your Registry Editor.
2. From the menu, choose Select Computer.
3. In the Select Computer dialog box, enter the name of the computer or select it from the browse list, and then click OK. The Registry Editor then displays the HKEY_LOCAL_MACHINE and HKEY_USERS subtrees from that computer. The title bar of each window displays the remote computer's name.
4. After you have finished working with the remote Registry, choose Close from the Registry menu, being sure that the remote Registry window is highlighted.

If you do not close the remote Registry windows, they reappear the next time you start the Registry Editor on your computer.

Summary

In this chapter, you explored how to configure the Windows NT installation. You reviewed the Control Panel applets and examined the Registry. In doing so, you were configuring the computer and environment settings.

Another way to configure, or administer, your computer is to create and manage user accounts, which is what we discuss next in Chapter 6, "Managing Users and Accounts."

QUESTIONS AND ANSWERS

1. What are the two Registry editors available with Windows NT?

   A. REGEDIT.EXE, the Registry Editor first made available with Windows 95, and REGEDT32.EXE, the Registry Editor first made available with Windows NT 3.1.

2. The System Policy file for Windows NT Workstation clients should be stored on the domain in _____ .

   A. The NETLOGON share. The system policies for Windows 9x clients would be stored in this same location as well.

3. The System Policy file for Windows 95 clients must be named _____ .

   A. The System Policy file for Windows 95 clients must be named CONFIG.POL. For Windows NT clients, it must be named NT CONFIG.POL.

4. The System Policy file for Windows NT Workstation clients must be named _____ .:

   A. The System Policy file for Windows NT clients must be named NTCONFIG.POL. For Windows 95/98 clients, it must be named CONFIG.POL.

5. True or False: All changes made to the Registry are immediate.

   A. True. All changes made to the Registry are immediate, although their effect may not be known until a refresh occurs. Many refreshes do not occur until the user logs off and back on.

CH
5

PRACTICE TEST

1. Which of the following keys in HKEY_LOCAL_MACHINE have corresponding directory files in the Windows NT system directory? More than one answer might be correct.

   a. SYSTEM
   b. SOFTWARE
   c. HARDWARE
   d. SECURITY

Answers a, b, and d are correct because the values are held within files beneath the CONFIG subdirectory. Answer c is incorrect because the HARDWARE key is built on each boot.

2. Which three of the following four features are a part of the Services applet in Control Panel?

   a. Running status
   b. Load order
   c. Hardware profile assignments
   d. Startup options

Answers a, c, and d are correct because they are features available from within the Services applet, whereas the Load Order (answer B) is not.

3. Which Control Panel applet creates and manages accounts?

   a. Disk Administrator
   b. User Manager
   c. Accessibility Options
   d. No Control Panel applet creates and manages accounts.

Answer a allows you to manage the disk but is not used to create or manage accounts and is not a Control Panel applet. Answer b allows you to create or manage accounts but is not a Control Panel applet. Answer c, although it is a Control Panel applet, does not allow you to create or manage accounts. **Answer d is correct because accounts are managed from the User Manager utility. This utility is available under the Administrative Tools menu choice and is not a Control Panel applet.**

4. Janice is a hearing-impaired account manager who has asked whether Windows NT provides any options appropriate for her. What can you do to help?

   a. Select Control Panel, Sounds and increase the volume for system sounds.
   b. Select My Computer, Properties and select the Accessibility tab to set Sound options.
   c. Select Control Panel, Accessibility Options and set the Sound options.
   d. Windows NT does not provide options for physically challenged persons.

Answer a is incorrect because increasing the sound does not help the hearing impaired. Answer b is incorrect because Accessibility is an applet in Control Panel, not a tab of My Computer. **Answer c is correct because Accessibility Options, a Control Panel applet, allows you to change the settings to have sounds visually displayed.** Answer d is incorrect; Windows NT does provide Accessibility features.

5. Antonio frequently travels for the company and accesses the network on his laptop via modem while on the road. When he is at the office, he docks his laptop at his workstation and uses the network card in the docking station to access the network. How can you facilitate the boot process between these two hardware configurations?

   a. Hardware profiles are a feature of Windows 95, not Windows NT 4.0.

   b. Create a hardware profile for each configuration—docked and undocked—and set a default timeout value for the most frequently used configuration.

   c. Modify the BOOT.INI file, and include a boot menu choice for a second hardware configuration using the \PROFILE:*filename* boot switch.

   d. Use Control Panel, Services and create a new profile from the HW Profiles button.

Answer a is incorrect; hardware profiles are also used in Windows NT. **Answer b is correct because two hardware configurations are needed—docked and undocked—to represent the two modes the computer can operate in. Using a default timeout of the most frequently selected choice saves the user from always making a menu selection.** Answer c is incorrect; you would not modify the BOOT.INI file to create a hardware profile. Answer d is incorrect; the Services applet is use to control services.

6. Martha wants to modify her mouse pointers. What is the most appropriate procedure for doing so?

   a. Choose Control Panel, Mouse and select the pointers through the Pointers tab.

   b. Right-click the desktop, choose Properties, and select the Settings tab.

   c. Start the Registry Editor, select HKEY_CURRENT_USER, and modify the Cursors subkey.

   d. Start the Registry Editor, select HKEY_LOCAL_MACHINE, and modify the System\CurrentControlSet subkey.

Answer a is correct because the Pointers tab of the Mouse applet, available through Control Panel, controls which pointers are utilized. Answer b does not bring up the mouse properties. Answer c is not the most appropriate procedure of those presented. Answer d is not the most appropriate procedure.

CH
5

7. You need to add the company's logo to the default Windows NT bootup screen. From which Registry subtree(s) can you make this modification?

    a. HKEY_LOCAL_MACHINE

    b. HKEY_CURRENT_USER

    c. HKEY_USERS

    d. This change can be made only through Control Panel, Service, Startup

Answer c is correct because HKEY_USERS holds the Registry settings for the default bootup screen logo, whereas answers a and b show the wrong locations. Answer d is simply incorrect.

8. Rick has added a new COM port adapter card to his computer and needs to configure it. Which applet should he use?

    a. COM

    b. Ports

    c. PCMCIA

    d. IRQ

Answers a and d are choices that do not exist as Control Panel applets. **Answer b is correct because Ports lets you add, modify, and delete parameters for your computer's COM ports.** Answer c lists the wrong Control Panel applet.

9. Having recently married, Jill is looking through the Registry for all locations where her last name appears. When she finds them, she intends to change the old value to her new last name. What value types should she look for?

    a. REG_DWORD

    b. REG_NAME

    c. REG_SZ

    d. REG_BINARY

Answers a and d are incorrect choices that do not hold text values. Answer b is a nonexistent value type. **Answer c is correct because names would be found in string (REG_SZ) values.**

10. Which tool should Kristin use to find system events related to devices that could not be initialized?

    a. Performance Monitor

    b. System Monitor

    c. Services applet

    d. Event Viewer

Answers a and c are choices that do exist but would not show Kristin the log files. Answer b is a tool that exists only in the Windows 9*x* world. **Answer d is correct because system events such as services that failed to start or devices that could not be initialized can be found in the log files viewed by Event Viewer.**

CHAPTER PREREQUISITE

Before reading this chapter, you should be familiar with the Windows NT 4.0 interface (see Chapter 4, "An Overview of the Windows NT 4.0 Interface"). It would also be useful for you to know how Windows NT modifies the Registry with configuration information (see Chapter 5, "Configuration and the Registry").

Managing Users and Accounts

— WHILE YOU READ —

1. True or False: Passwords and usernames are case sensitive.

2. A UNC path for a file named SCOTCH in a share named TAPE on a server named ROLL would be _____ .

3. True or False: The Password Never Expires check box overrides other parameters such as Maximum Password Age and User Must Change Password.

4. True or False: The Account Policy dialog box shows user rights that can be assigned to groups or individual users.

5. Audit policies can be configured to log what seven items (success or failure)?

This chapter describes the creation and management of accounts on Windows NT Workstation 4.0. Although you might not ordinarily think of creating multiple user accounts on a workstation computer, there are some compelling reasons for creating both user and group accounts on a Windows NT workstation. The information that you will learn in this chapter is also directly applicable to basic account management on Windows NT Server 4.0. Throughout this chapter, we will make reference to account management on a server to help compare and contrast that from the workstation.

Understanding User and Group Accounts

As you recall from previous chapters, the first screen that you see after booting and pressing Ctrl+Alt+Del is the Logon Security dialog box. It is here that you must enter your username and password to gain access to the workstation either through local or network authentication.

Key Concept

The user account is the first and foremost security object for access to local and network resources.

Each user and group account that is created is unique to Windows NT and as such has a unique security identifier associated with it. This identifier is called the Windows NT Security Identifier, more commonly referred to as the SID. All references made by Windows NT to any account, especially those dealing with security access and permissions, are linked to the SID. If you delete the user account and re-create it using exactly the same information, Windows NT will create a new SID for that user, and all security access and permissions will have to be reestablished. SAM The account information is stored in the Security Accounts Manager database (SAM), which you will recall is part of the Windows NT 4.0 Registry. If the account is local—in other words, an account that a user uses to log on to a specific workstation at the workstation—that account is included in the SAM database of that workstation's Registry. If it is a network account—meaning an account that is used to log on to the enterprise network from any given workstation—that account is included in the SAM database of the primary domain controller for the account domain of the enterprise.

Key Concept

A local account, in general, has access only to resources on the local workstation. A network or global account has access as provided to network resources such as shared printers, files, and folders.

Refer to Chapter 2, "Understanding Microsoft Windows NT 4.0," for a review of domain controllers and enterprise network models.

Default User Accounts

When you first install Windows NT Workstation 4.0, two default accounts are created for you: the Administrator and Guest accounts. Neither of these accounts can be deleted. For this reason, care must be taken to preserve the integrity of these accounts.

The Guest account provides the least amount of access for the user and is, in fact, disabled by default on both Windows NT Workstation and Server to prevent inadvertent access to resources. It is strongly recommended that you assign a password to this account and, for additional security, rename the account.

The Administrator account, as you might expect, provides the greatest amount of access and complete functional rights to the workstation (or the enterprise). Because this account is created by Windows NT by default, it also is the first account that a user has to log on to the workstation with. In reality, it is highly unlikely that the average user will need to log on to the workstation with full administrative privileges to do most everyday activities. Therefore, it is strongly recommended that this account be password-protected (with a unique, though memorable, password), and for additional security, it should also be renamed. After all, if you were a hacker trying to break in with administrative access, the first account name you would try would probably be "administrator," and then perhaps "supervisor" or "admin" or "XYZadmin," where "XYZ" is the company name. If we have exhausted your choices for alternative administrator account names, good! With Internet access especially prevalent, enterprise security has become an extremely significant and sensitive issue.

Another suggestion that Microsoft makes is to create a separate user account for everyday access. The user would then use this account to access his or her workstation and log on as administrator only when that level of access is required. Using a different account for everyday access eliminates a potential security "hole," that is, being logged in as administrator and leaving for lunch without locking the workstation or logging out. Leaving the workstation unattended may not be quite so significant when the user is logged on as a local administrator but becomes far more disconcerting when the user is logged on to a domain as a network administrator.

In some organizations, the Administrator account is not only renamed, but is also randomly assigned one of several different passwords. Also, the user is often not told the new name or password. Administrative tasks that must take place on the workstation must be performed by a designated workgroup administrator. This setup is not quite as limiting to the user as you might think, as you will discern later in this chapter.

**CH
6**

Default Group Accounts

When you first install Windows NT Workstation 4.0, six default groups are created for you: Administrators, Power Users, Users, Guests, Backup Operators, and Replicator. These groups are considered local groups in that they are used to provide a certain level of functional access for that local workstation. Any additional groups that you create will also be local and will be used primarily for administering access to resources on that local workstation. Table 6.1 describes the types of functional access associated with each group.

Table 6.1   Built-in Local Groups

Group	Description
Administrators	Members of this group can fully administer the computer or the domain. The Administrator account is automatically made a member of this group. Administrators, although they do not automatically have access to all files and resources, can gain access at any time.
Power Users	Members of this group have some of the same privileges that Administrators do but cannot fully administer the workstation or domain.
Users	Members of this group have the necessary level of access to operate the computer for daily tasks such as word processing, database access, and so forth. Every new user that you create becomes a member of this group.
Guests	Members of this group have the least level of access to resources. The Guest account is automatically a member of this group. Anyone in the network can potentially access a computer's resources through this group, so it is important that resource permissions be appropriately set. (See Chapter 7, "Windows NT 4.0 Security Model.")
Backup Operators	Members of this group have only enough access to files and folders as is needed to back them up or restore them on this workstation.
Replicator	When Directory Replication is configured, this group is used to identify the specific user account, often called a service account, that Windows NT uses to perform the replication function.

Table 6.2 lists functions and tasks and the groups that can perform them.

Table 6.2 Functional Tasks Assigned to Default Groups

Function	Groups Assigned
Assign user rights	Administrators
Create and manage users	Administrators, Power Users, Users
Create and manage groups	Administrators, Power Users
Create and manage shares	Administrators, Power Users
Create common groups	Administrators, Power Users
Format the hard disk	Administrators
Keep a local profile	Administrators, Power Users, Backup Operators
Lock the workstation	Administrators, Power Users, Everyone
Override the lock	Administrators
Share\stop sharing printers	Administrators, Power Users

Windows NT also creates and manages four groups, called internal or system groups, to "place" a user for accessing resources. These groups are Everyone, Interactive, Network, and Creator Owner, as described here:

- Everyone, of course, means just that. Every user who logs on to the workstation or accesses a resource on the workstation (or server) locally or remotely becomes a member of the internal group Everyone. It is interesting to note that Windows NT's philosophy for securing resources is not to secure them at all. By default, the group Everyone has full access to resources. It is up to the administrator to restrict that access and add security.

- Interactive represents to Windows NT the user who has logged on at the workstation itself and accesses resources on that workstation. Logging on this way is also referred to as logging on locally.

- Network represents to Windows NT any user who has connected to a resource on the workstation from another computer (remotely).

- Creator Owner represents the user who is the owner or has taken ownership of a resource. This group can, for example, be used to assign file access only to the owner of a file. Although Everyone may have read access to files in a directory, Creator Owner has full access; thus, although other users can read a file, only the owner of the file can make changes to it.

CH
6

The membership of these internal groups is fixed by the Windows NT operating system and cannot be altered. For example, if you create a file, you are the owner of that file, and Windows NT places you in the Creator Owner group for that file.

Group Management in Domains

This book is geared toward Windows NT Workstation 4.0 management issues. However, as your workstation is apt to be a member of a larger enterprise network, you should know a bit about domain group management as well.

When user accounts are created for participation in an enterprise network, these accounts are created and stored in the SAM database on a primary domain controller. This special Windows NT server acts as the authenticating server for users requesting logon and resource access throughout the network.

Group accounts are created and maintained there as well. However, two types of group accounts can be created in a domain:

- Local groups in a domain are local to the domain controller(s) in that domain and are used to manage resources local to the domain controller(s) just like they are used to manage resources local to a workstation. Local groups can be created on workstations, servers, and domain controllers.

- Global groups, on the other hand, are global to the domain. They can be used by any workstation or server that is a member of the domain to manage local resources. In other words, you don't have to create individual local groups of domain users on individual computers. You can use the same global groups of domain users who are available to all resource managers in the network. Global groups can be created and maintained only on domain controllers.

Three built-in global groups and three additional local groups are created on the domain controller. The Power Users group is not created for a domain controller. Table 6.3 describes each.

Table 6.3   Global and Local Groups on the Domain Controller

Group	Type	Description
Domain Admins	Global	This global group is used to assign its members administrative privileges on local computers by making it a member of the local Administrators group. It automatically becomes a member of the Administrators local group on the domain controller.
Domain Users	Global	This global group contains all domain user accounts that are created and is itself a member of the Users local group on the domain controller. If made a member of a workstation's local Users group, its members assume the user privileges that the local Users group has been given on that workstation.

Group	Type	Description
Domain Guests	Global	This global group contains the domain Guest account. If made a member of a workstation's local Guests group, the domain guest account also has guest access to the workstation resources.
Account Operators	Local	Members of this local group gain the ability to create and manage users, local groups, and global groups in the domain and to shut down the system.
Print Operators	Local	Members of this local group gain the ability to share and stop sharing printers and to shut down the system.
Server Operators	Local	Members of this local group gain the ability to create and manage shared directories, share and stop sharing printers, lock and unlock the server, format the hard disk, shut down the system locally and remotely, change the system time, and back up and restore files and directories.

Local groups can have as their members any local users, domain users, and global groups. They cannot have other local groups as members.

Global groups can have users only from their own domain as valid members.

Microsoft's group strategy for domains recommends that domain users be grouped into as many global groups as is appropriate. Local resource managers should then create local groups for maintaining access to the resources. The global groups are then used as members of the local groups. Whichever domain users are members of the global group get whatever level of access was given to the local group. Although this strategy may at first seem to be a bit of over-management, in large networks with hundreds or thousands of users, it makes a great deal of sense and can actually facilitate user management and resource access.

Planning for New User Accounts

Setting up new user accounts, especially on a domain controller, involves some planning. You should consider these four basic areas before creating new accounts:

- Account naming conventions
- How to deal with passwords
- Group membership
- Profile information

CH
6

If you are creating user accounts on a domain controller, you must also consider the following:

- Logon hours (when logon is possible)
- Which workstations the user can log on from

Naming Conventions

The choice of username determines how the user will be identified on the network. In all lists of users and groups, the account names are displayed alphabetically, so the choice of username can be significant. For example, if your naming convention is FirstnameLastinitial, your usernames for the following users would look like this:

User	Username
Charlie Brown	CharlieB
Lucy VanPelt	LucyvanP
Beetle Bailey	BeetleB
Dagwood Bumstead	DagwoodB
Dilbert	Dilbert

Now, what if you have several Charlies or Lucys, and so on. In a large corporation, having 20 or 30 persons with the same first name would not be uncommon. Looking through a list of users with the same first name and only a last initial to go by could become not only confusing, but irritating as well.

A more effective convention might be to use LastnameFirstInitial, like so:

User	Username
Charlie Brown	BrownC
Lucy VanPelt	VanpeltL
Beetle Bailey	BaileyB
Dagwood Bumstead	BumsteadD
Dilbert	Dilbert

With this convention, finding the appropriate user in a list is easier. Many organizations already have a network ID naming convention in place, and following that convention would be perfectly acceptable.

Usernames must be unique both locally and to the enterprise. Therefore, your naming convention must plan for duplicate names. Charlie Brown and Chuck Brown would both have the username BrownC according to the second convention suggested here. So, perhaps the convention could be altered to include middle initials in the event of a "tie"—for example, BrownCA and BrownCB—or include extra letters from the first name until uniqueness is achieved—for example, BrownCha and BrownChu. Usernames are not case sensitive and can contain up to 20 characters, including spaces, except the following:

" / \ { } : ; | = , + * ? < >

You might also consider creating user accounts based on function rather than the user's name. For example, if the role of administrative assistant is assigned from a pool of employees, then creating an account called AdminAsst or FrontDesk might make more sense. Using such a naming convention ensures that the assistant of the day has access to everything that person should have access to—as well as minimizes your administrative setup for that person.

Considerations Regarding Passwords

Besides the obvious consideration that requiring a password provides a greater level of security, you need to think about some other factors. One of them is who controls the password.

When you create a new user account, you have three password-related options to determine:

- ▪ User Must Change Password at Next Logon
- ▪ User Cannot Change Password
- ▪ Password Never Expires

Selecting User Must Change Password at Next Logon allows you to set a blank or "dummy" password for the user. When the user logs on for the first time, Windows NT requires the user to change the password.

Key Concept

It is important to set company policy and educate the users in the importance of protecting the integrity of their accounts by using unique and "unguessable" passwords. Among the most common choices for passwords are children's names, pets' names, favorite sports teams, or team members. Your users should try to avoid the obvious associations when choosing passwords.

User Cannot Change Password provides the most control to the administrator. This option is particularly useful for temporary employees or the administrative assistant pool account.

Password Never Expires ensures that the password does not need to be changed, even if the overall password policy requires changes after a set period of time has elapsed. Again, this option is useful for the types of accounts just mentioned or for service accounts.

Passwords are case sensitive and can be up to 14 characters in length. It is generally suggested among network administrators to require a minimum password length of eight characters, using alphanumeric characters and a combination of upper- and lowercase. For example, you might use as your password a combination of your initials and the last four digits of your Social Security number—two things you're not likely to forget, but not obvious to anyone else. For example, your password might be something like SDK4532, or it might be sdk4532, SdK4532, 4532sdK, 45sdk32, and, oh well, you get the idea.

Group Membership

The easiest way to manage large numbers of users is to group them together logically, functionally, departmentally, and so forth. Creating local groups for local resource access control is the most common use for creating groups on the workstation. You do not have to decide how to group users before creating the groups, but if you have already planned your groups, you can include the users' group memberships right up front while creating the account.

Determining User Profile Information

When referring to a user profile on a Windows NT workstation, we are usually referring to a local logon script or the location of the user's personal folder (directory). In the larger workgroup or enterprise, however, the user profile might be a file of environment settings stored on a specific computer and downloaded to whatever Windows NT-based computer the user is logging in from. The logon script and personal folder might also be located on a remote computer rather than on the local workstation; this location is especially useful if the user moves around a lot (like the pool of administrative assistants described earlier).

It is helpful, though not necessary, to determine ahead of time where this information will be kept and how much will be used. Will you need a user profile stored on a server for every user or only for administrative assistants? Does everyone need a logon script? Should personal files be stored on the local workstation or on a central computer? (Again, user profiles are useful for users who move around.)

You'll find a more thorough discussion of user profile files and login scripts later in this chapter.

Understanding the User Manager

User and group accounts are created and managed through an administrative tool called the User Manager. Account policies are also created and maintained through this utility; also, functional user rights are assigned, and security auditing is enabled. Functional rights define what functions a user can perform on a Windows NT computer. For example, shutting down the computer, changing the system time, formatting the hard disk, and installing device drivers are all functional rights.

On a domain controller, the User Manager utility is called the User Manager for Domains and includes additional management options appropriate for enterprise account management, such as logon hours, valid logon workstations, and trust relationships.

The User Manager acts as the database manager for user and group accounts stored in the SAM database, as shown in Figure 6.1. The four menu options are as follows:

- User creates and modifies user and group accounts.
- Policies sets account policies, assigns functional user rights, and enables security auditing.
- Options enables or disables confirmation and save settings, and sets display fonts for User Manager.
- Help displays the Windows NT help files specific to the User Manager.

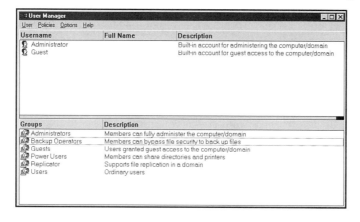

Figure 6.1
The User Manager displays the account database showing all user group accounts. Here, you see the two default users and six default groups created during installation.

**CH
6**

Creating a New User

In the User Manager, selecting New Under from the Under menu displays the New User dialog box shown in Figure 6.2. This screen, which is fairly intuitive, is described in the following list:

Username	This field indicates the logon ID that you have chosen for the user. Recall that this name must be unique in the database (or in the enterprise when you're creating the account on a domain controller), up to 20 characters including spaces, but excluding " / \ [ ] : ; l = , + * ? < >.
Full Name	This field indicates the user's full name. As with usernames, it is recommended that you determine a convention for entering this name (such as "Charles H. Brown") because the full name is used by Windows NT for determining the user account sort order.
Description	This field provides a simple description of the account or user, such as "Admin Assistant Account" or "Project Manager."
Password	The password is case sensitive and can be up to 14 characters in length. Recall the discussion of password integrity earlier.
Confirm Password	You must confirm the password here before Windows NT can create the account.
User Must Change Password At Next Logon	This password option forces the user to change his or her password the next time he or she logs on.
User Cannot Change Password	This password option prevents the user from being able to change his or her password. As mentioned earlier, this setting is useful for accounts for which the passwords should remain the same, such as temporary employees.
Password Never Expires	This password option prevents the password from expiring and overrides the Maximum Password Age set in the Account Policy dialog as well as User Must Change Password at Next Logon.
Account Disabled	This option prevents the use of the account. This setting is useful for users who are onv acation, on extended leave, or whose accounts otherwise should not be available for logging in to the network. It is always more appropriate to disable an account if there is any possibility of the user returning. Remember that deleting a user account also deletes the user's SID and thus removes all previous network resource access for that user.
Groups	This button displays the Group Memberships dialog box, which displays the user's group membership and from which group membership can be modified.

Profile   This button displays the User Environment Profile dialog box from
                             which a server-based profile can be referenced, logon script defined,
                             and home folder (directory) identified.

Dialin   This button displays the Dialin Information dialog box, which is used
                             to grant permission to use Dial-Up Networking to the user account
                             and set Call Back options.

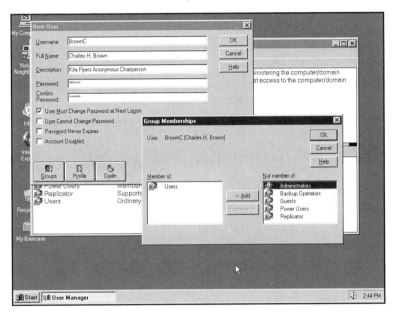

Figure 6.2
Here, the New User dialog box is filled in, and the Group Memberships window shows
the default membership in the Users local group.

As you can see, creating user accounts is a fairly straightforward process. By double-
clicking the account name in the User Manager window, or highlighting the username
and choosing Properties from the User menu, you can view these settings for each user
and modify them as appropriate.

User Manager for Domains: New User Options

When you're creating and managing users in the enterprise account domain, these additional options are available for the user accounts:

Hours   This button displays the Logon Hours dialog box from which you can
                             determine what times of the day the user can log on to the network.
                             This option is useful for dealing with shift employees or for identifying
                             backup times.

CH
6

Logon To	This button displays the Logon Workstations dialog box in which you can identify by computer name the computers at which this account can log on to the network. You can identify up to eight workstations.
Account	This button displays the Account Information dialog box in which you can specify an expiration date for the account and identify whether the account is a global domain account (default) or for a user from another untrusted domain who needs occasional access to your domain.

Creating a New Local Group

The process of creating a new local group is even more straightforward, as you can see by the New Local Group dialog box displayed in Figure 6.3.

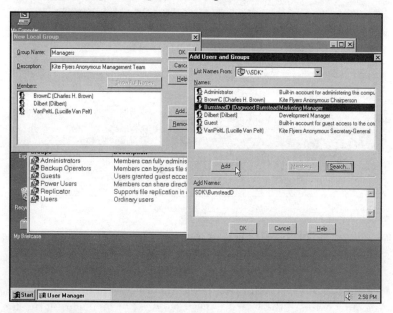

Figure 6.3
This New Local Group dialog box shows the new group name and description filled in, and the Add Users and Groups dialog box is also displayed.

New Local Group dialog box contains these options:

Group Name	This field indicates the name you have chosen for the local group. It can have up to 256 characters except the backslash (\), which, while descriptive, would be somewhat confusing in display lists of groups. Group names, unlike usernames, cannot be changed.
Description	This field provides a simple description of the group such as "Administrative Assistants" or "Project Managers."
Show Full Names	This button displays the full name associated with each user account displayed in the Members list box.
Members	This list displays all the current user accounts (or domain user and global group accounts) that are members of this local group.
Add	This button displays the Add Users and Groups dialog box from which you can select user accounts from your workstation SAM database, or domain user and global group accounts from the enterprise SAM database on a domain controller. (This dialog box is also shown in Figure 6.3.) In this dialog box, you select the workstation or account domain that has the desired user accounts from the List Names From list box, click the name of the user you want to add to the group in the Names list box, choose Add, and then click OK. You use the Search button to look for an account among all possible account databases. If you select a global group in the Names list box, you can choose Members to display the members of that global group. You also can select multiple accounts at one time by Ctrl-clicking the additional accounts.
Remove	This button deletes the selected account from group membership.

Here's a shortcut to populating a group: Before you create the group, select all the usernames you want in the group from the User Manager Username screen by Ctrl-clicking the additional accounts. Then create the group. The Members list box displays any user account that has been highlighted before the group was created.

User Manager for Domains: Group Options

CH
6

Creating a group in the enterprise account domain is pretty much the same as creating groups on the workstation. The difference is that, in addition to creating local groups, you can also create global groups. Recall that a global group is one that can be used by any workstation or server that participates in the enterprise for managing resource access.

When you create a new global group, you can select user accounts only from the account domain database, and they are the only accounts that are displayed for you.

Renaming, Copying, and Deleting Accounts

Recall from the discussion of the default Administrator and Guest accounts that for a higher level of security, you can rename these accounts. Renaming an account does not affect the account's SID in any way. Therefore, you can relatively easily change a username without affecting any of that user's access—whether it be changing the Administrator account to enhance its security, or changing a name because of a marriage or entrance into the Witness Protection Program. You can simply highlight the username in the User Manager, choose Rename from the User menu, and then enter the new username in the box provided. Group names cannot be renamed.

 Key Concept

If you choose to delete an account, remember that the account's SID is also deleted, and all resource access and user rights are lost. This means that if you re-create the account even exactly as it was before, the SAM database generates a new SID for the account, and you have to reestablish resource access and user rights for that account.

To delete the account, an action you should almost never do, highlight it and press Del on the keyboard, or choose Delete from the User menu. Windows NT warns you that the SID will be lost. Click OK, and the account is deleted.

You must keep in mind several points when you're working with user accounts:

- You cannot delete built-in user or group accounts.

- The Copy option under the User menu is useful for duplicating user account information that is the same for a group of users. Because you cannot rename a group, copying a group to a new name also duplicates its membership list and is the next best thing to renaming. Copying user and group accounts results in new accounts being created. As such, each new account has its own new SID assigned to it.

- When you copy a user account, the following settings are maintained: the Description, the password options that have been checked off, and if Account Disabled has been selected, it is unchecked for the copy. Also, group membership and profile information are maintained for the copied account. Copying accounts greatly simplifies the task of creating large numbers of similar users.

■ In the User Manager for Domains, the Logon Hours, Logon To workstations, and account expiration and type are also copied to the new account.

Creating and Managing Account Policies, System Rights, and Auditing

Account policy information and user rights are considered part of account management and as such are administered through the User Manager. Account policy information includes password-specific information, such as password age and minimum length, and account lockout options. User rights represent the functional rights that a user acquires for a given workstation when logging in. Auditing for file and directory access, print access, and so forth is accomplished by specifying the users or groups whose access you want to audit and is done at the file, directory, and print level. However, auditing for those security events must first be enabled for user and group accounts; that is done through the User Manager as well.

Account Policy

Figure 6.4 shows a typical account policy. The options presented in this dialog box should be very familiar to network administrators; they're described here in detail:

Maximum Password Age	You can set the password to never expire, or you can select a set number of days after which the user will be prompted to change the password. The default is set to 42 days.
Minimum Password Age	The default here is to allow users to change their passwords any time they want. Many organizations now prefer that passwords cannot be changed whenever the users want. The users must wait a specified number of days before they can change their passwords. This rule helps to maintain password uniqueness.
Minimum Password Length	The default, oddly enough, is to allow blank passwords. As you learned earlier, you will probably want to define a minimum length for the password. Most network administrators use 8 characters as the minimum length. The maximum length can be 14 characters.

**CH
6**

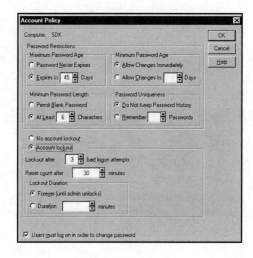

Figure 6.4
The password must be at least six characters long, and it expires every 45 days. Also, if the user forgets the password in three consecutive tries within 30 minutes, the account is locked out until an administrator releases it.

Password Uniqueness

The default is not to maintain a history of past passwords. This way, users can reuse passwords when they expire. Although being able to reuse passwords is convenient for the users, it is not always the most secure way to deal with passwords. Many organizations require passwords to be unique. This uniqueness is accomplished by specifying the number of passwords to be "remembered" by the system for each user (up to 24), requiring a maximum password age and a minimum password age. For example, if you set the maximum and minimum password age to 30 days and uniqueness to 24, the users would not be able to reuse their first passwords for two years. Setting the age like this, in effect, accomplishes uniqueness simply because the users are not likely to be able to remember that far back.

Account Lockout

The default is not to enable account lockout. Because enabling lockout does add additional resource overhead to the system, doing so is probably not truly necessary except on workstations that contain particularly sensitive data. Nevertheless, in an enterprise in which security is essential, this option is probably enabled and, in fact, is recommended.

Lockout After...	This option specifies the number of bad logon attempts (incorrect passwords) that the system will accept before locking out that account. The default is 5 and can be set from 1 to 999.
Reset Count After...	This number represents the number of minutes that the system will wait between bad logon attempts before resetting the bad logon count back to 0. For example, if you mistype your password, the bad logon count is set to one. If the reset count is 15 minutes, after 15 minutes, if you do not log on incorrectly again, the bad logon count is set back to 0. The default is 30 minutes and can be set from 1 to 99,999 minutes (or roughly 70 days, for those of you who couldn't help wondering).
Lockout Duration	You can require an administrator to reset the account after lockout. (This is one of our favorite radio button choices in Windows NT because of its name: "Forever.") You can also specify a length of time for the lockout to be in effect before letting the computer hacker try again. The default for this choice is 30 minutes and can be set from 1 to 99,999 minutes.
Users Must Log On In Order to Change Password	This option requires that the users log in to the system before making password changes. Normally, when passwords expire, the users are prompted during logon to change their passwords. With this option selected, the users cannot change the expired passwords, and the administrator needs to reset them. This option is useful for short-term employee accounts that expire in a specific amount of time to ensure that the employees cannot change the passwords on their own.

User Rights

As mentioned previously, user rights are functional rights and represent functions or tasks that a user or group can perform on a given workstation. Contrast this with permissions such as Read Only, Write, and Delete, which reflect resource access rights. User rights include shutting down the computer, formatting a hard disk, backing up files and directories, and so forth.

User rights are granted primarily to local groups. As you will learn in the next chapter, user rights maintain access control lists (ACLs). Groups and users represented by their SIDs are members of the ACL for each user right. Consequently, there is no way to select an account and see what user rights (or file permissions for that matter) have been assigned to that account because the rights do not "stay" with the account. Table 6.4 highlights the basic user rights and the default groups assigned to each.

CH
6

Table 6.4 User Rights	
User Right	Group(s) Assigned
Access this computer from the network	Administrators, Power Users, Everyone (no Power Users group on domain controllers)
Back up files and directories	Administrators, Backup Operators, (Server Operators on domain controllers)
Change the system time	Administrators, Power Users, (Server Operators on domain controllers)
Force shutdown from a remote system	Administrators, Power Users, (Server Operators on domain controllers)
Load and unload device drivers	Administrators
Log on locally	All built-in groups, including Everyone, except Replicator (all built-in local groups on domain controllers except Everyone, Users, and Guests)
Manage auditing and the security log	Administrators
Restore files and directories	Administrators, Backup Operators (Server Operators on domain controllers)
Shut down the system	All built-in groups except Guests and Replicator (all built-in local groups except Everyone, Users, and Guests on domain controllers)
Take ownership of files or objects	Administrators

Accounts assigned to the various user rights can be administered through the User Rights Policy dialog box, which you open by choosing User Rights from the Policy menu (see Figure 6.5). You can select the user right from the Right drop-down list. The default groups assigned this user right are then displayed in the Grant To list box. You can choose the Add button to display the Add Users and Groups dialog box and add user and group accounts to the user right's Grant To list, or you can choose Remove to delete members from the Grant To list.

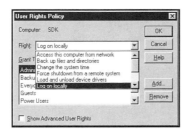

Figure 6.5
Here, Log On Locally has been selected as a user right, and in the Grant To box
behind the drop-down list, you can see the groups assigned this user right.

You can display advanced rights by checking that option at the bottom of the User Rights
Policy dialog box. These rights are for use primarily by developers. However, as an administrator on a network, you might need to modify two of these advanced user rights from
time to time:

Bypass traverse checking	This advanced user right allows the specified user or group accounts to change between directories and navigate directory trees even if permission has been denied to various directories. This right might be assigned to Power Users directories. This might be assigned to Power Users.
Log on as a service	This advanced user right is intended for user accounts that are used by certain background application tasks or Windows NT system functions such as Directory Replication. This right allows the service or function to log in as the specified account for the express purpose of carrying out that specific task. No other user needs to be logged in for the task to be performed.

Audit Policy

As stated earlier, auditing for events relating to file and directory access, print access, and
so forth is accomplished by specifying the users or groups whose access you want to audit.
You do so at the file, directory, and print levels. However, auditing for those security
events must first be enabled for user and group accounts; you enable auditing through
the User Manager by selecting Audit from the Policies menu (see Figure 6.6).

CH
6

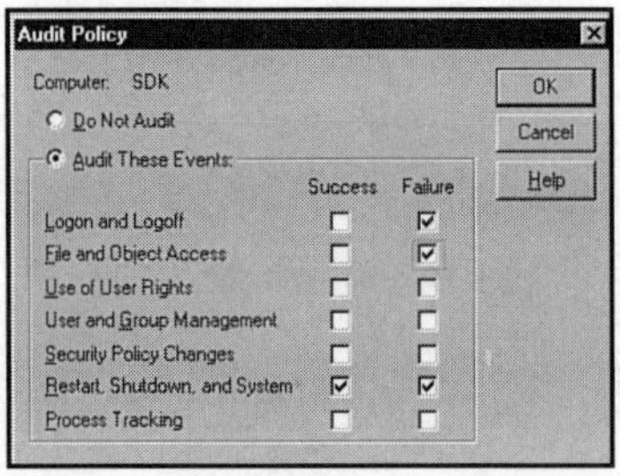

Figure 6.6
This audit policy has enabled auditing of failed logon and logoff attempts; unsuccessful file and object access; and any events relating to restart, shutdown, or system processes.

By default, auditing is not enabled because of the additional resources required to monitor the system for related events. Auditing can be enabled for the following seven areas:

Logon and Logoff	Monitors user logon and logoff of the workstation and network connections.
File and Object Access	Monitors user access of files, directories, or printers. This option enables the auditing. The users and groups that are audited are set up at the file, directory, and printer level.
Use of User Rights	Monitors when a user right is exercised by a user (such as formatting the hard disk).
User and Group Management	Monitors events relating to user and group management, such as the creation of new users, the modification of group membership, or the change of a password.
Security Policy Changes	Monitors changes made to user rights or account policy information.
Restart, Shutdown, and System	Monitors events related to these activities.
Process Tracking	Monitors events related to certain process activities, such as starting a program, indirectly accessing objects, and so on.

Successful and unsuccessful events can be logged in the security log, which can be viewed through the Event Viewer, another useful Administrative Tools utility. Generally, monitoring successful and unsuccessful events for all seven options would not be at all useful, even on a server, because of the resources involved and the volume of data that would be collected in the security log. Auditing, however, can be very helpful in troubleshooting events such as unsuccessful logins or unsuccessful file access.

Creating and Managing User Profiles

When we speak of the user profile in Windows NT 4.0, we are really talking about managing the user's working environment. Through the User Environment Profile dialog box (see Figure 6.7) in the User Manager (and the User Manager for Domains on the server), you can define various elements of the user's environment.

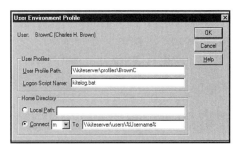

Figure 6.7
Here, BrownC's profile information is stored on a server called Kiteserver, KITELOG.BAT will be executed when he logs on, and his personal data folder is in a share called Users.

Elements you can define include the User Profile Path, which identifies the location of the Registry files and profile folders for the user, the Logon Script Name, which identifies the name and optional path of a set of commands that are executed when the user logs on, and the Home Directory, which identifies the location of the user's personal data folder.

Home Directory

The home directory simply represents a place where the user can routinely save data files. It is usually a folder (directory) that has been created on a centrally located server in the enterprise network; in small workgroups, however, it may actually be found on the user's local workstation—or not identified at all.

The advantage of placing the home directory on a centrally located server somewhere in the domain is primarily that of security. By using NTFS permissions, the users' folders can be secured quite nicely so that only they (and whomever they determine) can have access to them. In addition, these folders can then be included in regular server data backups, thus ensuring the availability of the files in the event of accidental deletion, corruption, or system crashes.

In the Home Directory section of the User Environment Profile dialog box (which you access by viewing the Properties of the user account and choosing Profile), you have two

CH
6

choices: Local Path and Connect To. The first represents the drive and path to an existing home directory folder, such as C:\USERS, in which the user's own profile folder can be created. The other represents a Universal Naming Convention (UNC) path that identifies the name of the server that contains an existing home directory share and a logical drive letter to assign to it that the user can use for saving files in applications, searching, exploring with Explorer, and so on.

A UNC name is very much like a DOS path in that it represents the path through the network to a network resource. In this case, the network resource is a directory that has been "shared" for the creation of a home directory folder for the user. UNC names take the following form:

> *servername\sharename\path*

servername represents the name of the server computer that contains the folder, *sharename* represents the name of the directory that has been made available for use as a resource (shared), and *path* represents an optional path to a subdirectory or specific file.

In Figure 6.7, the home directory is located on the server called Kiteserver under a directory called Users (which has been shared). Notice the use of an environmental parameter to identify the path. If you enter a specific directory name, Windows NT creates that directory if it does not already exist. If you use the variable %USERNAME%, as shown in this example, Windows NT creates a directory using the username as the directory name. This technique is particularly useful when you're using a template for creating large numbers of users. Recall that when you create a new user account by copying an existing account, the User Environment Profile information is also copied. If you use %USERNAME%, you can create individual user home folders by using each user's username as the directory name. Table 6.5, later in this chapter, displays a list of the environment variables that Windows NT 4.0 can use.

Logon Scripts

If you have had any dealings with networks before, you have encountered a logon script. Logon scripts are simply files that contain a set of network commands that need to be executed in a particular order. Often, as is the case with Novell NetWare, logon scripts have a specific command language and structure that should be used. In the case of Windows NT, these scripts are simply batch files and support all the Windows NT command-line commands, or in some cases, they are executables.

The following is an example of a Windows NT logon script called LOGON.BAT:

```
@echo Welcome to the NT Network!
@echo off
Pause
Net use p:\\server5\database
```

```
Net use r:\\server4\budget
Net time \\server1 /set /y
```

The name of the logon script is arbitrary. Windows NT does provide a place for storing logon scripts. In an enterprise setting, they are usually placed in the WINNT40\ SYSTEM32\REPL\IMPORT\SCRIPTS subdirectory on a domain controller. Because the user uses an available domain controller to gain access to the network, it makes sense that the logon scripts be stored there as well.

The advantage of storing the logon scripts on a domain controller is that, through a process called Directory Replication, the scripts can be distributed to all the domain controllers in the network. Because a user may authenticate at any one of the domain controllers, this provides a convenient way to ensure that the logon scripts are always available. Also, it provides the administrator with one central storage place for the scripts, making maintenance easier.

In the example in Figure 6.7 earlier in this chapter, notice that the entry for the Logon Script Name is simply the batch filename. Windows NT assumes that you will be storing this file in the Scripts subdirectory on the validating server. If you are logging on locally to the workstation, that directory can be found on the local hard drive, and Windows NT will look there. If you are logging on to an enterprise network, Windows NT assumes that the file is in that directory on a domain controller. If the logon script cannot be found, Windows NT records that fact and proceeds with validation. More environment variables are shown in Table 6.5.

Table 6.5 Additional Environment Variables for Home Directories and Logon Scripts

Variable	Description
%HOMEDIR%	Returns the logical mapping to the shared folder that contains the user's home directory
%HOMEDRIVE%	Returns the logical drive mapped to the home directory share
%HOMEPATH%	Returns the pathname of the user's home directory folder
%HOMESHARE%	Returns the share name of the folder that contains the user's home directory folder
%OS%	Returns the operating system of the user's computer
%PROCESSOR_ARCHITECTURE%	Returns the processor's base architecture of the user's computer, such as Intel or MIPS
%PROCESSOR_LEVEL%	Returns the processor type of the user's computer, such as 486
%USERDOMAIN%	Returns the name of the enterprise account domain in which the user is validating
%USERNAME%	Returns the user's logon ID (username)

**CH
6**

User Profiles

The user profile itself represents the user's environment settings, such as screen colors, wallpaper, persistent network and printer connections, mouse settings and cursors, shortcuts, personal groups, and Startup programs. These settings are normally saved as part of the Windows NT Registry and loaded when the user logs on to the system.

In Windows NT 3.51 and earlier versions, these settings were kept in the WINNT40\ SYSTEM32\CONFIG subdirectory with the other Registry files on the local computer, workstation, or server that the user logged in to. The next time the user logged on, the profile settings were made available and merged into the Registry for that session. If the user moved to another computer, whether the user logged on locally or on the network, a new profile would be created on that computer and saved locally.

Profiles in Windows NT 4.0 are still saved on the local computer at which the user logs on. However, all information relating to the user's profile is saved in a subdirectory structure created in the WINNT40\PROFILES subdirectory, which contains the Registry data file as well as directory links to desktop items. An example of this structure is displayed in Figure 6.8.

Figure 6.8
In this view of Windows Explorer, the WINNT40\PROFILES subdirectory with the profile folder structure for BROWNC is expanded. Notice the Registry file NTUSER.DAT.

Three default profile structures are created during installation: one for the Administrator's account, of course; one called Default User, from which new user accounts derive their initial environment settings; and one called All Users, which is used with the user's profile settings to assign settings that should be common to all users, such as startup items and common groups. The directory structure of the user's profile directory is outlined in Table 6.6.

When the user first logs on, the settings contained in Default User are used to create that user's own profile folders. In addition, the Registry data file, called NTUSER.DAT, is created and stored in the root of the user's profile folder (refer to Figure 6.8). As the user modifies the environment by changing settings, creating shortcuts, installing applications, and adding programs to the Start menu, Windows NT adds and modifies entries in the appropriate profile folder and updates the Registry file. For example, if BrownC (whose profile folders are shown in Figure 6.8) adds a shortcut to his desktop for Word 7, Windows NT would add an entry representing the shortcut to Word 7 in the Desktop folder under WINNT40\PROFILES\BROWNC.

The Registry data file NTUSER.DAT is actually a cached copy of the Registry subtree HKEY_CURRENT_USER and, as described in Chapter 5, contains information relating to the user's environment settings, such as color schemes, cursors, wallpaper, and so forth.

Table 6.6   Overview of the Profile Folder Directory Structure

Profile Folder	Description
Application Data	Contains references to application-specific data and is usually modified by the application during installation or when a user modifies a setting for the application
Desktop	Contains references to shortcuts created on the desktop and the Briefcase
Favorites	Contains references to shortcuts made to favorite programs and locations
NetHood	Contains references to shortcuts made to Network Neighborhood items, such as to shared folders
Personal	Contains references to shortcuts to personal group programs
PrintHood	Contains references to shortcuts made to print folder items
Recent	Contains references to items on the computer most recently accessed by the user
SendTo	Contains references to the last items that documents were "sent to" or copied, such as the A: drive or My Briefcase
Start Menu	Contains references to program items contained on the Start menu, including the Startup group
Templates	Contains references to shortcuts made to template items

By default the NetHood, PrintHood, Recent, and Templates folders are hidden from display in Windows Explorer. You can view them by choosing <u>V</u>iew, <u>O</u>ptions, <u>S</u>how All Files.

Server-Based User Profiles

As you have seen, user profile information is stored on the computer (or computers) that the user logs in on. If a user routinely logs on to several computers, it might be inconvenient for the user to create or modify preferred settings on each computer before beginning to work on that computer. It would be far more efficient if the user's work environment settings "followed" him or her to whatever computer the user logged on to. This type of user is known as a "roaming user," a concept that can be a bit disconcerting in the workplace, and this user's profiles are known as server-based, or "roaming," profiles, which perhaps might be even more disconcerting than the vagabond users. Actually, this type of profile is used more often in organizations to provide a level of consistency among their users' desktops rather than to accommodate roaming users.

Windows NT Workstation and Server 4.0 computers support two types of server-based profiles: roaming user profiles and mandatory user profiles. They both are user profile settings that have been copied to a centrally located server for access by the user when logging on. The location and name of the profile are identified in the user's User Environment Profile information through the User Manager (or the User Manager for Domains). When the user logs on to a computer, either a mandatory or roaming profile is downloaded to that computer. Changes made to the roaming profile are updated both on the local computer and the server. The next time the user logs on, whichever copy of the profile is more recent is loaded, and when the user logs off, both are updated again.

The primary difference between mandatory and roaming profiles is that the mandatory profile is created for the user and cannot be modified by the user.

 Key Concept

The user can change environment settings while in a particular session, but those settings are not saved back to the mandatory profile. Also, if the mandatory profile is not available to the user when trying to log on, the user cannot log on.

The roaming profile can be, and is meant to be, modified by the user, and it follows the user as a convenience.

Creating the Server-Based Profile

Windows NT Server 4.0 no longer provides the User Profile utility that you may be familiar with. Instead, management of user profiles has been built into the System applet in the Control Panel. To access it, start the System applet, and select the User Profiles tab.

The User Profiles tab displays the profiles that have been created and stored on that computer. Remember that a profile is created each time a user logs on. If you plan to delete a user account, you should delete the user's profile first through this tab. If you delete the user account first, you see an Account Deleted entry such as the one displayed in Figure 6.9. This is not really such a big deal; if the account is deleted anyway, it is a pretty safe bet that you can delete its profile information. Recall that all settings relating to a user account are linked to the user's SID. Deleting the account deletes the SID and renders all previous settings obsolete.

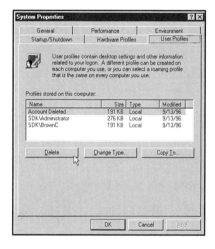

Figure 6.9
You can see that three user profiles are contained on this computer. One of them is for an account that has since been deleted. It should be removed to clean up the Profiles directory on the hard disk.

The first step in creating a roaming or mandatory profile is to identify the users or groups that require this type of profile. The Registry filename NTUSER.DAT cannot be changed, and it is this file that determines whether the profile is mandatory. The next step is to identify the central computer on which you plan to store the users' profiles. It should be a computer that is readily accessible by the users on that network or subnet, particularly if the profiles are mandatory. The directory should then be shared on the network. Within this directory, you can optionally create subdirectories for the different users or groups that will use various profiles you create.

x

Key Concept

If you permit several users or a group of users to use the same roaming profile, remember that the profile can be modified by the users. Multiple users may make multiple changes to the profile. Mandatory profiles are better used for groups of users. Individual roaming users should have their own roaming "changeable" profiles.

Roaming and mandatory profiles are then configured in the following manner:

1. Create a user account (or select an existing account), and make the appropriate changes to that account's work environment settings.
2. Select that account through the User Profiles tab in the System applet in the Control Panel, and choose Copy To.
3. In the Copy Profile To box, enter the UNC name to the share and directory that will contain the profiles, or choose Browse to look for the location.
4. Select Change, and from the Choose User dialog box that is displayed, select the user (Show Users) or groups that you are permitting to use this profile.
5. Click OK to save the profile and exit the System applet.

If you require the profile to become mandatory, you must use Windows Explorer to select the NTUSER.DAT file and change the extension to NTUSER.MAN.

Next, you must identify the profile file to the user or users in question through the User Manager utility:

1. Open the User Manager (or the User Manager for Domains).
2. From the User Properties of the user in question, choose Profile to display the User Environment Profile dialog box.
3. In the User Profile Path text box, enter the UNC path to the profile file. For example, if the profile NTUSER.MAN is located in the BROWNC directory in the share PROFILES on the server KITESERVER, you would enter **PROFILES\ BROWNC\NTUSER.MAN**.
4. Click OK to exit User Manager.
5. Test the profile by logging on as that user.

This discussion has not really distinguished between Windows NT Workstation and Server other than referencing both the User Manager and User Manager for Domains because server-based profiles are available for use on both Windows NT Workstation and Server. A single workstation or server computer that is part of a simple workgroup can just as easily be used to store these profiles and act as the profile "server" as a domain controller or server participating in a domain could. You are more likely to find the use of server-based profiles in a larger domain network than in a smaller workgroup setting.

A Profile Alternative

On a server or domain controller in an enterprise domain, the System Policy Editor can alternatively, and perhaps more effectively, be used to control user profile settings. This utility was described briefly in Chapter 5. It is available only on Windows NT servers. Through the System Policy Editor, you can modify the default settings for all users, or copy the settings and modify them by individual users or groups. The policy file is then saved as NTCONFIG.POL in the WINNT40\SYSTEM32\REPL\IMPORT\SCRIPTS subdirectory on all validating domain controllers.

Through the System Policy Editor, you can restrict user activity in the Display applet in the Control Panel; specify desktop settings such as wallpaper and color schemes; customize desktop folders; create custom folders and Start menu options; restrict use of Run, Find, and Shutdown; and disable editing of the Registry. With these capabilities, combined with computer system policies applied to the computer at which a user logs on, the administrator can get a finer level of granularity over controlling the user's work environment.

Troubleshooting Accounts, Policies, and Profiles

If you have been reading carefully, you already have the necessary building blocks for understanding and troubleshooting account management. The best tool for learning is to practice. Pay particular attention to user profiles; they can cause you some grief (as pointed out in the Key Concepts).

Most of the problems that you will encounter regarding user and group accounts have to do with permissions to use resources rather than with the account setup itself. Nevertheless, the following sections describe some points to keep in mind.

User Cannot Be Logged On by System

When a user cannot log on, fortunately the message or messages that Windows NT displays to the screen are self-explanatory. Usually, they involve the users incorrectly typing their usernames or, more likely, their passwords. Usernames are not case sensitive, but passwords are. Usernames and passwords can both have spaces, but the spaces tend to confuse users more than provide descriptive account names. Be sure to be consistent in your use of usernames. Educate your users in the importance of maintaining the integrity of their passwords, and expect a call every now and then from someone who has forgotten his or her password, or has the Caps Lock on when the password is in lowercase.

If a user forgets the Administrator password on a local workstation, you have few options. If you created an Emergency Repair Disk during installation, you can restore the SAM database, and thus the original Administrator account and password from it. However, if the Emergency Repair Disk has not been kept up-to-date, and additional accounts have been created in the meantime, the repair process will restore the original SAM database, thus causing you to lose all the additional account information. You can see now the importance of securing the Administrator account and password. If you need to, reread the sections in this chapter regarding the default Administrator account and password considerations.

Unable to Access Domain Controllers or Servers

Another possibility that can slow or inhibit a user's ability to log on successfully is the unavailability of a server. If the user is logging on locally, he or she is being validated on the local computer for access to resources on that computer. Unless the computer suddenly turns itself off, the user should be able to log on successfully. If the user is validating on an enterprise network domain controller, the domain controller must be accessible to the user, or the user might not be able to log on.

For example, if the primary domain controller is down, and no backup domain controller is identified to the network, the user cannot log on. If the user logged on successfully at the computer in a previous session, a message may indicate that the domain controller is unavailable and that the user will be logged on with cached information from the Registry. Any changes that have been made to your profile since the last session will probably not be available.

You troubleshoot this problem, of course, by verifying that the domain controller is up and that the computer in question has a valid connection to the network. If you are using TCP/IP as your protocol, you should check that the computer has a valid IP address and subnet mask and, if routing is involved, a valid default router address.

If the user cannot log on because a mandatory profile cannot be found, you can look at a couple of things. First, check that the path to the profile specified in the user's account properties is correct. Be sure that the share name specified is indeed "shared." Next, as with the domain controller, be sure that the server which contains the profile information is accessible by the user. Look at the same suggestions made in the preceding paragraph.

Sometimes network-based errors cannot be easily tracked down. For example, everything may seem to be functioning okay, but you just can't seem to access the network. Sometimes the network card can get confused, and the best approach is to shut down the computer and do a cold boot. A warm boot does not always reset the hardware—in this case, the network card.

Other Logon Problems

Other problems may be related to settings made through the User Manager for Domains. Recall that in this utility the administrator can additionally add logon hour and workstation restrictions for the user, as well as account expiration. Again, the messages that Windows NT displays are fairly obvious in this regard, so they will direct you to the appropriate account property to check and modify.

Summary

This chapter explored user and group accounts, including their creation and management. Account policies and system rights were examined, as well as creating and managing user profiles and troubleshooting issues.

The next chapter will describe an issue that is of paramount importance to any type of network, and one that we have alluded to but not pursued with great diligence: security. We will next discuss the Windows NT security model and how to apply security to resources and make those resources available to the users and groups we have created.

QUESTIONS AND ANSWERS

1. True or False: Passwords and usernames are case sensitive.

   A. False. Passwords are case sensitive, but usernames are not. In all of Windows NT, the operating system is said to be "case preserving," but it is "case sensitive" only with passwords.

2. A UNC path for a file named SCOTCH in a share named TAPE on a server named ROLL would be _____ .

   A. The UNC path would be \\ROLL\TAPE\SCOTCH.

3. True or False: The Password Never Expires check box overrides other parameters such as Maximum Password Age and User Must Change Password.

   A. True.

4. True or False: The Account Policy dialog box shows user rights that can be assigned to groups or individual users.

   A. False. The User Rights dialog box shows user rights that can be assigned to groups or individual users. In the Account Policy dialog box, you can set global parameters for passwords and lockouts.

CH
6

...continues

…continued

> **5.** Audit policies can be configured to log what seven items (success or failure)?
>
> A. Audit policies can be configured to log success or failure of the following seven items:
>
> Logon and Logoff
>
> File and Object Access
>
> Use of User Rights
>
> User and Group Management
>
> Security Policy Changes
>
> Restart, Shutdown, and System
>
> Process Tracking

PRACTICE TEST

1. Which of the following statements is true about the default user accounts created in Windows NT 4.0?

    a. The Administrator account is enabled and can be renamed; the Guest account is enabled and cannot be renamed.

    b. The Administrator account is enabled and cannot be renamed; the Guest account is disabled and cannot be renamed.

    c. The Administrator account is enabled and can be renamed; the Guest account is disabled and can be renamed.

    d. The Administrator account is disabled and cannot be renamed; the Guest account is enabled and can be renamed.

Answer a is incorrect because the Guest account is disabled and can be renamed. Answer b is incorrect because the Administrator account can be renamed, as can the Guest account. **Answer c is correct because, by default, the Administrator account is enabled and can be renamed; the Guest account is disabled and can be renamed.** Answer d is incorrect because the Administrator account is enabled and can be renamed, and the Guest account is disabled.

2. Everyone should be able to read the files in a certain directory. However, the user who created the file should be able to modify it. What do you need to do?

    a. Do nothing. By default, only the creator of a file has access to it. Windows NT restricts resource access by default.

    b. Give the group Everyone read access and the Creator Owner group change access. By default, Windows NT allows everyone complete access to resources.

    c. Give the group Everyone read access and the Creator Owner group change access. By default, Windows NT restricts resource access.

    d. Give the group Everyone read access and the Users group change access. Windows NT automatically determines who the owner of the file is and restricts the other users.

Answer a is wrong because doing nothing does not solve the problem. **Answer b is correct because, to meet the criteria given, you must assign Read access to Everyone and Change access to the Creator Owner group.** Answer c is wrong because NT does not, by default, restrict resource access. Answer d is incorrect.

3. Members of which group have some of the same privileges that Administrators do but cannot fully administer the workstation or domain?

    a. Replicator

    b. Users

    c. Power Users

    d. Supervisor

Answer a is incorrect because the Replicator group is used for Directory Replication. Answer b is wrong because members of the Users group have limited permissions. **Answer c is correct because members of the Power Users group have some of the same privileges that Administrators do but cannot fully administer the workstation or domain.** Answer d is not a group that exists on Windows NT.

4. What are the differences between a local group and a global group? Choose all that apply.

    a. Local groups can be created on workstations, servers, and domain controllers, whereas global groups can be created and maintained only on a domain controller.

    b. Local groups can contain local users, domain users, and global groups, whereas global groups can contain only users from their domain.

    c. Local groups can contain local users, domain users, global groups, and other local groups, whereas global groups can contain only users from their domain.

    d. Local groups can be used for managing resources only on the local computer, whereas global groups can be used to manage resources on any computer that participates in the domain.

CH
6

Answers a, b and d are correct because local groups can be created on any NT machine, whereas global groups can exist only on domain controllers. Additionally, global groups contain users only from their domains and are used to manage resources on any computer that participates in the domain. Answer c is incorrect because local groups cannot contain other local groups.

5. Which of the following sets of usernames and passwords are acceptable for Windows NT?

Username	Password
a. First Ass't Comptroller	FirstComp
b. FirstAsstCompt	1stComp
c. FirstAss*tCompt	COMP1
d. AsstComp1	123COMPTROLLER1

Answer a is invalid due to the apostrophe (') in the username. **Answer b is valid because the username is under 20 characters in length and does not contain invalid characters, and the password is under 14 characters in length and does not contain invalid characters.** Answer c is invalid due to the asterisk (*) in the username. Answer d is invalid due to the length of the password.

6. What is the tool to use to add new users to a Windows NT workstation?

a. User Manager for Domains

b. Server Manager

c. User Manager

d. Task Manager

Answer a is incorrect because User Manager for Domains exists only on NT Server, not NT Workstation. Answer b is incorrect because Server Manager is used for managing services on the domain and is not related to users on the workstation. **Answer c is correct because User Manager is used to add users to a Windows NT Workstation.** Answer d is incorrect because the Task Manager shows running applications and processes and does not allow you to add users.

7. Your boss has advised you that BrownC has left the company and asks you to delete his account from his workstation. Later, your boss hires BrownC back as a consultant and tells you to put his account back on the network. BrownC calls you the next day and informs you gruffly that he can no longer access any of the network resources that he used to. How do you troubleshoot?

a. Use the Registry to set BrownC's SID back to what it was before you deleted his account. He will then be able to access all the old resources.

b. Deleting BrownC's account also deleted his SID. Because security in Windows NT is linked to the user's SID, you need to reestablish all the network resource access that BrownC used to have.

c. Use the Emergency Repair Disk or your last network backup to copy BrownC's old account back to the Registry.

d. Restore the files from a backup tape.

Answer a is incorrect because it is not possible to reuse SIDs. **Answer b is correct because removing the account also removes the SID associated with the files.** Answer c is incorrect because restoring the Registry for one account is not a feasible solution. Answer d is an example of faulty logic. The problem lies not within the data of the files but with the fact that they are associated with the SID number of a user whose account has been deleted. The files restored from tape will still have the same SID associated with them.

8. Under which of the following situations would you disable the user account rather than delete it? More than one answer could be correct.

a. JaneD has left the company on maternity leave and plans to return in three months.

b. JohnB has taken an emergency medical leave of absence for possibly six or more months but hopes to return full time.

c. JaniceD has left the company to take a job at your competitor.

d. FrankP has taken a temporary team leader position in another department and will return when the project is completed.

Answers a, b, and d are correct because deleting a user account should never be undertaken unless leaving that account on poses a serious threat. Under all other circumstances, the account should be disabled. Answer c is incorrect because disabling the account could be a risk in this situation.

9. You are creating multiple user accounts for salespersons, marketers, and programmers. Each set of accounts belongs to the same relative groups (sales users in SALES, marketing users in MARKETING, and programmer users in PROGRAMMERS), uses the same logon scripts (SALES.BAT, MARKET.BAT, PROGRAM.BAT), and saves data in a home directory relative to each group (sales users under USERS\SALES, marketing users under USERS\MARKETERS, programmer users under USERS\PROGRAMMERS). What is the most efficient way to create these users?

a. Create a separate account for each user. As you create the user, use the %USERNAME% environment variable when specifying the home directory to let Windows NT create it for you.

b. Create a template for each type of user. Make the appropriate choices and entries for groups, logon script, and home directory. Use the %USERNAME% environment variable when specifying the home directory to let Windows NT create them for you. Then create each user account by copying the appropriate template.

CH
6

   c. Create all the user accounts without specifying group membership. After they are all created, select each group of users by Ctrl-clicking them, and create the appropriate group.

   d. You must create each user account individually.

Answer a is incorrect because using a template saves time over creating individual user accounts. **Answer b is correct because a template allows you to save a great deal of time over creating individual user accounts.** Answer c is incorrect because it adds additional steps that using a template can save. Answer d is a fallacy because you do not need to create each user account individually.

  10. To provide a greater level of security, you have decided to create an account policy that requires a minimum password length of eight characters, requires that users change their passwords at least once a month, and does not allow users to use the same password twice in two months. Which Account Policy settings are appropriate?

   a. Max Password Age: 60; Min Password Age: 30; Min Password Length: 8; Password Uniqueness: 2

   b. Max Password Age: 30; Min Password Age: 30; Min Password Length: 8; Password Uniqueness: 6

   c. Max Password Age: 30; Min Password Age: 10; Min Password Length: 8; Password Uniqueness: 6

   d. Max Password Age: 60; Min Password Age: 30; Min Password Length: 8; Password Uniqueness: 1

Answer a is incorrect because the password exceeds the maximum desired length of 30 days. Answer b is incorrect because the minimum age is set to the same as the maximum. **Answer c is correct because, to meet the criteria given, the parameters employed must be Max Password Age: 30; Min Password Age: 10; Min Password Length: 8; Password Uniqueness: 6.** Answer d is incorrect because the password exceeds the maximum desired length of 30 days.

CHAPTER PREREQUISITE

Before reading this chapter, you should understand the account management concepts described in Chapter 6 and be comfortable navigating the Windows NT 4.0 interface, especially Explorer (see Chapter 4). You should also be familiar with the Windows NT 4.0 architecture, as described in Chapter 2.

Windows NT 4.0 Security Model

WHILE YOU READ

1. When a user logs on to a domain controller, he or she is granted a(n) _____ that is compared to an access control list for an object to see whether he or she has access to it.

2. In the absence of a domain and the presence of a workgroup, what is the highest level security you can have?

3. True or False: Share permissions apply to local and remote users.

4. True or False: Shares are made hidden by making the first character of the name a dollar sign ($).

5. File ownership, and the transfer thereof, can be accomplished when NT is running on which file systems?

This chapter more thoroughly describes the Windows NT 4.0 security model. The security model itself applies both to Windows NT Workstation and Server 4.0, as does the method of applying permissions and sharing resources.

Examining the Windows NT 4.0 Security Model

All security provided by Windows NT 4.0 is handled through an executive service known as the Security Reference Monitor. When a user logs on, tries to perform a function at the workstation—such as formatting a disk—or tries to access a resource, the Security Reference Monitor determines whether and to what extent to allow access to the user. Logon provides security through password protection. User rights are functional in nature and define what actions a user can take at a given workstation, such as shutting down the workstation or formatting a disk. These issues were described in Chapter 6, "Managing Users and Accounts." Permissions define a user's access to network resources; they define what a user can do to or with a resource, such as delete a print job or modify a file. The terms *rights* and *permissions* are often used interchangeably and usually refer to resource access. With Windows NT, the term *rights* refers to those functional user rights that you can set through the User Manager and User Manager for Domains; the term *permissions* refers to resource access. These terms are used this way throughout this book.

Two types of permissions can be applied in Windows NT: share-level and resource-level. Share-level permissions define how a user can access a resource that has been made available (shared) on the network. This resource resides some place other than the workstation at which the user is sitting, and the user accesses it remotely. The owner or administrator of the resource makes it available as a network resource by sharing it. The owner or administrator of the resource also defines a list of users and groups that can access the resource through the share and determines just how much access to give them.

Resource-level permissions also define a user's access to a resource, but at the resource itself. The owner or administrator of the resource assigns a list of users and groups that can access the resource itself and the level of access to allow. Using these permissions, combined with share-level permissions, the owner and administrator of a resource can provide a high degree of security.

The most common resource-level permissions that you will encounter are those for files and folders. File and folder permissions are available only on NTFS-formatted partitions. If you do not have a partition formatted for NTFS, you can use only the FAT-level properties—Read Only, Archive, System, and Hidden. Under NTFS, you get a more robust set of properties including Read, Write, Delete, Execute, and Change permissions.

Shared devices, such as printers, also provide a means of assigning permissions to use the device—for example, printing to a print device, managing documents on the print device, and so on.

Key Concept

Any resource for which access can be determined is considered to be a security object. In other network operating systems, such as Novell NetWare, permissions to use resources are assigned directly to the user or group and stay with the user or group. This is not true with Windows NT. In all cases, it is important to note that permissions are assigned to and stay with the security object, not the user. A user's access to a resource is determined at the time he or she tries to access it, not when he or she logs on.

When a user logs on to Windows NT, whether at the local workstation or through a domain controller, he or she is granted an access token. Permissions ascribed to an object (resource) reside in an access control list (ACL) with the object. The Security Reference Monitor compares the user's access token information with that in the access control list and determines what level of access to grant the user. Let's explore these concepts further.

Exploring the Windows NT Logon Process

When a user logs on to Windows NT, the username, password, and point of authentication must be provided. This is part of the Winlogon service that monitors the logon process. The Winlogon service passes this information to the CSR (client/server) subsystem, which in turn passes it to the Security Reference Monitor (see Figure 7.1).

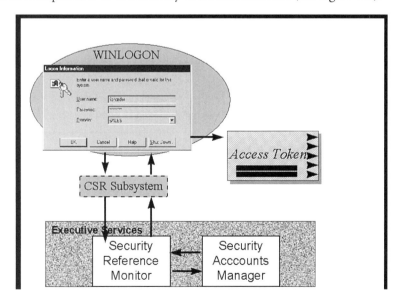

Figure 7.1
This diagram illustrates the Windows NT 4.0 logon process.

CH
7

The Security Reference Monitor checks the information entered against the Security Accounts Manager (SAM) database. If the information is accurate, the Security Reference Monitor authenticates the user and returns a valid access token back to the CSR subsystem and the Winlogon process. The user now has the ability to access the workstation and resources on the network.

The Account Access Token

Many companies that have secured areas provide access to those areas through an electronic key card. A magnetic stripe on the back of the card contains the user's information, such as a security ID. The card is read by a card reader at the point of entry. Often, the user may also have to enter in a security number or password on a keypad before the door is unlocked.

The access token is a lot like a key card. It contains important security information about the user. This information includes, most importantly, the user's SID. Recall that the SID is the unique security identifier that Windows NT assigned to the user's account when the account was created. All security-related requests made by the user are linked to and matched first and foremost against the user's SID. Other information includes the username and password, group memberships by name and group SIDs, profile location, home directory information, logon hours, and so on.

The access token is used by Windows NT to determine whether a user can gain access to a resource and how much access to provide.

Local Versus Domain Access Tokens

When a user logs on to a local Windows NT workstation participating in a workgroup model, the user's account resides in a component of the local Windows NT workstation's Registry (the SAM database portion). Hence, the user's access token is created on that local Windows NT workstation and can be used to access resources only on that workstation.

When a user logs on to a Windows NT workstation that is a member of a domain, the user's account resides in the domain SAM database on the domain controller. Recall that this type of account is called a domain, or global, account because the user can log on once and access any resource in the network that the account has been given permission to use. Hence, the user's access token is created on the domain controller for that domain and can be used (as it is a global account) to access any resource throughout the enterprise domain that the account has been given permission to use.

Because access to remote resources is determined by examining the SIDs for each account in the ACL with the SIDs listed in the user's access token, the point of logon validation affects the user's ability to access a resource.

In a domain, the user and group accounts are global and can be used in the ACL of any resource in the domain. When the user logs on to the domain, the access token contains the user's SID (and group SIDs per group membership) and is global to the network. Both access tokens and ACLs obtain their SIDs from the same SAM database. Thus, the user can access any resource that has given access permission to any SID contained in the user's access token (to the extent that the permission allows).

In a workgroup model, a user's access token is good only on the local Windows NT workstation. A remote resource's ACL consists of SIDs from the local SAM database on the Windows NT computer on which the resource resides. If the user has an account on that remote computer, the user's SID on that computer is necessarily different (see Chapter 6) from the SID the user gets when he or she logs on to his or her own computer. When the user tries to access the remote resource that has been shared in the workgroup, the two SIDs (access token and ACL) do not match, and the user is never able to access the resource.

Even if the administrator of the remote computer creates an account for the user, that account has a different SID.

Windows NT uses a process called pass-through authentication to validate the user on the remote computer. Windows NT takes the username and password from the user's access token on the local workstation rather than the SID and "passes it through" to the remote computer. There, the user is, in effect, logged on to the remote computer, and a new access token is created there with the user's account and group SIDs from the remote computer's SAM database. The user can then access resources on that computer to which the ACL grants permission.

This process works great as long as the username and password match on both the local workstation and the remote resource computer. If they do not, the user can still access the resource through pass-through authentication but has to supply a password as well. The user also has the option of connecting to a remote resource using a different account— that is, an account that is valid on the remote workstation.

Let's look at an example. If Computer1 has BrownC with password ABC, and BrownC wants to access a shared printer on Computer2, the first thing the print administrator must do is add BrownC to the ACL for the printer. However, in a workgroup setting, the administrator of Computer2 can only add members of Computer2's SAM database to the printer's ACL. This means that an account for BrownC must be created on Computer2 and added to the ACL for the printer. If BrownC's account on Computer2 also expects password ABC, then Windows NT uses pass-through authentication to pass "BrownC" and "ABC" from BrownC's access token on Computer1 to the Security Reference Monitor on Computer2 to be authenticated. A new access token is created for BrownC on Computer2. This token can be used successfully to access the printer because now the SID for BrownC on Computer2 matches the SID for BrownC in the ACL for the printer.

CH

7

If the passwords do not match, BrownC can still access the printer, but he has to connect to it by supplying the password for his account on Computer2. Similarly, if BrownC does not have an account on Computer2 but knows the username and password for a valid account on Computer2, say VanPeltL, he can connect to the printer by supplying both the username and password that are valid on Computer2.

Examining Access Control Lists

When a key card is read by the card reader, the information on the card is generally checked against a central database to see whether this user has the appropriate level of access to be let in the secured area. The database may indicate that the card holder has full access and allows the door to open, or the database may indicate that the card holder has minimum access and allows only a window in the door to open. If the access token is thought of as the key card for access to secured areas, an access control list can be thought of as the card reader database.

An access control list, hereafter referred to as the ACL, is just that—a list of users and groups that have some level of access to the resource. It is created at the object (resource or share) level and stays with the security object. It consists of user and group account entries that reference the accounts' SIDs rather than the accounts' names. These entries are called access control entries, or ACEs. Each entry has a particular level of permission associated with it, such as Read Only, Full Control, or No Access.

How ACLs Determine Access

When a user tries to access a resource, the request is passed once again to the Security Reference Monitor. The Security Reference Monitor acts here as the card reader. It checks the SID entries in the access token against the SID entries in the ACL (see Figure 7.2).

The Security Reference Monitor determines all matches, evaluates the permissions assigned to each matching entry, and calculates an overall permission level for the user, which becomes the user's effective access to the resource. It then returns that effective access as a security "handle" to the object—for example, Read and Write permissions for a file. The security handle becomes part of the access token for as long as the user accesses the object.

 Key Concept

As long as the user maintains access to the object, the same security handle is in effect, even if the owner or administrator of the resource changes the user's access. The changed permissions do not take effect for the user until the user releases control of the object and tries to access it again. For example, if BrownC has full access to a file he has opened, and the owner of the file decides to restrict BrownC to Read Only, BrownC continues to have Full Control until he closes the file and tries to open it again.

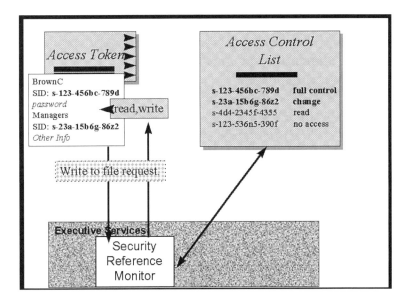

Figure 7.2
This diagram illustrates the security access process.

Sharing Resources and Determining Network Access

A resource such as a folder or printer is made available as a network resource by sharing it. For simplicity, we'll discuss printer sharing in Chapter 9, "Managing Printers."

Only a Power User or Administrator can share a resource on a workstation or server. In addition, the Server service must be running, and the network card must be operational. If you suspect a problem with the Server service or the network card, a good place to begin troubleshooting is the Event Viewer. Look for any devices or services that failed to start.

Sharing a folder is a relatively simple process. You share a folder by selecting the file or folder through Windows Explorer or My Computer, right-clicking it, and choosing Sharing, or through the object's Properties sheet. Figure 7.3 shows an example of a folder that has been shared.

Sharing is enabled by clicking the Shared As option. When you share a folder, the share name defaults to the folder name but can be changed to be more descriptive for its potential users. You can also indicate the number of users allowed to access the share at a time or accept the default of Maximum Allowed.

CH

7

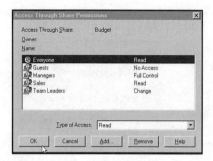

Figure 7.3
My Documents has been shared with the name Budget. Notice the list of groups and
the permissions assigned to each.

Recall that the maximum number of remote connections allowed on a Windows NT
workstation is 10. On a server, the number of connections is effectively unlimited, except
as defined by the license option chosen.

If you go no further, Windows NT shares this resource to any and all users. The default
permission for every shared resource is Everyone with Full Control.

Key Concept

Windows NT's philosophy of sharing resources is to make information readily
and easily available. Therefore, the default is to give every network user access
to the resource. Hence, the default permission is always Everyone with Full
Control.

If you want to add a layer of security to the shared folder, you must choose Permissions
and then Add to add the appropriate group and user accounts, modifying the permissions
as necessary. By doing so, you are creating and modifying the ACL for the folder.

Key Concept

It is recommended that you either remove the Everyone group and explicitly
assign permissions to specific users and groups, or give Everyone the least level
of access (Read) to provide a greater level of security. Do not give the Everyone
group No Access. Because every network user is automatically a member of
Everyone, giving this group No Access results in locking every user—even the
owner and administrator—out of that shared resource.

You can assign four share-level permissions in your ACL. They are defined in Table 7.1.

Table 7.1   Permissions for Shared Folders

Permission	Effect
Read	Displays the folder and filenames; allows files to be opened and programs to be run; allows similar access to subfolders.
Change	In addition to read permissions, allows changes to be made to files and folders, including creating and deleting files and folders.
Full Control	Allows complete access to the folder and its files and subfolders, including the ability to take ownership of files and change permissions of files and folders.
No Access	Denies access to the folder and its contents.

Key Concept

Note that share permissions take effect for a user accessing the resource remotely over the network. If the user sits down at a computer that has the folder, and no other permissions have been assigned, the user still has complete access to the folder and its files.

If two or more users attempt to access the same file at the same time, the first user is able to modify the file, and the rest see the file in a read-only fashion.

Permissions assigned to a folder also apply to all files and folders within the shared folder. For example, if you give Sales Read permissions for the folder DATA, the members of the Sales group also have Read permissions for all files and subfolders within DATA.

Effective Permissions

The Security Reference Monitor checks the user's access token against the entries in the ACL, as we have seen. When it identifies a match or matches, it then must determine the permissions to give the user. The effective share permissions are cumulative. The permissions explicitly assigned to a user, as well as permissions assigned to any groups that the user is a member of, are added together, and the highest level of permission is granted to the user. The only exception to this rule is the No Access permission, which always denies access regardless of the other permissions assigned.

For example, suppose BrownC is a member of Managers and Sales. BrownC has been given Change access, Managers has been given Full Control, and Sales has been given Read access to a shared folder. BrownC's effective permissions are Full Control by virtue of his membership in the Managers group.

CH
7

However, No Access always supersedes any other permission, even Full Control. Using the same example, if BrownC is given No Access explicitly, he is not able to access the shared folder, even though he is a member of the Managers group, which has Full Control.

It is important, therefore, that you take sufficient time to plan your shared folders and their permissions. Let's look at the home directory folders as an example. Suppose that users' home directories are created under a share called Users. By default, Users are shared to Everyone with Full Control. This means that all files and folders within Users also give Everyone Full Control. Thus, all network users can see all other users' files in their home directories. This is probably not a good idea.

So how can we fix this problem? Here is one suggestion: Change the share permissions for Users to remove Everyone, and add Administrators with Full Control (or at least Read). Share each home directory to the appropriate user explicitly with Full Control, and change the users' properties through the User Manager appropriately. Now, while Administrators can access everything for security reasons (and because they like the power), each user can access only his or her own home directory.

Administrative and Hidden Shares

When Windows NT is installed, it creates several shares, called administrative shares, all of which are hidden—except for NETLOGON. Hidden shares exist but cannot be seen by any user in lists of available shared resources. They are meant to be used either by the operating system for specific tasks and services, such as IPC$ and REPL$, or by an administrator for security access or troubleshooting, such as the root drive shares.

Table 7.2 summarizes these administrative shares.

Table 7.2   Administrative Shares

Share Name	Description
drive$	The root directory of every partition that Windows NT can recognize is assigned an administrative share name consisting of the drive letter followed by the $. Administrators, Server Operators, and Backup Operators can connect to these shares remotely.
Admin$	This administrative share is used by the operating system during remote administration of the computer; it represents the directory into which the Windows NT system files were installed (such as C:\WINNT40). Administrators, Server Operators, and Backup Operators can connect to these shares remotely.

Share Name	Description
IPC$	This administrative share represents the named pipes that are used for communication between programs and systems; it is used by the operating system during remote administration of a computer and when accessing another computer's shared resources.
Netlogon	This administrative share is created and used on domain controllers only for authenticating users logging on to the enterprise domain.
Print$	Similar to IPC$, this administrative share provides remote access support for shared printers.
REPL$	This administrative share is created and used on a Windows NT server computer when the Directory Replication service is configured and enabled. It identifies the location of the directories and files to be exported.

Hidden shares can be identified by the $ after the share name. As an administrator, you can view all the administrative shares on a computer by starting the Server applet from the Control Panel and viewing Shares (or by starting Server Manager on a Windows NT server, viewing a computer's properties, and then its shares).

You can also create hidden shares yourself by adding the $ to the end of the share name that you enter. This way, you can keep certain shares more secure. The only users who can connect to them are those who know the share name.

Accessing a Shared Folder

A user can access a shared folder in several ways (assuming that the user has been given permission to do so). Shares can be accessed by connecting directly to the resource through Network Neighborhood or the Find command, or by mapping a drive letter to a shared folder through My Computer or Windows Explorer.

All four utilities offer a point-and-click method of accessing the resource, which means that you do not necessarily have to know where the resource is exactly. With Network Neighborhood and Find, you do not waste a drive letter on the resource. With My Computer and Windows Explorer, you utilize a drive letter for every mapping you create—and the alphabet is not an unlimited list.

Network Neighborhood

Perhaps the easiest way to connect to a shared folder is to use Network Neighborhood, especially if you need only occasional or short access to the folder and its contents (see Figure 7.4).

CH
7

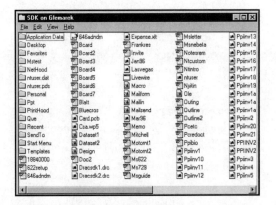

Figure 7.4
Network Neighborhood is used here to display the contents of the SDK folder shared
on the computer Glemarek.

To connect to a shared folder using Network Neighborhood, follow these steps:

1. Double-click Network Neighborhood.

   All members of your workgroup are listed under Entire Network.

2. Double-click the computer that has the shared folder to display a list of its shared
   folders.

3. Double-click the appropriate share name to see the contents of that folder.

Or, if you participate in a domain, follow these steps instead:

1. Double-click Network Neighborhood.

   All members of your workgroup are listed under Entire Network.

2. Double-click Entire Network and then Microsoft Network to see a list of domains.

3. Select your domain, and double-click to see a list of computers in the domain that
   contain shared folders.

4. Double-click the computer that has the shared folder to display a list of shared
   folders.

5. Double-click the appropriate share name to see the contents of that folder.

Find Command

The Find command on the Start menu can be used effectively to search for computers
that do not show up right away in a browse list like Network Neighborhood displays, or
for a specific file or folder in a shared folder whose name you cannot recall.

To find a computer, follow these steps:

1. Choose Start, Find, and then Computer from the taskbar.
2. In the Computer Name box, enter the name of the computer that has the shared folder.
3. Choose Find Now. Find displays a window showing the computer it finds.
4. Double-click the computer to display its shared folders.
5. Double-click the appropriate share name to display its contents.

Follow these steps to find a file or folder by name:

1. Choose Start, Find, and then Files or Folders from the taskbar.
2. In the Look In box, enter the name of the computer that contains the shared folder. Or you can choose Browse to browse the Network Neighborhood entry to find the computer.
3. In the Named box, enter the name of the file or folder that you are looking for.
4. Choose Find Now. Find displays a window with its search results. Double-click the appropriate file or folder to work with it.

All the Find options are available to help narrow your search, such as Date Modified and Advanced. For example, if you are just looking for a folder contained in some share on a computer, you can use Advanced to narrow the search only to folders.

My Computer and Windows Explorer

My Computer can be used to map a network drive to a shared folder on a computer. This process is similar to the way logical drives are assigned to Novell NetWare resources, if you are familiar with that network operating system (see Figure 7.5).

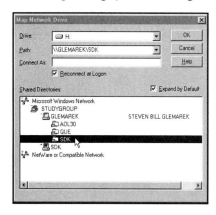

CH
7

Figure 7.5
Here, we are making the same connection as in Figure 7.4. Through My Computer, we expand through the Microsoft Windows Network to find the computer Glemarek in the workgroup Studygroup, and display its shares.

Using Windows Explorer is probably closest to using the File Manager in previous versions of Windows NT or Windows for Workgroups. It displays a Map Network Drive dialog box similar to that used with My Computer, and in fact, they both operate the same way.

To map to a shared folder using My Computer, follow these steps:

1. Right-click My Computer and choose Map Network Drive. Or you can start Windows Explorer, and choose Tools, Map Network Drive.

2. The next available drive letter is displayed in the Drive box. Select it or make another choice of letter.

3. Double-click the appropriate network entry in the Shared Directories list box to display a browse list of workgroups and domains.

4. Double-click the workgroup or domain that contains the sharing computer to display a list of computers with shared resources.

5. Double-click the appropriate computer to display its list of shared resources.

6. Select the appropriate shared folder from the list.

Or, if you do not see the computer or folder in the browse list but know the name of the computer and share, follow these steps:

1. Right-click My Computer and choose Map Network Drive. Or you can start Windows Explorer, and choose Tools, Map Network Drive.

2. The next available drive letter is displayed in the Drive box. Select it or make another choice of letter.

3. In the Path box, enter the UNC name to the shared folder using the convention *server**share*, where *server* represents the name of the computer that has the shared folder, and *share* represents the name of the shared folder.

4. Click OK.

In Figure 7.5, notice that the check box Reconnect at Logon is selected by default. This is known as a persistent connection. If you do not deselect this box, drive H is reconnected to the share every time the user logs in. If the user accesses this resource frequently, then this tool is convenient. If not, then you are just taking up extra system resources to locate the shared folder, make the connection, and monitor for access.

You can disconnect mapped drives when they are no longer needed by right-clicking My Computer and choosing Disconnect Network Drive, or by choosing Tools, Disconnect Network Drive Windows Explorer. Select the drive from the list that you want to disconnect, and click OK.

Also, you might need to access a resource on a computer on which you do not have a valid user account. Accessing a resource this way is particularly possible in workgroup configurations, or in the case of administrative access to various workstations or servers. If you know the name and password of a valid user account on that computer (including Guest), you can enter the UNC name in the Path box, as described in step 3 of the preceding steps, and then enter the name of the valid account in the <u>C</u>onnect As box. Windows NT asks you for the password, if it is required or different from your own, before connecting you to the resource.

Securing Folders and Files with NTFS Permissions

Up to this point, we have discussed how to make resources available to other network users, how to secure those resources that you share on the network, and how you access them. Yet another level of security can be applied to files and folders stored on an NTFS partition. Among the many benefits of formatting a partition as NTFS, Windows NT's own file system, is the ability to assign permissions directly to the file and folder—that is, at the resource level.

You set permissions for a file or folder by right-clicking the file or folder, displaying its Properties sheet, and selecting the Security tab. Choosing Permissions here displays the file or folders permissions dialog box from which you can make your choices.

Effective File and Folder Permissions

When you assign permissions to a folder or file, you are creating an ACL for that folder or file, much like you did for the share. The Security Reference Monitor checks the user's access token against the entries in the ACL, as we have seen. When it identifies a match or matches, it then must determine the permissions to give the user. The effective file or folder permissions are cumulative. The permissions explicitly assigned to a user, as well as permissions assigned to any groups that the user is a member of, are added together, and the highest level of permission is granted to the user at the file or folder level.

For example, suppose BrownC is a member of Managers and Sales. BrownC has been given Change access to a particular file, Managers has been given Full Control, and Sales has been given Read access to the file. BrownC's effective permissions for that file are Full Control by virtue of his membership in the Managers group.

The only exception to this rule is No Access. No Access always supersedes any other permission, even Full Control. Using the same example, if BrownC is given No Access explicitly, he is not able to access the file, even though he is a member of the Managers group, which has Full Control.

Unlike share permissions, which are effective for all files and folders within the share, folder and file permissions are effective only for the immediate folder and its contents, or for an individual file if applied to that file. The permissions for files in a folder, or for subfolders, can trickle down but can also be applied individually. If permissions have been applied to an individual file, the file permission always supersedes the folder permission.

For example, if BrownC has been given Read permission for the folder Data and Change permission to the file budget.doc, BrownC's effective permission for the file budget.doc is Change, even though, because of the folder permission, he has read permission to all the other files in Data.

As you can see, you have a great deal of discretion and control over the application of permissions to folders, subfolders, and files. It is important, therefore, that you take sufficient time to plan your folder and file permissions. Let's take a different look at the home directory folders as an example. Suppose that users' home directories are created under a share called Users. By default, Users are shared to Everyone with Full Control. If the home folders are on an NTFS partition, you can assign each user the NTFS permission Full Control to his own or her home folder only while assigning the Everyone group List access to the directory. This assignment effectively restricts access to each folder only to the owner of the folder.

Assigning File and Folder Permissions

Six individual permissions can be applied to files and folders. Table 7.3 describes these permissions.

Table 7.3   NTFS File and Folder Permissions

Permission	Folder Level	File Level
Read (R)	Can display folders, attributes, owner, and permissions	Can display files attributes, and file data owner and permissions
Write (W)	Can add files and create subfolders, change folder attributes, and display folder owner and permissions	Can change file contents and attributes, and display file owner and permissions
Execute (EX)	Can make changes to subfolders and display folder owners' attributes and permissions	Can run executable files and display file owner, attributes, and permissions
Delete (D)	Can delete a folder	Can delete a file
Change Permission (P)	Can change folder permissions	Can change file permissions
Take Ownership (O)	Can take ownership	Can take ownership of a folder of a file

Files and folders can be assigned these permissions individually or more often by using standard groupings provided by Windows NT security. The nine standard folder permissions include two choices for setting your own custom choice of folder permissions and file permissions to apply to all files in a folder. The five standard file permissions include an option for setting your own custom choice of file permissions per individual file. Tables 7.4 and 7.5 outline these permissions and what they allow the user to do.

Note that when you're viewing and setting permissions, Windows NT always displays the individual permissions in parentheses alongside the standard permission. For Folder permissions, the first set of parentheses represents the permissions on the folder, and the second set represents the permissions that apply to files globally, including any new file created in the folder.

Table 7.4   Standard Permissions for Folders

Permission	Access
No Access (None)(None)	Supersedes all other file permissions and prevents access to the file.
List (RX)(Not Specified)	Allows the user to view folders and subfolders and filenames within folders and subfolders. List is not available as a valid permission option for files.
Read (RX)(RX)	In addition to List access, the user can display file contents and subfolders and run executable files.
Add (WX)(Not Specified)	The user can add files to the folder but not list its contents. Add is not available as a valid permission option for files.
Add and Read (RWX)(RX)	In addition to Add, the user can display the contents of files and subfolders and run executable files.
Change (RWXD)(RWXD)	This permission allows the user to display and add files and folders, modify the contents of files and folders, and run executable files.
Full Control (All)(All)	In addition to Change, this permission allows the user to modify folder and file permissions and take ownership of folders and files.
Special Directory Access	This permission allows the selection of any combination of individual permissions (R,W,E,D,P,O) for folder access.
Special File Access	This permission allows the selection of any combination of individual permissions (R,W,E,D,P,O) for file access.

Table 7.5   Standard Permissions for Files

Permission	Access
No Access (None)	No access is allowed to the file.
Read (RX)	This permission allows the user to display file data and run executable files.
Change (RWXD)	In addition to Read, the user can modify the file contents and delete the file.
Full Control (All)	In addition to Change, the user can modify the file's permissions and take ownership of the file.
Special Access	This permission allows the selection of any combination of individual permissions (R,W,E,D,P,O) for a file.

Key Concept

The Folder permission Full Control provides the user an inherent ability to delete files in a folder even if the user is given No Access permission to a specific file. This is done to preserve Posix application support on UNIX systems, for which Write permission on a folder allows the user to delete files in the folder. This permission can be superseded by choosing the Special Directory Access standard permission and checking all the individual permissions.

You set permissions for a file or folder by right-clicking the file or folder, displaying its Properties sheet, and selecting the Security tab. Choosing Permissions here displays the file or folders permissions dialog box, as shown in Figure 7.6, from which you can make your choices.

Figure 7.6
The Public folder's permission list (ACL) shows that Administrators has Full Control, Everyone has Read, and Managers has Change. The Type of Access list box displays the standard permission options.

In the Directory Permissions dialog box shown in Figure 7.6, notice the two Replace choices: Replace Permissions on Subdirectories and Replace Permissions on Existing Files (which is selected by default).

Key Concept

The effect of Replace Permissions on Existing Files is to change any and all permissions that you set on individual files with the permissions that you set at the folder level. Because this option is selected by default, you can easily forget it when setting permissions at the folder level, and you can accidentally change permissions on files that you do not want to change. Bottom line: Read all screens carefully.

Choosing Replace Permissions on Subdirectories causes Windows NT to apply the permissions set at this folder level to all subfolders. If Replace Permissions on Existing Files is also left selected, the permissions are applied not only to the subfolders, but to their contents as well.

The Type of Access list box shows all the standard permissions that are available at the folder level, including the two special options, Special Directory Access and Special File Access, from which you can customize your choice of permissions.

As with share permissions, you can add or remove users and groups from the ACL by using the Add and Remove buttons.

Determining Access When Using Share and NTFS Permissions

A folder (and its contents) is made accessible across the network by sharing it. As we have discussed, an ACL can be created for the share. It defines which users and group accounts can access the share and the level of access allowed. We know that the effective permissions are cumulative at the share level.

When NTFS permissions are assigned to individual folders and files, the level of access can be further refined by creating an ACL at the file and folder level. We know that the effective permissions at the file and folder level are also cumulative.

When a user accesses a file or folder protected by NTFS permissions across the network through a share, the Security Reference Monitor determines the cumulative permissions at the share and the cumulative permissions at the file or folder. Whichever permission is most restrictive becomes the effective permission for the user.

For example, if BrownC, a member of the Managers group, has been given Read access individually and Change access through the Managers group to a share called Public, then BrownC's effective permission for Public is Change. If BrownC has been given Read access to the file budget.doc (contained in the folder that has been shared as Public) and Full Control through the Managers group, BrownC's effective permission at the file level is Full Control. However, BrownC's net effective permission to budget.doc, when accessing it through the network share, is Change, which is the more restrictive of the two permissions.

Through a shrewd use of share and file- and folder-level permissions, you can create a very effective security structure for resources stored on your Windows NT workstations and servers.

Understanding the Concept of Ownership

The user who creates a file or folder is noted by Windows NT to be the owner of that file or folder, and is placed in the Creator Owner internal group for that file or folder. A user cannot give someone else ownership of his or her files or folders. However, a user can give someone the permission to take ownership of his or her files and folders.

The Take Ownership permission is implied through Full Control but can also be assigned to a user or group through the Special Access permission options. A user who has this permission can take ownership of the file or folder. After ownership has been taken, the new owner can modify the file or folder's permissions, delete the file, and so on. Administrators always have the ability to take ownership of a file or folder.

Taking Ownership

If you're the user who has the Take Ownership permission, you can take ownership of a folder or file by following these steps:

1. Right-click the folder or file, and select Properties.
2. In the Properties sheet, select the Security tab.
3. On the Security tab, choose Ownership. The current owner is displayed.
4. Choose Take Ownership, and then click OK.

If any member of the Administrators group takes ownership of a file or folder or creates a file or folder, the owner becomes the Administrators group.

Taking ownership of files and folders can be useful, especially when users move around from department to department or position to position, or leave the organization. It provides a way to assign files and folders that are no longer being used by a user to an appropriate replacement.

Copying and Moving Files...and Permissions

When you copy a file from one folder to another, the file assumes the permissions of the target folder. When you move a file from one folder to another, the file maintains its current permissions. This concept sounds simple enough, except that a move isn't always a move. When you move a file from a folder in one partition to another, you are actually copying the file to the target folder and then deleting the original file. A move is only a move where permissions are involved when you move a file from a folder in one partition to another folder in the same partition.

Troubleshooting Security

The most likely problem that you will have with security is a user who is unable to access a resource. In this case, we cannot offer much additional advice besides what has been said already. In other words, you must go back and check the share permissions and file and folder permissions. Remember that, at the share level and at the file and folder level, permissions are cumulative. However, when comparing share permissions to file and folder permissions, Windows NT assigns the most restrictive permission to the user.

When changing permissions on a share, file, or folder, the user will not notice the effect of the change until the next time the resource is accessed because of the way Windows NT assigns the permission to the user. Recall that when the user's access token is compared to the ACL, and the effective permission established, the user's access token receives a permission handle to the resource. This handle remains in effect until the user releases the resource.

For example, BrownC has the effective permission Change to budget.doc. The owner of budget.doc decides to restrict BrownC to Read. While BrownC has budget.doc open and in use, his effective permission remains Change. When he closes budget.doc and opens it later, his effective permission is Read.

Suppose BrownC has established a logical drive mapping to the Data share and has the effective permission Change to the share. The owner of the share changes BrownC's permission to Read. BrownC continues to maintain Change permission to the share until he disconnects from it and reconnects, or until he logs off and logs back on.

Similarly, suppose BrownC is currently a member of the Managers group. BrownC has Read permission to the Data folder but Full Control effective permission through his membership in the Managers group. You take BrownC out of the Managers group to ensure that he has only Read access to the folder. When BrownC accesses the folder, he still has Full Control access to the folder because his access token still maintains that he has membership in the Managers group. Remember that the access token is created during logon. Thus, the group change is not effective until BrownC logs off and logs back on.

CH

7

Summary

This chapter explored all aspects of security, including permissions, shared folders, the logon process, and the security model.

In Chapter 8, "Managing Disk Resources," we will take a closer look at NTFS and what benefits it can offer. Also, we will begin a discussion of disk management through Windows NT 4.0, highlighting the Disk Administrator utility.

QUESTIONS AND ANSWERS

1. When a user logs on to a domain controller, he or she is granted a(n) _____ that is compared to an access control list for an object to see whether he or she has access to it.

    A. The user is granted a token. When you change a user's permissions, the changes become effective only when logged on. At the next logon, the user gets a new token.

2. In the absence of a domain and the presence of a workgroup, what is the highest level security you can have?

    A. The highest level security you can have is share level. In the presence of an authenticating server (a domain), the highest level of security you can have is user level.

3. True or False: Share permissions apply to local and remote users.

    A. False. Share permissions apply only to remote users, not to local users.

4. True or False: Shares are made hidden by making the first character of the name a dollar sign ($).

    A. False. Shares are made hidden by making the last character of the name a dollar sign ($), not the first.

5. File ownership, and the transfer thereof, can be accomplished when NT is running on which file systems?

    A. File ownership, and the transfer thereof, can be accomplished when NT is running on NTFS only.

PRACTICE TEST

1. A user's effective access to a resource is determined by _____.
   a. Comparing the rights of the user with the permissions assigned through the ACL of the resource.
   b. Comparing the permissions in the access token of the user with the permissions assigned through the ACL of the resource.
   c. Comparing the user and group SID entries in the user's access token with the permissions assigned through the ACL of the resource.
   d. Comparing the user and group SID entries in the user's access token with the user rights listed in the ACL of the resource.

Answers a and b are incorrect because user *and* group SIDs are compared. **Answer c is correct because a user's effective access to a resource is determined by comparing the permissions in the access token of the user with the permissions assigned through the ACL of the resource.** Answer d is incorrect because user rights are not examined by permissions assigned to the resource.

2. The Sales department recently acquired a laser-quality printer with an envelope feed that has been installed on its print server called SalesPrint. The sales staff are already members of the local group SALES on SalesPrint. The print operator shared the printer with the default permission. The sales staff can access the printer, but so can everyone else in the domain. What else must you do to ensure that only sales staff can access the printer?
   a. Assign the Sales group Print access to the printer.
   b. Assign the Sales group Print access to the printer, and remove the Everyone group.
   c. Do nothing else.
   d. Assign the Sales group Print access to the printer, and give the Everyone group Read access.

Answer a is incorrect because Everyone still has access. **Answer b is correct because the Sales group must be given access to the printer to use it, and removing Everyone prohibits others from using it.** Answer c is incorrect because it does not address the problem. Answer d is incorrect because you cannot assign Read access to a printer.

3. Where does the permission list defining access to a resource reside and what is it called?
   a. With the resource; it's called the access control list.
   b. With the user; it's called the User Rights Policy.

   c. With the user; it's called the access control list.

   d. With the resource; it's called the User Rights Policy.

Answer a is correct because the permission list defining access to a resource resides with the resource and is called the access control list (ACL). Answers b and c are incorrect because the permission list stays with the resource. Answer d is incorrect because the permission list is known as the access control list.

  6. Arlo, a member of the Developers group, is currently editing the file DOOM.DOC in the share TOOLS. The administrator of the share changes permission to the Developers group from Change to Read. Arlo continues to make changes to the document. What else must the administrator do to restrict Arlo's access?

   a. Take Arlo out of the Developers group.

   b. Give Arlo No Access explicitly.

   c. Disconnect Arlo from the resource.

   d. Nothing. Arlo must disconnect from the share and then reconnect before the new permission will take effect.

Answers a and b do not address the issue that Arlo must get a new access token. Answer c is incorrect because it does not address the problem. **Answer d is correct because the user must disconnect from the share and access it again to get a new (updated) token.**

  7. The administrator of the TOOLS shared folder wants to limit access to the folder only to the Developers group. To do so, she gives the Everyone group No Access and the Developers group Change access. The Developers complain that they cannot access any file in TOOLS. What else must the administrator do?

   a. Share the files in the TOOLS folder.

   b. Remove the Everyone group.

   c. Give the Developers group Full Control.

   d. Format the partition as NTFS, and assign NTFS permissions in addition to the share permissions.

Answers a and c are incorrect because Everyone can still access the folder. **Answer b is correct because Everyone includes Developers, and leaving the Everyone group there would effectively give No Access to the Developers.** Answer d is incorrect because it does not address the problem in a logical manner. The problem relates to permissions, and formatting the drive is a larger undertaking than needed to solve the problem.

8. Ned is a member of the Developers group at Springfield Technologies. This group has been recently assigned additional responsibilities. As a result of the new assignments, Ned needs to edit the DOOM.DOC file in the Tools folder but does not have Write access. What must you do to give Ned—and other Developers—access to DOOM.DOC?

   a. Do nothing. The next time Ned logs on, his permissions will change.

   b. Change the Developers group permission to Change.

   c. Add Ned to the Team Leaders group, and have him log in again.

   d. Change the Team Leaders group permission to Full Control.

Answer a is incorrect because avoidance does not solve the problem. **Answer b is correct.** Changing the Developers group permission to Change solves this problem. Answers c and d are incorrect because no Team Leaders group is mentioned.

9. The TOOLS folder has been shared with the Developers group with Change permission. DOOM is a subdirectory under TOOLS. Team Leaders should have access only to DOOM with Read permissions. What can you do to give these permissions?

   a. Add Team Leaders to the TOOLS share with Read permission.

   b. Create a new share called DOOM, and give Team Leaders Read permission to it.

   c. Add Team Leaders to the TOOLS share with Change permission.

   d. Add Team Leaders to the TOOLS share with No Access and to the DOOM subdirectory with Read.

Answer a is incorrect because the rights will accumulate. **Answer b is correct.** Creating a new share called DOOM and giving Team Leaders Read permission to it will address the needs. Answer c is incorrect because the rights will accumulate. Answer d is incorrect because the Team Leaders still need access to TOOLS.

10. The manager of the Accounting department wants to make next year's budget templates available for the staff accountants to review beginning next month. Staff accountants are already members of a global group called Accountants in CORPDOMAIN. The templates will be stored on the department resource server called ACCT1 in a folder called BUDGET97 on an NTFS partition. The folder has been shared with the default permission, which you do not want to change. What tool can you use to perform these operations on Windows NT Workstation?

   a. User Manager for Domains

   b. User Manager

       c. Server Manager

       d. None of the above.

Answer a is incorrect because User Manager for Domains is the correct tool to use, but it exists only on NT Server, not NT Workstation. Answer b is incorrect because the User Manager cannot work with global groups. Answer c is incorrect because the Server Manager is the wrong tool for working with users and does not exist on NT Workstation at all. **Answer d is correct.** The User Manager for Domains is the correct tool to use, but it exists only on NT Server, not NT Workstation.

CHAPTER PREREQUISITE

Before reading this chapter, you should be familiar with basic disk concepts such as drives, partitions, folders, and files. You should also be comfortable with the security concepts described in Chapter 7, "Windows NT 4.0 Security Model."

Managing Disk Resources

— WHILE YOU READ —

1. NTFS supports disks to a theoretical size of _____.

2. File compression can be accomplished from the command line with what utility?

3. What is the type of backup that includes only files and folders that have changed since the last backup and sets their archive bit off?

4. True or False: Backups can be automated with the CRON utility included with NT.

5. True or False: The Backup utility included with Windows NT Workstation 4.0 can be used to back up the local Registry.

Throughout the first half of this book, we examined installation issues, configuration methods and concerns, the Windows NT Registry, account management, and resource security. In the rest of this book, we'll cover additional management topics such as disk and printer management, application support, network connectivity, and suggestions for tuning Windows NT. As always, we are approaching these topics from the workstation point of view. Nevertheless, concepts described here are nearly always applicable within the larger enterprise environment. As before, wherever practical, we will continue to call your attention to specific information relating to Windows NT Server 4.0 as a point of comparison.

Understanding Partitions

Before a computer can be used effectively, an operating system must be installed. Before an operating system can be installed, the computer's hard disk or disks must be partitioned into the storage space required by the operating system and the user, and formatted with a file system supported by the operating system, such as File Allocation Table (FAT).

Many types of partitions are supported by Windows NT Workstation and Server 4.0. The most common that you will encounter are primary and extended. Others include volume sets and stripe sets. Windows NT Server 4.0 adds fault-tolerant partition options, such as stripe sets with parity and disk mirroring.

In MS-DOS, the primary partition contains the boot files needed to start MS-DOS and initialize the system. It is also called the active partition, and it cannot be subdivided any further. Under Windows NT 4.0, a primary partition usually holds the operating system files for Windows NT or an alternate operating system but can also designate simply another data or application storage place. Up to four primary partitions are supported per physical disk device under Windows NT 4.0. MS-DOS can recognize only one primary partition per physical disk device, and to dual-boot to MS-DOS (or Windows 95), that partition must also be marked as the active partition.

An extended partition offers a way to get beyond the four-partition limit and subdivide a partition into more than four logical drives. Consequently, an extended partition usually comprises the remaining free space on a disk after the primary partition is created. Because MS-DOS recognizes only one primary (active) partition per physical disk, logical drives in an extended partition provide a way to support a larger number of "drives" under MS-DOS. A logical drive is virtually the same as a partition, except that from the MS-DOS and Windows NT point of view, it is a division within a partition. The use of logical drives allows greater control and flexibility for the disk administrator over the storage of applications and data on the physical disk.

There is also the matter of simple arithmetic in the way that Windows NT counts partitions. This counting scheme becomes more of a concern for Windows NT when the

CH
8

partition scheme changes frequently or when troubleshooting with a boot disk among a variety of Windows NT computers because it involves the ARC path to the Windows NT system files.

The ARC path, as you may recall from Chapter 3, "Installing Windows NT Workstation 4.0," specifies the physical location of the partition that contains the Windows NT operating system files (the WINNT40 installation directory). The following is an example of an ARC path used by the BOOT.INI file:

    multi(0)disk(0)rdisk(0)partition(2)

According to this path, the WINNT40 directory can be found on the second partition of the first physical drive attached to the first physical controller card. Because the ARC path involves the physical path—which includes the controller, disk device, and partition number—if partition schemes change frequently, the partition number of the Windows NT system partition could also change.

Windows NT always counts the active primary partition first, or the first primary partition on each additional physical disk, then other primary partitions from the first to the last physical disk, and then the logical drives from the first physical disk to the last (see Figure 8.1).

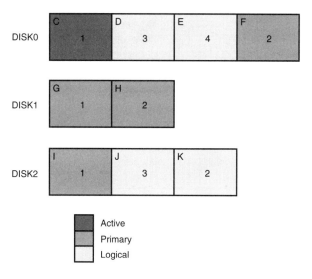

Figure 8.1
In this partition scheme, you see primary, extended, and logical partitions. They are numbered as Windows NT would number them when it boots. Notice that primary partitions are counted before logical drives in an extended partition.

Key Concept

Windows NT refers to the partition from which the computer system boots as the *system partition*. For Windows NT, this partition contains the files that Windows NT uses to boot (NTLDR, NTDETECT.COM, BOOT.INI, NTBOOTDD.SYS, and BOOTSECT.DOS). The partition that contains the Windows NT system files such as NTOSKRNL.EXE (the WINNT40 installation directory) is called the *boot partition*. In other words, the system partition contains the operating system boot files, and the boot partition is the partition that contains the Windows NT directory. This terminology is used for the remainder of this chapter.

Exploring File System Support in Windows NT 4.0

After the partition scheme has been decided and applied to the physical disk or disks, the disk or disks must then be formatted with a file system that the operating system can understand. MS-DOS and Windows 95 support the FAT file system. Windows NT supports FAT and its own NTFS (New Technology File System). All support the CD-ROM file system (CDFS). Windows NT 4.0 does not support Windows 95's FAT32, however.

Previous versions of Windows NT provided support for IBM OS/2's HPFS (High Performance File System). This support is no longer available under Windows NT 4.0.

An Overview of FAT

FAT support under Windows NT is somewhat expanded from that offered under MS-DOS. For example, FAT under Windows NT supports long filenames. The following are some characteristics of FAT as supported under Windows NT 4.0:

- FAT is required for the system partition if you intend to dual-boot between Windows NT and MS-DOS or Windows 95.
- FAT supports filenames of up to 255 characters.
- The filename can have multiple sections, separated by periods and, as such, can be considered multiqualified. The last section is treated as the file extension.
- Filenames must begin with an alphanumeric character and can contain any characters, including spaces, but excluding the following:
  " / \ [ ] : ; | = , ^ * ?
- FAT offers only the traditional file attributes—Read, Archive, System, and Hidden. As such, it does not provide the range of security that NTFS permissions can.
- Folders in a FAT partition can be shared.
- FAT supports a maximum partition (file) size of 4GB.

- FAT is considered most efficient for file access on partitions of less than 400MB in size.
- Formatting a partition as FAT requires less than 1MB of overhead for the file system.
- The system partition of RISC-based systems must be at least 2MB, formatted as FAT.

Key Concept

Since the release of Windows NT 4.0, Windows 95 and subsequently Windows 98 have been released with a new file system: FAT32. This file system is not supported by Windows NT Workstation 4.0, nor is it recognized.

An Overview of NTFS

NTFS provides the most features and benefits for securing your data. However, it is recognized only by Windows NT computers. Also, your old MS-DOS-based disk utilities most likely do not recognize NTFS-formatted partitions, nor do your MS-DOS– or Windows 95-based applications. Although NTFS is used extensively on Windows NT Server 4.0 computers to provide a high level of security and fault tolerance, it can also be used on Windows NT 4.0 Workstation computers for those end users who require added security and a higher level of support. They include developers, network administrators, secure data system users, and so on.

The following are some characteristics of NTFS:

- NTFS supports long file and folder names of up to 255 characters, including extensions.
- Filenames preserve case but are not case sensitive, except when using Posix-based applications for which case sensitivity is supported.
- File and folder names can contain any characters, including spaces, but excluding the following:

  " / \ < > : | * ?

- NTFS supports a theoretical partition (file) size of up to 16 exabytes. However, on most hardware, this translates to file size limits of 4GB to 64GB, and to a functional partition size of up to 2TB, due to industry standard limitations of disk sectors.
- NTFS is considered more efficient on partitions larger than 400MB.
- Formatting a partition as NTFS requires between 4MB and 5MB of system overhead, making it impossible to format a floppy disk with NTFS.

- NTFS provides support for built-in file compression. File compression is treated as a file and folder attribute and is enabled through the properties of the file or folder.

- NTFS offers automatic Transaction Tracking, which logs all disk activity and provides a means of recovery in the event of a power failure or system crash.

- NTFS offers automatic Sector Sparing, also called hot fixing, in which so-called bad clusters are determined and marked, and the data contained therein is moved to a new good cluster.

- Through the Services for Macintosh feature on Windows NT Server 4.0, NTFS provides support for Macintosh files.

- NTFS provides the highest level of security for files and folders through its permission set (see Chapter 7).

- NTFS maintains a separate Recycle Bin for each user.

As you can see, NTFS is quite a robust file system, but perhaps not always the preferred choice on all workstations.

Converting a FAT Partition to NTFS

Formatting a partition as NTFS right away, or during installation, is certainly not necessary. One of the nicest things about NTFS is its capability to be applied to an existing FAT partition.

Windows NT provides a conversion tool that you can use to apply NTFS to an existing FAT partition. It is called CONVERT.EXE and can be found in the WINNT40\ SYSTEM32 subdirectory. No data is lost during the conversion process because this is not a reformatting operation. The syntax of the command is as follows. At an MS-DOS prompt, you type

CONVERT D: /FS:NTFS

where D: represents the drive letter of the partition to be converted.

If Windows NT is currently accessing the drive in some way—for example, the pagefile is located on it—or you have the drive window open through My Computer or Windows Explorer, Windows NT displays a message to that effect and offers to schedule the conversion for the next boot. If you choose to accept the offer, when Windows NT boots, it detects that the partition is marked for conversion. It reboots and performs the conversion; then it reboots again to start the operating system and lets the user log in.

Considering Long Filenames

Both FAT and NTFS under Windows NT 4.0 support long filenames for files and folders. However, not all Microsoft Network clients support or recognize long filenames.

For example, MS-DOS and Windows 3.x-based computers and their applications do not recognize long filenames. Windows NT has allowed for this variety in operating systems. When you create a file or folder using a long filename to identify it, Windows NT automatically assigns an 8.3 format version of the name. This way, DOS- and Windows-based systems can "see" the files and folders. You do have several considerations to keep in mind as you work with long filenames.

How 8.3 Names Are Created

The internal algorithm that Windows NT uses to autogenerate an 8.3 name from a long filename is really quite simple within the first four iterations. Windows NT takes the first six characters of the name, minus spaces, and adds a ~ (tilde character) followed by a number increment. Notice the convention followed in this example:

Filename	8.3 Name
1995 Budget Summary Spreadsheet.XLS	1995Bu~1.xls
1995 Budget Detail Spreadsheet.XLS	1995Bu~2.xls
Budget Overages.DOC	Budget~1.doc

As you can see, the short filename does not give anywhere near the level of description that the long filename does. Do you see another consideration? Notice that if several long filenames start with the same characters within the first six, the 8.3 versions can be identified only by the number increment. After the fifth iteration, Windows NT's algorithm performs a name hash, retaining the first two characters of the long filename and generating the remaining characters randomly, as shown in this next example:

Filename	8.3 Name
KiteFlyers Corp Budget - January.XLS	KiteFl~1.XLS
KiteFlyers Corp Budget - February.XLS	KiteFl~2.XLS
KiteFlyers Corp Budget - March.XLS	KiteFl~3.XLS
KiteFlyers Corp Budget - April.XLS	KiteFl~4.XLS
KiteFlyers Corp Budget - May.XLS	Kia45s~1.XLS
KiteFlyers Corp Budget - June.XLS	Ki823x~1.XLS

On a network with a variety of clients that include Windows NT, MS-DOS, and Windows 95, the short names can become a source of confusion for users using those clients and applications that support and display only the short names. Consequently, in a mixed environment, you should try to keep the long filenames unique within the first six characters.

Additional Thoughts on Long Names

The following are some additional considerations to ponder:

- When you refer to long names at a DOS prompt, most DOS commands require that you place the name in quotation marks. For example, if you're copying the file MY BUDGET SPREADSHEET.XLS from C:\Apps to the D:\Data directory, you would need to type it as follows:

  COPY "C:\Apps\MY BUDGET SPREADSHEET.XLS" D:\Data
- Some DOS and Windows 16-bit applications save files by creating a temporary file, deleting the original file, and renaming the temporary file to the original name. This process deletes not only the long filename, but also any NTFS permissions associated with the file.
- Third-party DOS-based disk utilities that manipulate the FAT can also destroy long filenames contained in the FAT because they do not recognize those entries as valid DOS files.
- You can display the 8.3 version of the long filename at a DOS prompt by typing **DIR /X** at the prompt.
- Every long filename utilizes one FAT directory entry for the 8.3 name (called the alias) and a hidden secondary entry for up to every 13 characters of the long filename. MY BUDGET SPREADSHEET.XLS, for example, uses one FAT directory entry for the 8.3 name—MYBUDG~1.XLS—plus two secondary entries for the long filename (25 characters divided by 13), for a total of three. The FAT root directory has a hard-coded limit of 512 directory entries. Therefore, you can run out of directory entries if you use very long filenames consistently.

As you can see, if you are supporting a variety of clients in a Windows NT network enterprise, the use of long filenames must be duly considered, and if widely used, explained thoroughly to the end users who will encounter them.

In Chapter 5, "Configuration and the Registry," we made a concerted effort to dissuade you from ever modifying the Registry if a utility is available to you. That having been said, on some occasions, you can only, or best, effect a change by modifying the Registry. Let's look at an example of that for your Windows NT 4.0 workstation.

You can prevent the support of long filenames on FAT partitions altogether by modifying a Registry entry. To do so, you use the Registry Editor to expand the HKEY_LOCAL_MACHINE subtree to the following subkey:

```
HKEY_LOCAL_MACHINE\SYSTEM\CurrentControlSet\Control\FileSystem\
```

Here, you can change the parameter setting for Win31FileSystem from 0 to 1. This technique is particularly useful when several clients are accessing files stored on a central server and there is any chance of confusion among them. They are only able to name files and folders following the 8.3 convention on the FAT partitions.

Exploring File Compression Under NTFS

When a partition is formatted as NTFS, among the features provided is the capability to compress files and folders. Compression is treated as another attribute of the file and folder and is, in fact, enabled through the General Properties for the file or folder. This compression is handled on-the-fly and, like all compression algorithms, although resulting in greater disk capacity, can result in a performance decrease, especially when accessed across networks with heavy traffic.

NTFS compression follows a roughly 2:1 ratio with slightly more for data files and slightly less for executables. In general, compression can be most effective for those files that are not accessed on a regular basis but that cannot be archived because ready access is required. Good file candidates also are going to be fairly large in size and located on disk partitions whose storage space is at a premium.

NTFS does not support compression on NTFS-formatted partitions whose cluster size is greater than 4KB. You can determine cluster size by starting the Windows NT Diagnostics utility in the Administrative Tools group and viewing the specific partition's Properties on the Drives tab. You multiply the bytes per sector by the number of sectors per cluster.

How to Enable Compression

As you learned earlier, compression is considered an attribute of the file or folder on an NTFS partition. To enable compression for either a file or a folder, right-click the file or folder, and display its Properties sheet. On the General tab, select Compress.

If a folder's Compress attribute is set, any new files placed in the folder also have their Compress attribute set. Also, for folders, you can choose to apply the Compress attribute down through that folder's subfolders. You disable compression for folders and files by deselecting the Compress attribute.

You can configure Windows Explorer to display compressed files and folders in blue on the screen. You can do so by choosing View, Options and selecting Display Compressed Files and Folders with Alternate Color.

The WINNT40 installation folder and all its files and subfolders can be compressed if disk space is an issue. However, because Windows NT accesses these folders and files rather frequently, compressing them almost certainly results in a noticeable decrease in performance on that computer. Compressing the folder and its files is especially unwise on a Windows NT Server 4.0 computer or domain controller. NTLDR and the current pagefile can never be compressed.

Managing Compression from the Command Prompt

Windows NT provides a command prompt utility called COMPACT.EXE that you can use to enable and disable file and folder compression on NTFS partitions (see Table 8.1). The basic syntax is one of the following:

```
COMPACT /C d:\path\filename

COMPACT /C d:\foldername

COMPACT /?.
```

Table 8.1   COMPACT.EXE Switches

Switch	Description
/C	Enables compression of specified files and folders.
/U	Disables compression of specified files and folders.
/S	Applies the command to files in the specified folder and to all subfolders.
/A	Displays hidden and system files (omitted by default).
/I	Continues the operation even if errors are encountered. By default, COMPACT stops when it encounters an error.
/F	Forces compression on all specified files, even if previously marked as compressed. If a file is being compressed when power is lost, the file may be marked as compressed without actually being compressed.
/Q	Displays summary information about the operation.

Like NTFS permissions, when you copy a file from one folder to another, that file assumes the compression attribute of the target folder. Similarly, if the file is moved from one folder to another, it retains its compression attribute. Of course, a move is considered a move only when the operation takes place between folders on the same partition.

Managing Disks with the Disk Administrator

Now that we've explored partitions and file systems, we'll next take a look at another utility in the Administrative Tools group called the Disk Administrator.

My favorite way of introducing the Disk Administrator is to call it a GUI FDISK. You should remember the MS-DOS FDISK utility that you used to create the primary and extended partition and logical drives. The Disk Administrator does the same for your Windows NT Workstation and Server, plus a whole lot more.

Creating and Managing Partitions

To start working with the Disk Administrator, let's begin with the simplest task—creating a new partition. Recall that you can create up to four primary partitions per physical disk and one extended partition that can contain many logical drives. Refer to Figure 8.2 as we continue this discussion.

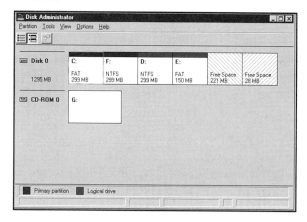

Figure 8.2
This sample Disk Administrator screen will help you interpret the text.

To create a partition, follow these steps:

1. Start the Disk Administrator by choosing Start, Programs, Administrative Tools.
2. Click an area of free space on a physical disk.
3. Choose Partition, Create to create a new primary partition. Or choose Partition, Create Extended to create an extended partition. The Create Primary or Create Extended Partition dialog box appears, showing you the smallest size (2MB) and the largest size partition you can create.
4. In the Create Partition of Size text box, enter the size partition you want to create.
5. Click OK. The new primary partition is displayed in the Disk Administrator as Unformatted. The new extended partition is set apart from any additional free space with an opposing cross-hatch.

If a primary partition already exists, when you create the next two to four primary partitions, Windows NT displays a message to the effect that the partition scheme may not be compatible with MS-DOS. NT displays this message because MS-DOS cannot recognize more than two primary partitions on the same physical disk. If you dual-boot between DOS and Windows NT on the same computer, DOS can see only the primary active partition. Users connecting to your computer through a share will be able to see all your partitions.

After you create an extended partition, you need to create logical drives within it to store data and other files. You can create a logical drive following the same basic set of steps:

1. Click an area of free space in the extended partition.

2. Choose Partition, Create to create a new logical drive. The Create Logical Drive dialog box then appears, showing the smallest size (2MB) and the largest size drive you can create.

3. In the Create Logical Drive of Size spin box, enter the size drive you want to create.

4. Click OK. The new logical drive is displayed in the Disk Administrator as Unformatted.

The Format Process

The next step, of course, is to format the new primary partition or logical drive. Before you can do that, you must confirm your partition changes to Windows NT. Do so by choosing Partition, Commit Changes Now. The Disk Administrator asks that you confirm your changes and then reminds you to update the Emergency Repair Disk with this new configuration information by using the RDISK.EXE command-line utility. This utility is described in Chapter 12, "Tuning, Optimizing, and Other Troubleshooting Tips," along with other tools for tuning and optimization.

To format the new primary partition or logical drive, follow these steps:

1. Select the partition or drive.

2. Choose Tools, Format. The Format Drive dialog box is displayed. If you are formatting an already-formatted drive or partition, the Capacity text box displays its size. Otherwise, it simply says Unknown Capacity.

3. In the File System list box, select either FAT or NTFS.

4. Specify an Allocation Unit Size. Unless you know something different, stick with Default.

5. Enter a Volume Label if you want. The label appears in the Disk Administrator and Windows Explorer and helps to make the drive and its contents more descriptive.

6. Select Quick Format if the disk has been previously formatted and you know it is not damaged. Quick Format removes files and does not perform a scan for base sectors before formatting. It is faster, but potentially more risky.

7. Select Enable Compression if you are formatting as NTFS and want to turn on the compression attribute for the entire drive or partition.

8. Choose Start. The dialog box charts the progress of the format operation. Click OK when formatting is complete, and then choose Close.

Deleting Partitions and Drives

Deleting a partition is as simple as choosing Partition, Delete. The Disk Administrator warns you that, if you delete the partition or drive, you will irrevocably lose any data stored on the partition. Always check the contents of a drive or partition before you delete it to ensure that you will not inadvertently lose something valuable—and that you don't have backed up!

Disk Management Extras: Drive Letters, Properties, and Display Options

Besides the Format option, the Tools menu gives you the ability to assign a specific drive letter to a logical drive or primary partition. By default, Windows NT assigns the next available drive letter to your primary partition or logical drive. Some programs require that a particular drive letter be used for the partition that holds the application files. Or you can choose to assign drive letters for consistency. Sometimes, a persistent connection to a mapped drive takes up a drive letter that you would prefer to assign to a logical drive or primary partition after you have disconnected.

To assign a drive letter, follow these steps:

1. Select the drive or partition in the Disk Administrator.
2. Choose Tools, Assign Drive Letter.
3. In the Assign Drive Letter text box, select the desired drive letter. Only available drive letters are shown. If a drive letter you want to use is currently in use by a persistent connection, disconnect that mapping first to release the drive letter.

You have the option of not assigning a drive letter at all. Because the alphabet has a limited number of letters, and some are reserved up front, this option allows you to create additional drives and partitions now and assign drive letters to them as you need to access them. This kind of activity is not recommended on the average end user's desktop because it can lead to confusion and possible misplacement or loss of data.

You can quickly display the Properties sheet of any partition or logical drive by selecting that drive and choosing Tools, Properties. From here, you can see usage statistics, change the volume label, run volume scan and defragmentation tools, and view sharing information for the drive.

As you create primary partitions, logical drives, volume sets, and so forth using the Disk Administrator, it uses various color codes and cross-hatching to facilitate your interpretation of the disks' partition and formatting schemes. The Options menu includes options for changing Colors and Patterns used in the legend, whether to show partition and drive sizes to scale through Disk Display, and whether and how to show a specific physical disk only through Region Display. By choosing Customize Toolbar, you can even create and customize your own icon toolbar to facilitate your most frequent activities.

System, Boot, and Active Partitions

As you learned earlier, Windows NT refers to the partition that contains the Windows NT boot files (NTLDR, NTDETECT.COM, NTBOOTDD.SYS, BOOT.INI, and BOOTSECT.DOS) as the system partition and the partition that contains the WINNT40 installation directory as the boot partition. Only one partition can be marked as active. On MS-DOS computers, it is usually the C: drive. In Windows NT, on dual-boot computers (booting between both Windows NT 4.0 and MS-DOS or Windows 95), it is probably still the C: drive. However, it must be the partition that contains the Windows NT boot files. You might have multiple operating systems on your computer, such as Windows NT 4.0 and UNIX or Windows NT 4.0 and OS/2. Each expects its boot files to be on the partition marked active. You are most likely to find this type of configuration on developers' workstations or test servers.

You use the boot manager utility that comes with the other operating system to mark the Windows NT system partition as the active partition when you want to restart your workstation and boot into Windows NT. When you are in Windows NT and are ready to restart your system and boot into another operating system, you use the Disk Administrator as your boot manager.

To change the active partition marker, follow these steps:

1. Start the Disk Administrator.
2. Select the partition to be marked active (primary partitions only).
3. Choose <u>P</u>artition, Mark <u>A</u>ctive. The Disk Administrator displays a confirmation message that the partition has been marked active and will boot with whatever operating system is on it the next time you restart your system.

You can spot the active partition if you look very closely in the color bar above the drive letter. The active partition is marked with a star. You can see it better if you choose <u>O</u>ptions, <u>C</u>olors and Patterns and change the color bar to something other than dark blue.

Creating and Managing Volume Sets

You can think of a volume as any partition or logical drive on any physical disk that can be accessed as a single unit. In Windows NT, a volume can be a single contiguous area of disk space or a collection of noncontiguous areas of disk space. The latter is called a volume set.

A volume set can consist of from 2 to 32 areas of free disk space on one or more physical disk drives. They are combined and treated by Windows NT as though they were one large volume, and can be formatted as either FAT or NTFS. After these areas have been combined, they cannot be split apart. Consequently, deleting any part of a volume set deletes the entire volume set.

You can use volume sets to clean up areas of free space that, by themselves, may not be large enough to be useful, or to create storage areas larger than any one physical disk can provide.

The following are some more facts about volume sets:

- Volume sets can contain areas of free space from different drive types such as SCSI, ESDI, and IDE.

- Data is written to each member of a volume set in turn. That is, when one member is filled, the next member is written to, and so on. Therefore, a volume set really does not improve disk I/O performance.

- Windows NT system and boot partitions cannot participate in a volume set.

- Like NTFS, on workstations that dual-boot between Windows NT and MS-DOS or Windows 95, volume sets cannot be accessed by MS-DOS or Windows 95.

- If any member of a volume set fails, or the disk that a member resides on fails, the entire volume set is corrupted.

When you choose areas of free space of very disparate sizes, the Disk Administrator sizes each member of the volume set proportionate to the amount of free disk space selected. For example, if you choose to create a 50MB volume set out of a 10MB and 200MB area of free space, you might expect the Disk Administrator to use all the 10MB space for the first member of the volume set, and then 40MB from the remaining 200MB free space for the second member of the volume set. However, the Disk Administrator determines, as you can see in Figure 8.3, that proportionate to the size of the free areas selected, the first member is 4MB and the remaining is 47MB. This same note applies to extended volume sets.

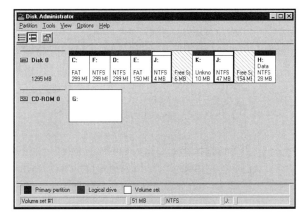

Figure 8.3
In this example, note that the volume set J: consists of two noncontiguous areas of disk space and has been formatted as NTFS.

Creating and Formatting a Volume Set

To create a volume set, follow these steps:

1. Start the Disk Administrator.

2. Select from 2 to 32 areas of free disk space by clicking the first and then Ctrl-clicking the rest.

3. Choose Partition, Create Volume Set. The Create Volume Set dialog box is displayed, showing the smallest size (2MB) and largest size volume set you can create from your selections.

4. In the Create Volume Set of Total Size text box, enter the total size you want for the volume set.

5. Click OK. The Disk Administrator displays the new volume set similar to the example shown in Figure 8.3.

6. Format the new volume set as FAT or NTFS.

Extending a Volume Set

If you have formatted a partition, logical drive, or volume set as NTFS, and you are running out of space on it, never fear. You can extend NTFS-formatted space into free space without any loss of data and without having to reformat the space. This process is called *extending the volume set.*

Extending the volume set can be particularly helpful in adding extra print spool space to a partition or allowing for the growth of a database.

To extend a volume set, follow these steps:

1. From the Disk Administrator, select the NTFS partition, drive, or volume set.

2. Ctrl-click an area of free space that you want to add on.

3. Choose Partition, Extend Volume Set to display the Extend Volume Set dialog box. The minimum and maximum total sizes for the extended volume are shown.

4. In the Create Volume Set of Total Size text box, enter the total size you want the volume set to be.

5. Click OK. The Disk Administrator creates what appears to be a volume set and applies NTFS to the new volume set member (see Figure 8.4).

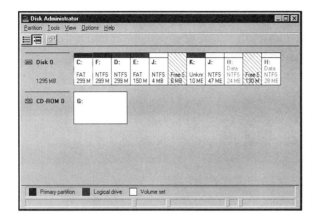

CH
8

Figure 8.4
Note how drive H: has been extended from 28MB to a total of 52MB. Because the drive was formatted as NTFS, NTFS is automatically applied to the extended volume.

Creating and Managing Stripe Sets

A stripe set in Windows NT is quite similar to a volume set in that both involve combining areas of free disk space into a single large volume. The similarities end there, however.

A stripe set consists of free space from at least 2 and up to 32 different physical drives. The area of free space chosen on each disk must be the same size on each disk. For example, if you have three disks with 100, 200, and 300MB of free space each, and you want to combine all three to create a stripe set, the largest any member can be is the smallest of the areas of free space, or 100MB, providing a total stripe set across all three disks of 300MB (100MB * 3 disks). Or you can combine two 200MB areas from the second and third disks to create a total stripe set of size 400MB. It's all just simple arithmetic.

Unlike volume sets, in which the first member gets filled up before the second member is written, in stripe sets, data is written uniformly in 64KB blocks across all members of the stripe set (see Figure 8.5). Because data can be written concurrently across the physical disks, a stripe set can result in an overall disk I/O performance increase.

The following are some more facts about stripe sets:

- Windows NT system and boot partitions cannot participate in a stripe set.
- Like NTFS, on workstations that dual-boot between Windows NT and MS-DOS or Windows 95, stripe sets are not accessible by MS-DOS or Windows 95.
- If any member of a stripe set fails, or the disk that a member resides on fails, the entire stripe set is corrupted.

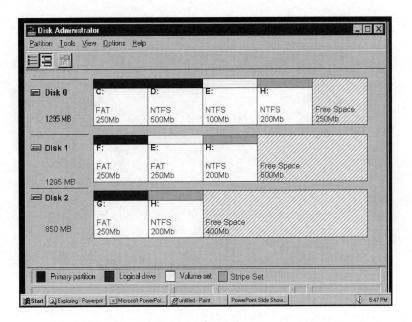

Figure 8.5
Drive H: in this example represents a 600MB stripe set distributed across three physical disk drives.

To create a stripe set, follow these steps:

1. From the Disk Administrator, select from 2 to 32 areas of free disk space on different physical disks. Click the first area, and Ctrl-click the remaining areas. The areas should be of approximately the same size. If they are not, the Disk Administrator sizes the stripe set based on the smallest area of disk space selected.

2. Choose Partition, Create Stripe Set to display the Create Stripe Set dialog box. The minimum and maximum total sizes for the stripe set are shown.

3. In the Create Stripe Set of Size text box, enter the total size stripe set you want.

4. Click OK. The Disk Administrator displays the equal-sized members of the stripe set distributed across the physical disks selected.

5. Format the stripe set.

6. Quit the Disk Administrator, or choose Partition, Commit Changes Now to save your changes in the Registry.

The System Partition and RISC

The system partition on a RISC-based computer must be formatted as FAT because these computers can boot only from FAT. There is no way to protect the system partition in this environment with local security. However, the Disk Administrator provides an additional menu choice called Secure System Partition. When this option is selected, only administrators on that computer are able to access the system partition.

CH
8

Disk Administrator Options on Windows NT Server 4.0

In addition to the partition, volume set, and stripe set options that you have seen, the Disk Administrator on Windows NT Server 4.0 provides additional disk fault-tolerant options. From the menu option Fault Tolerance, you can create stripe sets with parity, also called RAID 5, and disk mirroring, as well as regenerate data lost because of failed stripe sets with parity or mirrored disks.

We are talking about software-based fault tolerance that is built into the Windows NT operating system. When enabled, it places additional stress on the processor for resource management and disk I/O. Also, when a member of a stripe set fails, or a disk mirror fails, Windows NT must be shut down, the drive replaced, and the data regenerated. Hardware-based fault-tolerant systems generally allow for hot-changing failed disks without shutting down Windows NT. However, Windows NT's software-based fault tolerance is considerably less expensive than its hardware counterparts. If you are just getting started and need to secure your servers with fault tolerance, this is a good way to go. Look for more information on these options in the *Windows NT Server 4.0 Exam Guide* from Que.

Backing Up and Restoring Data

By now, if you have spent any length of time working with microcomputers, especially within a network environment, you have heard the words "backup and restore" at least once. Perhaps you heard them uttered yourself, as in "Why didn't I...?"

Backing up data and having the ability to recover it are perhaps the most important parts of disk management, especially within an enterprise network environment. As companies move faster and closer toward electronic media for conveying information—and in spite of rhetoric to the contrary, believe that it is happening—the backup process has taken on a much more prominent and integral role in securing data.

You can follow several strategies in implementing a backup procedure, and you have just about as many hardware and software options to choose from. This section is not intended to drive home the importance of developing and implementing a sound backup/restore policy, however. If you haven't yet been convinced, you will be—the first (and last) time that you lose $20 million worth of financial records because the incremental daily backup failed to occur and no one monitored it.

The purpose of this section is to introduce you to the Backup/Restore utility included with your installation of Windows NT Workstation and Server 4.0, explain some terms that Microsoft uses (and that you are apt to encounter on the Workstation exam), and to posit a couple of backup and restore strategies.

Requirements, Terms, and Strategy

The Windows NT Backup utility is designed for use with a Windows NT-compatible tape backup device. To determine whether your tape backup device is compatible, consult—as with any new piece of hardware—the Windows NT 4.0 Hardware Compatibility List (HCL).

The Windows NT Backup utility is meant primarily as a file and folder backup product and does not back up data at the sector level. Consequently, Windows NT's Backup utility cannot be used to perform volume recovery. If you need this kind of functionality or want built-in scheduled backups and so on, you should review the many third-party backup programs available now for Windows NT. Nevertheless, the Windows NT Backup utility is a fine product and does allow the backup of the Registry.

The following persons can perform the backup and restore function:

- Administrator
- Members of the local Backup Operators group
- Members of the local Server Operators group
- Users granted the user right Backup (Restore) Files and Directories
- Users who have Read permission for files and folders

As for strategy, Microsoft promotes the following three areas of consideration when planning your backup procedure:

- What do you need to back up? You need to determine the significance of the data.
- Where are you backing up from? You need to determine whether it is centrally stored data or locally distributed.
- How often do you need to back up? You also need to determine the frequency with which the data should be backed up to provide recovery.

The significance of the data is always subjective. For purposes of your strategy, you need to determine how much data is significant so that you can plan for the appropriate number of backup devices, right-sized media, location of devices, and so on.

Data stored centrally tends to be easier to maintain than data stored at local computers. For one thing, although you can back up users' data remotely with Windows NT's Backup utility or various third-party products, you rely more heavily on the user either to back up his or her own data or make his or her computer available for making remote backups, sharing folders, closing files, and exiting applications. The backup of centrally stored data is usually the responsibility of one or two persons who can monitor network usage and ensure that important files are closed and can be backed up regularly.

Key Concept

The obvious recommendation, then, is to store critical files in a central location and always back them up. Files that you cannot live without—including the Registry, especially on the domain controller (SAM and Security databases)—should be backed up regularly, perhaps daily. Files that change infrequently or are of less importance might also be backed up on a regular basis, perhaps weekly. However, you probably never need to back up temporary files and files that are used once and forgotten.

Table 8.2 lists some backup terms that Windows NT uses and that you may already be familiar with.

Table 8.2   Backup Types

Term	Effect
Normal	Backs up selected files and folders and sets their archive attribute.
Copy	Backs up selected files and folders but does not set the archive attribute. This option is generally used for creating tape copies outside the regular backup routine.
Incremental	Backs up only selected files and folders that have changed since the last backup and sets their archive attribute.
Differential	Backs up only selected files and folders that have changed since the last time they were backed up but does not set their archive attribute.
Daily	Backs up only files and folders that changed that day without setting their archive attribute.

The use of the archive attribute is significant for any backup strategy. The archive attribute indicates whether the file has been previously backed up. Let's examine the difference between a differential and incremental backup as an example.

According to Table 8.2, differential and incremental backups do precisely the same thing except for setting the archive attribute. The incremental sets it, and the differential does not.

Let's say that you have a data folder in which users make frequent contributions and modifications. If you employ an incremental backup each day of the week, starting with a normal backup on Monday, the backup would proceed like this:

Monday	Back up all files and set their archive attribute.
Tuesday	Back up all files that are new or have changed since Monday and set their archive attribute.
Wednesday	Back up all files that are new or have changed since Tuesday and set their archive attribute.
Thursday	Back up all files that are new or have changed since Wednesday and set their archive attribute.
Friday	Back up all files that are new or have changed since Thursday and set their archive attribute.

By the end of the week, you have created five backup tapes, each containing data that has changed since the previous day. If data is lost in the folder on Friday, all tapes can be employed to recover the data that is lost because you would not know necessarily which day's data is lost. The backup process is faster, but the restore process can potentially take longer.

Now let's back up the same folder using a normal backup on Monday and a differential the rest of the week:

Monday	Back up all files and set their archive attribute.
Tuesday	Back up all files that are new or have changed since Monday, but do not set their archive attribute.
Wednesday	Back up all files that are new or have changed since Monday, but do not set their archive attribute.
Thursday	Back up all files that are new or have changed since Monday, but do not set their archive attribute.
Friday	Back up all files that are new or have changed since Monday, but do not set their archive attribute.

Notice that each day's tape contains files that are new or have changed since the beginning of the week. This backup process takes a little longer, but if data is lost from the folder on Friday, only the Monday and Thursday tapes need be restored because Monday contains all the original data, and Thursday contains everything that has changed since Monday.

Another twist on these strategies is to perform a complete normal or copy backup once every week or every month, and archive that tape offsite. By designating a series of tapes in rotation, you can cycle your offsite archive tapes into the regular routine and always maintain a valid and timely recovery system that includes offsite data storage.

Table 8.3 lists some additional terms that Microsoft uses regarding the backup process.

Table 8.3 Backup Terms

Term	Description
Backup set	The group of files and folders backed up during a backup session. A tape may contain one or more backup sets.
Family set	The group of tapes that contain files and folders backed up during a single backup session.
Backup log	The backup text file that the Backup utility creates to record details relating to the session, such as the date, type of backup, which files and folders were backed up, and so on.
Catalog	A graphical representation of the backup that is loaded during the restore process and that displays the backup sets on a tape, and the files and folders contained in a backup set.

Initiating Backup

The first step in initiating a backup is to determine what you will be backing up (see Figure 8.6). It helps to know ahead of time what files and folders you want to back up and where they are located. For example, if you are planning on backing up files located in a remote server or a user's workstation, the folder containing the files must first be shared, and then you must connect to that share from the computer that is doing the backup. All files, of course, must be closed because the Backup utility cannot operate on open files. After you have made these preparations, you can start the Backup utility. Unfortunately, you cannot back up the Registry from a remote computer.

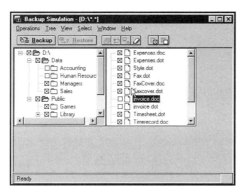

Figure 8.6
In this backup example, notice that you can select the files and folders on drive D: by simply pointing and clicking.

To back up files and folders, follow these steps:

1. Start the Windows NT Backup utility (by choosing Start, Programs, Administrative Tools, Backup).

2. In the Backup dialog box, select the drives, folders, or files to be backed up by pointing and clicking the appropriate check boxes.

   Your selections are hierarchical in that if you select a drive or folder, you automatically select its contents and subfolders (see Figure 8.6).

3. Choose Operations, Backup, or just click the Backup button to display the Backup Information dialog box shown in Figure 8.7.

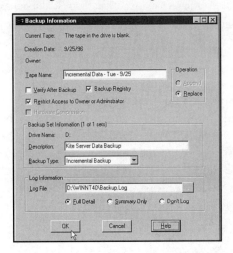

Figure 8.7
This tape for the files selected on Kite Server includes an incremental backup of the Registry and is restricted to the user who performed the backup.

4. In the Tape Name text box, enter a name for the tape up to 32 characters. If you are appending to an existing tape, the Tape Name box is not available.

5. Choose the appropriate tape options. See Table 8.4 for a description of these tape options.

6. Enter a Description for the backup set you are creating.

7. Choose a Backup Type.

8. In the Log File text box, enter the name and path for the text file you want to use to record details about the backup operation, and select whether you want to capture all backup information (Full Detail); only major operations such as starting, stopping, and failing to open files (Summary Only); or Don't Log at all.

9. Click OK. Backup displays the status of the operation as it takes place and a summary when it is complete, as shown in Figure 8.8.

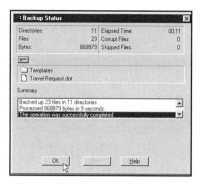

Figure 8.8
Here, you see the statistics compiled for a successful backup of the files and folders selected in Figure 8.6.

10. Click OK to complete the operation.

11. Store your tape in a safe place.

Table 8.4   Tape Options

Option	Description
Append	Adds a new backup set to an existing tape.
Replace	Overwrites the data on an existing tape.
Verify After Backup	Compares files selected with files backed up and confirms that they are backed up accurately.
Backup Registry	In addition to the files selected, copies the Registry to the backup set. (At least one file in the volume containing the Registry must have been selected for the Registry to be backed up successfully.)
Restrict Access	Allows access to the backup set only to Administrators, Backup Operators, or the user who performed the backup for purposes of recovery.
Hardware Compression	Enables data compression if the tape drive supports it.

Initiating a Restore

The restore process is much the same as the backup process, but in reverse. The same rules apply regarding who can perform the operation, and your restore strategy pretty much depends on what type of backup strategy you implemented. Refer to the two backup examples outlined earlier in the section "Requirements, Terms, and Strategy."

Also, as with backup, the first step in initiating a restore is to determine what you will be restoring. You will make good use of the backup logs created during the backup process to determine which files and folders you want to restore, on what backup set they are located, and where you need to restore them to. For example, if you are planning on restoring files to a remote server or a user's workstation, you must connect to the appropriate drive on that computer. Unfortunately, the Registry cannot be restored to a remote computer.

To restore files and folders, follow these steps:

1. Start the Windows NT Backup utility. The Tapes window displays the name of the tape in the device and information regarding the first backup set on the tape.

2. To see additional backup sets, load the tape catalog by choosing Operations, Catalog. The Catalog Status dialog box is displayed.

3. Click OK when the process is complete. A new window with the tape's name is displayed.

4. In this window, select the appropriate backup set to load its catalog.

5. Select the drives, folders, and files to be restored by selecting the appropriate check boxes. Your selections are hierarchical in that if you select a drive or folder, you automatically select its contents and subfolders.

6. Choose Operations, Restore, or just click the Restore button to display the Restore Information dialog box, shown in Figure 8.9.

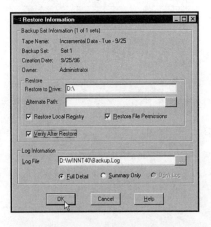

Figure 8.9
This operation restores the selected files and folders to the original D: drive, as well as the Registry, and maintains the original permission settings.

7. In the Restore to <u>D</u>rive text box, the original drive and path are displayed. If you like, you can select an <u>A</u>lternate Path.

8. Select the appropriate restore option. See Table 8.5 for a description of the three options.

9. Enter the name and path for the text file you want to use to record details about the restore operation in the <u>L</u>og File text box, and select whether you want to capture all restore information (<u>F</u>ull Detail); only major operations, such as starting, stopping, and failing to restore files (<u>S</u>ummary Only); or D<u>o</u>n't Log at All.

10. Click OK. Restore displays the status of the operation as it takes place and a summary when it is complete, as shown in Figure 8.10.

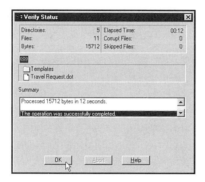

Figure 8.10
This dialog box shows the summary statistics for the restore operation you began in Figure 8.9.

11. Click OK to complete the operation.

Table 8.5   Restore Options

Option	Description
Restore Local Registry	Restores the local Registry to the target computer.
Restore File Permissions	Restores the NTFS permissions to the files as they are recovered. If this option is not selected, files assume the permissions of the target folder. If you restore to a different computer, be sure that you have valid user and group accounts, or your permissions may be inaccurate.
Verify After Restore	Compares files selected with files restored and confirms that they are restored accurately.

Troubleshooting Backup and Restore

You are not likely to encounter any problems with the Backup utility provided you are using a supported tape device and have the appropriate level of permission to perform the operation, either by virtue of membership in the Administrators, Backup Operators, or Server Operators group; by assignment of the Backup (Restore) Files and Directories user right; or through Read permission to the files and folders.

If you have chosen to log the backup and restore operations, any exceptions to the process, such as open files that couldn't be backed up, are duly recorded there. You can use that file to troubleshoot what did and did not get backed up, where it was backed up from, what backup set it can be found in, and so on.

Also, you should review the catalog for the selected backup set before restoring files. Corrupted files and folders are highlighted with a red X. Obviously, you should probably not restore them.

Scheduling a Tape Backup

Windows NT provides a command-line backup utility that you can use in combination with Windows NT's AT command to schedule a tape backup operation. To schedule a backup, you need to create a batch file that contains the backup command syntax and then use the AT command to schedule the batch file to run.

The basic backup command syntax is

```
NTBACKUP BACKUP path\filenames options
```

where `path\filenames` indicates the location of selected files, and `options` are any selected from Table 8.6.

Table 8.6 NTBACKUP Options

Option	Description
/A	Adds (appends) the backup set to the existing tape
/b	Backs up the local Registry
/d "text"	Adds a description for the backup set
/e	Creates a summary log rather than a detail log
/l filename	Assigns a filename to the backup log other than the default
/r	Restricts access to Administrators, Backup Operators, Server Operators, or users who perform the backup
/t type	Indicates the type of backup (Copy, Incremental, Differential, Daily) other than the default Normal
/v	Verifies that files were backed up accurately
/hc:on/off	Turns on or off hardware compression for tape devices that support the option

If you need to connect to a remote share to back up files, begin the batch file with a connection to that remote share using the syntax

```
CMD /C net use d: \\server\share
```

where `d:` represents the logical drive mapping, and `\\server\share` represents the UNC path to the remote share. At the end of the batch file, include the same line with a `/d` at the end to disconnect from the share.

Following is an example of a batch file called DATABACK.BAT; it connects to a share called DATA on server ACCT1; does an incremental backup of the files in that share, the Registry; restricts access; and verifies the backup:

```
CMD /C NET USE M: \\ACCT1\DATA
NTBACKUP M: /a /t Incremental /b /r /v
CMD /C NET USE M: /D
```

To use the `AT` command to schedule this batch file, you must have the Scheduler Service running. You use the Services applet in the Control Panel to enable and configure this service.

The `AT` command uses the syntax

```
AT \\computer time options batchfilename
```

where `computer` represents a remote computer (otherwise the local computer is assumed), `time` indicates the 24-hour time in hour:minute (00:00) notation for the operation to take place, `options` are as described in Table 8.7, and `batchfilename` indicates the command or batch file that you want to execute.

For example, if you want to schedule your ACCT1 backup to occur at 11:00 p.m. every weekday, you would enter the following AT command:

AT 23:00 /every:M,T,W,Th,F DATABACK.BAT

Table 8.7   AT Command Options

Option	Description
/delete	Cancels a scheduled command by the ID number assigned to it.
/interactive	Lets the job interact with the currently logged-on user.
/every:date	Runs the command on the specified day or days of the week (M, T, W, Th, F, S, Su) or one or more days of the month using numbers (1 to 31). The default is the current day.
/next:date	Runs the command on the next occurrence of the day or days specified or one or more days of the month.

Troubleshooting Disk Management

As with all the troubleshooting sections so far in this book, if you have read the material and understand it, and have taken the opportunity to experiment with the utilities described, you already have the basic tools you need to troubleshoot most problems. The following sections describe a few more considerations.

Saving Disk Configurations

When you have made changes to the partition and format scheme on your computer, updating that information is important. Of course, the current Registry settings are updated. However, if you are using the Emergency Repair Disk as a recovery tool, then you must remember to update it also. You can do so by running the RDISK command at the command line. Running this command updates the Emergency Repair information with any Registry changes, including the disk configuration.

You can also choose Partition, Configuration, Save from the Disk Administrator menu bar to save assigned drive letters, volume sets, stripe sets, stripe sets with parity, and mirror sets to a blank disk or the Emergency Repair Disk. This information can be particularly useful when you're planning migrations, software upgrades, and so on.

Other Considerations

If Windows NT fails to recognize a drive, it is most likely an incompatibility problem or driver problem. Always check the HCL before upgrading any hardware on your Windows NT 4.0 computer. Detected hardware errors are listed in the Registry in the key HKEY_LOCAL_MACHINE\Hardware.

You generally should delete corrupted files and folders and restore good versions from your most recent backup. Worst cases require that you reformat the disk and then restore from backup.

When you're dual-booting to MS-DOS, running some third-party MS-DOS-based utilities that modify the FAT entries can result in corruption or loss of data in Windows NT, especially if long filenames are in use. Don't use these utilities to avoid file corruption or loss, or disable long filename support for FAT partitions.

One-gigabyte IDE disk drives that follow the EIDE standard have a BIOS limit of 1,024 cylinders, which restricts Windows NT's capability to access all the available storage space on these disks. Either the BIOS needs to be able to get around the limit through sector translation or relative cluster addressing, or Windows NT needs to be able to communicate with the disk's controller. Windows NT currently supports Western Digital 1003-compatible controllers.

Summary

In this chapter, you learned about partition support and management through the Disk Administrator utility, Windows NT file system support, stripe sets and volume sets, and Microsoft's Backup and Restore utilities.

Next on our agenda is a trip through the wonderful world of network printing—still an adventure after all these years. Before you journey on, be sure to try the review questions and lab for this chapter.

CH 8

QUESTIONS AND ANSWERS

1. NTFS supports disks to a theoretical size of _____.

   A. 16EB (exabytes).

2. File compression can be accomplished from the command line with what utility?

   A. The COMPACT utility.

3. What is the type of backup that includes only files and folders that have changed since the last backup and sets their archive bit off?

   A. Incremental. Other backup types include copy, full (normal), differential, and daily.

4. True or False: Backups can be automated with the CRON utility included with NT.

   A. False. The CRON service/daemon is not included with Windows NT. Backups can be automated with the AT utility included with NT.

5. True or False: The Backup utility included with Windows NT Workstation 4.0 can be used to back up the local Registry.

   A. True. Although it cannot back up remote registries, the Backup utility included with Windows NT Workstation 4.0 can be used to back up the local Registry.

PRACTICE TEST

1. Lucy has been appointed the backup coordinator for the network. What must you do to enable her to accomplish this task and still maintain security on the data? Choose all that apply.

   a. Make Lucy a member of the local Backup Operators group on each computer that needs to be backed up.

   b. Make Lucy a member of the Server Operators group on each server computer that needs to be backed up.

    c. Assign Lucy the Backup Files and Directories user right.

    d. Give Lucy Full Control over all files and folders.

Answers a, b, and c are correct. You must make Lucy a member of the local Backup Operators group on each computer that needs to be backed up, you must make Lucy a member of the Server Operators group on each server computer that needs to be backed up, and you also must assign Lucy the Backup Files and Directories user right. Answer d is incorrect because giving Lucy Full Control is much more power than she needs, and doing so defeats security.

  2. You need to extend a FAT partition to allow more space for a growing database. Which option best explains your strategy?

    a. Use the Disk Administrator to select the FAT partition and an area of free space, and choose Partition, Create Volume Set.

    b. Use the Disk Administrator to select the FAT partition and an area of free space, and choose Partition, Extend Volume Set.

    c. Use the Disk Administrator to select the FAT partition and an area of formatted space, and choose Tools, Combine Volume Sets.

    d. Convert the drive to NTFS, and create a volume set.

Answer a is incorrect because a FAT volume set is not a good idea; after it's created, it cannot change size. Answer b is incorrect because a FAT volume set cannot be extended. Answer c is incorrect because volume sets cannot be combined. **Answer d is correct because converting the drive to NTFS and creating a volume set address the problem.**

  3. You are ready to implement your backup strategy and want to back up files from all Windows NT computers remotely to an archive directory on your local computer. All remote shares have been implemented. What is the best solution?

    a. Connect to the shares, start Backup, and select the files and folders to be backed up. Choose Backup and enter the UNC path to the target archive directory in the Backup Path text box.

    b. Connect to the shares, start Backup, and choose Operations, Select Target from the menu. Enter the path to the archive directory in the Backup Path text box.

    c. Connect to the shares, start Backup, and redirect the backup path by choosing Tools, Options.

    d. You cannot back up to disk.

Answers a, b, and c are incorrect because backups must be done to removable media. **Answer d is correct because you cannot use NTBACKUP to back up to disk.**

4. You need to convert a partition from FAT to NTFS with no loss of data. How can you best accomplish this task?

    a. Use the Disk Administrator to select the partition, and choose Tools, Format. Then select NTFS.

    b. Use the command-line utility CONVERT.EXE to convert the partition.

    c. Format the partition for NTFS and restore the data.

    d. You cannot convert a FAT partition to NTFS without loss of data.

Answers a and c are incorrect because format operations erase data. **Answer b is correct because you must use the command-line utility CONVERT.EXE to convert the partition.** Answer d is incorrect because the CONVERT utility allows you to do this.

5. Which of the following statements are true regarding volume sets and stripe sets? Choose all that apply.

    a. Stripe sets can contain the system partition, but volume sets cannot.

    b. Stripe sets must combine areas of equal size, whereas volume sets can combine areas of any size.

    c. Volume sets can contain the system partition, but stripe sets cannot.

    d. Stripe sets write to all members of the set concurrently, whereas volume sets fill each member of the set in turn.

Answers a and c are incorrect because stripe sets cannot contain the system partition. **Answers b and d are correct because stripe sets *must* combine areas of equal size, whereas volume sets can combine areas of any size.** Additionally, volume sets can contain the system partition, but stripe sets cannot.

6. What does Windows NT call the active primary partition?

    a. Boot partition

    b. System partition

    c. Startup partition

    d. Extended partition

Answers a, c, and d are incorrect because the active partition is known as the system partition. **Answer b is correct because NT refers to the active partition as the system partition.**

7. You need to recover a lost folder for a user. Before you do so, what can you do to minimize errors?

a. Review the backup set catalog for any corrupted files before proceeding with the backup.

b. Review the backup log file to see whether any files were missed during the backup process.

c. Select the verify files restore option.

d. Do nothing. Windows NT automatically verifies files while restoring to disk.

Answers a, b, and c are correct. Never restore files from a corrupted backup, make certain the files you need were included on the backup, and do not restore the entire backup, but select the needed files before starting. Answer d is incorrect because Windows NT does not automatically verify files during a restore.

8. Which of the following statements are true regarding FAT and NTFS? Choose all that apply.

a. FAT supports long filenames, and so does NTFS.

b. NTFS supports long filenames, but FAT does not.

c. FAT supports a maximum partition size of 4GB, and NTFS supports a maximum partition size of 16EB.

d. Formatting a partition as FAT requires less than 1MB of overhead, whereas NTFS formatting requires at least 4MB.

Answers a, c, and d are correct. FAT and NTFS support long filenames. FAT supports a maximum partition size of 4GB, and NTFS supports a maximum partition size of 16EB. Formatting a partition as FAT requires less than 1MB of overhead, whereas NTFS formatting requires at least 4MB. Answer b is incorrect because both FAT and NTFS support long filenames.

9. Which of the following statements accurately describe NTFS? Choose all that apply.

a. NTFS provides built-in Transaction Tracking.

b. NTFS supports file compression as a file property.

c. NTFS requires less than 4MB of overhead for formatting.

d. NTFS offers file- and folder-level security.

Answer a, b, and d are correct. NTFS provides built-in Transaction Tracking. It also supports file compression, and does so as a property (or attribute) of the file. NTFS also offers file- and folder-level security. Answer c is incorrect because NTFS requires between 4 and 5MB.

10. You are deciding whether to support long filenames on FAT partitions for your server. You have a variety of client platforms that connect to the server, including MS-DOS and Windows 95. Some of the platforms support older 16-bit applications. Which of the following considerations would you make?

    a. There are no significant concerns. All applications support long filenames on all platforms in a Microsoft network.

    b. Most Microsoft applications support the long filenames, but some older applications save changes by deleting the old file and renaming a temporary file to the original filename. This process could eliminate the long filename.

    c. Long filenames saved in the root of the drive require one directory entry for the alias and one for up to every 13 characters of the name. Because the root is hard-coded for 512 directory entries for FAT partitions, you could run out of entries.

    d. If long filename support is disabled for the FAT partition, it is disabled for all partitions on that computer, including NTFS.

Answer a is incorrect because not all older applications support long filenames. **Answers b and c are correct.** Most Microsoft applications support the long filenames, but some older applications save changes by deleting the old file and renaming a temporary file to the original filename. This process could eliminate the long filename. Also, long filenames saved in the root of the drive require one directory entry for the alias and one for up to every 13 characters of the name. Because the root is hard-coded for 512 directory entries for FAT partitions, you could run out of entries. Answer d is incorrect. While a uniform policy should be in place, what is set for one partition does not affect another.

CHAPTER PREREQUISITE

Before reading this chapter, you should be familiar with the Windows NT 4.0 architecture as described in Chapter 2, "Understanding Microsoft Windows NT 4.0." You should also be comfortable navigating in Windows NT 4.0 (see Chapter 4, "An Overview of the Windows NT 4.0 Interface").

Managing Printers

WHILE YOU READ

1. When does the print process start in NT?

2. In the printing process, the local _____ service makes an RPC connection to the print server and copies the print job to the print server spooler directory.

3. True or False: By default, NT sends a separator page between print jobs.

4. True or False: The most common print job type is RAW.

5. What is the highest print priority?

This chapter will introduce you to the Windows NT 4.0 printing process. A couple of significant changes from Windows NT 3.51 to Windows NT 4.0 will serve to enhance the management process for you. As with previous topics, the concepts and procedures described in this chapter apply to both workstation and server installations. Also, because Windows NT is predominantly a network-based operating system, we will concentrate on network-related issues regarding the Windows NT 4.0 printing process.

Introducing and Examining the Windows NT 4.0 Print Process

In the past, printing was an adventurous prospect, not only on the local desktop, but also across the network. And it still is. However, great effort has been made among operating system developers and printer manufacturers to streamline the process and facilitate management of the print process, particularly on the network.

Microsoft has been especially mindful of the problems associated with network printing and has throughout its history tried to enhance the process. For example, every MS-DOS application generally requires its own print driver to be loaded in order for that application to successfully talk with a given printing device. With Windows, Microsoft introduced a single set of print drivers that could be used with all Windows applications. In other words, Windows required the installation of one driver that all its applications would use instead of a driver for each application.

Windows NT follows this same concept—one driver that can be used by all applications running under Windows NT. It takes the concept a step further in version 4.0, however, by not requiring a driver for every installation of Windows NT, as we will see shortly.

First, let's explore some terminology used throughout this chapter and that you will encounter as you read through materials published by Microsoft and others.

When we speak of a printer in Windows NT 4.0, we are referring to the print driver. The actual hardware box that does the printing is called the print device. The print request is called the print job and can be sent to either a local print device connected directly to the user's local computer or a remote print device that is attached to or managed by another computer on the network.

The printer interacts with the print device to ensure that the print device receives a print job that has been formatted appropriately for that device. The printer also provides the print management interface from which print jobs can be viewed and manipulated. You could call it the print queue as well because it displays the status of jobs that have been spooled for that print device.

After a print device has been made available to users on the network, any valid Microsoft network client (Windows NT, DOS, Windows 95, Windows for Workgroups,

Windows 3.1, LAN Manager 2.x, NetWare, Macintosh) and even OS/2 and UNIX clients are able to direct print jobs to that device.

Key Concept

UNIX clients need to run SMB software or use a TCP/IP port on the NT system. Macintosh requires Services for Macintosh.

When you make a print device available as a remote printer, you are not actually sharing the device itself. Rather, you are sharing the printer—that is to say, the management interface. A given print device might have several printers associated with it, each with a different set of characteristics, priorities, or permissions. We will explore this concept further later in this chapter.

Windows NT 4.0 Print Process

When an application makes a print request, the print process begins. One of the innovative things Microsoft has done with Windows NT regards its Windows NT (all versions) and Windows 95 clients. Although clients need a print driver to process print requests, these clients do not require that a print driver be installed locally. Instead, Windows NT checks to see whether a local driver exists. If it does not, or if its version is older than that on the print server, the print server downloads a copy of the print driver to the client computer, where it is cached for that session. If the client's driver is newer, then the newer local driver is used.

As a result, the printing administrators can provide a greater number and variety of print devices easily to their clients without running around and installing a bunch of drivers on everyone's computer. Figure 9.1 gives a graphic representation of the print process.

Step 1.   When an application makes a request for printing on a print device attached to a print server, the client computer checks to see whether it has a local print driver installed. If it does not, or if the local copy is older than the copy on the print server, the print server sends a copy of the print driver to the client. The print driver is loaded into memory on the client computer.

Step 2.   The GDI component of the client operating system creates a print job in enhanced metafile format. This job is sometimes called a journal file, and it represents the print job formatted to print on most any print device type, such as HPPCL or PostScript. It is sent to the local spooler.

Step 3.   The local spooler service makes an RPC connection to the corresponding service on the print server (not unlike your mapping a logical drive) and copies the print job there. The bulk of the print process now continues on the print server.

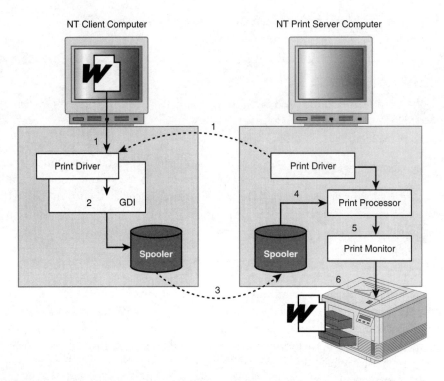

Figure 9.1
The Windows NT 4.0 print process for Windows NT and Windows 95 clients.

Step 4.   The print job is routed to the appropriate print processor, where the print job is further rendered into a format compatible for the specific print device. This file is usually referred to as a RAW file. If a separator page has been requested, it is attached to the beginning of the print job.

Step 5.   The print job is then passed to the appropriate print monitor that controls access to print devices, directs jobs to the correct port, monitors status of the job, and so on.

Step 6.   The print device receives the print job from the print monitor and generates the final print product.

Printing from other clients is essentially the same, except that the appropriate print driver must be installed on that local computer. The fully formatted RAW print job file is generated locally and routed to the print server spooler. Because no further rendering is needed, a separator page is added if required, and the print monitor sends the print job to the print device.

Windows NT 4.0 supports MS-DOS-based applications and Windows-based applications. In general, these applications take advantage of the Windows NT print driver and print successfully. Some MS-DOS applications that produce graphic print output, however, probably require that the print driver native to that application be installed for that application. It is safe to say that if the print output from MS-DOS- or Windows-based applications is not correct, you need to install an application-specific driver.

Exploring Print Process Components

CH
9

So far in this chapter, you've learned about four basic components of the print process: the print driver, spooler, print processor, and print monitor. We'll now explore each in more detail.

Print Driver

As you learned earlier, the print driver interacts with the print device to allow applications to generate printed output. It also provides the graphic interface through which the print device and queue can be managed. The print driver consists of three pieces: two dynamic link library files (DLLs) and a characterization data file.

The printer graphics driver DLL converts the print job output from an application into a print device-ready format.

The printer interface driver DLL provides the interactive management screen through which the print jobs and the print device can be manipulated.

The characterization data file provides information concerning device-specific characteristics of the print device, such as the amount of memory, internal cartridges, additional form trays, and so on.

Print Spooler

The print spooler actually refers to the spooler service running in Windows NT 4.0. It is responsible for making a connection to the spooler on a remote print server. It tracks print jobs, sending them to the appropriate ports and assigning them an appropriate print priority.

You could consider the spooler to be the print queue for the Windows NT print process. As such, the spooler can get "stuck" if a print job hangs, the system crashes, or some other such thing. If a print job hangs, or the spooler does not seem to be responding, you must purge the spooler. Purging it is actually quite easy, although all jobs in the spooler are also purged.

Because the spooler is a Windows NT service, you can control it through the Services applet in the Control Panel. To do so, simply select the spooler service from the list, choose STOP, and then choose START. This way, you can effectively purge any print jobs waiting in the spooler.

Using the printer interface to try to pause or delete a problem job is always preferable to stopping and starting the spooler service so as not to lose any other jobs in queue.

By default, print job files are spooled to the WINNT40\SYSTEM32\SPOOL\ PRINTERS directory. Depending on the size of the partition, as well as the number and size of the print jobs spooled there, it is indeed possible to run out of disk space because of SPOOL folder capacity.

Key Concept

You could use the folder compression attribute described in Chapter 8, "Managing Disk Resources," to compress the spool files and conserve disk space. However, keep in mind that compression does add additional overhead to your system and could, with large print files, result in a performance decrease.

If you were using an NTFS partition, you could use the Disk Administrator to extend the volume into available free space (you see, there is a good reason for doing it). Windows NT also provides a Registry entry through which you can modify the location of the SPOOL folder globally for all printers, as well as for individual printers.

Use the Registry Editor to select the HKEY_LOCAL_MACHINE subtree and expand through to find the following key:

    SYSTEM\CurrentControlSet\Control\Print\Printers

Look for a parameter entry called DefaultSpoolDirectory, and modify its value to correspond to the new spool location. This change affects all printers installed on the computer.

On the next level below the Printer key is an entry for each printer you created on the computer. Each of these entries also has a SpoolDirectory entry that, if modified, will change the spool location just for that printer.

As you can see, when you plan your installation of Windows NT 4.0, especially if your installation will be a server or provide server-related activities such as print serving, you need to allow for enough disk space for those activities as well.

Print Processor

The print processor is responsible for carrying out any further formatting or rendering of the print job required for the specific printer to understand it. The default print processor for Windows NT 4.0 is WINPRINT.DLL. It recognizes and renders the print job types listed in Table 9.1.

Table 9.1 WINPRINT.DLL Print Job Types

Type	Description
Raw Data	This print job type is the most common. It represents a print job that has been fully rendered and ready for the specific print device, such as PostScript.
Enhanced Metafile (EMF)	This portable format can be used with any print device.
Text	This print job type represents a print job rendered with raw, unformatted ASCII text and minimal control codes (linefeeds, carriage returns).
PSCRIPT1	Used on Windows NT servers running services for Macintosh, this print job type represents PostScript code from a Macintosh client destined for a non-PostScript print device on a Windows NT print server.

CH
9

Print Monitor

Whereas the spooler tracks the location of the job and ensures that the print job reaches the appropriate destination, the Windows NT 4.0 print monitor is responsible for tracking the status of the print job. It controls the stream of jobs to the printer ports, sends the job to its destination print device, releases the port when finished, returns print device messages like "out of paper" or "out of toner," and notifies the spooler when the print device has completed the generation of print output.

Table 9.2 outlines the print monitors supplied by Windows NT 4.0. The print monitor installed depends on the print driver you are using; the print device type, such as PostScript, HPPCL, or DEC (Digital Equipment Corporation); as well as the network protocol used to direct print traffic.

Table 9.2 Windows NT 4.0 Print Monitors

Print Monitor	Description
LOCALMON.DLL	Monitors print jobs targeted for print devices connected to local ports.
HPMON.DLL	Monitors print jobs targeted for Hewlett-Packard network print devices. The DLC protocol must be installed on the print server and the printer "port" identified by supplying the print device's hardware address.

…continues

Table 9.2 continued	
Print Monitor	Description
SFMMON.DLL	Monitors Macintosh print jobs routed using AppleTalk protocol to network print devices.
LPRMON.DLL	Monitors print jobs targeted for print devices communicating through the TCP/IP protocol, such as UNIX print devices and print spooler services.
DECPSMON.DLL	Monitors print jobs targeted for DEC's Digital PrintServer and other DEC print devices. Either the DECnet protocol or TCP/IP can be used to communicate with these print devices. It obtains the DECnet protocol from DEC.
LEXMON.DLL	Monitors print jobs targeted for Lexmark Mark Vision print devices using DLC, TCP/IP, or IPX to communicate.
PJLMON.DLL	Monitors print jobs targeted for any bidirectional print device that uses the PJL (Printer Job Language) standard, such as the HP LaserJet 5Si.

More About LPD Devices

The Line Printer Port print monitor (LPRMON.DLL) is loaded when the TCP/IP Printing Support is installed on the print server. It is designed to facilitate the routing and tracking of print jobs destined for network-ready print devices that communicate using the TCP/IP protocol or print devices that are connected to UNIX-based computers.

Windows NT provides two command-line utilities for directing and monitoring print jobs targeted for UNIX host printers; they're called LPR.EXE and LPQ.EXE. If you are familiar with the UNIX environment, you probably have used these commands before.

To direct a print job to a UNIX host print device, open a command prompt window and enter the command

LPR -S *IP address of UNIX host* **-P** *Printer Name filename*

where *IP address of UNIX host* is the TCP/IP address of the printer or host computer to which the printer is attached, *Printer Name* is the shared name of the printer, and *filename* is the name of the print job that you are directing.

To receive queue information on the print server, enter the following command:

LPQ -S *IP address of UNIX host* **-P** *Printer Name* **-l**

Keep in mind that LPR and LPQ command switches are case sensitive. Further note that a few (mostly older) flavors of UNIX do not support this implementation of lpq/lpr.

Managing the Print Process

In the following sections, you will learn how to create and share printers, set their characteristics and properties, assign security, manage print jobs, and do other fun printer stuff.

Creating a Printer

Recall the definition of a printer: When you speak of a printer in Windows NT 4.0, you are referring to the print driver, the interface through which you interact with the print device and from which you can monitor and manipulate print jobs.

The first step in creating a printer is to ensure that the print device is compatible with Windows NT 4.0. This information can be verified in the Hardware Compatibility List (HCL).

CH
9

As you might also expect, only certain users have the ability to create printers and share them on the network. Administrators, of course, have this ability by default. However, members of the Print Operators and Server Operators groups on domain controllers and Power Users group members on any other Windows NT workstation or computer can perform this task as well.

The advantage of using something like the Print Operators group can be summed up in one glorious word: delegation. Recall our discussion in Chapter 6, "Managing Users and Accounts," regarding the tasks and rights granted the different built-in groups. The Print Operators group, for example, allows its members to create and manage printers but not perform any other administrative tasks. These capabilities can be particularly useful for administering remote print servers.

You create and connect printers by using the Add Printer Wizard, which you can access through the Printers folder in My Computer or by choosing Start, Settings, Printers. Let's walk through the process of creating a new printer that is connected to a local computer. The local computer (workstation or server) will act as a print server for users on a network (workgroup or domain-based).

To create a new printer, follow these steps:

1. From the Printers folder, start the Add Printer Wizard by double-clicking Add Printer (see Figure 9.2).

2. If the printer is connected directly to this computer, keep the default setting My Computer. Network Printer Server will be used later to connect to a remote printer. Choose Next.

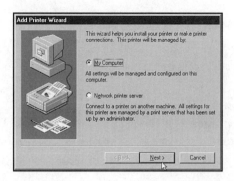

Figure 9.2
Add Printer Wizard dialog box.

3. Select the port that the printer is attached to (see Figure 9.3). Use Configure Port to modify transmission retry or baud settings of the designated port. If the print device is a network printer or is identified through a hardware or IP address, choose Add Port to provide that information, select or add the appropriate print monitor, or load another or third-party print monitor. You also have the option of enabling a printer pool. Printer pools and their benefits will be discussed later in this chapter. Choose Next.

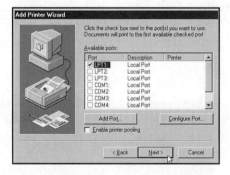

Figure 9.3
In the ports dialog box, the print device is attached to LPT1.

4. The list of print driver options has grown tremendously and so has Microsoft's support (see Figure 9.4). Microsoft has very wisely divided the onscreen listing into choices of device manufacturer and print device. If the device you are installing is not represented in the list, and you have an OEM disk with the Windows NT-compatible driver on it, choose Have Disk to install it. Choose Next.

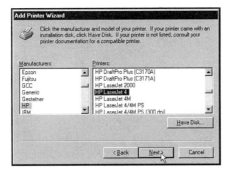

Figure 9.4
Here, the print driver to be installed is for the HP LaserJet 4.

5. Enter a printer name that is descriptive of the print device (see Figure 9.5). This is the name that print administrators will use to identify the printer. Also, if the printer is being installed for local use, identify it as the default printer for use by applications if you like. The first installed printer is always designated as the default. Choose Next.

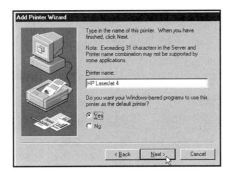

Figure 9.5
The printer name will remain the default name of the print device and will be the default print device for applications run on this computer.

6. If you want to share the printer now, you can do so by selecting Shared, but you can always share it later, especially if you are not clear on how to set the printer permissions. Enter a Share Name that will be descriptive for the users who will connect to this printer (see Figure 9.6).

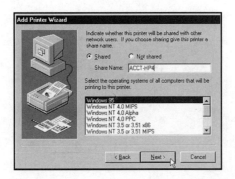

Figure 9.6
This printer has been shared using the name ACCT-HP4. Note that Windows 95 has been identified as a client that will print to this printer.

Also, in the list box on the lower portion of this dialog box, you can find a list of alternate driver platforms that you can support with this printer. For example, if Windows 95 clients will be accessing this printer, and you want to download the driver to each client rather than install it separately on every Windows 95 client, then select Windows 95 from the list. Windows NT will prompt you later for the Windows 95 source files, however, so be sure to have them ready. Again, you can always modify this information later.

Choose Next.

7. The wizard asks whether you want to print a test page to the print device. Printing this page is usually a good idea, especially if you are identifying a network print device through a hardware or IP address. Choose Finish.

8. As Windows NT installs the print driver, note the various driver files, DLLs, monitor files, and so forth being loaded. If you're asked, supply the path to the location of the Windows NT source files.

9. As the installation completes, the wizard adds an icon to represent the printer in the Printer folder (see Figure 9.7) and asks whether the test page printed successfully. If it did, you are done. If it did not, you have the opportunity to go back and modify your settings. The new printer icon is your access to the print manager for that printer, its jobs, and its print device(s).

Figure 9.7
Notice the new HP LaserJet 4 icon created in Printers and the print manager window that it displays.

Sharing and Securing a Printer

If you chose not to share the printer while you were installing it, you can do so later. As we mentioned before, it is probably not always a good idea to share a printer without knowing how you will secure it. The default permission for shared printers, as you probably guessed, allows everyone to print to it. Not adequately securing the printer can be particularly embarrassing if the printer is the Graphics department's expensive network-connected color laser print device, and users from all over the network are printing party invitations or banners on it. Even if you did share it during installation, your next step should be to secure it.

To share a printer, follow these steps:

1. Display the printer's properties (by right-clicking and then choosing Properties).
2. Select the Sharing tab.
3. Enter a user-friendly share name. This is the name that users will see when they are determining which printer to connect to. Make it descriptive and informative (within eight characters).
4. Optionally, choose to install an alternate platform printer driver if needed.
5. Click OK. The printer is then shared.

Printer share names, as is true with all share names, must remain within the eight-character range in order for non-Windows NT and Windows 95 clients to be able to see the names. If your share name is longer than eight characters, some network clients may not be able to connect to the printer.

Setting Permissions for the Shared Printer

Recall that, when sharing folders, you have the option of setting permissions for the share. These permissions interact with any NTFS permissions set on the files and folders to produce effective permissions for the users. You cannot set any permissions directly on a printer share. Instead, you set permissions on the printer itself. Four permissions can be used to secure a printer in Windows NT 4.0:

- No Access means just that, as always. Regardless of whatever permission you have been assigned through group membership, if you get No Access explicitly or through a group, you cannot access the printer to print or view the print jobs.

- Print permission is the default permission for the Everyone group. It allows users to connect to the printer, send print jobs to the printer, and manage their own print jobs—such as delete, pause, resume, or restart print jobs owned by the user.

- Manage Documents allows all the permissions of Print and extends job management to all print jobs.

- Full Control, in addition to the permissions allowed for Manage Documents, lets the users modify printer settings, enable or disable sharing, delete printers, and modify permissions.

Like file and folder permissions, the permission list is actually the access control list (ACL) for the printer. By default, Administrators and Power Users are given Full Control on Windows NT workstations and servers, and Administrators, Print Operators, and Server Operators have Full Control on Windows NT domain controllers. On all Windows NT computers, Everyone has Print permission, and Creator Owner has Manage Documents. Recall that the Creator Owner group is a special internal group that Windows NT uses to identify the owner of a file, folder, or in this case, a print job. By assigning it the Manage Documents permission, you are in effect saying that only the owner of any given print job has the ability to pause, delete, resend, or cancel it.

To secure a printer:

1. Display the printer's properties (by right-clicking and choosing Properties).
2. Select the Security tab.
3. Choose Permissions to display the Permissions dialog box. The current ACL for the printer is displayed in the Name list box (see Figure 9.8).
4. Modify the access of the current ACL entries by selecting the entry and choosing a Type of Access. Choose Remove to remove entries from the list (like Everyone, Print), or choose Add to add user and group accounts from the local or domain SAM database.
5. Click OK to save the permissions.

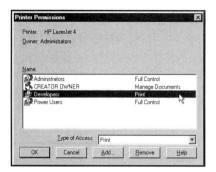

Figure 9.8
In the printer permissions for HP LaserJet 4, the Everyone group has been removed, and the Developers group has been added with Print permission.

Auditing and Taking Ownership of the Printer

As with files and folders, access to a printer can be audited, provided auditing has been enabled in the User Manager. The audit events are saved as part of the Security log, which you can view through the Event Viewer utility (see Figure 9.9).

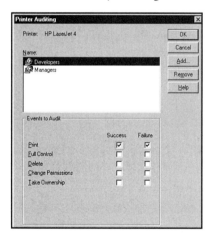

Figure 9.9
Users who are members of the Developers and Managers groups that access this printer to print are recorded in the Security log of the Event Viewer.

You can configure auditing for the printer by selecting Auditing from the Security tab of the printer's Properties sheet. Recall that you audit the activities of specific users and groups regarding the printer rather than general access to the printer.

In the Printer Auditing dialog box, select Add to display the account database. Then select the users and groups for whom you want to record printer activity. In the Events to Audit section, select the activities you want to audit.

Key Concept

Auditing places additional strain on resources and the processor. It is designed as a troubleshooting technique rather than as a reporting tool.

As with files and folders, the user who creates the printer becomes the owner of the printer. If, for some reason, that user is no longer able to manage the printer, you can take ownership of it like you might take ownership of a file or folder. Remember that ownership must be taken; it cannot be bestowed.

Members of the Administrators, Print Operators, Server Operators, and Power Users groups have the ability to take ownership of a printer. Also, any other user or group that has been given Full Control permission for the printer can take ownership of that printer.

To take ownership of the printer, select Ownership from the Security tab on the printer's Properties sheet, and choose Take Ownership.

Working with Printer Properties

You were undoubtedly lured to explore the other Properties tabs while sharing and securing your printer. Let's explore them further.

General Tab

As you can see in Figure 9.10, the General tab of the printer's Properties sheet gives you the option of entering a descriptive comment about the printer, such as who can use it, what options it provides, and so on. Also, you can enter a descriptive location for the printer. This information is useful when users are browsing for printers, viewing print manager screens, or receiving device-specific messages.

Here, you also can identify a Separator Page, choose an alternate Print Processor, and print a Test Page.

A separator page, sometimes called a banner page, identifies and separates print output. This page is printed before the document to indicate who submitted the document and the date and time it printed. However, it also has the function of switching a printer between modes. Windows NT provides three separator pages, which are located in WINNT40\SYSTEM32, as shown in Table 9.3.

Figure 9.10
A comment and descriptive location have been added here. When users view the printers or receive device-specific messages, they will see the location as well.

Table 9.3   Windows NT 4.0 Separator Pages

Separator File	Description
SYSPRINT.SEP	Causes a page to print before each document and is compatible with PostScript print devices
PCL.SEP	Causes the device to switch to PCL mode for HP devices and prints a page before each document
PSCRIPT.SEP	Causes the device to switch to PostScript mode for HP devices and does not print a page before each document

A separator page is a text file and can be created and saved with an .SEP extension in the WINNT40\SYSTEM32 directory using any text editor. Control characters that you can use to customize a separator page include \N, which returns the name of the user who sent the document; \D, which returns the date the document was printed; \T, which returns the time the document was printed; and \Hnn, which sets a printer-specific control sequence based on a specified hexadecimal ASCII code.

You can find more information about creating custom separator pages in the online books that come on the Windows NT Workstation and Server CD. Just start up Books, choose Find, and search for "separator."

You can choose Print Processor at the bottom of the General tab to specify an alternate print processor for the print device and port and modify the job types it creates to accommodate your applications. For example, WINPRINT offers five default print job types, including RAW, the default; RAW (FF appended); and RAW (FF auto). Let's say that the application that sends jobs to a particular printer always leaves the last page stuck in the printer. It is not adding a form feed to the end of the document. You might choose RAW (FF appended) to force a form feed on the end of any document sent to the printer or RAW (FF auto) to let the print processor decide.

Ports Tab

You use the Ports tab of the Properties sheet for a number of different activities. First, you can use it to see which port the printer and print device is associated with and what kind of print device it is.

However, you could also change the port associated with a given printer. For example, if the LPT1 port has failed, and you move the print device to the LPT2 port, you need only change the port designation here rather than create a new printer.

On another note, you could also use the port associations listed here to redirect print output from one printer to another. For example, if the printer stalls for some reason—perhaps because of a failed port, broken printer, or problem print job—you can redirect the output of the printer from the current printer to, perhaps, a remote printer (see Figure 9.11). Testing this type of redirection before implementing it would be prudent. If the spooling has been done in extended metafile format (EMF), the print job will print correctly. If not, the remote print device needs to be identical to the printer you are redirecting from.

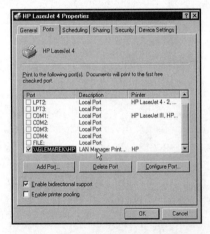

Figure 9.11
Here, the HP LaserJet 4 has been redirected from LPT1 to a remote printer on a server named Glemarek.

You can use Add Port near the bottom of the tab to add additional ports, such as a network port IP address for an LPD-enabled print device. For example, if you need to redirect print jobs from an existing printer to a network printer, you can use Add Port to add the remote printer to the list of ports and then select it from the list on the Ports tab. Use D̲elete Port to delete ports that you no longer need. Use C̲onfigure Port to modify the transmission retry value, COM port settings, and so on.

When the print device associated with the printer you installed supports the sending of setting and status information back to the printer, it provides bidirectional support. Any extra information about the print process that you can get will be helpful. If the print device supports this feature, select E̲nable Bidirectional Support.

Print Pools

Perhaps the most useful activity you can perform with ports is the creation of a print pool. A print pool represents one printer associated with two or more print devices. In other words, the same printer driver and management window are used to interact with two or more print devices that are compatible with that printer driver. This type of arrangement is particularly efficient on a network with a high volume of printing. Print jobs sent to the pool print on the next available print device, thus reducing the time jobs stay in queue. In addition, you need to manage only one printer rather than several.

For example, as you can see in Figure 9.12, three print devices are available for use on the computer. An HP LaserJet 4 is connected to LPT1 and LPT2, and an HP LaserJet III is connected to COM1. You could create a separate printer for each print device. However, creating separate printers doesn't stop users from favoring one printer over another. They may, for example, rarely send to the HPIII printer because of its slower performance. Consequently, print jobs may get stacked up on the other two printers.

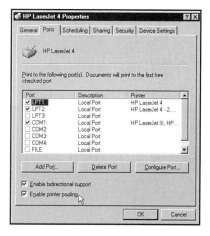

Figure 9.12
Three printers have been configured as a print pool in this example.

CH
9

If you associate one printer with all three devices, users have only one shared printer choice to make and their print jobs are serviced by the next available print device. However, the users do not know on which printing device the job printed.

To set up a print pool, follow these steps:

1. Choose E<u>n</u>able Printer Pooling on the Ports tab.
2. Check off the ports connected to the print devices you want as part of the pool.

As you can see, this process is very straightforward.

Key Concept

When you're pooling printers, be sure that the print devices you associate with the printer drivers in the pool support those print devices. If they do not, print output may be unintelligible. For example, although the HP LaserJet 4 printer driver is downward-compatible with an HP LaserJet III print device, it definitely does not support an HP LaserJet 5Si. The print drivers, then, must be compatible with the print devices in the print pool.

Print pools can be combined with other printers to produce a variety of output control options for the print manager. Suppose you create three shared printers: one each for Developers, Accountants, and Managers. You can then set up the permissions so that members of each group can print only to their specified printer. However, it is important that Managers' print jobs get printed as quickly as possible. You therefore can make the Managers' printer into a print pool by associating it with the other two print devices. Now, Developers and Accountants each have one print device that services their print jobs, but Managers' print jobs can be printed on any of three—that is, the next available print device.

Scheduling Tab

The Scheduling tab of the Properties sheet, besides allowing you to define when the printer can service jobs, lets you set a priority for the printer and define additional spool settings as well, as shown in Figure 9.13. All three of these option settings help the crafty print manager to further refine how and when print jobs are serviced.

Defining when the printer can service jobs is fairly straightforward. To do so, select Available: <u>F</u>rom, and then select the time range you want. Print jobs sent to this printer will still be spooled but will not print until the designated time.

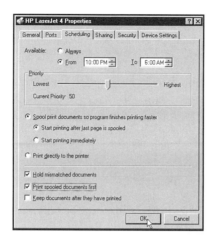

Figure 9.13
This printer will begin sending print jobs to the print device after 10:00 p.m. It will also wait until the entire job has been spooled before sending the job and will print jobs that have finished spooling ahead of jobs that are still spooling.

For example, suppose that you have a color laser print device to which several different groups of users send print jobs. One group, Graphics, tends to send very large graphics files that cause the other groups' print jobs to wait in the spooler. You could create a separate printer for that print device and assign only the Graphics group print access. Then you could set the printing time to print at off-peak hours. The Graphics group's print jobs will then wait in queue until the print time for their printer is reached.

Priority

When you set a priority for a printer, you are really setting a priority for all print jobs received by that printer. In the Priority section of the Scheduling tab, you can set the printer priority from 1 (lowest) to 99 (highest).

Setting a priority really makes sense only when you want documents sent to the same print device to have different priorities on that device. The key to making the priority effective is to associate two or more printers with the same print device. This is the exact opposite of a print pool in which one printer is associated with two or more print devices.

After you have created and associated the printer with two or more print devices (reread the Key Concept in the "Print Pools" section), you can set a priority for each by using the sliding bar under Priority.

Let's use the same example posited for Print Pools. Say you have three groups: Managers, Developers, and Accountants. They all use the same HP LaserJet 5Si network print device. Accountants tend to send large spreadsheets to the HP5Si, but Developers send pretty hefty blocks of code. Managers always want their documents to print as soon as possible.

You can create three printers and associate each with the same HP LaserJet 5Si print device. To do so, you can set permissions so that each group can print only to their respective printer. You can set the priority for each printer as follows:

99 (highest) for the printer used by Managers

50 (medium) for the printer used by Accountants

1 (lowest) for the printer used by Developers

Whether the Developers let you get away with these priority settings is a separate discussion. Nevertheless, you have accomplished your task. Because the Managers' printer has been given the highest priority, their print jobs print ahead of Accountants and Developers. Likewise, because the Accountants' printer has been given a medium priority, their print jobs print ahead of Developers. Because the Developers' printer has the lowest priority, their print jobs always wait until Managers' and Accountants' jobs finish printing.

Priorities do not affect a job that has begun printing. If a Developer's print job has begun printing, the Manager's print job waits until it is finished. However, any subsequent Developer's print job will wait until Managers' and Accountants' print jobs have completed.

Other Spool Options

You can use several cool options on the Scheduling tab to determine how jobs are spooled. In combination with print pools and priorities, these options give the print administrator many choices for affecting how, when, and where print jobs are printed.

The first option is Spool Print Documents So Program Finishes Printing Faster. This option, which is the default, simply means that print requests are spooled to a file rather than sent directly to the printer, resulting in a faster return to the application for the user.

The other option is Print Directly to the Printer. In this case, the print job is not spooled. It decreases printing time because the rendered print job is sent directly to the print device. However, the user must wait until the print job is complete before control is returned to the application.

If you choose Spool Print Documents, you have two "suboptions" to consider. The default, Start Printing Immediately, indicates that the print job will be sent to the print device for printing as soon as enough information has been spooled. Printing, of course, will be faster overall. The other option, Start Printing After Last Page Is Spooled, indicates that the print job will not be sent to the print device for printing until the entire job has been spooled. When used with printers of different priorities, this option can effectively prevent large documents from "hogging" the print device. Smaller documents will be printed first because they will be spooled first.

Did you ever experience the problem of sending a legal size print job to a print device that had only a letter size tray? The print job hangs up at the print device. The Hold Mismatched Documents option is designed to prevent that situation from happening by comparing the format of the print job with the configuration of the printer. If they do not match, the print job is held in queue and not allowed to print while other print jobs in the queue proceed.

The Print Spooled Documents First option allows print jobs that have completed spooling to print ahead of those that are still spooling, even if their priority is lower. When this option is used with the option Start Printing After Last Page Is Spooled, it virtually assures that smaller print jobs will print ahead of larger print jobs. If no print jobs have finished spooling, larger jobs will print ahead of smaller jobs.

When a print job finishes printing, the spooler deletes the print job from the queue, thus from the printer management window. If you would like to keep the document in queue to see its "complete" status, to keep open the option of resubmitting the job, or to redirect it to another printer if it prints incorrectly, choose Keep Documents After They Have Printed. After the print job is completed, it will be held in the spooler rather than be deleted, and its status will be displayed. For example, if you have an end-of-month report that is difficult to reproduce and you would like to resubmit it, you can use this option to keep the job in the spooler. On the other hand, the jobs remain in the spooler directory taking up space, and it becomes the responsibility of the print administrator to remove these jobs when they are no longer needed. Consider this option seriously before selecting it.

Device Settings Tab

You use the Device Settings tab of the Properties sheet to assign forms to paper trays, indicate the amount of memory installed in the print device, specify font cartridges, and configure other device-specific settings such as soft font or halftone.

Configuring these options is as easy as selecting the option you want to configure and choosing a setting from the list box displayed in the lower portion of the dialog box. The options available and their settings depend on the print device and the printer you installed to manage it. For example, whereas an HP LaserJet 4 has only one paper tray, an HP LaserJet 5Si may have several, including an envelope feed. The Device Settings tab reflects these device features.

Some printers offer page protection as a feature, and this option is displayed on the Device Settings tab. Page protection ensures that the print device prints each page in memory before creating the output page. If you regularly send print jobs whose pages are composed of complex text and graphics, enabling this option helps ensure that the print device will print the page successfully rather than possibly breaking up the page as it prints.

Managing the Printer and Its Documents

When you double-click a printer icon in the Printers folder, its printer management window appears. You can choose from four menu options: Printer, Document, View, and Help. View and Help are fairly self-explanatory. You will spend most of your time with Printer and Document, though.

From the Printer menu, you can pause the printer, change the default printer for the computer, manage sharing and permissions, purge all documents from the spooler, and, of course, manage printer properties. In addition, you can set document defaults that apply to all print jobs sent to the printer. Among the options that can be set are the paper size, paper tray, number of copies, orientation, and resolution settings.

From the Document menu, you can pause, resume, restart, and cancel print jobs. Each print job also has individual properties, which can be set much like the properties for the printer itself.

Document Properties

You can set properties for individual print jobs just like you do for printers, though print jobs don't have as many. However, the most important options—such as scheduling a time and priority for the job—are available (see Figure 9.14). Only users who have Full Control or Manage Documents permissions or the owner of the document can modify the print job's properties.

Figure 9.14
The BUDGET document is scheduled to print between 12:00 midnight and 1:30 a.m. with the highest priority.

You can display a print job's properties by highlighting the document in the printer management window and selecting <u>D</u>ocument, P<u>r</u>operties.

The General tab of the Properties sheet displays statistics about the print job, such as its size, number of pages, its owner, and when it was submitted. In addition, you can specify a user account to send a message to when the print job is complete.

You can set an individual priority for the job on this tab like you did for the printer. However, the priority selected here overrides the printer priority. Thus, if one particularly large print job that needs to be printed as soon as possible has been sent to a low-priority printer, you can set its priority higher.

Finally, you can set a time range within which the document can be printed for the individual print job. Using Figure 9.14 as an example, you can see that the BUDGET document is a large job that has been sent to the low-priority Developer's printer. Other jobs have undoubtedly been sent to the Managers' and Accountants' printers, which have higher priorities. BUDGET's individual property settings ensure that it will print with the highest priority between 12:00 midnight and 1:30 a.m.

Using the Page Setup and Advanced tabs of this Properties sheet, you can set additional options for the particular document, such as the paper size, paper tray, number of copies, orientation, and resolution settings.

Troubleshooting Printing

Let's start this discussion with some basic troubleshooting steps to follow when the printing process fails—steps that most of you have certainly followed in the past. The following bullets outline this troubleshooting checklist:

- Check to see whether the print device is turned on and online.
- Check to see whether the print device connection is good. Swap out cables; then check the network card, IP address, and so on.
- Verify that the printer driver installed is compatible with the print device.
- Confirm that the printer is available and has been selected. Verify that sharing has been enabled and that the permissions allow printing to take place for the users affected.
- Verify that the appropriate printer port has been selected and configured by printing a test page.
- Monitor network traffic in the case of remote printing to verify that print jobs are being routed correctly and not being dropped.

CH
9

- Check the amount of disk space available for spooling. Recall that the default spool directory is WINNT40\SYSTEM32\SPOOL. The installation partition often contains only the Windows NT files and is kept purposefully small. If not enough space is available for the spooled files, printing will fail. You either can add more disk space (extend the partition if it is NTFS) or move the spool directory to a disk with adequate space through the Registry. You could also turn on compression for the spool directory. However, compressing the directory could have a negative effect on printing performance for large print jobs.

- Determine whether the printing problem is the result of a specific application error or it occurs with all applications. Some MS-DOS and Windows 16-bit applications may require their own print drivers installed to successfully print their documents.

- Resubmit the print job to print to a file, and then copy the file to a printer port. If the job prints successfully, the problem may be related to the spooler or transmission process. If not, the problem is probably related to the application or printer driver.

Another source of help for troubleshooting printing problems is the built-in Windows NT Help program. It also provides a set of troubleshooting steps and tips to help resolve printing-related problems. You can access help for printing problems by following these steps:

1. Select Help, Help Topics from the menu of any window opened through My Computer or Network Neighborhood.

2. Choose the Contents tab on the Help dialog box.

3. Double-click the contents entry titled Troubleshooting.

4. Select the topic If You Have Trouble Printing.

5. Find the problem you are having, and click it. Help then guides you through a series of questions and suggestions to help resolve the problem.

6. Exit Help when you are finished by closing the Help window.

Additional Considerations

As noted earlier, you are most likely to experience problems because of inadequate disk space, incorrect port or address settings, or restrictive permissions. Also, recall that most older MS-DOS–based applications and some Windows-based applications require that their own printer driver be installed. Be sure to consider these possibilities as well when you're troubleshooting.

Windows-based applications print just like they do under Windows. Settings saved in WIN.INI and/or CONFIG.SYS are copied into the Windows NT Registry and are used for these applications printing under Windows NT. Applications that produce PostScript-specific graphics will probably print incorrectly or not at all. If no default printer has been selected, these applications will produce an out-of-memory error message when loading or not allow selection of fonts.

If print jobs stall in a printer, or no one is able to print to it any longer, the spooler has probably stalled. You can purge the spooler of its documents and restart by stopping and restarting the spooler service accessed through the Services applet in the Control Panel. Stopping and restarting the spooler service will purge all documents in the spooler, so caution should be used.

If your print server and clients happen to be of different or mixed platforms, and you still want the print server to download the appropriate driver to all the Windows NT work-stations, you need to install the appropriate platform drivers on the print server. A given print server may have multiple platform drivers installed for just this purpose.

For example, suppose that your print server is a RISC-based DEC Alpha computer. The Windows NT clients connecting to shared printers on the print server are Intel-based computers. You need to install the Windows NT 4.0 Alpha printer driver for the print server to interact successfully with the print device. However, you cannot download the Alpha driver to the Windows NT Intel clients. You could go around to each of the clients and install the Intel drivers on each. An easier solution is to also install the Intel platform driver on the print server. When an Intel client accesses the shared printer, the Intel driver is downloaded to it. The Alpha print server, in turn, uses the Alpha driver to manage the print job on the print device.

Summary

In this chapter, you examined the Windows NT 4.0 print process and explored print process components. This chapter also addressed managing the print process and troubleshooting techniques.

UNIX clients need to be running SMB software or using a TCP/IP port on the NT sys-tem for printing, whereas servicing of Macintosh clients requires Services for Macintosh.

When you're pooling, be sure that the print device you associate with the printer driver in the pool supports that print device. If it does not, print output may be unintelligible.

In the next chapter, we will look at the subsystem architecture that Windows NT uses to run applications more closely. In particular, we will discuss just how Windows NT does run those MS-DOS- and Windows-based applications you hear so much talk about.

CH
9

QUESTIONS AND ANSWERS ────────

1. When does the print process start in NT?

   A. The print process starts in NT when an application makes a print request.

2. In the printing process, the local _____ service makes an RPC connection to the print server and copies the print job to the print server spooler directory.

   A. In the printing process, the local *spooler* service makes an RPC connection to the print server and copies the print job to the print server spooler directory. This is the third step in the printing process.

3. True or False: By default, NT sends a separator page between print jobs.

   A. False. By default, NT does not send a separator page between print jobs.

4. True or False: The most common print job type is RAW.

   A. True. The most common print job type is RAW.

5. What is the highest print priority?:

   A. The highest is 99, and the lowest is 1.

PRACTICE TEST

1. Which of the following sets of Windows NT network clients do not require print drivers to be installed on the local computer?
   a. All Microsoft Network clients
   b. Windows NT and Windows 95
   c. Windows NT, Windows 95, and Windows for Workgroups 3.11
   d. Windows NT, Windows 95, and LAN Manager v2.x for DOS

Answer a is incorrect. All clients other than Windows NT and Windows 95 require the drivers to be manually installed on the local computer. **Answer b is correct because all clients other than Windows NT and Windows 95 require the drivers to be manually installed on the local computer.** Answer c is incorrect. Windows for Workgroups 3.11 clients require the drivers to be manually installed on the local computer. Answer d also is incorrect. LAN Manager v2.x for DOS clients requires the drivers to be manually installed on the local computer.

2. Which of the following steps apply to the Windows NT 4.0 print process on Windows NT computers? Choose all that apply.

a. The GDI component of the client computer generates an enhanced metafile print job.

b. The bulk of the print process completes in the spooler on the client before forwarding the print job to the print server.

c. The print monitor controls access to the print devices and device ports, and it monitors status of the print job.

d. The local printer spooler makes a remote connection to the print server spooler and copies the print job there.

Answer a is correct. The GDI component of the client computer generates an enhanced metafile print job. Answer b is incorrect. The bulk of the print process does not complete in the client computer spooler. **Answer c is correct.** The print monitor controls access to the print devices and device ports, and it monitors status of the print job. **Answer d also is correct.** The local printer spooler makes a remote connection to the print server spooler and copies the print job there.

3. Jeanette calls to say that her print jobs seem to have stopped running. You check the printer she sent the jobs to and see that the jobs are stuck in queue. What steps should you take to clear the stuck jobs? Choose all that apply.

a. Select the stuck jobs and choose Document, Cancel.

b. Select Printer, Purge Printer.

c. Use the Control Panel's Service applet to stop and restart the Spooler service.

d. Select each stuck job and change its priority.

Answers a, b, and c are correct because they are legitimate steps that could solve the problem. Answer d is incorrect because it does not solve the problem with a stuck job.

4. Several users have called you within the past half hour to complain that their print jobs are not printing. In fact, they get system messages telling them that the spooler is not responding. You have verified that the spooler directory partition does not have adequate free space to hold all the print jobs sent to it. What one step should you take to resolve this situation?

a. Use the Control Panel's Services applet to stop and restart the Spooler service more frequently to keep the print jobs from becoming fragmented.

b. Change the location of the spool directory to a partition with enough disk space by modifying the HKEY_LOCAL_ MACHINE\System\ CurrentControlSet\Control\Print\Printers DefaultSpoolDirectory parameter.

CH
9

    c. Change the location of the spool directory to a partition with enough disk space by modifying the HKEY_Current_User\ Control\Print\Printers\ Spool SpoolDirectory parameter.

    d. If the partition is formatted with NTFS, compress the spool directory.

Answer a is incorrect. Stopping and restarting the spooler service frequently is not recommended. **Answer b is correct.** Changing the location via the Registry solves the problem. Answer c is incorrect. It points to the wrong Registry key. Answer d is incorrect. You could compress the spool directory, but it is not the best answer because compressing adds additional overhead to your system and could decrease performance.

  5. If the final print output is corrupted, which print process component should you check?

    a. Spooler service on the client computer

    b. Spooler service on the print server

    c. Print processor on the print server

    d. Print monitor on the client computer

Answers a, b, and d are incorrect because the print processor is responsible for the final output. **Answer c is correct because the print processor is responsible for the final output.**

  6. Which print monitor is loaded with TCP/IP and tracks print jobs targeted for TCP/IP print hosts?

    a. IPMON.DLL

    b. LPDMON.DLL

    c. LPRMON.DLL

    d. LOCALMON.DLL

Answers a and b are invalid DLLs that do not exist or relate to printing at all. **Answer c is correct because the Line PRinter MONitor, or LPRMON.DLL, is responsible for this process.** Answer d is used in printing, but it monitors print jobs targeted for print devices connected to local ports.

  7. What is the purpose of the print monitor SFMMON.DLL?

    a. SFMMON.DLL monitors Macintosh print jobs routed using AppleTalk protocol to network print devices.

    b. SFMMON.DLL is the System File Manager print monitor that tracks print jobs sent directly to or printed directly from a file.

    c. SFMMON.DLL is the software print job compression DLL that compresses the print job before it is routed from the local print spooler to the print server.

    d. SFMMON.DLL is not a valid print monitor.

Answer a is correct because SFMMON.DLL monitors Macintosh print jobs routed using AppleTalk protocol to network print devices. Answers b, c, and d are incorrect because none of them represent the purpose of SFMMON.DLL.

8. A print job can be routed directly to a UNIX host print device and its status can be checked using which two command-line utilities?
   a. LPD and LPR
   b. LPD and LPQ
   c. LPR and IPCONFIG
   d. LPR and LPQ

Answer a is incorrect because LPD is a service, not a utility. Answer b is incorrect because LPD is a service, not a utility. Answer c is incorrect because IPCONFIG has nothing to do with printing. **Answer d is correct because LPR is used to submit a print job, and its status can be checked with LPQ.**

9. Nelson has been selected to assist you as a printing administrator in the Dry Gulch office because you are unable to travel there frequently, though you would really like to. What is the minimum level of access you need to give Nelson so that he can perform basic print management tasks, such as creating and sharing printers and managing print jobs?
   a. Make Nelson a member of the Print Operators local group on his print server.
   b. Make Nelson a member of the Server Operator local group on his print server.
   c. Make Nelson a member of the Administrators local group on his print server.
   d. Give Nelson Full Control permission for each printer on his print server.

Answer a is correct. Making Nelson a member of the Print Operators local group on his print server gives him the needed ability and does not jeopardize any other security. Answers b, c, and d are incorrect because they do not give Nelson the "minimum level of access" that making him a member of the Printer Operators group does.

10. You have created four printers. Each of them will be used by a specific group of users. Name all the steps that are required to successfully make the printer available to the appropriate users.
   a. Share each printer.
   b. Set the share permissions for each printer so that only the appropriate group has access.
   c. Set the printer permissions for each printer so that only the appropriate group has access.
   d. Create a printer pool so that each group can access all the print devices.

CH
9

Answers a and c are correct because the printer must be shared before it can be made available. After the printer is shared, you must set the printer permissions for each printer so that only the appropriate group has access. Answer b involves share permissions rather than printer permissions, making it incorrect. Answer d creates a pool of multiple devices and has nothing to do with the scenario at hand.

Running Applications Under Windows NT 4.0

WHILE YOU READ

1. The process of converting 16-bit code to 32-bit code is known as
   _____.

2. Applications can be started at different priority levels from the command line via what utility?

3. What is the default priority level for a normal job?

4. What does the acronym NTVDM stand for?

5. True or False: WIN32 and POSIX applications run only on the platform for which they have been compiled.

In this chapter, we will explore how applications run under Windows NT 4.0. This material is not development oriented, but rather an overview of how the Windows NT subsystems support applications running under Windows NT. In particular, we will review the subsystem architecture and some key points about application support, and give particular focus to MS-DOS and Windows 16-bit applications and how they are supported under Windows NT 4.0.

Reviewing the Windows NT 4.0 Subsystem Architecture

As we noted in Chapter 2, "Understanding Microsoft Windows NT 4.0," an integral part of any understanding of Windows NT is a discussion of the internal architecture of the Windows NT operating system. As you will recall, the Windows NT 4.0 architecture consists of two primary processing areas: User (or Application) mode and Kernel (or Privileged Processor) mode.

The User mode, as its name implies, provides operating system support primarily for user applications and the environment, which is what we are concerned with in this chapter. The Kernel mode provides operating system support for just about everything else, including kernel processing, memory management, hardware access, and so forth. These services are referred to collectively as the Executive Services.

User (Application) Mode

The User mode of the operating system provides application processing and logon support. Four subsystems run in User mode (see Figure 10.1). The OS/2 and POSIX subsystems provide environment support for OS/2 1.x applications and POSIX applications, respectively. The Security subsystem is loaded at boot time and is used solely for managing the Windows NT logon process.

The primary subsystem, which is also loaded at boot time, is CSR, or the Client/Server subsystem. CSR supports both 32-bit Windows and Windows 95 applications, as well as 16-bit DOS and Windows applications. It also provides graphics-based support to the environment subsystems and support to any other applications that are not written for the Windows NT application interface, error handling, or shutdown process.

Any application program calls from the two environment subsystems (OS/2 and POSIX) that read or write to the display are forwarded to the CSR subsystem. Any other calls to drivers or other Executive Services are communicated directly to the Kernel mode.

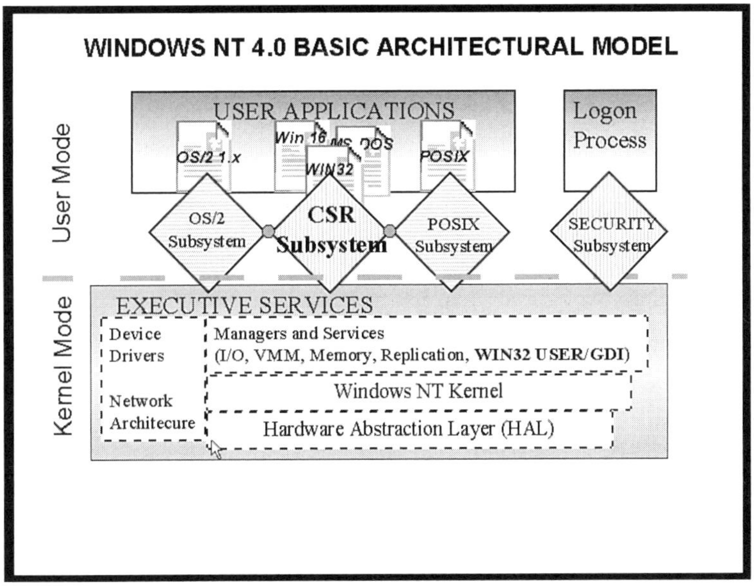

Figure 10.1
Basic Windows NT 4.0 Architecture Model showing application support subsystems.

As you may recall from Chapter 2, in Windows NT version 3.51, the USER and GDI portions of the operating system were included in what was then called the WIN32 subsystem. The USER is the window manager and responds to user input on the screen. The GDI processes graphics primitives such as pixels, lines, fills, and so on. The GDI also performs graphics rendering for print files.

If an application needed either of these two portions for processing, it had to create an InterProcess Communication (IPC) connection to it. This process involved a context switch from User mode to Kernel mode (ring 0 to ring 3 of the processor), as well as 64KB buffering. Then another context switch would take place back to User mode. This process, obviously, involved some time and decreased overall performance.

Windows NT 4.0 moves the USER, GDI, and graphics device drivers into the Kernel mode as part of the Executive Services. This move significantly improves application performance by eliminating the 64KB buffer and leaving only a kernel transition, such as one context switch. You can see the benefit particularly in those applications that involve direct draw to the screen such as Pinball and multimedia applications such as QuickTime.

Kernel (Privileged Processor) Mode

Kernel mode provides support for all major operating system functions. For example, it controls access to memory and the execution of privileged instructions. All Kernel mode processes run in the protected mode of the processor, ring 0. As such, the applications running in User mode are effectively buffered from direct access to hardware. Thus, 16-bit applications designed to access hardware directly do not run successfully under Windows NT.

The Kernel mode consists of these three main parts:

- The Executive Services, the largest part of Kernel mode, provide support for window management and graphics device interaction, processes, threads, memory management, I/O, IPC, and security. It is here that most Windows NT services and process managers are executed. Device driver support also is provided here, including Windows NT's network architecture support drivers, protocols, and so forth.
- The Windows NT Kernel provides support for thread scheduling and context switching, synchronization among services and processes in the Executive Services, multiprocessor load balancing, and exception and interrupt handling.
- The Hardware Abstraction Layer (HAL) provides hardware platform support. It isolates specific platform details from the Executive Services and the Windows NT Kernel. HAL is largely responsible for those 16-bit applications that like to talk directly to hardware not being able to run.

Examining WIN32-Based Application Support

Each application written to the WIN32 API is offered the full benefit of OpenGL graphics support, OLE (across both WIN32 and WIN16 applications), DirectX, multithreading, and multiprocessing.

Every WIN32-based application has one or more threads of execution associated with it. Each thread is independent of the other process threads and can be processed concurrently. Further, through Windows NT's Virtual Memory Manager, each WIN32-based application is given its own memory space of up to 2GB. By virtue of multithreading and virtual memory addressing, it is almost impossible for one WIN32-based application to interfere with or cause another to fail.

A Word About OpenGL and DirectX

OpenGL, an industry standard programming interface in which Microsoft participates, allows applications to produce high-quality two- and three-dimensional color graphics.

However, whereas other OpenGL implementations such as UNIX support VGA 256-color graphics, Windows NT 4.0 supports VGA 16-color mode.

Windows NT offers five 3D screen savers that conform to the OpenGL standard. They are 3D FlowerBox, 3D Flying Objects, 3D Maze, 3D Pipes, and 3D Text. Because they require additional processor resources for management, they are not recommended on computers that require processor resources for integral applications.

DirectX further adds to the robustness of multimedia support by providing accelerated video and audio support for multimedia applications, as well as network interaction between the applications through regular network interface or dial-up access. Whereas OpenGL gets its performance through dedicated processors on video cards, DirectX gets its performance through direct access to the multimedia device.

The next time you play 3D Pinball, think OpenGL and DirectX.

WIN32 applications are source compatible across platforms. That means the version of a WIN32 application that runs on an Intel computer cannot run on a DEC Alpha. The application must be specifically recompiled for that platform.

MS-DOS–based applications are sensitive to the DOS memory model, requiring 640KB for application support, 384KB for upper memory driver loading, and expanded and extended memory addresses. Windows 95 and Windows NT 4.0 use a flat memory model, discarding those distinctions in address. The MS-DOS application, however, needs that security blanket. What is there to do?

Like Windows before it, Windows NT 4.0 generates a Virtual DOS Machine (NTVDM) within which the MS-DOS–based application will load and run. This NTVDM essentially reproduces the MS-DOS environment configuration determined by the PIF and expected by the application to run successfully.

Every NTVDM created is given one thread of execution. As such, it is independent of all other threads, and if the NTVDM should fail, only its one process thread is affected. No other Windows NT application is affected by the failed NTVDM.

The NTVDM is supported by four elements in Windows NT 4.0. When the MS-DOS application is loaded, the NTVDM is created first by the NTVDM.EXE. It emulates and manages the DOS environment for the application based in part on the PIF settings for the application. Two more files, NTIO.SYS and NTDOS.SYS, are loaded; they emulate the two MS-DOS system files that provide basic operating system functions to the application. Finally, because MS-DOS applications want to interact with basic hardware directly but cannot do so under the Windows NT architecture, virtual device drivers are supplied for application interaction with the keyboard and mouse, printer, video, and other ports.

On RISC-based systems, an additional Instruction Execution Unit (IEU) is loaded with the NTVDM to emulate the Intel 486 processor for the application. Thus, for all practical purposes, the MS-DOS-based application thinks it is running in its native DOS when, in reality, it is being faked out by the NTVDM.

Configuring the NTVDM

The NTVDM is configured through the PIF created for each MS-DOS application. Remember, regardless of whether you create one, Windows NT always loads a PIF for an MS-DOS-based application, even if only the default settings. Therefore, it is to your advantage to create a PIF that more accurately determines memory and other needs of the MS-DOS application.

Two major changes have been made to the PIF editor from its earlier Windows and Windows NT versions. In Windows NT 4.0, the PIF settings have been implemented as properties of the MS-DOS application; therefore, you can access them by right-clicking the program executable. So, you see, Windows NT will always use PIF settings to generate the NTVDM.

The PIF settings themselves have not changed dramatically from earlier versions (see Figure 10.2), so we will not go into each one in great detail. However, we will review the general areas that can affect the application's NTVDM environment.

Figure 10.2
The PIF properties for the DOS initialization files, including an application-specific AUTOEXEC and CONFIG file.

The MS-DOS application's Properties sheet consists of six tabs for the six environmental areas that you can change: General, Program, Font, Memory, Screen, and Misc.

- General settings include an informational display of the application path and size; created, modified, and last accessed dates; and DOS attributes (Read, Archive, Hidden, and System). You can set the attributes on this tab.

- On the Program tab, you can change the icon and name that are associated with the application; the path and executable; the working directory; and whether to run it maximized, minimized, or in a normal window. Perhaps the most significant addition to the PIF settings is the option of creating and naming, through the

Windows NT button on this page, AUTOEXEC and CONFIG files that are specific to the application.

Under Windows 3.x, because Windows is a DOS-based application whose core runs in conventional memory, you pretty much have to manage your DOS environment before loading Windows. When a DOS application is loaded in Windows, Windows creates its virtual machine by "cloning" the DOS environment. In other words, before Windows is loaded, you have to look at all the DOS applications that might run under Windows and load drivers high to provide the best common denominator environment that would suit Windows and the DOS applications it would need to support.

Windows NT 4.0 uses a flat memory model with no AUTOEXEC.BAT or CONFIG.SYS and no references to conventional, upper, or high memory, so there is no DOS environment to clone for the NTVDM. However, Windows NT does provide default AUTOEXEC.NT and CONFIG.NT files, which you can modify if you like. Most of the settings you usually make in these files are addressed by a PIF setting. However, if you want to run a particular TSR or want to load a particular device driver, you can do so for each individual application. You can create as many different AUTOEXEC and CONFIG files as you want and reference them in each application's properties. This way, you have far greater control over how the application will perform under Windows NT than you ever had under Windows.

■ On the Misc tab, you can set background operation options, idle processing time, termination warnings, and reserved shortcut keys.

This information taken altogether, perhaps you can understand the earlier statement that the MS-DOS–based application might indeed experience a performance increase running under Windows NT 4.0. It certainly should not run any worse.

Key Concept

Any MS-DOS–based application that interacts directly with hardware, such as modem dial-out programs or disk management utilities, cannot run under Windows NT because these functions are isolated from the application through the HAL.

Examining WIN16 Application Support

Windows-based 16-bit applications are also supported under the Windows NT 4.0 WIN32 API. Recall that Windows runs in conventional memory and uses extended memory for application support. Because Windows requires MS-DOS to run, it should seem logical that Windows applications also require an NTVDM to run successfully under Windows NT 4.0.

Just as the NTVDM is designed to emulate the MS-DOS environment for MS-DOS–based applications, the NTVDM for WIN16 applications also is designed to emulate the Windows environment. Windows NT provides an addition to NTVDM called WOW. WOW, which stands for WIN16 on WIN32, is a 32-bit user mode program that allows a 16-bit Windows application to run in the WIN32 environment. And it is a pretty cool concept.

When 16-bit applications run in Windows 3.1, they make 16-bit calls to various Windows 3.1 functions and DLLs. Windows NT 4.0, on the other hand, uses 32-bit functions and DLLs. The WOW intercepts these 16-bit calls, translates them into 32-bit calls, and passes them on to WIN32, and vice versa. This process is called thunking. Lest you feel that this process results in a performance degradation, any loss in performance through the translation function is more than compensated for by the increased performance gained by WIN32 processes.

So it is the WOW that provides 16-bit Windows applications with the nonpreemptive multitasking environment within which they expect to run. In addition to the four NTVDM support files, five additional files support the WOW. WOWEXEC.EXE and WOW32.DLL provide Windows 3.1 environment emulation. KRNL386.EXE, GDI.EXE, and USER.EXE correspond to the same files in Windows 3.1 and manage the thunking process for each one's specific function set.

Key Concept

As with MS-DOS–based applications, WIN16 applications that require direct interaction with hardware through DLLs, DOS interrupts, or virtual device drivers do not run successfully under Windows NT 4.0.

When a WIN16 application starts, Windows NT creates a single NTVDM within which all subsequent WIN16 applications will also run—again just as they do in Windows 3.1. The NTVDM itself has one process thread associated with it that is preemptively multitasked with all other Windows NT processes and their threads. WIN16 applications are nonpreemptively multitasked (time-sliced) within the NTVDM. Consequently, it stands to reason that if one WIN16 application fails—because they all share the same NTVDM—all WIN16 applications in the NTVDM can also be affected. However, a failed Windows NTVDM does not affect any other WIN32 functions or their threads.

Of course, this same scenario would also be true running under Windows 3.1, so nothing lost, nothing gained. However, there must be some benefit in the NTVDM scenario, and the answer is in multiples.

Managing WIN16 Applications with Multiple NTVDMs

Under Windows NT 4.0, each WIN16 application can be run in its own NTVDM, and thus in its own memory space. Doing so effectively gives each WIN16 application its own process thread.

As you might expect, running WIN16 applications this way eliminates the concern that a so-called "poorly behaved" WIN16 application could adversely affect the others. Also, because running each WIN16 application in its own memory space gives each its own process thread, even if one WIN16 application is busy, the others are accessible. In fact, WIN16 applications that tended to bog down Windows because of processor or resource memory requirements may actually experience a performance boost when run in their own memory space. Here's what I mean.

Most everyone who has worked with Windows 3.1 applications has at one time received an "out of memory error" because of a lack of resource memory (called resource heaps). A limited amount of resource memory is allocated in Windows 3.1. An application referred to as a resource "hog" could easily use up most of the available resource memory space just for its own functions. When competing for resources with other applications, one often runs out of resource memory space, prompting the "out of memory error" and subsequent system hang.

When you run the same application in its own memory space under Windows NT 4.0, the application is still a resource hog. However, it no longer has to compete with the other WIN16 applications. Thus, it should run as well or better than it did under Windows 3.1.

Giving the WIN16 Application Its Own Space

You can start a 16-bit Windows application in its own memory space in three ways. You can issue a command-line command to execute it in its own memory space; you can make the selection through the Start, Run dialog box for that application or its properties (see Figure 10.3); or you can modify the application's run association through Windows Explorer.

Figure 10.3
CONVERT.EXE is a WIN16 application that you can run in a separate memory space by modifying the properties of its shortcut or from the Start, Run dialog box as shown.

You can start a 16-bit Windows application in its own memory space from the command line like this:

1. Open the MS-DOS Command Prompt window.
2. Enter **START /SEPARATE** *path/ executable*, indicating the location and filename of the application's executable file.

Follow these steps to start a 16-bit Windows application in its own memory space from the Start menu:

1. Choose Start, Run.
2. Enter the path to the WIN16 application executable file.
3. Select the option Run in Separate Memory Space.

To configure the application to always start in its own memory space, follow these steps:

1. Create a shortcut for the application on the desktop or the Start menu.
2. View the properties of the shortcut.
3. On the Shortcut tab, select Run in Separate Memory Space.

You can modify the 16-bit Windows application's run association like this:

1. Find the application executable through Windows Explorer.
2. Choose View, Options.
3. Choose the file type for the application, and select Edit.
4. Select open from the Actions list, and double-click or choose Edit.
5. In the Application Used to Perform Action text box, modify the entry to include the following immediately in front of the entry: **CMD /C STAR /SEPARATE**.
6. Choose OK twice to exit from the Properties sheet.

Key Concept

Although each WIN16 application can be run in its own memory space, only one NTVDM can have multiple WIN16 applications running in it. For example, if you want to run Word 6, Excel 5, PowerPoint 4, and Access 2 simultaneously, you could run each in its own memory space using any of the methods described. You could also run Word and Excel together in one memory space and PowerPoint and Access in individual memory spaces. However, you cannot run Word and Excel in one NTVDM and PowerPoint and Access in another. Only one multiple application WOW NTVDM can be running per session.

Considerations

If all the WIN16 applications are well behaved, OLE and DDE are fully supported among them. If the applications are not well written or rely on running in shared memory to exchange data, then OLE and DDE-based functions may fail. These applications have to be run together in one NTVDM to provide this level of information exchange.

Key Concept

Each WIN16 application that is run in its own memory space creates a new NTVDM. Each time an NTVDM is created, it requires up to 2MB of additional pagefile space, depending on the memory configuration of your system, and 1MB of additional RAM. Taking up this extra space can have an overall negative impact on performance, especially on computers where RAM and disk space are a premium.

On Windows NT Workstation 4.0, the WOW environment for the Windows NTVDM is loaded automatically when Windows NT is booted, though the NTVDM is not. Loading the NTVDM automatically reduces startup time when launching WIN16 applications. On Windows NT Server 4.0, the WOW is loaded on demand—that is, when the 16-bit Windows application is started. This optimization technique is designed to improve server performance. If you consider that you don't usually use Windows NT Server to run 16-bit Windows applications, loading WOW this way makes a world of sense.

You can view the WOWEXEC and NTVDM processes loading and the percent of processor time each is commanding by starting the Windows NT Task Manager (by right-clicking the taskbar and choosing Task Manager) and selecting the Processes tab.

Reviewing OS/2-Based Application Support

The OS/2 subsystem supports only 1.x-based applications on Intel-based computers. There is no OS/2 subsystem support for any other OS/2 application platform (such as OS/2 2.11 or Warp). Some OS/2 applications are considered bound applications. That means that the application prefers to be run in the OS/2 subsystem but can be forced to run in an NTVDM instead. If the application is bound, then you can run it in an NTVDM on any platform by issuing the forcedos command followed by the executable at the command prompt.

The OS/2 subsystem is not loaded at Windows NT boot time. It is loaded only when an OS/2 1.x application is executed and is supported by the files OS2.EXE, OS2SRV.EXE, and OS2SS.EXE. It communicates with the Windows NT Executive Services through the

CSR subsystem for screen-oriented I/O and graphics rendering. When the application is closed, the OS/2 subsystem files remain in memory until the system is restarted or until the memory space is needed by another activity.

Microsoft now offers an add-on subsystem to provide support for OS/2 1.x Presentation Manager applications. This add-on replaces the default OS/2 subsystem support files with updated versions and additional files. The additional files that support this add-on include PMSHELL.EXE, the Presentation Manager desktop interface; PMNTDD.SYS, the Windows NT support device driver; PMSPOOL.EXE, the Presentation Manager Print Manager utility; and PMCPL.EXE, the Presentation Manager Control Panel. When an OS/2 1.x Presentation Manager application is started, the add-on subsystem creates a separate desktop for the Presentation Manager desktop interface.

Configuring the OS/2 Subsystem

OS/2 subsystem configuration information is stored in the Windows NT Registry. Under OS/2, applications are run based on driver, environment, and other information supplied either in the OS/2 CONFIG.SYS file or the STARTUP.CMD file. The first time the OS/2 subsystem is invoked, it looks for these two files to determine its environment and other settings and then adds the information to the Windows NT Registry. Subsequent loads of the subsystem use the Registry entries to create the CONFIG.SYS file. Subsystem support file information is stored in HKEY_LOCAL_MACHINE\SYSTEM\ CurrentControlSet\Control\Session Manager\SubSystems. CONFIG.SYS and STARTUP.CMD information is stored in HKEY_LOCAL_MACHINE\SOFTWARE\ Microsoft\OS/2 Subsystem For NT\1.0\Config.sys and OS2.ini.

The best way to change the OS/2 environment before the subsystem is ever loaded is to create an appropriate CONFIG.SYS or STARTUP.CMD for the application or applications that you want to support. When the subsystem loads, it updates the Registry. To modify it afterward, you either can modify the appropriate Registry entries or start an OS/2 application and modify the CONFIG.SYS file created with an OS/2-based text editor.

Reviewing POSIX-Based Application Support

POSIX is an application standard created for UNIX-based operating systems that meet United States Federal Information Processing Standard 151. Hence, you're most likely to come across these applications in a government office or an underground silo somewhere. POSIX applications that require access to file system resources under Windows NT can only do so on an NTFS partition. POSIX applications that do not require such access can run under any file system.

NTFS provides compliance with the POSIX.1 Library of function calls. For example, NTFS preserves case-sensitive naming for POSIX applications; for example, README.TXT and readme.txt in the same directory are two different files under POSIX.1 Library compliance.

Like the OS/2 subsystem, the POSIX subsystem is loaded only when a POSIX application is started. It communicates with the Windows NT Executive Services through the CSR subsystem for screen-oriented I/O and graphics rendering. When the application is closed, the POSIX subsystem files remain in memory until the system is restarted or until the memory space is needed by another activity.

The POSIX subsystem is supported by three components. PSXSS.EXE is the main support file for the subsystem. POSIX.EXE tracks and manages interaction between the subsystem and the Windows NT Executive. PSXDLL.DLL provides application support to PSXSS.EXE.

Unlike OS/2 1.x applications, POSIX applications can run on other platforms such as RISC or PowerPC. However, you need to obtain the version of the application compiled for that platform. POSIX applications are source compatible in this regard.

**CH
10**

Considerations for Troubleshooting Application-Related Issues

Most of the problems that you are likely to experience regarding application support under Windows NT 4.0 have already been addressed in one way or another in this chapter and generally are the result of some incompatibility on the part of the program or lack of memory, and so on. We'll recap them here:

- MS-DOS or Windows-based applications that interact directly with hardware through interrupt calls or virtual device drivers, such as disk utilities or memory managers, do not function successfully or at all under Windows NT 4.0. Recall that these hardware requests are designed to be handled by the Kernel mode of the operating system, particularly the microkernel and the HAL. The CSR subsystem simply blocks these calls from the application.

- WIN32 and POSIX applications run only on the platform for which they have been compiled. Intel versions do not run successfully on a RISC-platform computer.

- OS/2 applications that can be forced to run in an NTVDM (bound applications) can be run on other hardware platforms. OS/2 1.x Presentation Manager applications cannot run natively in Windows NT 4.0. However, they are supported with the Presentation Manager Subsystem add-on product.

■ A new NTVDM is created for each MS-DOS-based application that you run
under Windows NT 4.0. A new WOW NTVDM is created for every WIN16
application run in its own memory space. Each NTVDM requires up to 2MB
additional pagefile space and 1MB of RAM. On a computer where RAM and disk
space are at a premium, running too many NTVDMs can result in the system
running out of RAM or disk space and freezing up. You should monitor the use of
RAM closely when you're running multiple NTVDMs.

■ By default, all WIN16 applications run in the same WOW NTVDM. If any of
the WIN16 applications hang or fail, the others may also be affected. Resource
memory is distributed among all the WIN16 applications. If one or more applications overutilize the resource memory, the result can be an "out of memory" message, and the NTVDM could fail. One solution would be to run the application
or applications in question in their own WOW NTVDM, keeping in mind the
preceding bullet point regarding RAM and disk space.

In addition to these reminders, you need to consider the following when dealing with
application support: thread priority, responsiveness, and the Task Manager.

Thread Priority

Recall that every application or process that executes under Windows NT 4.0 has at least
one execution thread associated with it. A thread is a basic unit of code to which the
processor can assign processing time. Every NTVDM is given one thread.

The Windows NT kernel assigns thread priorities based on the type of activity associated
with the thread. Priority levels range from 0 (lowest) to 31 (highest). In general, User
mode activities such as application execution are given a "normal" priority of 8, whereas
Kernel mode activities such as those relating to the operating system (I/O management,
memory allocation, and so on) are given a 16 or higher.

You can force an application to start with a higher or lower priority by entering the following syntax at the command prompt:

START /*startoption executable*

Here, *startoption* represents one of four possibilities—described in Table 10.1—and
executable represents the path and filename of the application file.

Table 10.1   Priority Start Options from the Command Line

Start Option	Sets to This Priority Level
/LOW	Base priority 4, three below normal
/NORMAL	Base priority 8
/HIGH	Base priority 13, six above normal
/REALTIME	Base priority 24, same level as kernel mode functions; available only to Administrators; can result in overall decrease of performance to operating system tasks

When an application is started with a different priority, Windows NT still balances priority loads on the processor on its own, and the application may eventually be returned to a priority closer to normal. Some developers also build priority preferences into the application threads. These priorities can also affect overall performance of threads.

The Windows NT 4.0 Resource Kit contains a process thread viewer called PVIEWER through which you can monitor thread activity, alter priorities, and terminate threads. You have a greater degree of control over how the threads can be managed than you would with the Task Manager utility. PVIEWER is strictly a "use at your own risk" utility that is, like most Resource Kit utilities, not supported by Microsoft.

Modifying Application Responsiveness

As noted in the preceding section on priorities, the Windows NT kernel manages and balances priority loads on the processor. When the kernel is dealing with application threads, whether the application is running in the foreground or background affects the priority level of the application's thread or threads. Windows NT provides a utility in the Control Panel's System applet through which you can adjust how Windows NT changes the priority based on foreground and background activity. A change here affects all applications, whereas the START command option affects a particular application.

The Performance tab on the System applet's Properties sheet provides three settings that affect foreground application responsiveness:

- Maximum gives the application a two-level priority boost from 8 to 10 when the application is running in the foreground. Background applications continue to run at the normal level of 8. This setting is the default for foreground responsiveness.

- The middle setting boosts the priority level of a foreground application by one level from 8 to 9, again leaving the background applications at the normal level. You can set the priority to the middle setting when it is not critical that foreground applications receive additional CPU consideration. For example, you might play Solitaire while your database is being sorted with this setting, but you would probably not work on your budget spreadsheet at the same time without putting the setting back to Maximum.

■ None leaves the foreground and background settings both at the normal level. In other words, Windows NT does not adjust processor time given to the application based on whether it is running in the foreground or the background. This setting might be good to use on a Windows NT server on which you need to occasionally use a utility. The utility should not at all decrease performance of the activities of connected clients.

Task Manager

Windows NT contains a utility that displays basic information about processes currently running on your system: the Windows NT Task Manager. You can access it by right-clicking the taskbar and selecting Task Manager. The Task Manager offers three tabs with information for your consideration and tracking: Applications, Processes, and Performance. At the bottom of the Task Manager window is a statistics bar that shows the total number of processes running and total CPU and RAM usage.

The Applications tab displays a list of the applications currently running on the computer and their status. If an application has failed or is hung, its status entry reflects that state. On this tab, you can choose End Tasks, especially to end those tasks that have failed or hung; choose Switch to move to other application windows; or load another application by selecting New Task. Choosing New Task actually brings up the Run dialog box in which you can enter the path and filename of the application executable, and choose to run WIN16 applications in their own memory space.

The Processes tab displays a list of User and Kernel mode processes that are running. If your WIN16 application and MS-DOS-based applications are not displayed here, select Options, Show 16-bit Tasks from the menu to include them. This option is generally selected by default. You can end any process by selecting it and choosing End Process. You can also right-click any process to end it or to change the priority of the process. These "use at your own risk" options should be used only to terminate or alter the priority of a process that you know is application-related (not kernel-related) and that has become unresponsive or bound to a processor.

The default screen lists the process name and ID number assigned by the Windows NT kernel, the percentage of CPU usage and CPU time that each process commands, and the amount of RAM used by the process. However, you can use nine additional columns to customize the display screen. To access them, choose View, Select Columns.

Additional choices include Memory Usage Delta, Page Faults (the number of requests for data from the page file or disk), Page Faults Delta, Virtual Memory Size (size of the virtual address space currently in use by the process), Paged Pool (number of bytes of data that can be paged to the pagefile), Non-Paged Pool (number of bytes of data that cannot be paged to the pagefile but must remain in memory), Base Priority (normal, low, high), Handle Count, and Thread Count.

The Performance tab is not a cover charge for using Task Manager. Rather, it offers a dynamic graphic overview of the CPU and RAM usage for the current session, as well as summary totals for threads, handles, commit limits (physical plus virtual memory), and kernel memory. If you have multiple processors in the computer, you can choose to show each processor in its own graph.

When the Task Manager is running, it places a CPU usage icon at the far right end on the taskbar. This icon graphically displays CPU usage; if you right-click it, it displays the percent of CPU usage at that point in time.

Also, clicking the column header above each column of data sorts that column's data alternately from greatest to lowest and from lowest to greatest.

**CH
IO**

Summary

In this chapter, you reviewed the Windows NT 4.0 subsystem architecture and examined Windows NT support for MS-DOS-based applications. You also examined Windows NT support for 16-bit Windows applications and support for WIN32, OS/2-based, and POSIX-based applications. Rounding out the chapter were considerations for troubleshooting applications.

Up to this point, we have been staying pretty close to home, meaning our computers. Though we have talked about network issues, we have not yet explored Windows NT network architecture. The next chapter, "Network Connectivity and Remote Support," will tackle this area of Windows NT Workstation 4.0.

┌─ QUESTIONS AND ANSWERS ──────────────────────────

1.   The process of converting 16-bit code to 32-bit code is known as

_____.

A. The process of converting 16-bit code to 32-bit code is known as thunking. Going from 16 to 32 is known as "thunking up," and going from 32 to 16 is known as "thunking down."

2.   Applications can be started at different priority levels from the command line via what utility?

A. Applications can be started at different priority levels from the command line via the START command.

3.   What is the default priority level for a normal job?

A. The default priority level for a normal job is 8.

4.   What does the acronym NTVDM stand for?

A. NT Virtual DOS Machine.

5.   True or False: WIN32 and POSIX applications run only on the platform for which they have been compiled.

A. True. WIN32 and POSIX applications run only on the platform for which they have been compiled.

└──

PRACTICE TEST

1. Which two subsystems are loaded when Windows NT boots?

   a. CSR and Security subsystems
   b. CSR and OS/2 subsystems
   c. Environment and Security subsystems
   d. OS/2 and POSIX subsystems

Answer a is correct because the Client/Server (CSR) and Security subsystems are loaded at boot. Answer b is incorrect because the OS/2 subsystem is not loaded when NT boots. Answer c is incorrect because there is not a subsystem called Environment. Answer d is incorrect because neither the OS/2 nor the POSIX subsystems are loaded when NT boots.

2. Following the power-on self-test, what does NT load?

    a. Environment settings

    b. Master boot record

    c. OS Kernel

    d. OS system file

Answers a, c, and d are incorrect because NT loads the MBR following the POST. **Answer b is correct because the master boot record (MBR) is loaded following the POST.**

3. What are the two primary phases of the NT boot sequence?

    a. Boot and load

    b. Boot and initialize

    c. Load and initialize

    d. Startup and shutdown

Answer a is correct because boot and load are the two primary phases of the NT boot sequence. Answer b is incorrect because initialize is not a primary phase of the boot sequence. Answer c is incorrect because initialize is not a primary phase of the boot sequence. Answer d is incorrect because neither startup nor shutdown are primary phases of the boot sequence.

4. Where are the operating system choices displayed during bootup stored?

    a. The Registry

    b. The master boot record

    c. BOOT.INI

    d. CONFIG.SYS

Answers a, b, and d are incorrect because the BOOT.INI file holds the startup choices. **Answer c is correct because the text file BOOT.INI holds the startup choices.**

5. Which files are read before NT displays the blue screen (check all that apply)?

    a. BOOT.INI

    b. CONFIG.SYS

    c. NTLDR

    d. COMMAND.COM

Answers a and c are correct because both BOOT.INI and DTLDR are read before the blue screen appears. Answer b is incorrect because the CONFIG.SYS file is not necessary and is not read prior to the blue screen. Answer d is a file used in the MS-DOS operating system.

CH

10

6. Mandy is running Pinball, the DOS Editor, Word 6, Excel 5, and Microstomp, which is a 16-bit, third-party Windows Web surfing program. Microstomp has been configured to run in its own memory space. Microstomp has hung up because of low resource memory. What other applications will be affected?

   a. No other applications

   b. No other applications except the DOS Editor

   c. No other applications except Pinball

   d. No other applications except the other WIN16 applications

Answer a is correct because the applications are isolated, and no other applications will be affected by the hanging of the one. Answers b, c, and d are incorrect because all applications run in their own environment.

7. Which of the following statements are true about the NTVDM?

   a. Each NTVDM has one thread of operation associated with it.

   b. Each NTVDM is designed to emulate the Windows memory environment, and it provides a set of support files to do so.

   c. Each NTVDM is configurable by modifying the properties of the MS-DOS application.

   d. Each NTVDM is configurable through one AUTOEXEC.BAT file and one CONFIG.SYS file read when Windows NT boots.

Answers a and c are correct because each NTVDM is configurable and has one thread of operation. Answer b is incorrect because NTVDM is intended for DOS, not Windows. Answer d is incorrect because these files are read when the application is run, not when NT boots.

8. Angela has an older MS-DOS program that she needs to run on her Windows NT 4.0 workstation. The application requires a specific environmental variable set and device driver loaded. How can you help Angela configure her program to run successfully?

   a. Configure the program to run in its own memory space.

   b. Create AUTOEXEC.BAT and CONFIG.SYS with the appropriate settings to load when Windows NT boots.

   c. Create specific AUTOEXEC and CONFIG files for the application and reference them in the application's properties (PIF).

   d. Install the application using the ADD Application applet in the Control Panel, and reference the environment variable and device driver during installation.

Answer a is incorrect because the separate memory space still does not perform the needed configuration. Answer b is incorrect because these files are read when the application runs, not when NT boots. **Answer c is correct because AUTOEXEC and CONFIG files can be created for every application as long as the PIF holds the information to find them.** Answer d is incorrect because there is no such applet.

9. Which of the following statements accurately describe a WIN16 application running under Windows NT 4.0?

    a. All WIN16 applications run in the same NTVDM by default.

    b. All WIN16 applications are nonpreemptively multitasked within the NTVDM.

    c. Through a process called thunking, 16-bit calls are translated into 32-bit calls.

    d. WOW emulates the Windows 3.1 memory environment for WIN16 applications.

All the above are correct. WIN16 applications run in the same NTVDM by default, are cooperatively multitasked, run via WOW (Windows On Windows), and their code is translated in both directions via thunking.

10. Mandy is running Pinball, the DOS Editor, Word 6, Excel 5, and Microstomp, which is a 16-bit, third-party Windows Web surfing program. Microstomp occasionally hangs because of low resource memory. This problem affects her other Windows applications. What can you suggest to alleviate this problem?

    a. Configure Microstomp to run in its own memory space.

    b. Configure each WIN16 application to run in its own memory space.

    c. Modify the PIF for Microstomp to increase its resource memory allocation.

    d. Modify the PIF for the WOW NTVDM to increase resource memory allocations for all the Windows applications.

Answer a is correct because isolating the application to its own memory space will alleviate the problem. Answer b is incorrect because only the application in question need run in its own memory space. Answers c and d are incorrect because resources are not the problem. The interaction between it and other applications—specifically memory sharing—is the problem.

Network Connectivity and Remote Support

WHILE YOU READ

1. An enhancement to the PPP protocol is _____ .

2. True or False: The tunneling protocol can work with NetBEUI PPP packets over TCP/IP.

3. The administration of the Web service is done through

   _____ .

4. What is the client component of RAS?

5. True or False: Auditing on RAS features can be enabled to track remote connection processes such as logging on and dialing back users.

In this chapter, we will review the Windows NT 4.0 network architecture, including the protocols supported by NT 4.0, a brief overview of TCP/IP, and the newest advantages of this release. We'll also review the functions of services related to network activity, client support for NetWare networks, and remote access support. This description is not meant to be exhaustive; instead, we'll focus on networking as it pertains to Windows NT Workstation 4.0.

Exploring the Windows NT 4.0 Networking Model

As described in Chapter 2, "Understanding Microsoft Windows NT 4.0," networking capabilities are fully integrated into Windows NT Workstation and Server 4.0. Network support is supplied for Microsoft network clients, such as Windows 95 and Windows for Workgroups, and also for Apple Macintosh clients (through Services for Macintosh on the Windows NT Server), NetWare clients and servers (through a variety of NetWare connectivity products for both Windows NT Workstation and Server 4.0, but primarily for the Server), and TCP/IP systems, such as Internet connectivity and UNIX hosts. In addition, dial-in capabilities are also supported and fully integrated.

The Windows NT 4.0 network architecture is positioned as part of the Executive Services running in Kernel mode. In fact, the Windows NT 4.0 network architecture is itself a three-tiered model that is an integrated part of the Windows NT Executive Service called the I/O Manager (see Figure 11.1). The I/O Manager is primarily responsible for determining whether a request for resource access is locally or remotely directed. If it is remotely directed, the request enters the layers of the network model.

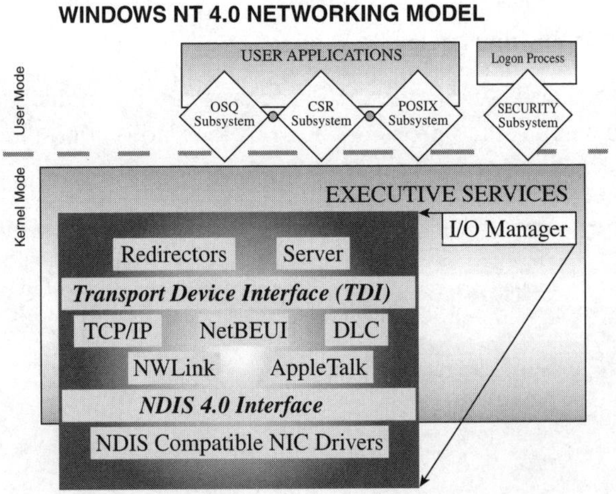

WINDOWS NT 4.0 NETWORKING MODEL

Figure 11.1
The Windows NT 4.0 networking model.

The three layers are the File System (or Redirector) layer, the Protocol layer, and the NIC (or Adapter) layer. Each layer is separated but bound by a boundary or transmission interface through which the request must pass to get to each layer.

Comparing the OSI Model to Windows NT's Network Model

You may be familiar with the Open Systems Interconnection (OSI) network model created by the International Organization for Standards (ISO). This seven-layer model begins with the Application layer and concludes with the Physical layer. The seven layers of the OSI model are Application, Presentation, and Session, corresponding to the File System layer in Windows NT's model; Transport and Network, corresponding to the Protocol layer in Windows NT's model; and Data Link and Physical, corresponding to the NIC layer in Windows NT's model.

Microsoft decided to simplify the model and path the requests took through the layers by synthesizing it into three layers connected by two boundary interfaces.

When the request is made, a path to the location of the resource is established by finding the most appropriate "path" through the layers of the client computer, through the network connection, and up through the layers of the server computer—the computer that has the resource. These paths through the layers are known as the bindings for that computer. The established connection between a client and server computer is called the interprocess communication (IPC) mechanism that enables data to flow between the computers. This type of interaction is often referred to as distributed processing. A computer may have several bindings to various protocols to enable the establishment of various IPC mechanisms for different networking platforms, such as NetWare IPX or UNIX TCP/IP. Some of these mechanisms are outlined in Table 11.1.

CH
II

Table 11.1 IPC Connections

Type of Connection	Description
Named Pipes	A two-way connection channel that guarantees data is sent, received, and acknowledged by both computers.
Mailslots	A one-way connection channel in which data is sent with no acknowledgment of receipt. NetBIOS broadcasts are examples of mailslot IPC connections.
Windows Sockets	A Windows application-based programming interface (API) that enables two-way acknowledged data transfer between the computers and provides communications support with NetWare Loadable Modules (NLMs).

...continues

Table 11.1 continued	
Type of Connection	*Description*
NetBIOS	Another application-based programming interface (API) that enables two-way acknowledged data transfer between the computers.
Distributed Component Object Model (DCOM)	A new IPC model in Windows NT 4.0 that enables the distribution of processes across multiple servers in the Windows NT network for the purpose of optimizing access and performance of network-based programs.

Now we'll take a look at the various components of the Windows NT 4.0 network architecture.

File System Layer

The File System layer is also known as the Redirector layer because the Windows NT I/O Manager determines where to "redirect" the request for the resource in this layer. If the request is for a local resource, a file on an NTFS partition, the request is kept local and directed to the appropriate file system—in this case, to NTFS on the partition.

If the request is for a resource on another computer in the network, the request must be "redirected" to that remote location. As you learned, the remote location might be on another Windows NT workstation or server; therefore, the I/O Manager redirects the request to Windows NT's own built-in network redirector, RDR.SYS, also known as the workstation service. Every Windows NT computer, whether workstation or server, has a workstation service configured to load and run automatically upon booting Windows NT. Every Windows NT computer has the capability of making, and does make, requests for resources on other computers.

However, the requests could be for a resource on a NetWare server or a UNIX host; therefore, the requests must be "redirected" accordingly. In the case of NetWare, redirecting involves loading another redirector that can interpret requests meant for a NetWare server and find the appropriate binding and IPC connection to send the message. On a Windows NT Workstation, this additional redirector is the Client Services for NetWare service (CSNW) that comes with Windows NT Workstation 4.0 as an installable service. You might need to obtain other network redirectors from the network manufacturer.

Protocol Layer

Protocols are responsible for creating the packets of information sent from one computer to another across the network connection. Various networks support or require specific protocols when communicating with a computer in that network. UNIX hosts require TCP/IP, for example, whereas NetWare networks prefer IPX/SPX.

Windows NT 4.0 supports five protocols. TCP/IP, a routable protocol supporting enterprise networking and NetBIOS connections, is used to connect to the Internet and UNIX hosts. NWLink IPX/SPX is Microsoft's 32-bit implementation of IPX/SPX. It also is routable and supports enterprise networking among Windows NT network clients, as well as connection to Novell servers. NetBEUI is a fast, efficient, but nonroutable protocol used within smaller networks and thus is not well-suited for enterprise networking. The Data Link Control (DLC) protocol is used to provide connection support to SNA mainframe computers and network-connected printers. AppleTalk is used primarily on Windows NT Server 4.0 computers providing remote access support for Apple Macintosh computers through Services for Macintosh. TCP/IP, NWLink, and NetBEUI will be examined in more detail later in this chapter.

Windows NT 4.0 supports the installation of one or more protocols in each Windows NT computer.

Network Adapter (NIC) Layer

The Network Adapter layer is the hardware layer consisting of the NDIS 4.0-compatible network interface card (NIC) drivers that initialize and manage communications through the hardware device connected to the network. Windows NT 4.0 supports the installation of one or more network interface cards in each Windows NT computer, provided that the card is compatible with Windows NT (read: on the HCL) and has an NDIS 4.0-compatible driver available to support it.

CH
II

Transport Device Interface

The Transport Device Interface (TDI) is a boundary interface between the Redirector layer and protocols. It provides a common programming interface that any redirector can use to build a path (bind) to any and all appropriate installed protocols. This capability allows the redirectors to remain independent of the protocols installed and makes it extremely easy (and attractive) for network manufacturers to write redirectors for Windows NT. The TDI provides the translation necessary to enable the redirector to "talk" successfully with the protocol. This process is called "binding" the redirector to a protocol.

NDIS 4.0 Interface

The NDIS 4.0 boundary interface does for network cards what the TDI does for redirectors. It provides a common programming interface between the protocols and the NICs. Protocols are written to communicate with the NDIS 4.0 interface. NIC drivers are also written to communicate with the NDIS 4.0 interface. Consequently, only one set of drivers needs to be written for either a protocol or an NIC. In other models, each protocol would require drivers to communicate with every NIC installed in a computer. This is no longer necessary in Windows NT 4.0. As with the TDI interface, this capability makes it attractive and easy to write protocol and card drivers to work with Windows NT.

Benefits of TDI and NDIS 4.0

The ultimate benefit from Windows NT's network model is that the TDI and NDIS 4.0 interfaces do all the work of finding the appropriate path for a resource request out on the network. They provide the "bindings" between the layers. As a result, you can install any number of compatible protocols, redirectors, and NICs in a given Windows NT computer. TDI and NDIS 4.0 neatly manage communications among them.

Furthermore, each network card can have multiple protocols bound to it. Thus, your Windows NT workstation can "talk" with any computer on the network running any of your installed protocols. For example, it would be possible for your computer to have two NICs installed on your Windows NT 4.0 workstation. One NIC could use the NetBEUI protocol to communicate with computers on one subnet, while the other NIC could use TCP/IP to communicate with computers on another subnet. You can access resources on computers in either subnet with this arrangement.

As the administrator, you have the ability to fine-tune these bindings, even turn them off if they're not being used. We will explore this ability in a later section in this chapter.

Examining NetBEUI, NWLink, and TCP/IP

Of the five communication protocols supported by Windows NT 4.0, three are most likely to be used for computer-to-computer communications: NetBEUI, NWLink, and TCP/IP. In the preceding sections, we briefly reviewed each. Here, we will look at them in a bit more detail as they relate to Windows NT networking.

NetBEUI

As stated earlier, NetBEUI is a fast, efficient networking protocol used mostly for small, single subnet local area networks (LANs) rather than large, multiple subnet wide area networks (WANs) because NetBEUI is not a routable protocol.

This protocol relies heavily on network broadcast messages to find and complete IPCs and thereby provide communications between computers. Subsequently, NetBEUI LANs have a relatively high level of broadcast traffic. Think of a broadcast as a computer calling out its name with a request for a specific computer, or a response to another computer's request.

NetBEUI has no configuration parameters in Windows NT 4.0.

NWLink IPX/SPX Compatible Transport

NWLink IPX/SPX Compatible Transport is Microsoft's 32-bit NDIS 4.0-compatible implementation of the IPX/SPX protocol; it enables Windows NT 4.0 computers to establish connections with other computers or networks running IPX/SPX (such as NetWare networks). NWLink supports the NetBIOS over IPX and Windows Sockets APIs described previously.

Being an IPX/SPX-compatible protocol, NWLink enables any computer running IPX/SPX, such as NetWare client computers, to communicate with client/server applications running on Windows NT computers. For example, NetWare clients running IPX/SPX could interact with an SQL database running on a Windows NT 4.0 server that is using NWLink as its networking protocol.

NWLink is configurable on Windows NT 4.0. Three options can be set on Windows NT computers. They are the frame type, the network number, and, new to Windows NT 4.0 servers, the Routing Information Protocol (RIP).

The network adapter card formats the data packet for transmission on the network. A number of factors determine how this packaging occurs as the request passes through the layers of the Windows NT network model. One of the factors is the network protocol. NWLink requires that a frame type associated with the topology of the network be part of the packet format. The data packet can be serviced only by computers formatted for the same frame type.

NWLink supports Ethernet II, 802.2, 802.3, and SNAP for Ethernet topologies; 802.5 and SNAP for Token Ring; and 802.2 and SNAP for FDDI (Fiber Distributed Data Interface). NetWare networks default to 802.3 for versions 3.11 and older and 802.2 for versions 3.12 and later.

Windows NT computers using NWLink, by default, automatically detect the frame type being used on the network topology and switch to this frame type. This capability is particularly useful if you are not sure what frame type is being used. However, if multiple frame types are detected—for example, both NetWare 3.11 and 3.12 servers are on the network—then NWLink defaults to 802.2.

Key Concept

Because NWLink defaults to 802.2 when multiple frame types are detected on the network, communications might not take place among some of the computers—those with differing frame types. If this is true on your network, you need to configure NWLink manually to recognize multiple frame types and include them in the packet format for your network.

CH
II

Configuring NWLink Frame Types

If you need to configure your Windows NT 4.0 computer to recognize multiple frame types, the method is somewhat different for workstations and servers.

On a Windows NT 4.0 server, you can make your selections from the frame type list on the General tab for NWLink properties.

However, on a Windows NT 4.0 workstation, you must make the change in the NT Registry. To do so, start the Registry Editor, and expand it to find the key

```
HKEY_LOCAL_MACHINE\System\CurrentControlSet\Services\NwlinkIpx\NetConfig\
network adapter card1
```

where *network adapter card1* is the entry for your network adapter card. Look for the parameter PktType. This multistring parameter is set to ff for autodetecting frame types. You can specify multiple frame types by removing ff (the default value) and adding the appropriate values for each frame type, each on its own line in the string editor dialog box, according to the following legend:

0   Ethernet II

1   Ethernet 802.3

2   Ethernet 802.2

3   Ethernet SNAP

4   ArcNet

Another parameter that you sometimes need to set in the network properties for NWLink is the network number. The IPX machine address is made up of two parts: one is the network address; the other is the node address. They are normally represented as DEADDEAD: 00000000. The network number represents the internal network number used for Windows NT and identifies the computer to the network by assigning a logical hexadecimal address to the network interface card. The default is 00000000. In general, especially if you have only one network interface card installed, you do not need to change the default. However, if you have installed multiple network interface cards in your computer or are communicating with services such as SQL or SNA whose applications may require such identification, then you need to provide a network address for each network interface card installed.

New to Windows NT 4.0 is the capability to enable your Windows NT server to act as an IPX router. You do so by enabling the RIP (Routing Information Protocol) setting for NWLink. Turning on this setting enables the Windows NT server to broadcast IPX routing information such as network addresses to other IPX routers, thus enabling IPX/SPX communications packets to be easily transmitted from one IPX subnet to another. If you have multiple network cards installed in your Windows NT server connected to different subnets, you can enable RIP for each and let the Windows NT server route between the cards.

TCP/IP Protocol

You can consult mountains of books, magazine articles, Web sites, and friends of friends to obtain some excellent (and poor) information about TCP/IP and Internet communications. The purpose of this section is to relate TCP/IP as it applies to Windows NT Workstation 4.0.

As you know, TCP/IP is the communications protocol of the nineties. Well, it is the Internet communications protocol, and it is the default protocol choice selected during your installation of Windows NT Workstation and Server 4.0.

TCP/IP is designed with the enterprise network in mind. Originally developed by the United States Department of Defense and subsequently endorsed by certain educational institutions as a research data-sharing mechanism, TCP/IP is network independent and eminently routable. It does not matter what network operating system you may use internally within your organization. If you use TCP/IP to connect to the Internet, you can communicate with any other organization's network that is also connected to the Internet through TCP/IP.

In addition, on a Windows NT 4.0 computer with at least two network interface cards, each card can receive its own IP address, and the computer can then be configured to act as an IP router. A Windows NT 4.0 computer configured in this way is referred to as a multi-homed computer.

TCP/IP is a suite of protocols, each designed to handle a specific element of network communications. For example, the IP part of TCP/IP, which stands for Internet Protocol, provides addressing and routing functions. The TCP part, which stands for Transmission Control Protocol, provides connection-oriented guaranteed packet delivery with error checking. Also included in the suite are Windows Sockets, NetBIOS over TCP/IP, User Datagram Protocol (UDP) providing connectionless broadcast communications, Address Resolution Protocol (ARP) resolving the IP address of a computer to the hardware address of its network interface card, and Simple Network Management Protocol (SNMP) providing network management data required by Management Information Base (MIB) program servers.

TCP/IP comes with a variety of built-in and add-on utilities supplied in the Windows NT 4.0 installation of this protocol. They are used to support data transfer and troubleshooting. Some of them are described in Table 11.2.

CH

II

Table 11.2	TCP/IP Utilities
Utility	Description
PING	Tests and verifies communications between IP addresses
IPCONFIG	Displays current TCP/IP settings associated with the computer, such as IP address, default gateway address, subnet mask, and WINS server address
FTP	Provides a bidirectional file transfer mechanism between two TCP/IP configured computers
Telnet	Provides a terminal emulation mechanism to another TCP/IP host computer running a Telnet host program
Internet Explorer	Facilitates searching for and locating data on the Internet through a GUI interface
Finger	Retrieves configuration information from another computer running TCP/IP

Of these utilities, PING and IPCONFIG are of particular value as troubleshooting devices.

You can use PING (Packet Internet Groper) to verify that the IP address information, especially to routers and remote hosts, is correct and the routers and hosts can be contacted. At a command prompt, you type **PING** followed by the IP address of the other host or router. If the connection is made, PING responds with four "reply from" messages from the other host.

You can use IPCONFIG to verify address parameters associated with a particular host computer. For example, if you want to see what your computer's current IP address and subnet mask are, you can type **IPCONFIG** at a command prompt, and the information is displayed. IPCONFIG offers several command-line switches that are displayed with descriptions when you type **IPCONFIG /?** at a command prompt. The /ALL switch additionally displays hardware address information and DHCP and WINS address information.

The three most important pieces of information you need to provide when configuring TCP/IP are the IP address, the subnet mask, and the default gateway address. The IP address, of course, is the address of your computer (called a host) on the network. It is a 32-bit address more commonly displayed as a four-part decimal address separated by dots—for example, 121.132.43.5. Each host address must be unique in the network, and each host must have an address.

The subnet mask is used to identify the IP addresses of one network from those of other networks. It is also used within an organization to identify networks (often referred to as subnets) within the organization from other networks connected by routers. It does so by blocking out, or "masking," a portion of the address by performing a binary "and" of the IP address with the subnet mask. All the addresses associated with a specific subnet mask resolve to the same result when the calculation is performed. Those that do not are not considered part of the local network.

When a data packet is sent to another computer within a subnet, the IP address of the source and target hosts along with the subnet mask determine that the data packet remains within the subnet. Further address and name resolution then takes place to ensure that the data packet arrives at its destination. Likewise, when a data packet is destined for a target host on another subnet, the subnet mask is used to determine that the target host address is not on this subnet. As a result, the data packet is sent to a router configured to send the data packet along to its appropriate subnet destination.

The default gateway address is the specific router to which these "nonsubnet" packets are sent for further address resolution. Routers maintain lists of subnet addresses and masks to which they are connected to facilitate the sending of packets from one subnet to another. Routers themselves may have default gateways for data packets whose address and subnet mask information is not in the router's table.

Through the combination of IP addresses, subnet masks, and routers, a data packet can take one of possibly several routes to get from here to there successfully, even if a router is down along the way. This is partially why the entity is referred to as the "Web." It is a web-like network of routers through which data packets can "ping-pong" like balls in a pinball machine, but with a more determined direction rather than just a random pattern. *Web* primarily refers to the HTML/HTTP protocol used by the World Wide Web and references the links that connect Web pages like threads of a spider's web.

IP Address Considerations

You can see the significance of having the appropriate, unique addresses and subnet masks identified for each computer on the network. An inaccurate IP address or subnet mask can result in communications failure all the way around.

Furthermore, if a computer is moved from one subnet to another, all the address information must be adjusted to correspond with the new location. The old TCP/IP parameters configured on that computer will likely not apply to the new subnet. Adjusting this information requires a high level of documentation and attention to the details of your network.

Windows NT does include a Server service that can provide the appropriate TCP/IP configuration data to a computer automatically, foregoing the need to configure each computer itself. It is available for all Microsoft Windows NT, Windows 95, Windows for Workgroups, and MS-DOS clients (with an appropriate add-on) and is called Dynamic Host Configuration Protocol, or DHCP. DHCP is a Windows NT Server service only and is not available for Windows NT workstations.

The DHCP service enables you to create and maintain a range of IP addresses available for a subnet, along with the appropriate subnet mask information, default gateway information, and other IP information options. Currently, Microsoft DHCP clients accept and use the following additional information options:

- DNS Server—Specifies a list of Domain Name System (DNS) servers available to the client listed in order of preference and with at least one IP address referenced.

- WINS Server (NetBIOS Name Server, or NBNS)—Specifies a list of RFC 1001/1002 NBNS name servers listed in order of preference and with at least one IP address referenced.

- NetBIOS Node Type—Allows configuration of NetBIOS node type options as described in RFC 1001/1002. They include B-node, P-node, M-node, and H-node.

- NetBIOS Scope ID—Specifies the scope parameter for the client as described in RFC 1001/1002.

When a client configured to use DHCP is booted, it requests its IP configuration parameters from the DHCP server. The DHCP server then assigns the client an address from its pool of addresses and also provides the supplementary information (subnet mask and so on).

This service effectively eliminates the need for you to closely monitor the configuration parameters of each computer. For example, if the computer moves from one subnet to another, when it boots, it merely asks the DHCP server on that subnet for its address information. The computer is, in effect, oblivious to the fact that it has moved. You can obtain the current assigned address information for any given computer by using the IPCONFIG command at that computer.

Another address-related component essential to successful communication between computers is the NetBIOS name of the computers. The computer name that you assigned during Windows NT installation is the NetBIOS name of the computer. This name is the one broadcast when the computer is booted and the name that you see when browsing for resources. It is also the name you generally use to establish connections between computers using TCP/IP rather than typing in an IP address.

When you attempt to establish communications using a computer's NetBIOS name—for example, mapping a network drive through Windows Explorer—TCP/IP needs to be able to resolve that name to that computer's IP address. If the computer you are mapping to is on the same subnet, this resolution takes place as a NetBIOS name broadcast. However, if the computer you are mapping to is on a different subnet, a NetBIOS name broadcast does not resolve the address. Another method must be used. This has generally been done through a name and address table known as an LMHOSTS file that is maintained on every computer in the network. TCP/IP doesn't maintain the LMHOSTS file; rather, the administrator must modify it manually when adding or removing computers from the network or changing a computer's name. You can see the compounded mess that ensues when a computer moves.

The list can be dynamically maintained on a "host name" server in several ways. Windows NT provides another server-based service that collects and maintains NetBIOS names, and provides name-to-address resolution. It is called Windows Internet Name Service, or WINS for short.

WINS eliminates the need for separate host files on each computer by compiling name and address information in its own database. When a request for name-to-address resolution is made on the network, WINS responds to it by providing the information it has collected to the requesting computers.

You will learn more about DHCP and WINS as you continue your education process with Windows NT Server 4.0. They are mentioned here because Windows NT 4.0 workstations are compatible with, and often are configured to use, these services, and you are likely to see references to them on the Windows NT Workstation 4.0 exam.

Configuring and Installing Network Options

Network-based options are installed, configured, and maintained through the Network applet in the Control Panel and are also accessible through the Network Neighborhood properties (see Figure 11.2). The applet has five tabs, three of which are of particular interest to the current discussion. The five tabs are Protocols, Adapters, Bindings (the first three being of interest to us), Identification, and Services.

CH

II

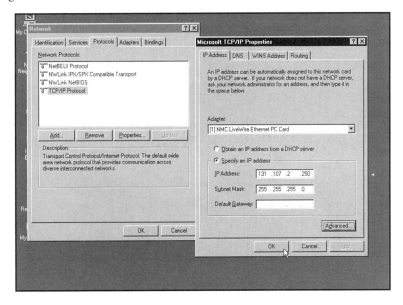

Figure 11.2
The Network applet showing the Protocols tab and the Properties sheet for the TCP/IP protocol.

The Protocols tab displays a list of the currently installed network protocols. Choosing Add displays a list of all the protocols that are available for installation through Windows NT or through an OEM disk. You can choose Remove to remove the protocols from the computer or Update to update a protocol driver. Protocols are configured during installation of the protocol, or you can configure them by selecting the protocol from the list and choosing Properties. For example, notice the TCP/IP configuration parameters displayed in Figure 11.2. You can specify the usual required IP address and subnet mask, but you can also specify Domain Name Service parameters, indicate the location of the WINS server, and configure IP routing. You can determine whether the IP information is obtained from a DHCP server, and you can even specify IP configuration by network adapter card.

The Adapters tab, shown in Figure 11.3, displays the installed network adapter cards. Again, if you choose Add, Windows NT displays a list of all supported adapter cards for which Windows NT supplies an NDIS-compatible driver. You can also install a card using a manufacturer-supplied driver, provided it is NDIS compatible. You also can choose Remove and Update to remove and update drivers, respectively. Network adapter card drivers are configured during installation of the card, or you can configure them by selecting the card from the list and choosing Properties. Settings associated with the card are displayed in a dialog box similar to the one shown in Figure 11.3. Settings such as IRQ level, DMA base, I/O base, and transceiver type can be viewed and modified here.

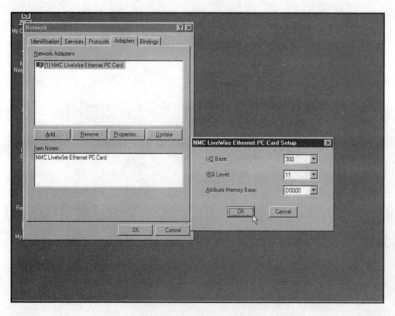

Figure 11.3
Through the Adapters tab, you can add adapter cards and configure adapter card settings.

The Bindings tab displays in a graphic format the "paths" that network-bound communications can take to complete their tasks. Because this tab is arranged like Windows Explorer, you can easily expand through a protocol or service to see what that protocol or service is bound to. For example, in Figure 11.4 you can see that an application using NetBIOS will communicate with the network through NWLink NetBIOS that is bound to NWLink IPX/SPX, or through NetBEUI to other computers running NWLink or NetBEUI.

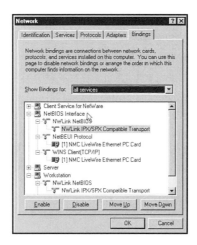

Figure 11.4
This tab shows some of the bindings for NetBIOS and Workstation.

As you can also see from the available buttons on the Bindings tab, you can enable or disable bindings and change their order. If you think of network bindings as being a path that a communications request can take, all enabled bindings are possibilities, and Windows NT will check each one to find the best path to take. Further, it will search the paths in the order it encounters them. Therefore, you can improve network performance somewhat by moving the "paths" most likely to be taken up in the list so that they are encountered and chosen ahead of the others, or by disabling paths that are infrequently used.

For example, suppose that you can communicate with several computers throughout your network using TCP/IP and NWLink. Some of the computers have only NWLink, but most use TCP/IP or both. You most frequently communicate with the computers using TCP/IP. If NWLink appears ahead of TCP/IP in the bindings list, Windows NT has to check the NWLink binding first before choosing TCP/IP (which it usually winds up choosing anyway because you most frequently talk with the TCP/IP computers). If you move the bindings for TCP/IP ahead of NWLink, then for those computers that you most frequently talk with using TCP/IP, Windows NT has to check only the first binding for TCP/IP and never go any further.

As another example, say that you maintain an archive computer on your subnet so that you can back up data once a month using NetBEUI. There is no particular reason to leave the binding for NetBEUI active because you use it only once a month. It is taking up resources and very probably sending out many broadcast messages that can affect network traffic. In this case, you could disable the binding for NetBEUI and enable it only when you need to use the protocol to communicate with the archive computer.

The Identification tab of the Network applet displays the current computer (NetBIOS) name and workgroup or domain that the computer participates in. You can change either setting through the Change button. You'll explore this tab in more detail later in this chapter.

The Services tab displays Windows NT services that are currently installed on the computer. Recall that services are programs and processes that are added to the Executive Services portion of the Windows NT operating system to perform specific tasks. For example, if you want your Windows NT 4.0 workstation to be able to log in to a NetWare server, you need to install Client Services for NetWare on your computer. You add that service through the Services tab by selecting Add and choosing it from the list of available services.

We'll look at three services in particular next. They are Workstation, Server, and Computer Browser.

Reviewing Workstation and Server Services

The Workstation and Server services are both integral to your ability to share and access resources on the network. You may recall earlier the reference to the redirector that determines which network and binding a resource request is meant for. The Windows NT 4.0 redirector file is RDR.SYS and is more commonly called the Workstation service. In addition to accessing network resources, the Workstation service provides the ability to log on to a domain, connect to shared folders and printers, and access distributed applications. It is your "outgoing" pipe to the Windows NT network.

The "incoming" pipe is the Server service. The Server service enables the creating and sharing of network resources such as printers and folders. It also accepts incoming requests for resource access, directs the request to the appropriate resource (or file system such as NTFS), and forwards resources back to the source computer.

Now let's try to put the whole process together. A request for a Windows NT network resource is made and sent to the I/O manager on a computer. The I/O manager determines that the request is not for a local resource and sends it to the appropriate network redirector, in this case, the Workstation service. Through the redirector and the bindings, the appropriate protocol is chosen and packet created and sent through the network interface card onto the network.

The resource request is received by the target computer (determined by NetBIOS name, or IP address, or NWLink hardware address, or frame type, and so on). It is serviced by the Server service on the target computer that determines which resource is required and where it is located (local printer, NTFS folder, and so on) and directs it there. After the access control list for the resource determines the effective access to the resource, the appropriate resource response (printer driver, file, and so on) is forwarded back through the now-established IPC connection to the client computer.

Two additional components play a part in determining name and redirector resolution for network requests. The Multiple Universal Naming Provider (MUP) enables the client computer to browse for and request network resources by their UNC name. Recall this is the syntax in which a resource path is established by naming the server and share name for the resource. For example, a folder shared as DATA on server ACCT1 can be accessed by mapping a network drive in Windows Explorer to \\ACCT1\DATA—its UNC name. Along with the MUP, the Multiple Provider Router (MPR) ensures that on computers with multiple redirectors to multiple networks, requests for network resources are routed to the appropriate network redirector. After a connection has been established to a network, it is cached for that session, and the MPR provides the "route" again for additional requests for that network.

Introducing the Computer Browser Service

CH

II

The Computer Browser service is an interesting Windows NT service over which you have about as much control as watching the sun rise in the east. Well, you have a little more control than that, but not much.

Computer Browser's primary mission is to provide lists of network servers and their resources to waiting clients (see Figure 11.5). For example, when you choose Tools, Map Network Drive in Windows Explorer, the dialog box displays a list of networks detected, domains and workgroups, computers in each that have shared resources, and finally the resources shared on each computer. This list is collected, maintained, and provided by the Computer Browser service.

Browser lists are maintained on specific computers called browsers. There are various types of browsers, each with a specific role to play in the process. They are described in Table 11.3.

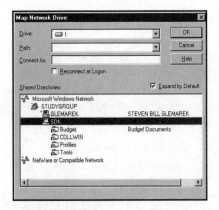

Figure 11.5
The Computer Browser Service creates and maintains the list of computers and shared resources displayed when mapping a network drive.

Table 11.3 Browser Computer Types and Roles	
Type	Role
Master Browser	This browser computer compiles and maintains the master list of computers and their shared resources. Every workgroup or domain subnet has its own master browser. It distributes copies of its list to backup browsers, or to a domain master browser if applicable, on a periodic basis.
Domain Master Browser	This browser computer is always the primary domain controller (PDC) in a domain-based enterprise network. It compiles and maintains an enterprise-wide list of network resources collected from all the master browsers in the domain, as well as from other domain master browsers for other domains in the enterprise. It distributes copies of its list to the master browsers in the domain, as well as to other domain master browsers on a periodic basis.
Backup Browser	This browser computer gets a copy of the master list from a master browser in its workgroup or domain subnet that it distributes to client computers on request (as when mapping a network drive through Windows Explorer).
Potential Browser	This computer has not yet assumed a browser role but has the potential of becoming a backup or master browser.
Non-Browser	This computer has been configured to never become a browser computer of any role.

It is important to realize that a finite number of computers assumes a particular browser role. Every domain has one domain master browser. Every workgroup or domain subnet has one master browser and at least one backup browser. For every 32 computers in a workgroup or domain, an additional backup browser is configured. It is equally important to remember that these browser roles are determined with virtually no input from you.

Browser Elections

Computers assume their browser roles through an election process. If you check your Event Viewer's system log first thing in the morning, you will notice several entries relating to the browser. Closer inspection will show that they are actually browser election events in which your Windows NT workstation participated.

Consider first the presidential election process—simplified a great deal. Several people want to be elected president. They each publish criteria they feel make them appropriate for the office. The candidates are whittled down in primaries and decided in a general election. When the president is elected, he or she names members to the Cabinet based on their qualifications. These Cabinet members are often chosen from among those who ran for president.

The browser election process is quite similar. When computers boot up, they announce their criteria to become a browser computer. Of course, they would like to be a master browser. The master browser is determined by the computer with the highest criteria— the best credentials for the job. For example, a primary domain controller always becomes a domain master browser because being a PDC is about the coolest thing a computer can do in a domain. (You get the idea.)

Criteria that decide browser roles include the operating system type and version; current browser role—master browser, backup browser, or potential browser; the server type— primary domain controller, secondary domain controller, or member server; and length of time it has been a browser. For example, if your computer is already a master browser, it is not likely to resign that role unless a truly more appropriate computer comes along. If all else is equal, the computer with the lexically lower name becomes the browser.

So these election packets are broadcast on the network and received by a browser. Their criteria are compared, and those with lower criteria are discarded and the process continued until a master browser is elected. The master browser then assigns one or more computers the role of backup browser, again based on election criteria.

If the master browser should become unavailable, the backup browser detects that status and forces another election to determine the new master browser.

Configuring Browsers

As you learned previously, you have little control over the election process. In fact, the most you can do is make some determinations for your Windows NT computer as to whether it should participate in the election process or not. No utility is provided in Windows NT—for example, in the Control Panel—to bring about these modifications. This being the case, the configuration must be done in the Registry.

The Registry key you are looking for is HKEY_LOCAL_MACHINE\ System\ CurrentControlSet\Services\Browser\Parameters. Look for a parameter entry called MaintainServerList. By default, this entry is set to Auto. This means that the computer will participate in the election process and could become a master or backup browser. You can set this value to No to have it never become a browser. Setting the value to No is convenient for laptop computers or computers that are frequently shut down and restarted. You can also set this value to Yes, which indicates that it should always try to become at least a backup browser.

Another parameter that you can add to the Registry key is Preferred-MasterBrowser. You can set it either to 1 (Yes) or 0 (No). If this parameter is set to Yes, this computer is given an election boost to master browser among computers where the criteria are essentially the same. If this parameter is set to No, the computer will never become a master browser.

How Does Browsing Work?

The browser process is really quite simple and, on a certain level, elegant. When computers boot or share a resource, they announce themselves to the master browser. Computers announce themselves once a minute for the first 5 minutes after booting and then every 12 minutes thereafter. The master browser compiles a list of computers and their available resources and sends a copy of the list to the backup browser or browsers approximately once every 15 minutes.

When a client computer requests a list of resources, it actually begins by asking the master browser for a list of backup browsers in the computer's workgroup or domain subnet. Then the client asks the first available browser for a list of network computers and subsequently for a list of shared resources.

If a computer sharing resources is shut down normally, it announces that fact to the master browser, which then takes that computer off the list. At the next announcement interval, the updated list is distributed to the backup browser or browsers (and domain master browser). However, if the computer crashes, loses power, or is powered off without shutting down, the master browser is not notified. The master browser waits for three announcement periods (12*3=36 minutes) until it revises its list. At the next announcement interval, it then updates the list.

You therefore could wait for a half hour or longer before the browse list you see is updated. In the meantime, the computer still remains on the list, and you won't know it is down until you try to double-click it and the system seems to take forever to respond with a message like "Path to computer not found."

Similarly, backup browsers contact the master every 15 minutes and announce that they are shutting down. However, if they crash, the master browser again won't know for three announcement periods, or in this case, up to 45 minutes. This wait can pose a performance problem for your users who rely on browse lists to make connections. Because clients get the list from the backup browser, if there are two and one crashes, the master browser won't select another for up to 45 minutes. All browse list requests are now being serviced by just one backup browser, and it can get backed up with requests.

What can you do about this problem? Nothing. This process is strictly internal. But you should be aware of the timing issues involved when computers become unavailable, and when they become first available or make additional resources available.

When a computer is booted, or you share a new resource on a computer, that computer or resource might not be listed right away in the browse list because the browse list is cached and not updated immediately by the master browser (up to 15 minutes). This does not mean, however, that the computer or its resources are not available.

Key Concept

The Browser service is only a list provider and does not affect the availability or unavailability of network resources. You can always access a computer and its resources by using its UNC name either through a net use command at a command prompt or through the Path box when you're mapping a network drive.

Browsing and browser elections can sometimes adversely affect network traffic with the number of announcements made. Under certain circumstances, disabling the Computer Browser service altogether may be advisable. For example, if your users' network resource access is predetermined through System Profiles or login scripts, and they never map their own connections, then you should disable the service. By doing so, you eliminate the traffic associated with the service and improve network response. Remember, the Computer Browser service is only a list provider. It does not affect access to a resource.

Becoming a Member of a Domain

Chapter 2, described the various models of network computing available with Windows NT and compared workgroup computing with domain computing. When you participate in a workgroup, you are part of a logical grouping of computers that may or may not share resources with each other and for which there is no single point of logon or authentication. Recall that every computer in the workgroup (workstation or server) maintains its own account database. When a user logs on at a computer, that user is authenticated on that local workstation and receives an access token for resource use on that local workstation.

As your network grows and as workgroups merge together, migrating to a domain or enterprise model may become appropriate. Recall that a domain centralizes account information in one or more domain controllers. Thus, users have a single point of logon. They can log on to the domain from any computer that participates in the domain, be authenticated by a domain controller for the domain, and receive an access token that can be used to access any resource available within the domain.

You can switch your computer's participation from workgroup computing to a domain through the Identification tab in the Network applet accessible through the Control Panel (or through the properties of Network Neighborhood). For your Windows NT computer to join a domain, it must have a computer account created for it on the domain controller. This account can be created ahead of time by a domain administrator, or during the change process by providing the name and password of a valid administrator's account.

Only Windows NT Workstation computers require a computer account in a Windows NT domain. Other Windows NT network clients do not.

Key Concept

Be sure that the computer name you are using is unique in the domain you are joining. If it is not, you can run into some serious connection problems in the domain. If you need to change your computer name to make it unique, modify the entry in the Computer Name text box in the Identification Changes dialog box.

As you can see in Figure 11.6, choosing the Change button on the Identification tab displays an Identification Changes dialog box. Select the Domain option, and enter the name of the domain your computer is joining. If the computer account for your computer has already been created, click OK and wait for Windows NT to confirm that you have successfully joined the domain.

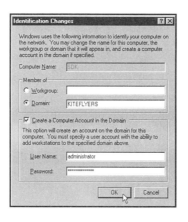

Figure 11.6
This computer is about to join the Kiteflyers domain by using the administrator's account from that domain to create a computer account for it there.

If you do not have a computer account already created but know the name and password of a valid administrator account for the domain, select the option Create a Computer Account in the Domain. Enter the administrator account name in the User Name text box and the valid password in the Password text box. Then click OK.

After you create the computer account for your computer, you can move back and forth between a workgroup and a domain. However, you cannot be a member of both simultaneously.

Understanding Dial-Up Networking and Remote Access Services

What is commonly referred to as Remote Access Services (RAS) in Windows NT 4.0 actually consists of two basic components that share some common elements: Dial-Up Networking services, which are installed on a Windows NT 4.0 workstation; and Remote Access Service services, which, when installed on a Windows NT 4.0 workstation, support 1 inbound dial-in connection, and when installed on a Windows NT 4.0 server, support up to 256 inbound dial-in connections.

RAS provides the Windows NT network with standardized WAN-based remote access support. Dial-Up Networking is the service a client computer uses to connect to remote network resources through a RAS server. Through RAS, clients using Dial-Up Networking can access network resources through regular telephone lines (Public Switched Telephone Networks, or PSTN) using a modem, through X.25 connections using a packet-switching protocol (X.25 PAD) and an X.25 adapter, or through digital ISDN connections with an ISDN adapter installed at both the client and server computers.

CH
II

Both Serial Line Internet Protocol (SLIP) and Point-to-Point Protocol (PPP) can be used to establish connections to RAS servers. SLIP is an older standard for establishing remote connections and provides little security. Although it supports TCP/IP, it cannot take advantage of DHCP, thereby requiring a static IP address assigned to the client. Also, it does not support IPX/SPX or NetBEUI.

PPP, on the other hand, does support several protocols in addition to TCP/IP, can use DHCP and WINS to assign IP addresses and resolve names, and takes advantage of Windows NT's security features. Besides IPX/SPX (which gives remote Windows NT clients using Client Services for NetWare [CSNW] the ability to dial into NetWare servers) and NetBEUI, PPP supports Point-to-Point Tunneling Protocol (PPTP), AppleTalk, DECnet, and Open Systems Interconnection (OSI).

PPP support on RAS servers enables remote clients to dial in using any PPP-compliant dial-in software with a protocol enabled on the server side but must provide at least the level of security that the RAS service is configured to require. The correct protocol, or for that matter another vendor's dial-in software, can gain access to any domain resource as if it were directly connected to the network.

In addition to PPP, Windows NT 4.0 has introduced the PPP Multilink Protocol based on the IETF standard RFC 1717. On computers that have multiple modems, X.25 or ISDN adapters, each with its own analog or digital communications line installed, PPP Multilink Protocol enables them to be combined into logical groups, thus increasing the bandwidth for transmissions. For example, a Windows NT 4.0 workstation with two 14.4 modems and two phone lines can use PPP Multilink Protocol to create one 28.8 logical connection to a RAS server also using PPP Multilink. For this setup to be effective, the workstation and the server must both have the same number of communications lines and connections available.

The RAS Server can act as a de facto router for the network. When RAS is installed on a Windows NT 4.0 server, it automatically integrates whatever protocols have been installed on the server. The RAS administrator can enable gateway services for any or all of the network protocols installed on the server. For example, if NetBEUI, NWLink, and TCP/IP have been installed, the RAS gateway can be enabled for any or all of them. This capability effectively enables a remote client using any one of these protocols to not only access the RAS server, but also to access network resources located anywhere in the domain using any of the three protocols installed on the RAS server to get there. RAS on the server can also act as IP and IPX routers to link LANs and WANs together. Indeed, just about every function that a client computer enjoys while directly connected to an Ethernet or Token Ring network, it will also enjoy, though in decreased line speed, through dial-in networking to a RAS server.

Introducing Point-to-Point Tunneling Protocol

If an organization maintains access to the Internet either directly or through an Internet provider, its users can gain access to the organization's network through the Internet using a new network technology supplied by Microsoft in Windows NT 4.0: Point-to-Point Tunneling Protocol (PPTP).

Clients using PPTP on their Windows NT 4.0 workstations can connect securely to a RAS server in their company network either directly through the Internet—if they are themselves directly connected—or through their local Internet provider. Connecting this way is known as Virtual Private Networking, or VPN. A Virtual Private Network provides the ability to "tunnel" through the Internet or other public network to connect to a remote corporate network without sacrificing security. The transmissions are encrypted and secure, and usually less costly than modem, X.25, or ISDN connections. Because the RAS server can act as a gateway to the company network, you need to have only one RAS server connected to the Internet.

Key Concept

PPTP supports multi-protocol encapsulation. This means that Dial-Up Networking clients can use any protocol for their PPP connection. PPTP encapsulates the PPP packet within IP packets and sends it across the Internet using TCP/IP, making it possible to use the Internet as a NetBEUI or IPX/SPX backbone. The client and RAS server must be using TCP/IP only to access the Internet.

When PPTP is provided by a user's Internet provider, the Virtual Private Network support is completely transparent to the user. VPN is enabled when the user connects to his or her provider.

When PPTP is configured on the user's workstation through the Network Properties dialog box, the user can connect to any Internet provider, even those that do not provide PPTP in their points of presence. In addition to installing PPTP, the user creates a phone book entry for the VPN, including the IP address of the PPTP server in the corporate network that he or she is connecting to in place of the phone number entry.

The Virtual Private Network uses RAS security. When the user connects through PPTP, the user account is validated in the Windows NT domain database just as though he or she was directly connected to the network. In addition, through RAS, the username, password, and data can all be additionally encrypted. On the PPTP server side, PPTP filtering can be enabled to allow only PPTP-enabled users to connect to the PPTP server through the Internet. It also supports the use of firewalls to screen access to the network.

RAS Security

RAS actually implements several additional security features over and above what Windows NT offers. RAS, of course, supports Windows NT's domain security, requiring dial-in users to authenticate using the domain account database before resource access can take place. The RAS server also maintains an ACL that identifies which domain users have permission to dial in.

In addition, however, RAS enables all logon information and data transmitted to be further encrypted, an especially nice feature when public telephone lines are used for dial-in. Auditing can be enabled to track remote connection processes such as logging on and dialing back users.

RAS servers can be configured to use callbacks to provide an extra layer of security. When a client calls in, the RAS server can be configured to call back the client at a predefined number, such as to a particular office location or at a user-defined number, perhaps a hotel room or client site.

Callback to hotel rooms may be tricky given that most hotel phones are routed through a hotel operator, making callback unusable. Some hotels, however, are now providing data access lines with separate phone numbers.

RAS servers support the addition of third-party security hosts and firewalls. Firewalls screen incoming and outgoing access to network computers through the use of passwords or security codes.

When connecting through PPTP, the RAS server must have a connection to the Internet either directly or through a firewall allowing connections to the PPTP port. This type of connection can become a security issue because the computer is left relatively open to packets other than PPTP. Fortunately, PPTP provides a security feature called "filtering" that, when enabled, disables all other protocols from using the network adapter that provides PPTP connection to the Internet.

Installing and Configuring RAS and Dial-Up Networking

If you intend to use your Windows NT 4.0 workstation to dial into a RAS server, you need only install and configure Dial-Up Networking. It may have been installed during Windows NT installation; if not, you can do so later through the Dial-Up Networking program in Accessories.

If you intend to dial into your Windows NT 4.0 workstation, you need to install RAS services on the workstation and configure it for dial-in. For example, if you want to be able to dial into your office desktop from home, you can install RAS services on the office desktop Windows NT computer.

Because the most likely configuration for a Windows NT 4.0 workstation is as a dial-in client, this chapter will concentrate on that aspect of configuring remote access. However, an overview of the RAS services setup will be presented.

Understanding and Configuring TAPI

Dial-Up Networking is a TAPI-compliant application in Windows NT 4.0. TAPI, which stands for Telephony Application Programming Interface, provides a set of standards for communications programs to manage and control data, voice, and fax dial-up functions, such as establishing calls, answering and hanging up, transferring calls, holding, conferencing, and other common phone system functions.

Among the dialing properties configurable for TAPI-compliant applications are phone book entries, area and country codes, outside line access, calling card data (encrypted, of course), and line control codes such as disabling call waiting.

You can configure these TAPI properties by using the Telephony applet in the Control Panel; just open the My Locations tab of the Properties sheet. The options here are fairly self-explanatory, as you can see in Figure 11.7.

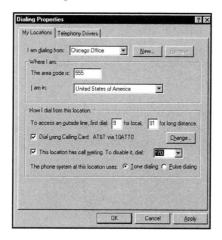

Figure 11.7
This tab shows some typical TAPI location settings.

Here, you can choose or enter a descriptive name for your calling location in the I Am Dialing From box. Choose New to add additional locations. In the Where I Am section of the dialog box, you can enter your area code and country. In the How I Dial From this Location section, you can specify the number you must dial (if any) to reach an outside local line or to place a long-distance call. Select the Calling Card option if you are using a calling card to charge the call, and choose Change to specify the calling card, the call number, and any rules applicable for the card. If you need to disable call waiting, you can choose to disable it here by specifying the line code to do so. Finally, you can indicate whether the phone uses Tone or Pulse dialing.

Dial-Up Networking

TAPI properties are used to configure the location you are dialing from. The Dial-Up Networking program lets you configure the phone book entry of the location you are dialing to. It establishes the connection and monitors the call.

You access the Dial-Up Networking program through the Accessories group. The first time you access it, a dial-up wizard prompts you for the first phone book entry. You need to provide a descriptive name for the entry; whether you are calling the Internet or a non-Windows NT server and how to deal with that; and the country code, area code, and phone number of the target location. Subsequent access will display the Dial-Up Networking dialog box that you see in Figure 11.8.

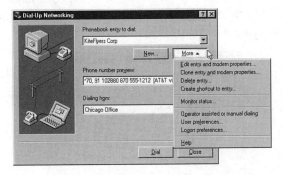

Figure 11.8
This Dial-Up Networking dialog box shows the modification options available.

You can select a phone book entry from the Phonebook Entry to Dial list, or you can choose New to create a new entry. The phone number for the entry is displayed using any TAPI location properties you specified for the Dialing From location.

The More button displays a list of additional options for modifying the dial-up data. For example, choosing Edit Entry and Modem Properties opens the Edit Phonebook Entry dialog; in this dialog, not only can you modify the basic entries, but you also can specify the dial-up access type (SLIP, PPP, PPTP) and protocols of the target server, dial-up scripts that you want executed, and the level of security you want to use for this connection (see Figure 11.9).

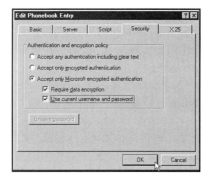

Figure 11.9
For this dial-up entry, the highest level of security possible is chosen. Here, Microsoft authentication will be used with the current user's account and password, and data transmitted during this session will be encrypted.

You also can specify parameters relating to redial attempts and callback options by choosing More, Logon Preferences in the Dial-Up Networking dialog box. By choosing More, User Preferences in this dialog, you can enable the autodial feature. Autodial automatically associates the phone book entry used to map to a network resource. When the resource mapping is reestablished at the next logon, the appropriate RAS server is called automatically.

Finally, you can choose Dial at the bottom of the dialog to dial out and establish the connection with the target location. After the connection has been made and any authentication has taken place, in the case of Windows NT RAS servers, you now have access to network resources to which you have been given permission.

Configuring RAS on the Server

On the server side, RAS is configured as a Windows NT service. As such, you select and install it through the Services tab of the Network applet accessible through the Control Panel or the Network Neighborhood properties. Recall that a Windows NT service is installed like any other protocol or adapter. You choose Add, select the service from the list of available services, and click OK. You then are prompted for a modem selection and configuration, as well as a RAS setting configuration. You must shut down and restart Windows NT for the Registry to be updated, the bindings to be put into effect, and the new service to start.

Follow these same steps to configure RAS services on your Windows NT 4.0 workstation if you intend to use it as a dial-in server.

CH
II

After you install RAS, you can select it from the list of services on the Services tab of the Network applet and configure its properties. You have the option of configuring the RAS server to act as a dial-out or dial-in server only, or to accept both. Depending on the dialing option you choose, you can specify which protocol to use for dial-out or to accept through dial-in. As you can see in Figure 11.10, clients dialing in using TCP/IP will be able to access the entire network and will receive their IP address from a DHCP server as well. Notice, too, that Microsoft authentication has been selected. Only clients whose Dial-Up Networking has been configured to use Microsoft authentication will be able to access this server.

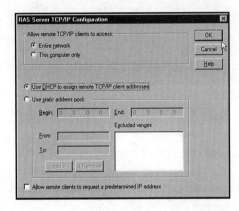

Figure 11.10
The configuration box to configure TCP/IP for inbound connections. This server has been configured for both dial-out and dial-in. All protocols have been enabled for both.

Encryption settings are also set for dial-in clients.

Key Concept

The encryption setting you select for dial-in clients (refer to Figure 11.9) represents the level of encryption that the client is configured to use rather than what the server uses. For example, if the Windows NT workstation client's Dial-Up Networking is configured to use Microsoft authentication, that client can access any RAS server configured to accept any authentication, encrypted authentication, or Microsoft encrypted authentication. Conversely, if the client is configured to use clear-text, but the RAS server is configured to accept only Microsoft authentication, that client will not be able to establish a connection with the RAS server.

Each of the network protocol options can be configured similarly to the way they are configured for the computer itself. For example, the IPX option lets you specify a range of network numbers to assign to the clients as they dial in. TCP/IP options include a range of IP addresses assigned by the RAS server or IP addresses assigned by a DHCP server. All three protocols include the option (selected by default) to enable gateway access to the entire network. If you want to restrict dial-up access to the RAS server only, you must disable gateway access for each protocol.

Troubleshooting

Troubleshooting either Remote Access Services or Dial-Up Networking is largely a matter of checking settings, phone numbers, dial access codes, and so on. In addition, you should always check the Event Viewer for events related to Remote Access Services or Dial-Up Networking because the descriptions of the events usually are quite good at pointing you to the root of the problem.

You can use the authentication options as a troubleshooting mechanism. If a client is having difficulty establishing a connection, you can set the server option to the lowest security setting: Allow Any Authentication. If the client can establish a connection with that setting, you can try again with the next highest security option, and so forth, until the connection fails. This technique indicates at what level of security the client is configured and at what level of security he or she must be set.

Finally, you can enable a log file that tracks PPP connections through the Windows NT Registry. Look for the key System\CurrentControlSet\Services\Rasman\PPP. Here, look for the parameter Logging, and change its value to 1. Setting this value to 2 initiates a "verbose" mode and will cause Windows NT to record even more detailed information. Windows NT creates the text file PPP.LOG, records PPP session information in it, and stores it in the WINNT40\SYSTEM32\RAS directory. The information contained in the log includes the time the PPP packet was sent, the protocol used (such as LCP), the packet type, length, ID, and the port connected to.

CH
II

Windows Messaging

A new feature of Windows NT Workstation and Server 4.0 is the Windows Messaging client (Microsoft Exchange 4.0). It is a universal inbox client that can create, send, receive, and organize electronic mail. Although it is optimized for use with Microsoft Exchange Server and other Microsoft Exchange clients, it can be used with other mail systems and client software.

To install Windows Messaging, double-click the Inbox icon on the desktop to initiate the installation wizard. You need to know the location of the mail server and its post office to fully complete the installation. When Windows Messaging is installed, its intuitive interface and Help files will guide you through any additional setup and configuration that need to take place.

Introducing Peer Web Services

Microsoft has long established the goal of improving Internet access, developing utilities to facilitate the implementation of Internet and intranet services, and the inclusion of Internet and intranet development tools in its future product rollouts.

Most people are now familiar with the Internet—the global network of computers communicating using a common protocol (TCP/IP) whose main interface is the World Wide Web (WWW) service. An intranet, on the other hand, is an internal Internet-like system used to communicate and publish information using Internet technology such as HTTP and FTP.

With Windows NT 4.0, Microsoft has introduced two new products designed to provide Windows NT 4.0-based computers the capability to develop and publish resources and services such as home pages, FTP services, and Web services. For Windows NT Server 4.0, Microsoft has included the Internet Information Server (IIS). For Windows NT Workstation 4.0, it has included Peer Web Services (PWS).

Both products provide publishing and access services through Hypertext Transfer Protocol (HTTP), File Transfer Protocol (FTP), and Gopher service on Windows NT networks using the TCP/IP protocol. They offer the capability to publish files; create links to other files and Internet sites; provide security for resources using the Windows NT security system; and provide full integration with SQL server, SNA, and other BackOffice applications. The primary difference between IIS and PWS is in the intended audience. IIS is optimized for heavy volume usage, whereas PWS is optimized for departmental or workgroup-sized traffic.

Both products are installed on their respective Windows NT 4.0 installations through the Services tab of the Network applet. Be sure you have the Windows NT 4.0 source CD available as well as enough disk space (about 3.5MB if you install everything). You also need an NTFS partition to secure data accessed through IIS or PWS. Because the installation and configuration proceed pretty much the same for both IIS and PWS, this discussion will focus on PWS.

Installation Process for PWS

When you begin the installation process for Peer Web Services, you are presented with seven component options (see Figure 11.11). They are described in Table 11.4.

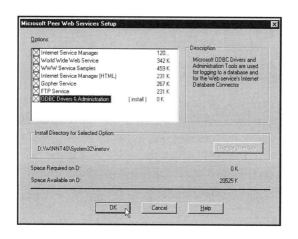

Figure 11.11
This Microsoft Peer Web Services Setup dialog box has all options selected for installation.

Table 11.4   PWS Component Options

Component	Function
Internet Service Manager	Provides an administration interface for managing PWS services such as WWW or FTP
World Wide Web Service	Provides a WWW publishing service for the Windows NT 4.0 workstation
WWW Service Samples	Provides sample HTML files that can be used as models to create your own
Internet Service Manager (HTML)	Provides additional HTML browsing services to the Internet Service Manager enabling you to manage the services through the browser
Gopher Service	Provides a Gopher publishing service for the Windows NT 4.0 workstation
FTP Service	Provides a file transfer publishing service for the Windows NT 4.0 workstation
ODBC Drivers and Administration	Enables access and administration of ODBC-based applications (like SQL databases) from the WWW Service

In addition to installing the ODBC Drivers and Administration for PWS, you need to set up the ODBC drivers and data sources through the ODBC applet in the Control Panel if you want to provide access to ODBC databases through PWS. Before you configure the ODBC options, you should close all ODBC applications first.

Now you can select the appropriate components and continue. Windows NT creates a directory called WINNT40\SYSTEM32\INETSRV unless you tell it otherwise.

Next, the PWS setup indicates the drive and directory structures it will create for each of the component services you selected on the boot partition. You either can change them to point to a different NTFS partition or simply accept the defaults. Windows NT creates the directories and installs the components for you.

After the installation is complete, you will notice a new folder called Microsoft Peer Web Services beneath the Administrative Tools group folder on the Start menu. Through this folder, you can gain access to the Internet Service Manager utilities; the Key Manager to secure data transmissions to selected servers through the use of security keys; the PWS setup utility to add, modify, or remove components; and a demonstration program.

You use the Internet Service Manager (ISM) to configure the PWS services. Through ISM, you can manage remote servers, specify user connection, log on and authenticate parameters, specify home directories, log server activity, and secure access through keys for each component service. You can also provide welcome and exit messages for the FTP service.

If you are using WWW service to publish files and other data through PWS, you can use the built-in Internet Explorer program to navigate, access, and browse that data. You simply redirect it to look at your PWS home page.

Providing Connectivity to NetWare Servers

Windows NT provides many options for connecting Windows NT network clients to a NetWare network. Most of them are server-based services that are described briefly in Table 11.5. However, the service covered here is Client Services for NetWare (CSNW).

Table 11.5   Windows NT Server 4.0 NetWare Connectivity

Service	Description
Gateway Service	This service for NetWare (GSNW) connects a Windows NT 4.0 server to a NetWare server via a service account established on the NetWare server. Trustee rights and permissions are administered at the NetWare server. Through a gateway service, NetWare file and print resources can be shared to Windows NT network clients. Consequently, any Windows NT network client that needs occasional access to a NetWare resource can do so by accessing the gateway share.
File and Print Service (FPNW)	This add-on service effectively makes a Windows NT 4.0 server look like a NetWare server to NetWare client computers. NetWare clients can log in to, attach to, and access resources on a Windows NT 4.0 server just as they would do with a NetWare server. This service is handy when you're migrating users from a NetWare environment to a Windows NT environment.

Service	Description
Directory Service Manager (DSMN)	This add-on service enables NetWare accounts to be copied to and managed by a single Windows NT domain controller with changes propagated back out to the NetWare servers as required.
Migration Tool for NetWare	This utility lets you merge NetWare account and group information into the Windows NT account database. It also lets you migrate any or all of the NetWare system volumes to an NTFS partition, preserving all rights and permissions assigned through NetWare.

Client Services for NetWare (CSNW) and NWLink IPX/SPX Compatible Protocol provide basic file and print access to NetWare 3.x and 4.x servers on your Windows NT 4.0 workstation. CSNW supports NetWare Core Protocol as well as NetWare's Directory Services (NDS), which enables shared resources to be organized into a tree-like hierarchy.

Services tab (Network applet)Services tab (Network applet)CSNW is installed and configured like most services—through the Services tab of the Network applet. After the service is installed, Windows NT adds a CSNW applet icon to the Control Panel. Through this applet, you can choose a preferred NetWare server to connect to during logon.

Key Concept

The Windows NT WINLOGON process passes the Windows NT username and password on to the preferred NetWare server for authentication there. Therefore, you log in to both the Windows NT network and a NetWare server.

Being able to choose the NetWare server implies—and rightly so—that you should have a valid login account on the NetWare server that matches the Windows NT username, and to be completely transparent, the passwords should also be matched exactly. A lot of administration can be involved, but Windows NT does provide DSMN just for this purpose (see Table 11.5).

Being able to choose the NetWare server does not mean, however, that you cannot maintain separate passwords or even nonmatching user accounts on the NetWare server. If the password or username does not match, you receive an error message when logging in to the Windows NT 4.0 workstation to the effect that you could not be validated on the preferred NetWare server.

Using the CSNW applet in the Control Panel, you can set the preferred server setting to "none." Setting the preferred server to "none" means that the you will not be validated on a NetWare server during the logon process to Windows NT. However, you can always connect to a NetWare resource on a server that you have accessed through Windows Explorer or Network Neighborhood. Both offer the option of mapping a network drive to a resource as a specific user. By specifying the name of a valid user account on the NetWare server and confirming the password, you can access any resource that has been allowed access.

Follow these steps to map a network drive as a specific user through Windows Explorer:

1. Start Windows Explorer by choosing Start, Programs, Windows Explorer.
2. Select Tools, Map Network Drive to display the Map Network Drive dialog box.
3. Select a drive letter that you want to assign to this mapping from the Drive list box.
4. Enter the path to the NetWare server and resource you want to access in the Path text box.
5. In the Connect As text box, enter the name of the NetWare user account that you want to log in with, and click OK.
6. When Windows NT prompst you for the password, enter the correct password and click OK. Windows NT then connects you to the directory and adds the mapped drive to your Explorer window.

Follow these steps to map a network drive as a specific user through Network Neighborhood:

1. Right-click the Network Neighborhood icon on the desktop to display the short-cut menu.
2. Select Map Network Drive from the menu.
3. Enter the path to the NetWare server and resource you want to access in the Path text box.
4. In the Connect As text box, enter the name of the NetWare user account that you want to log in with, and click OK.
5. When Windows NT prompts you for the password, enter the correct password and click OK. Windows NT then connects you to the directory and adds the mapped drive to your Explorer window.

By using the CSNW applet in the Control Panel, you also can select a default NDS tree and context to define the default NDS name and position of the username you will use to log in. All resources in the default tree specified can then be accessed without further password prompts.

You can define print options to add a form feed at the end of a print job sent to a NetWare print queue, receive a notification when printing is completed, and include a banner page with each print job.

New to Windows NT 4.0 is the capability for CSNW to interpret and execute NetWare login scripts. Select this option if you want the NetWare login scripts to execute.login scriptslogin scripts

After Client Services for NetWare is installed, you will notice a new entry for NetWare networks in your browse lists. Expand this entry to see available NetWare servers that you can map to. When you're mapping to a resource on a NetWare server, if your Windows NT account matches the NetWare server account, you can connect just like you would to a Windows NT resource—just point and click. However, if the NetWare server account is different, use the Connect As text box to enter the logon ID of the valid NetWare account to complete the connection.

For your Windows NT user account to have administrator privileges on the NetWare server—that is, become a NetWare Admin account—you must give your NetWare user account supervisory equivalence on the NetWare server. You do so by using NetWare's interface utilities, such as Syscon.

Network Troubleshooting

CH
II

If you encounter network-related difficulties, they are more likely the result of traffic problems, protocol incompatibilities, or hardware failures than anything else. You can troubleshoot your Windows NT network like you troubleshoot any other network. A good network traffic analysis tool, such as the Windows NT Network Monitor utility that comes with Windows NT Server 4.0, would be beneficial for a network administrator.

If you experience a network problem after the first installation of Windows NT workstation or after the installation of an adapter card, double-check the adapter settings. You may recall from Chapter 3, "Installing Windows NT Workstation 4.0," that Windows NT uses the default factory settings for most network interface cards. As a result, if you did not change the settings, your card may not be properly configured for the network.

Performance Monitor (also described in Chapter 12, "Tuning, Optimizing, and Other Troubleshooting Tips") also provides objects and counters relating to the protocols installed, as well as to the Workstation and Server services. For example, for each protocol installed on a Windows NT 4.0 workstation (or server), you can chart total bytes per second, session timeouts and retries, frame bytes sent and received, packets sent and received, and adapter failures. TCP/IP object counters become available when the SNMP service is installed.

Other tips include double-checking protocol configuration options. For example, be sure that the TCP/IP address and subnet mask are correct, and that the IP address is unique. If you're using WINS, be sure that the correct address to these servers has been configured for the workstation. Recall that NWLink autodetects the network frame type. If multiple frame types are detected, NWLink simply defaults to 802.2, which may restrict access to certain resource servers. If necessary, determine what frame types are in use on the network, and manually configure NWLink to recognize them.

Check the Services applet in the Control Panel and the Event Viewer to see whether any network-related services failed to start and why. If the Workstation service is not running, you cannot connect to network resources. Similarly, if the Server service is not running, you cannot share resources or service network requests.

Summary

This chapter explored the Windows NT 4.0 networking model. You looked at NetBEUI, NWLink, and TCP/IP protocols, as well as the Workstation and Server services. This chapter also introduced the Browser service and Peer Web Services. You learned how to configure and install network options, as well as how to become a member of a domain. Dial-Up Networking and Remote Access Services were also covered.

The final stop on your journey through NT is learning about optimizing, tuning, and troubleshooting. Throughout the book, you encountered optimizing, tuning, and troubleshooting issues as they related to the topics at hand. This final chapter will look at some additional considerations and tools to help you administer your Windows NT 4.0 workstations in particular.

QUESTIONS AND ANSWERS

1. An enhancement to the PPP protocol is _____ .

   A. Point-to-Point Tunneling Protocol (PPTP).

2. True or False: The tunneling protocol can work with NetBEUI PPP packets over TCP/IP.

   A. True. The tunneling protocol can work with NetBEUI PPP packets over TCP/IP. PPTP can work with NetBEUI, IPX/SPX, or TCP/IP.

3. The administration of the Web service is done through _____ .

   A. The Internet Service Manager.

...continues

> **4.** What is the client component of RAS?
>
> A. Dial-Up Networking (DUN).
>
> **5.** True or False: Auditing on RAS features can be enabled to track remote connection processes such as logging on and dialing back users.
>
> A. True. Auditing on RAS features can be enabled to track remote connection processes such as logging on and dialing back users.

PRACTICE TEST

1. RAS accepts what kinds of inbound connections? Choose all that apply.

   a. ISDN

   b. Modem

   c. X.25

   d. PPP

All the above are correct because RAS accepts inbound ISDN, modem, X.25, and PPP connections.

2. Which technology allows RAS to utilize two ISDN channels? Pick one.

   a. PPTP

   b. PPP

   c. Multilink PPP

   d. SLIP

Answers a, b, and d are incorrect because Multilink allows the combination of multiple connections into one—in this case, allowing RAS to utilize two channels. **Answer c is correct because Multilink PPP allows RAS to utilize the two ISDN channels. Multilink is always used to combine multiple connections into one.**

3. The Point-to-Point Tunneling Protocol does what? Pick one.

   a. Establishes a connection via the modem for the RAS server and RAS client to communicate

   b. Establishes a connection via X.25 for the RAS server and RAS client to communicate

   c. Enhances authentication with a longer key

   d. Encrypts all data between the client and server

Answers a, b, and c are incorrect because PPTP is a tunneling protocol used for the purpose of encryption. **Answer d is correct; PPTP encrypts all data between the client and server and is often used in the creation of Virtual Private Networks.**

CH
11

4. How can callback security be set up? Choose all that apply.

    a. Not to call back

    b. To call back to a predefined number

    c. To call back to a user-assigned number

    d. To call back and require a voiceprint match

Answers a, b, and c are correct because callback can be configured to not be utilized, to call back to a preset number, or to call a number the user provides when a connection is established. Answer d is incorrect because neither the NT operating system nor the RAS service includes the ability to do voiceprint authentication.

5. With browsing, how often does the master browser compile a list of computers and their available resources and send a copy of the list to the backup browser?

    a. Every 2 minutes

    b. Every 5 minutes

    c. Every 10 minutes

    d. Every 15 minutes

Answers a, b, and c are incorrect because the browse list is sent to the backup browsers approximately every 15 minutes. **Choice d is correct; the master browser compiles a list of computers and their available resources and sends a copy of the list to the backup browser every 15 minutes.**

6. RAS supports what protocols? Choose all that apply.

    a. TCP/IP

    b. IPX/SPX

    c. NetBEUI

    d. DLC

Answers a, b, and c are correct because RAS supports TCP/IP, IPX/SPX, and NetBEUI. Choice d is incorrect because RAS cannot support DLC.

7. To create a log file that tracks PPP connections, you turn on auditing via what?

    a. Network Monitor

    b. User Manager

    c. Remote Access Admin

    d. Editing the Registry

Answers a, b, and c are incorrect because the only way to turn on auditing for PPP connections is to edit the Registry. **Answer d is correct because you must edit the Registry to turn on auditing for PPP connections.**

8. What is a Windows application-based programming interface (API) that enables two-way acknowledged data transfer between the computers and provides communications support with NetWare Loadable Modules (NLMs)?

- **a.** Mailslots
- **b.** Windows Sockets
- **c.** Named Pipes
- **d.** NetBEUI

Answer a is incorrect because Mailslots are one-way connections sent without acknowledgment. **Answer b is correct because Windows Sockets are Windows application-based programming interfaces (API) that enable two-way acknowledged data transfer between computers.** Answer c is incorrect; Named Pipes are not API-based. Answer d is incorrect because NetBEUI is a networking protocol for small networks, not an API-based means of communication.

9. Which of the following statements would be true of an IP address? Choose all that apply.

- **a.** It is a 32-bit address.
- **b.** It is most commonly written as a five-part decimal address separated by colons.
- **c.** One must be assigned to every host.
- **d.** The address must be unique in the network.

Answers a, c, and d are correct because IP addresses must be 32-bit binary numbers, be assigned to every host, and be unique within the network. Answer b is incorrect because addresses are most commonly displayed as a four-part decimal address separated by dots.

10. Which service allows Windows NT Workstation clients to directly connect to NetWare servers?

- **a.** Gateway Services for NetWare
- **b.** NetWare Migration Tool
- **c.** Client Services for NetWare
- **d.** File and Print Services for NetWare

Answer a is incorrect because the Gateway Service for NetWare (GSNW) is installed on an NT Server to allow clients to access a NetWare server through the NT Server, not directly. Answer b is incorrect because the NetWare Migration Tool is used to move your company from NetWare servers to NT Servers. **Answer c is correct because Client Services for NetWare (CSNW) is used to allow NT clients to connect directly to NetWare servers.** Answer d is incorrect because File and Print Services for NetWare (FPNW) is an add-on product used to allow NetWare clients to directly access an NT Server.

CH
II

CHAPTER PREREQUISITE

Before reading this chapter, you should have read all preceding chapters and be comfortable with making changes to the Windows NT operating system through configuration utilities.

Tuning, Optimizing, and Other Troubleshooting Tips

WHILE YOU READ

1. To effectively use statistics gathered in the Performance Monitor, you must gauge them against a(n) _____ .

2. What is the default view in the Performance Monitor?

3. True or False: The first division of the system in the Performance Monitor is objects.

4. What is the default filename for a dump file?

5. What three NT Server log files can the Event Viewer look at?

We have reached the final leg of our journey through Windows NT Workstation 4.0. We've covered a lot of ground, but we still have a few things to discuss.

This chapter covers topics that can loosely be termed tuning and optimization related. Otherwise, they might be termed "miscellaneous stuff that didn't quite fit in anywhere else." We'll examine the Virtual Memory Manager more closely and also the use of page-files. We'll review the use of the Event Viewer and Windows Diagnostics as troubleshooting tools. We'll also get an introduction to the Performance Monitor utility and examine how it can be used to track system and, to a certain extent, network performance.

Understanding Virtual Memory Management

One of the Executive Services managers is the Virtual Memory Manager. The memory architecture of Windows NT 4.0 is a 32-bit, demand-based, flat, linear model. This model allows the Virtual Memory Manager to provide each process running in Windows NT up to 4GB of memory—generally far more than the amount of physical RAM installed in most computers.

If you remember the Windows swap file model, you will recall the two types of swap files: permanent and temporary. Both swap files manage available RAM in 4KB pieces using an internal Windows algorithm called the LRU (Least Recently Used). Essentially, the LRU determines that the piece of code in memory that was least recently accessed by a process is liable to be swapped to disk when more RAM is needed for a current process. On computers with the minimum required RAM running Windows, a considerable amount of swapping could take place. The main difference between permanent and temporary swap files is that a permanent swap file has a preallocated amount of space reserved on the disk. Temporary swap files begin at 2MB and then "grow" as needed to a predetermined amount. Thus, although a permanent swap file provides better swap performance because space is always there and available, it also reduces the amount of available disk storage. Similarly, although temporary swap files do not reduce the amount of disk storage available up front, more resources are expended to find additional storage space when the swap file needs to "grow."

Windows NT combines the "best" of these swap files. The Windows NT pagefile (PAGEFILE.SYS) is created when Windows NT is installed. It generally defaults to an initial, preallocated size (a la permanent swap files) of 12-plus physical RAM and a maximum size of three times physical RAM (depending on the amount of disk space available). For example, on a computer with 16MB of physical RAM, the default initial pagefile size would be 28MB (12 + 16MB), and the maximum size would be about 48MB (3×16MB). Windows NT boots with the initial size pagefile available. The pagefile subsequently grows as applications are loaded and demands for physical RAM increase.

Windows NT maps memory addresses in 4KB blocks, or pages. The virtual memory address space can accommodate up to 1,048,576 pages, or 4GB of addresses. It is important to realize that while Windows NT allows virtual addressing of up to 4GB of memory, the Virtual Memory Manager allocates up to 2GB of virtual storage for each application. The other 2GB is allocated for all system (Kernel mode) processing.

The Virtual Memory Manager addresses application memory as follows (see Figure 12.1):

1. When an application is loaded, the Virtual Memory Manager assigns it virtual memory addresses in its own virtual memory space.

2. It maps available physical RAM to the virtual memory addresses. The mapping is transparent to the application.

3. As the data is needed by the application, it calls for the virtual memory addresses.

4. The Virtual Memory Manager moves those pages on demand into available locations in physical RAM.

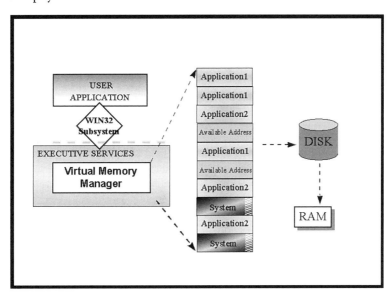

Figure 12.1
Windows NT 4.0 virtual memory model.

Key Concept

This process of assigning virtual addresses to the application effectively hides the organization of physical RAM from the application. The various pages of the application may wind up in noncontiguous space in physical RAM, but as the Virtual Memory Manager provides the addresses, this isn't a problem—because the organization of physical RAM is hidden. In this way, Windows NT makes the most efficient use of available physical RAM and provides an overall performance increase for application processing.

Exploring and Optimizing Pagefile Usage

The default size of the paging file (PAGEFILE.SYS) created by Windows NT Workstation during installation is 12MB + physical RAM. Thus, if you have 16MB of RAM installed, the initial pagefile size is 28MB. The minimum size the pagefile can be is 2MB, and the maximum tends to be about 3×physical RAM (see Figure 12.2). In Windows NT Server, the paging file's initial size is equal to RAM only.

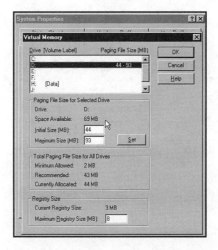

Figure 12.2
This computer has 32MB of RAM installed because the pagefile initial size is 44MB (12+32). In the Space Available field, you can see that not enough room is available on the D: drive for the maximum pagefile size.

Even though the minimum can be 2MB, when you're planning your computer configuration, you should plan so that the total memory commitment (physical RAM + pagefile) to Windows NT and its processes is at least 22MB. This amount is considered the minimum for Windows NT 4.0. Windows NT, as a rule, will take 10MB of physical RAM for its own use (Kernel mode operations) upon booting. Therefore, to determine the minimum size pagefile that can support Windows NT on a given system, you can use the following formula: (RAM – 10MB) + pagefile = 22MB. For example, on a computer with 16MB of RAM, the minimum pagefile size should be no less than 16MB: (16MB – 10MB) + 16MB (pagefile) = 22MB. Similarly, on a computer with 32MB of RAM or more, no pagefile is necessarily needed: (32MB – 10MB) + 0 = 22MB. If Windows NT does not consider the pagefile to be properly sized, it displays a message to that effect upon every boot and also displays the Virtual Memory dialog box so that you can fix the pagefile size.

 Key Concept

The calculations presented here are considered minimum calculations only and do not necessarily represent an optimal operating environment on a heavily used workstation or server. It is strongly suggested that you maintain the sizes Windows NT recommends for the pagefile.

During installation, Windows NT looks for a disk partition large enough to hold the pagefile it creates. It is often the same as the installation (boot) partition, but it may be another formatted partition.

Because the pagefile is apt to be "hit" quite often by the system, maintaining it on a hard disk that is not itself "hit" frequently by other processes should make sense. The boot partition contains the Windows NT system files and, as such, is accessed frequently by the operating system quite apart from the pagefile. Keeping the pagefile on the same partition as the Windows NT system files can result in an overall decrease in disk performance because of excessive I/O on that one disk drive.

Therefore, an optimization suggestion for the pagefile, which will also improve overall disk performance, is to move the pagefile to a partition on a different disk drive. Moving it effectively eliminates the competition for disk I/O between system file and pagefile requests.

Moving the Pagefile to Another Disk

All pagefile configuration takes place through the Virtual Memory dialog box (see Figure 12.3).

You can move the pagefile to another disk like this:

1. Start the System applet in the Control Panel, and switch to the Performance tab. The Virtual Memory section shows the current total page file size for all disk volumes.
2. Select <u>C</u>hange. The Virtual Memory dialog box is displayed.

CH
12

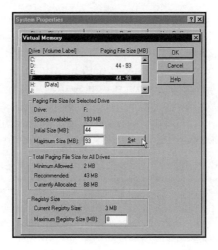

Figure 12.3
The pagefile is being prepared to move from the D: drive to the F: drive in this example. The next step is to delete the current pagefile from the D: drive.

3. In the Drive list box, note the location of the current pagefile and its initial and maximum sizes.

4. Highlight the drive on which you want to place the pagefile. In the Paging File Size for Selected Drive section of the dialog box, be sure that the Space Available on the selected drive will accommodate the pagefile size needs.

5. In the Initial Size box, enter the initial size of the pagefile. It should be at least as large as the original initial size you noted in step 3.

6. In the Maximum Size box, enter the maximum size of the pagefile. It should be at least as large as the original maximum size you noted in step 3.

7. Choose Set.

8. In the Drive list box, highlight the drive that contains the original pagefile.

9. In the Initial Size box, delete the size entry.

10. In the Maximum Size box, delete the size entry.

11. Choose Set.

12. Click OK. Windows NT then prompts you to restart the system to make the changes take effect.

Right-Sizing the Pagefile

When Windows NT boots, it loads the initial pagefile. As additional page space is needed, the Virtual Memory Manager adds to, or expands, the pagefile to accommodate the need. Of course, every time the pagefile needs to grow, additional disk I/O is expended to find and allocate the space and write the pages.

The pagefile grows and shrinks within the range specified, but it is important to note that it is not cleaned up in any way. It shrinks, for example, only when the pages at the end of the pagefile are no longer needed or deleted.

Although you can use Windows Explorer to monitor the size of the pagefile, the size shown for the pagefile stored on an NTFS volume is probably inaccurate because in NTFS, file size is not updated while the file is open. The size is updated only when the file is closed. Of course, the pagefile is always opened to its initial size when Windows NT boots.

There is a way around this phenomenon: You can try to delete the pagefile through Windows Explorer. When you do, you get a message to the effect that the file is in use by another process (of course, Windows NT). Then you can refresh Windows Explorer or type **dir** at a command prompt to display the correct pagefile size.

If you are running several large applications simultaneously, which is quite probable on a Windows NT server or on power users' workstations, determine what the "expanded" size of the pagefile is. Then you can modify the pagefile size so that the initial size matches the expanded size. This way, you are starting with a "right-sized" pagefile and can eliminate the disk I/O involved with expanding the pagefile. Voilá! You will have increased performance all the way around.

To change the pagefile size, follow these steps:

1. Start the System applet in the Control Panel, and switch to the Performance tab. The Virtual Memory section shows the current total page file size for all disk volumes.
2. Select <u>C</u>hange. The Virtual Memory dialog box is displayed.
3. In the <u>D</u>rive list box, highlight the drive that contains the pagefile whose size you want to change.
4. In the <u>I</u>nitial Size box, enter the new initial size.
5. In the Ma<u>x</u>imum Size box, enter a new maximum size if necessary.

Key Concept

If you have increased the initial size of the pagefile, you should increase the maximum size proportionately. Be sure that the drive can accommodate the increased sizes specified.

CH

12

6. Choose Set.

7. Click OK. Windows NT then prompts you to restart the system to make the changes take effect.

Creating Multiple Pagefiles

Another optimization technique is to create multiple pagefiles—for example, one on each physical disk drive. With Windows NT, unlike Windows 3.1 and Windows for Workgroups, you are not restricted to only one pagefile. In fact, if the computer's disk controller supports contiguous disk I/O, creating a pagefile on each disk can significantly improve disk performance (see Figure 12.4).

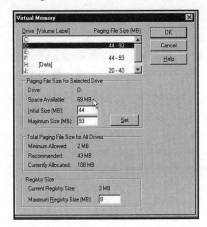

Figure 12.4
In this example, three page files have been created on three different disk drives (D:, F:, and J:) to improve overall performance and alleviate the lack of disk space for the maximum pagefile size on drive D:.

Windows NT writes pages to the pagefile separately. Two writes are allowed to be outstanding for each pagefile. The pagefile with the most free space is always written to first. Thus, placing a pagefile on each disk drive effectively distributes pagefile requests across all available pagefiles on all disk drives.

From another point of view, if you determine that the original pagefile is not large enough or cannot expand sufficiently because of a lack of disk space, creating an additional pagefile can help alleviate the demand of the original pagefile. Because room now exists for "expansion," system performance is improved.

Key Concept

The performance of the pagefile and accompanying disk I/O is directly related to the performance of your applications and any other system processes as a result of the way virtual memory maps physical addresses to virtual addresses. If an application makes a request for RAM and not enough is available, the Virtual Memory Manager moves the least recently used pages from RAM to the pagefile to accommodate the application's request. If the pagefile performance is poor, the application's performance will ultimately reflect that fact. If the pagefile's capability to react to the page request is prompt, the application's performance will be enhanced.

Follow these steps to create multiple pagefiles:

1. Start the System applet in the Control Panel, and switch to the Performance tab. The Virtual Memory section shows the current total page file size for all disk volumes.

2. Select Change. The Virtual Memory dialog box is displayed.

3. In the Drive list box, note the location of the current pagefile and its initial and maximum sizes.

4. Highlight the drive on which you want to place the additional pagefile. In the Paging File Size for Selected Drive section of the dialog box, be sure that the Space Available on the selected drive will accommodate the pagefile size needs.

5. In the Initial Size box, enter the initial size of the pagefile. Because Windows NT writes to the pagefile with the most free space, you should probably size all your pagefiles with the same initial size, though doing so is not required.

6. In the Maximum Size box, enter the maximum size of the pagefile. Because Windows NT writes to the pagefile with the most free space, you should probably size all your pagefiles with the same maximum size, though doing so is not required.

7. Choose Set.

8. Repeat steps 4 through 7 for each additional pagefile you want to create.

9. Click OK. Windows NT then prompts you to restart the system to make the changes take effect.

CH
12

Using the Event Viewer to Troubleshoot Windows NT

Any events generated by the Windows NT operating system—missing an application or security auditing—are collected in log files that can be viewed with the Event Viewer utility. The failure of a driver to load, a stalled service, an unsuccessful logon, or the corruption of a database file are typical events that are recorded by Windows NT and can be viewed through the Event Viewer in one of three log files. The System Log records events generated by the operating system, such as failed drivers, disk space limits, pagefile errors, and so on. The Application Log records events generated by applications, such as corrupted temporary files or resource allocation errors. The Security Log records events relating to audit events that only Administrators can view. Auditing is enabled through the User Manager and then configured for files, folders, and printers through their properties. Events, such as the successful writing of a file or the failed attempt to delete a folder, are recorded in the Security Log (see Figure 12.5).

Figure 12.5
This sample System Log shows the event detail for a Stop error.

Three types of System and Application Log errors and two types of Security Log errors are recorded. They are described in Table 12.1.

Table 12.1   Event Log Entry Types

Event Type	Description
Information	Denoted by a blue "i" icon, it indicates that an infrequent but significant event has taken place, such as a Browser election or successful synchronization of domain controllers.
Warning	Denoted by a yellow "!" icon, it represents an event that may or may not be significant but could lead to future concerns, such as low disk space or unexpected network error.
Error	Denoted by a red "stop sign" icon, it represents a significant problem that has, or could lead to, a service failure or loss of data, such as a driver failing to load.
Success Audit	Denoted by a "key" icon, this Security Log event represents an audited security event that was successful, such as a successful logon or access to a printer.
Failure Audit	Denoted by a "lock" icon, this Security Log event represents an audited security event that was unsuccessful, such as an attempt to delete a file to which a user did not have access.

The Event Viewer is one of the Administrative Tools utilities. You can access it by selecting Start, Programs, Administrative Tools, Event Viewer. The default view is the System Log. By default, events are listed in descending time order from most recent to least recent.

Each entry records the icon type of the event, the date and time it occurred, the source of the event (usually related to a service or function), a category or classification (such as Logon and Logoff or Policy Change), an event number (to be referenced when speaking with a Microsoft product support representative for Security Logs), the name of the user involved, and the computer on which the event occurred.

You can obtain more details about each entry by double-clicking the entry (refer to Figure 12.5). Besides a hexadecimal display of the event frame, the event detail also provides a brief description of the problem. This description usually points you in the right direction for troubleshooting but might be nothing more than another error code that you can look up in the Windows NT Resource Kit or provide to a Microsoft product support representative. Nevertheless, the recorded events can be useful when you want to track down the cause of a problem.

For example, many services maintain dependencies on other services. If one service in the dependency fails to start or otherwise perform its task, the dependent services may also fail or not perform their tasks. This problem usually manifests itself at boot time with the message "Dependency or service failed to start." This message, in and of itself, is not terribly informative; however, the Event Viewer is.

To troubleshoot this message, you can start the Event Viewer and look for the first event log entry (an information entry) for the approximate time and date that the error occurred. The stop message right above it will likely be the source of the error.

CH
12

Service dependencies can be viewed through the Services tab in the Windows NT Diagnostics utility. The event logs, by default, are 512KB in size and keep only seven days' worth of events. This means that when the event log grows to 512KB in size, or after seven days' data has been collected, the oldest events are eligible to be dropped from the log if the space is needed.

You can change these defaults through the Log, Log Settings menu option. You can change the size of the log and the number of days' worth of data stored for each individual log. Rather than save a specified number of day's data, you could choose to overwrite events as needed or not to overwrite events at all. If you choose not to overwrite events, the Event Viewer collects data up to the specified size and then stops, requiring the administrator to manually clear the log. Because the event logs can grow rapidly, especially if auditing has been enabled, changing the default size significantly is not recommended unless disk space is not of concern to you.

As you grow accustomed to using the Event Viewer to track events, you will become more familiar with the Source and Category entries. Using the View menu options, you can change the order of all events displayed in the log; use Find to find a specific entry by event type, source, category, and so forth; and choose Filter Events to do just that.

In the Filter dialog box, you can select events to display by specific or range of date and time, type, source, category, user, computer, and event ID. For example, if you just want to see all stop events, you can use the filter to select only Error event types and deselect the other types. Or, if you want to see errors relating to service management, you can select Error event types, as above, and also select Service Control Manager as the Source type, as shown in Figure 12.6.

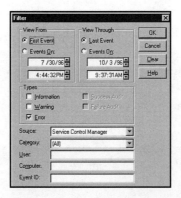

Figure 12.6
Here, the Event Viewer System Log has been filtered to display only error messages whose source is the Service Control Manager.

Exploring the Windows NT Diagnostics Utility

Windows NT Diagnostics is an enhanced and GUI version of Microsoft's MS-DOS–based MSD (Microsoft Diagnostics). This utility gives detailed information culled directly from the Windows NT Registry relating to system configuration (see Figure 12.7). This version actually provides a greater level of detail than previous Windows NT or Windows versions. You can even print the information screens. You access it through the Administrative Tools group.

Figure 12.7
Here, you can view the status of the Messenger service that has stopped. Dependencies of the Messenger service—both service and group related—are visible as well.

Windows NT Diagnostics provides the following nine tabs of data relating to your system's configuration:

- The Version tab displays general information about this installation of Windows NT such as its build and version number and who it is registered to.

- The System tab displays more details about the BIOS installed on the computer and of each processor installed. It also specifies what type of Hardware Abstraction Layer (HAL) has been installed.

Key Concept

Recall that the HAL performs the majority of application-to-hardware calls. Sometimes certain models of computers require a BIOS-specific HAL for hardware interaction to be successful. If you experience a hardware failure on a specific model computer for an application that runs successfully under Windows NT on other models of computers, you need to find out what HAL has been installed and then contact the manufacturer to see whether it has a BIOS-specific HAL for that model computer.

- The Display tab shows BIOS information, adapter settings, video memory allocation, and driver data. Again, this information can be helpful when you're trying to determine compatibility problems.

- The Drives tab displays a list of logical drives on the computer by type (floppy, CD-ROM, local) or by drive letter. You can display any drive's properties by selecting the drive and choosing the Properties button at the bottom of the Windows NT Diagnostics utility window. From here, you can determine the amount of free space left on the disk, as well as sector and cluster size.

- The Memory tab gives detailed statistics concerning RAM, kernel memory, commit memory (RAM+pagefile), and pagefile size and usage.

- The Services tab shows a list of Windows NT services and devices available and their current status. Although you cannot affect the status of the service or device here, you can view more details about them. By selecting an entry and choosing the Properties button at the bottom of the Windows NT Diagnostics window, you can view general information and service and process flags, as well as dependencies this service or device has on other services or devices. Going back to the Event Viewer example, if a service fails as the result of a dependency, but you are not sure what other services it depends on, you can use Windows NT Diagnostics to find out. Now you know what else to look for, either in the Event Viewer or in the Services or Devices applets in the Control Panel.

- Through the Resources tab, you can view summarized or detailed properties for IRQ settings, I/O port addresses, DMA channels, and memory addresses. In addition, you can view a summary of all this information by device. To get really technical, you can view the same information as it relates to HAL resource usage.

- The Environment tab displays both system and user environment variables such as ComSpec and Temp, respectively, and their current values.

- Finally, the Network tab provides general information about the network configuration for the computer, such as the user access level, the domain you're participating in, the current user, and where the user was validated. In addition, you can view transport data, session settings (such as session timeout and buffer size), network frame statistics for the given session (such as bytes received and sent), SMBs (system message blocks) sent and received, open network sessions, and failed sessions.

All in all, you get a lot of bang for your buck with Windows NT Diagnostics. It can be a useful informational tool when you're troubleshooting or gathering statistics about your computer. And you can print from it as well!

Monitoring System Performance with the Performance Monitor

Windows NT 4.0 contains a performance tracking tool called the Performance Monitor, which collects data about system resources and presents them in a graphical chart-based format. This section serves as an introduction to the Performance Monitor and how you can use it as a troubleshooting utility.

The Performance Monitor treats system resources as objects with characteristics, or counters. Multiple occurrences of an object and counter, or variations on them, are called instances. For example, the processor is an object that can be monitored. It has counters that can be charted, such as the total percent of processor usage, the percent of the processor used by the Kernel mode, and so on. If you have multiple processors, you can track each processor's total percent of usage, and so on, for each instance of the processor.

With the Performance Monitor, you can also create and view log files, view summary statistics, and create system alerts based on monitored values.

The Performance Monitor is used primarily for two purposes: creating baselines of performance and monitoring aberrations from the baseline—that is, troubleshooting.

Key Concept

It does you no good as an analyst to turn on the Performance Monitor to monitor system activity after a problem has been detected if you have no "normal" baseline of activity against which to measure the problem.

About 20 objects, each with numerous counters, are available by default. Every additional protocol, service, driver, and in some cases application, you install on your Windows NT workstation or server will likely add additional objects and counters to the list. The number of instances varies greatly with each object. However, four specific objects are of particular concern when you're troubleshooting your system: processor, process, disk, and memory.

CH
12

We're not saying that monitoring other objects isn't important. These objects are simply the ones most often looked at first to determine aberrations from the baseline and bottlenecks in the system. After all, if the system is running with poor performance, it is likely slowing as a result of poor performance at the processor (too many I/O requests for its power), in memory (not enough to handle all address requests), on disk (not enough disk space or excessive paging), or with the process itself (an application that overuses resources).

Configuring Performance Monitor

Performance Monitor with the other Administrative Tools. Just follow these basic steps when configuring a Performance Monitor chart:

1. From the taskbar, select Start, Programs, Administrative Tools, Performance Monitor.

2. Choose Edit, Add to Chart to display the Add to Chart dialog box.

3. In the Computer text box, enter a computer name, or browse for the computer you want to monitor. If you have a valid administrator's account or participate in a domain in which you are a domain administrator, you can monitor other Windows NT computers remotely.

4. Select the Object that you want to monitor.

5. As you select an object, the Counter list displays counters associated with the chosen object that you can chart. Select the counter that you want to track. You can select multiple counters by clicking the first and then Ctrl-clicking the others.

6. If you are unsure about what a counter measures, select Explain to display descriptive text about the counter.

7. If appropriate, choose an Instance for each object counter.

8. Modify the legend characteristics as you desire (Color, Scale, Width, and Line Style).

9. Choose Add to add the counter(s) to the chart window.

10. Repeat steps 3 through 9 for any additional objects you want to monitor.

11. Choose Done when you are finished.

Performance Monitor, by default, displays a line chart that charts activity for every second in time. You can modify these defaults by selecting Options, Chart to display the Chart Options dialog box.

Most of the options in the Chart Options dialog box are self-explanatory. However, note the Update Time section. The Periodic Interval is set to 1 second, the default. If you want to capture information in smaller or larger time intervals, modify the value accordingly. The value you enter will affect the Graph Time value on the Statistics bar at the bottom of the graph itself. At a setting of 1 second, completing one chart pass in the window will take 100 seconds. A setting of 2 seconds will take 200 seconds to make a complete pass. A setting of .6 second will take 60 seconds, or one minute, to complete a pass.

To save chart settings for future use, such as for creating a chart to compare against baseline activity, choose File, Save Chart Settings. You then can load the chart settings later to monitor system activity as designed.

Creating a Monitor Log

As was mentioned before, charting values really is ineffective unless you have some baseline values against which you can compare activity. Object counter values can be collected and saved in a log file.

Follow these steps to create a log file:

1. Start the Performance Monitor.
2. Choose View, Log to display the log window.
3. Choose Edit, Add to Log. Select all the objects whose data you want to capture, and choose Add. Choosing this option causes the log to record activity for every counter associated with each object. Choose Done when you are finished.
4. Choose Options, Log.
5. Enter a name for the log file and a directory to save it in, and set the Periodic Update interval if you want.
6. Choose Start Log to begin recording system activity.
7. Monitor the file size counter (shown in bytes) until the file grows as large as you like, or simply use your watch to collect data over a specific period of time.
8. After you have collected the amount of data you want, choose Options, Log and then select Stop Log.
9. Choose Options, Log and then select Save to save the log file.

You can view the contents of a log file like this:

1. Start the Performance Monitor.
2. Choose View, Chart to display the chart window.
3. Choose Options, Data From to display the Data From dialog box.
4. Choose Log File and enter the path and filename of the log file, or browse for it. Click OK.
5. Choose Edit, Add to Chart. The only objects listed will be those you captured in the log file. Select the object, and the appropriate counters for each, for which you want to view chart values; then choose Add to add them to the chart. A static chart view is then created.
6. Adjust the time view of the chart by choosing Edit, Time Window, and make your adjustment.

The Performance Monitor does not have a facility to print charts. However, you can press Print Screen to capture a chart window to the Clipboard, paste it into a word processing document, and print it that way. You could also export the data to an Excel spreadsheet and use its utilities to create graphs and analyze the data.

Objects to Monitor

The four basic objects to monitor—especially when you're creating a baseline of "normal" system activity—are processor, process, logical disk, and memory. The following sections describe some specific counters that can be useful to chart for each.

Processor Object

The processor object monitors processor usage by the system. You might want to chart four counters: %Processor Time, %User Time, %Privileged Time, and Interrupts/Sec.

%Processor Time—shown in Figure 12.8—tracks the total processor usage and gives a picture of just how busy the processor is. This counter, in and of itself, is not enough to tell you what is driving the processor to this level of usage, but it does help to indicate whether the problem or bottleneck is related in any way to the processor. %User Time and %Privileged Time define processor usage by displaying what percentage of the total usage pertains to User mode (application) and Kernel mode (operating system) activities, respectively. Again, these counters do not indicate what specific activities are driving the percentages. These three, in general, should remain below 75 to 80 percent depending on computer use. For example, you would expect these values to be lower on a desktop computer but consistently high on a server running Microsoft Systems Management Server.

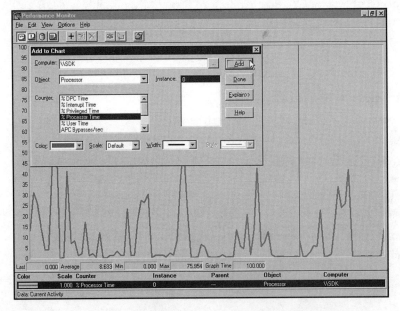

Figure 12.8
The total percent of processor usage for the computer is shown here. Note that only one processor is installed, so there is only one instance to track.

Interrupts/Sec tracks the number of device interrupt requests from hardware devices, such as network cards or disk controllers, serviced by the processor. The number of requests considered optimum varies from processor to processor. For example, you would expect a Pentium to handle perhaps three times as many requests as a 486 processor. In general, the higher the number (greater than 1000 suggested for 486), the more likely the problem is hardware related. You would next monitor queue lengths for various suspected hardware devices, such as the disk controller or network card. Optimally, only one request should be waiting in queue. Queue lengths greater than two indicate which device is the likely culprit and may need to be replaced or upgraded.

Key Concept

Processor object counters, as with all object counters, should never be monitored alone. As pointed out in the preceding paragraphs, the mere indication of activity beyond the norm does not in itself point to the processor as the focus of the problem. You should use these and the other object counters recommended to draw attention to a problem. Then you can add additional object counters to help pinpoint and troubleshoot the problem.

Process Object

For every service that is loaded and application that is run, a process is created by Windows NT and monitored by the Performance Monitor. Each process is considered an instance in this case, and each object instance has several counters that can be charted.

Notice that the %Processor Time can be tracked for each process instance (see Figure 12.9). This way, you can determine which specific process is driving the processor to higher than normal usage.

Another useful process counter is the Working Set. This counter actually tracks the amount of RAM required by the process and can be used to help determine when additional RAM is necessary.

CH
12

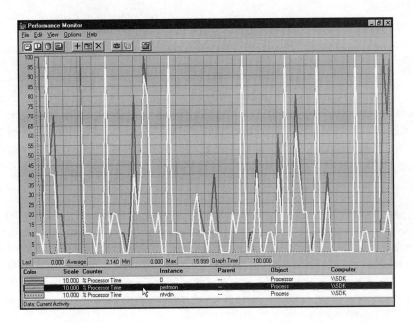

Figure 12.9
The Performance Monitor (perfmon in the legend—the white chart line) is driving the total percent of processor usage. You can also see from the dotted chart line (NTVDM in the legend) when the screen capture program took the snapshot of this chart and contributed to an overall increase in processor usage.

Memory Object

Perhaps the most common problem encountered on heavily used computers is inadequate RAM for the processes to perform at their optimum rates. In this case, two memory counters can be of particular service to you:

- Commit Limit indicates the number of bytes that can be written (committed) to the pagefile without extending, or growing, it. As this number falls, the pagefile is more likely to grow. You can use this counter to help determine whether you need to "right-size" your pagefile (review the section "Right-Sizing the Pagefile" earlier in this chapter).

- Pages/Sec indicates the number of pages requested by an application or other process that were not in RAM and had to be read from disk. In itself, this value should remain rather low—less than 5 is recommended. Multiply this counter's average value by that of the Logical Disk object's Avg. Disk Sec/Transfer counter. This counter indicates the average number of seconds for each disk I/O. The resulting value shows the percent of disk I/O used by paging. Microsoft suggests that if this value consistently exceeds 10 percent, paging is excessive and you probably need more RAM. The actual threshold is based on the function of the particular computer. You might expect more paging to occur on an SQL server than on a desktop, for example.

Consider that you have determined paging is excessive by multiplying the Memory object's Pages/Sec counter by the Logical Disk object's Avg. Disk Sec/Transfer counter and got a value of 20 percent. You presume that you need additional RAM. But how much?

You have also been tracking the %Processor Time for the processor as a whole and for several suspect processes, and you note three that really push the processor.

For each process, you also monitor that process' Working Set counter. Recall that this is the amount of RAM required by the process. Make note of the amount of RAM used by each process. Now you can terminate one of the processes and then check the percent of disk I/O used by paging. Has it dropped below the acceptable threshold (10 percent, as recommended by Microsoft)? If so, then the amount of RAM required by that application is the minimum amount of additional RAM to add to your computer. If not, terminate another application and check the results again. Keep repeating this step until the pagefile I/O drops to an acceptable level, and then add up the working set values for the terminated processes. The total represents the minimum amount of RAM to add to your computer. Programmers often round up this value to the nearest multiple of four.

Disk Objects

Two objects are actually related to disk activity: Physical Disk and Logical Disk.

The Physical Disk object counters track activity related to the disk drive as a whole and can be used to determine whether one disk drive is being used more than another for load-balancing purposes. For example, if the activity of a disk is particularly high as a result of operating system requests and pagefile I/O, then you might want to move the pagefile to a disk that is being underutilized, especially if the disk controller can write to each disk concurrently. The number of instances will be the number of physical drives installed on the computer.

The Logical Disk object counters track activity related to specific partitions on each disk and can be used to locate the source of activity on the disk—that is, on what partition the pagefile is located. The number of instances will be the number of partitions created by drive letter.

Both objects have pretty much the same group of counters for tracking activity. Four of these counters in particular can be useful:

■ One counter, Avg. Disk Sec/Transfer, you saw when reviewing Memory object counters. It shows the average amount of time for disk I/O to complete and can be used with the Memory object's Pages/Sec counter to determine whether paging is excessive.

CH
12

- Disk Queue Length represents the number of requests for disk I/O waiting to be serviced. This number should generally be less than 2. Consistently high numbers indicate that the disk is being overutilized or should be upgraded to a faster access disk.

- Disk Bytes/Sec indicates the number of bytes of data that are transferred during disk I/O. The higher the average value, the more efficient the performance.

- %Disk Time represents the amount of time spent servicing disk I/O requests. A consistently high number, of course, indicates that the disk is being heavily used. You may choose to determine which processes are driving this usage and partition or move the applications to a less heavily used disk to load-balance disk activity.

These counter values, used with the others previously discussed, can help you determine bottlenecks and possible courses of action to alleviate problems.

Key Concept

Disk object counters, although they are visible in the Add to Chart dialog box, are not enabled by default because the resource required to monitor disk activity is itself rather demanding. Disk object monitoring must be enabled before any charting can take place; otherwise, your chart will always display a flat line graph.

You can enable disk monitoring by typing the following command at a DOS command prompt

**DISKPERF -Y *computername*

where *computername* optionally references a remote computer whose disk activity you want to monitor.

When you are finished capturing your data, type

**DISKPERF -N *computername*

to disable disk monitoring.

Reviewing the Emergency Repair Process

The Emergency Repair Disk is usually created during the NT installation process (see Chapter 3, "Installing Windows NT Workstation 4.0"). However, you can create (and update) it at any time by running the Windows NT utility RDISK.EXE at the Windows NT command prompt.

The Emergency Repair Disk contains setup information relevant to your installation of Windows NT, including the location of source files and computer configuration, disk configuration, and security information from the Registry, including the SAM database. You can use it to replace corrupted or missing boot files, recover account information, and restore Windows NT to the master boot record (MBR) of the computer boot partition if it has been modified.

To use the Emergency Repair Disk, you must first boot the computer using a Windows NT Startup disk. This disk was created during the Windows NT installation process, unless you chose to do a diskless installation (see Chapter 3).

Key Concept

If you do not have a Windows NT Startup disk but have access to the original installation files, you can create one by accessing the installation file directory and typing the command **WINNT /O** at a command prompt (refer to Chapter 3 for a complete discussion of this and other installation switches). Be sure to have three disks available, and label them as instructed.

Initiating the Repair Process

choose Startup, Repair. The repair process offers four options:

1. Inspect Registry Files. This option prompts you for replacement of each Registry file, including System and SAM.

Key Concept

The security files on the Emergency Repair Disk overwrite the security files in the Registry. If you created or modified accounts but did not update the Emergency Repair data with the changes, you will lose the new and modified information when you perform the repair process. For this reason, this method is not the best way to recover damaged security or account information. A backup will be much more useful in maintaining the integrity of existing account entries.

2. Inspect Startup Environment. This option checks the BOOT.INI file for an entry for Windows NT. If it doesn't find one, it adds one for the next boot attempt.

3. Verify Windows NT System Files. This option verifies whether the Windows NT system files match those of the original installation files. For this option, you need to have access to the original installation files. This option also looks for, and verifies, the integrity of the boot files.

Key Concept

If you updated Windows NT with a service pack, you need to reinstall the service pack after initiating a repair.

4. Inspect Boot Sector. This option checks the MBR for NTLDR. If NTLDR is missing or corrupt, this option will restore the boot sector.

If you know specifically which file is missing or corrupt, you can replace the file directly from the source files by using the NT EXPAND * utility. At a Windows NT prompt, type **EXPAND -R** followed by the compressed filename. If Windows NT is inoperable on your system, you can use another Windows NT system to expand the file and then copy it to your computer.

Keep the Emergency Repair information up-to-date by running the RDISK.EXE utility after every major configuration change, or after modifying or creating accounts or setting permissions. On a Windows NT workstation, this information is not likely to change frequently, and the Emergency Repair information can be kept on a secure diskette. However, on a Windows NT server, particularly a domain controller, the account database itself is likely to exceed the capacity of the disk many times. Windows NT does keep a copy of the Emergency Repair information in the subdirectory WINNT40\REPAIR. However, in the event of a disk failure, that will not do you much good. As noted in the previous caution, in this situation it is best to have established a regular backup routine, which includes the Registry from which you can more reliably recover lost information.

Creating and Using a Windows NT Boot Disk

Another useful tool to have in your troubleshooting toolkit is a Windows NT boot disk. It is not a disk formatted with NTFS. Rather, it is a disk that has been formatted under Windows NT with copies of the boot files on it.

When you format a disk under Windows NT, Windows NT creates a boot sector on that disk that references NTLDR. Through Windows Explorer, you can set your view options to show all files and folders, particularly hidden files. You can copy the appropriate boot files from the root directory of the active system partition of your computer to this disk, and you have a Windows NT boot disk. This disk can be used in any number of Windows NT computers because it is not unique to each installation. The only file you might need to modify, for obvious reasons, is the BOOT.INI file because it references the location of the Windows NT system files (boot partition) by ARC path (see Chapter 3).

The boot files you will want to copy to the Windows NT boot disk include NTLDR, NTDETECT.COM, BOOT.INI, BOOTSECT.DOS, and NTBOOTDD.SYS (if your system boots through a SCSI controller). In addition, it is recommended that you copy the NTOSKRNL.EXE file from the WINNT40 system directory. You now have all the files you need to easily replace missing or corrupt boot files.

Key Concept

You can format a disk from My Computer. To do so, right-click the A: drive icon and select Format. Make the appropriate selections, and click OK.

Reviewing System Recovery Options

On rare occasions, your Windows NT 4.0 workstation may experience a stop error that causes the system to halt and Windows NT to be restarted. Troubleshooting this problem is difficult because you cannot do anything at that time except restart Windows NT.

Windows NT does provide a recovery utility in which you can specify how Windows NT should handle such an error. Its options can be set through the Startup/Shutdown tab of the System applet in the Control Panel. You can set the following four recovery options. These options are not enabled by default on Windows NT Workstation 4.0, but they are enabled by default on Windows NT Server 4.0.

- The first option—Write an Event to the System Log—is perhaps the most useful, given the discussion in this chapter. It, of course, causes the stop error to be recorded in the System Log and viewed through the Event Viewer.

- The next option—Send an Administrative Alert—sends an alert to all administrators that the stop error has occurred and on what computer it occurred. This option is useful if the stop error is intermittent.

- You can choose Write Debugging Information to write to a specified file or the default dump file. This option writes all memory registers to the pagefile. For this option to work, the pagefile must be at least as large as physical RAM, and it must reside on the boot partition (Windows NT system file partition). When Windows NT restarts, this information is copied to a specified dump file (WINNT40\MEMORY.DMP by default). This file can be used by Microsoft Technical Support or with the DUMPEXAM.EXE program supplied on the Windows NT CD-ROM to debug the problem.

- Finally, you can choose Automatically Reboot to restart the computer automatically after the stop error occurs. This option is extremely handy on server installations.

CH

12

Summary

In this chapter, you explored virtual memory management and pagefile usage. You also looked at the Event Viewer, the Windows NT Diagnostics utility, and the Performance Monitor. Finally, you reviewed the Emergency Repair process, ways to use a Windows NT boot disk, and system recovery options.

QUESTIONS AND ANSWERS

1. To effectively use statistics gathered in the Performance Monitor, you must gauge them against a(n) _____ .

    A. To effectively use statistics gathered in the Performance Monitor, you must gauge them against a baseline.

2. What is the default view in the Performance Monitor?

    A. The default view in the Performance Monitor is the Chart view.

3. True or False: The first division of the system in the Performance Monitor is objects.

    A. True. The first division of the system in the Performance Monitor is objects.

4. What is the default filename for a dump file?

    A. The default filename for a dump file is Memory.Dmp.

5. What three NT Server log files can the Event Viewer look at?

    A. The three NT Server log files the Event Viewer can look at are System (the default), Security, and Application.

PRACTICE TEST

1. Frederick has recently loaded two more C++ applications to modify on his Windows NT 4.0 Workstation. He has noticed that when he boots and loads all his applications, Windows NT takes longer to respond to application requests. You use the Performance Monitor and notice that pagefile usage has increased and that the Commit Limit for the pagefile drops rapidly when the applications are loaded. What is the best solution you can offer Frederick based on this data?

    a. Purchase more RAM for Frederick's computer.

    b. Move the pagefile to another disk partition.

    c. Increase the initial size of the pagefile so that it doesn't have to grow right away as the applications load.

    d. Move the C++ applications to another disk partition.

Answers a and b are not the best answers because they do not change the initial size of the pagefile. **Answer c is correct because the best solution in this environment is to the increase the initial pagefile size and allow it plenty of room within which to operate without needing to grow immediately.** Answer d solves nothing. Regardless of the partition the applications are on, the issue is with the pagefile.

2. Desiree, a Visual Basic developer, has noticed that her system's performance has decreased since she began work on a large VB application. You have used the Performance Monitor to determine that the pagefile usage has increased. You also notice that the pagefile, Windows NT system files, and the VB application are all stored on the same partition. In addition, the working set for the VB application shows that it consistently requires 16MB for itself. What solutions can you recommend? Choose all that apply.

    a. Add more RAM in the computer.

    b. Move the pagefile to a disk partition other than the system or application partition.

    c. Increase the maximum size for the pagefile.

    d. Create multiple pagefiles.

Answer a is correct. Adding more RAM allows the system to utilize memory more and the pagefile less. **Answer b is correct.** Moving the pagefile to another partition prevents the drive from competing between the applications and pagefile. Answer c does not solve the problem given the resource scenario presented. To solve this problem, you must isolate the applications from the pagefile, utilize more than one pagefile, or add more RAM. **Answer d also is correct.** Creating multiple pagefiles lessens the burden on the one that now services the operating system and applications.

3. Which Processor object counter would be useful to determine how much processor time is being utilized by application requests?

    a. %Processor Time

    b. %User Time

    c. %Application Time

    d. %Privileged Time

Answer a is incorrect because it does not show how much processor time is being utilized by application requests. Rather, it shows how busy each processor is if you have multiple processors. **Answer b is correct because %User Time would be used to determine how much processor time is being utilized by application requests.** Answer c does not exist. Answer d shows only User mode and Processor mode.

CH

12

4. Which Process object counter would be useful in determining the amount of memory required by an application?

a. %Application Memory

b. Commit Limit

c. Working Set

d. Avg. Disk Sec\Transfer

Answer a is invalid. Answer b shows only the limit on committed memory. **Answer c is correct because Working Set is needed for determining the amount of memory required by an application.** Answer d shows disk activity.

5. Which Memory object counter would help to identify when to right-size the pagefile?

a. %Pagefile

b. Commit Limit

c. Working Set

d. %Disk Time

Answer a is invalid. **Answer b is correct because Commit Limit should be consulted to identify when to right-size the pagefile.** Answer c shows the amount of memory required by an application. Answer d shows disk activity.

6. On your Windows NT 4.0 development workstation, you have concluded that performance as a whole has decreased. You are not sure which process is driving this performance problem, but you have noticed that your disk drive has had a lot more activity lately. What objects should you monitor through the Performance Monitor to help troubleshoot this situation?

a. Check the Processor>%Processor Time counter, determine the percent of disk I/O used for paging through the Memory>Pages/Sec counter and the Logical Disk>Avg. Disk Sec/Transfer counter, and check the Process>Working Set for every process running.

b. Check the Processor>%Processor Time counter, and determine the percent of disk I/O used for paging through the Memory>Pages/Sec counter and the Logical Disk>Avg. Disk sec/Transfer counter. Track the Process>%Processor Time counter for every process running to determine which processes are pushing the processor excessively. Monitor the Process>Working Set counter for these processes in particular.

c. Check the Processor>%Processor Time counter, determine the percent of disk I/O used for paging through the Logical Disk>Disk Queue Length counter, and check the Process>Working Set for every process running.

d. Check the Processor>%User Time counter, determine the percent of disk I/O used for paging through the Logical Disk>%Disk Time counter, and check the Memory>Commit Limit counter for the pagefile.

Answer a is not a valid choice. **Answer b is correct because you must examine all the counters related to the Processor, Logical Disk, and Processes to get a full view of the situation.** Answer c does not give the numbers you are looking for. By concentrating only on the Logical disk, you are overlooking the much needed memory figures. Answer d does not show the processes desired. The processes are never examined to see what values they are generating.

7. What is the utility to verify the validity of a Memory Dump file?

   a. Dumpflop.exe

   b. Dumpexam.exe

   c. Dumpchk.exe

   d. Dump.exe

Answer a is incorrect because this tool is used to dump files to floppies. Answer b is incorrect because this tool is used to find the cause of the error. **Answer c is correct because Dumpchk.exe verifies the validity of a Memory Dump file.** Answer d is not a valid tool.

8. Which of the following counters provides you with the total number of bytes transferred during disk I/O for all the disks in your computer? Choose the best answer.

   a. Logical Disk>Disk Bytes/Sec, Total instance

   b. Logical Disk>Disk Bytes/Sec, for each partition instance

   c. Physical Disk>Disk Bytes/Sec, Total instance

   d. Physical Disk>Disk Bytes/Sec, for each disk instance

Answer a does not show more than the partition. Answer b does not show more than the partition. **Answer c is correct because the Physical Disk looks at all partitions, and the Total instance shows all activity.** Answer d is an inferior choice to c.

9. Which objects would be most beneficial to include in a log file when you're creating a baseline measurement of your system's performance? Choose all that apply.

   a. Memory

   b. TCP/IP

   c. Processor

   d. Physical and Logical Disk

Answers a, c, and d are correct because Memory, Processor, and Disks must all work together. To get a true view of how your system is working, all must be taken into account. Answer b is invalid because network statistics do not measure individual system performance.

CH
12

10. You plan to use the Performance Monitor to help predict and troubleshoot server activity under various conditions. Which of the following would be the best way to begin?

a. Create and monitor a real-time chart during peak activity, and note the percent of processor usage during these periods.

b. Create a series of baseline logs of specific objects (processor, memory, disk, and network), each representing a different condition. Use them to predict activity under those conditions and to troubleshoot abnormal system activity.

c. Create a baseline log measuring system activity during periods of average activity. Compare this log against real-time charts created during peak activity on the system.

d. Network Monitor would be a better tool to predict system activity.

Answer a is valid but not the best choice because it completely ignores a crucial element: baselines. **Answer b is correct because baselines must always be established before any further actions can take place.** Baselines should be created for all major components and referenced against all future monitoring. Answer c examines only peak activity and compares it to the logs. You must look at the system during all activity, not just peak. Answer d does not address the question and uses a tool available only in NT Server.

Glossary

access control entry (ACE)—An entry in an access control list that defines a set of permissions for a group or user.

access control list (ACL)—A list containing access control entries. An ACL determines the permissions associated with an object, which can be anything in a WIN32 environment.

access time—If a file is executable, the last time it was run; otherwise, the last time the file was read or written to.

ACE—See access control entry.

ACK—Short for acknowledgment. A control character sent to another computer in a conversation. Usually used to indicate that transmitted information has been received correctly when using a communications protocol, such as Xmodem.

ACL—See access control list.

active window—The window the user is currently working with. Windows identifies the active window by highlighting its title bar and border.

Advanced Program-to-Program Communications (APPC)—A method of interprogram communication, usually used by applications intended for use with IBM SNA-based networks.

Advanced Research Project Agency (ARPA)—The agency responsible for the formation of the forerunner to the Internet. See also Defense Advanced Research Projects Agency.

agent—Software that runs on a client computer for use by administrative software running on a server. Agents are typically used to support administrative actions, such as detecting system information or running services.

Alerter Service—A Windows NT Executive Service that notifies selected users or computers of system-generated administrative alerts.

American National Standards Institute (ANSI)—A standards-making organization based in the United States of America.

American Standard Code for Information Interchange (ASCII)—A scheme that assigns letters, punctuation marks, and so on, to specific numeric values. The standardization of ASCII enabled computers and computer programs to exchange data.

ANSI—See American National Standards Institute.

ANSI character set—An 8-bit character set used by Microsoft Windows that enables you to represent up to 256 characters (0 to 255) using your keyboard. The ASCII character set is a subset of the ANSI set. See also American National Standards Institute.

API—See application programming interface.

APPC—See Advanced Program-to-Program Communications.

application—A computer program that is designed to do some specific type of work. An application is different from a utility that performs some type of maintenance (such as formatting a disk).

application programming interface (API)—A list of supported functions. Windows NT 4.0 supports the MS-DOS API, Windows API, and WIN32 API. If a function is a member of the API, it is said to be a supported or documented function. Functions that make up Windows but are not part of the API are referred to as undocumented functions.

ARPA—See Advanced Research Project Agency.

ASCII—See American Standard Code for Information Interchange.

ASCII character set—A 7-bit character set widely used to represent letters and symbols found on a standard U.S. keyboard. The ASCII character set is identical to the first 128 characters in the ANSI character set.

association—The process of assigning a filename extension to a particular application. When an extension has been associated with an application, Windows NT 4.0 will start the application when you choose to open the file from Windows Explorer. Associations are critical to the concept of document-centric computing.

attribute—A characteristic of a file that indicates whether it is hidden, system, read-only, archive, or compressed.

Audio Video Interleaved (AVI)—The format of the full-motion video files used by Windows NT 4.0.

audit policy—A definition of the type of security-related event that will be recorded by the Event Viewer.

authentication—The validation of a user's access to a computer or domain by either the local computer (local validation) or a backup domain controller for the domain that the user is accessing.

AUTOEXEC.BAT—A file in the root directory of the boot disk that contains a list of MS-DOS commands that are automatically executed when the system is started. AUTOEXEC.BAT can be created by either the user or the operating system. Windows NT 4.0 Setup examines the AUTOEXEC.BAT file looking for configuration information such as user environment variables.

auxiliary audio device—An audio device whose output is mixed with the Musical Instrument Digital Interface (MIDI) and waveform output devices in a multimedia computer. An example of an auxiliary audio device is the compact disc audio output from a CD-ROM drive.

AVI—See Audio Video Interleaved.

background window—Any window created by a thread other than the thread running in the foreground.

backup domain controller—The NT controller server that performs the validation of user logon requests. The backup domain controller obtains a copy of the master account database for the domain from the primary domain controller.

Basic Input/Output System (BIOS)—The bootstrap code of a PC. The low-level routines that support the transfer of information among the various parts of a computer system, such as memory, disks, and the monitor. The BIOS is usually built into the machine's read-only memory (ROM); it can have a significant effect on the performance of the computer system.

batch program—A file that contains one or more commands that are executed when you type the filename at the command prompt. Batch programs have the .BAT extension.

binding—The process that links a protocol driver and a network adapter driver.

BIOS—See Basic Input/Output System.

BIOS enumerator—In a Plug and Play system, the driver responsible for identifying all the hardware devices on the computer's motherboard.

bit—Short for binary digit, the smallest unit of data a computer can store. Bits are expressed as 1 or 0.

bitmap—Originally, an array of bits but now expanded to include arrays of bytes or even 32-bit quantities that specify the dot pattern and colors that describe an image on the screen or printed paper.

BMP—The extension used for Windows bitmap files.

Boot Loader—A feature that defines the location of the NT boot and system files.

boot partition—The partition that contains the NT system files.

Bootstrap Protocol (BOOTP)—An internetworking protocol that is used to configure TCP/IP networks across routers.

branch—A segment of the directory tree, representing a directory and any subdirectories it contains.

browse—To look through a list on a computer system. Lists include directories, files, domains, or computers.

buffer—A temporary holding place reserved in memory, where data is held while in transit to or from a storage device or another location in memory.

APP
A

buffering—The process of using buffers, particularly to or from I/O devices such as disk drives and serial ports.

bus enumerator—A driver responsible for building the hardware tree on a Plug and Play system.

byte—8 bits.

Card Services—A protected-mode VxD, linked with the PCMCIA bus drivers. Card Services passes event notifications from socket services to the PCMCIA bus driver, provides information from the computer's cards to the PCMCIA bus driver, and sets up the configuration for cards in the adapter sockets.

cascading menu—A menu that is a sub-menu of a menu item. Also known as a hierarchical menu. The menus accessed via the Windows NT 4.0 Start button are cascading menus.

CCITT—See International Telephone and Telegraph Consultative Committee.

CD-DA—See Compact Disc-Digital Audio.

CD-ROM—See Compact Disc Read-Only Memory.

CD-ROM/XA—See Compact Disc-Read-Only Memory Extended Architecture.

CD-XA—See Compact Disc-Extended Architecture.

CDFS—See Compact Disc File System.

central processing unit (CPU)—The computational and control unit of a computer; the device that interprets and executes instructions. The CPU or micro-processor, in the case of a microcomputer, has the ability to fetch, decode, and execute instructions and to transfer information to and from other resources over the computer's main data-transfer path, the bus. The CPU is the chip that functions as the "brain" of a computer.

character—A letter, number, punctuation mark, or a control code. Usually expressed in either the ANSI or ASCII character set.

character mode—A mode of displaying information on the screen, where all information is displayed using text characters (as opposed to graphical symbols). MS-DOS applications run in character mode.

check box—In the Windows NT 4.0 interface, a square box that has two or three states, and is used by the user to select an option from a set of options. A standard check box is a toggle, with two states: checked and unchecked. A three-state check box has an additional state: disabled (grayed).

class—For OLE, a data structure and the functions that manipulate that data structure. An object is a member of a class. For hardware, a grouping of devices and buses for the purpose of installing and managing devices and device drivers, and allocating the resources used by them. The Windows NT 4.0 hardware tree is organized by device class.

clear-to-send—A signal sent from one computer to another in a communications conversation to indicate readiness to accept data.

client—A computer that accesses shared network resources provided by another computer, called a server. See also server.

code names—A name assigned to conceal the identity or existence of something or someone. The code name for Microsoft Windows NT 4.0 was "SUR," which sometimes appears as an identifier in several places in the released product, including hardware setup files.

codec—Compression/decompression technology for digital video and stereo audio.

COMMAND.COM—The command processor for MS-DOS. Windows NT 4.0 loads its version of COMMAND.COM (compatible with MS-DOS version 5.0) to process commands typed in MS-DOS mode or in an MS-DOS prompt.

communications resource—A device that provides a bidirectional, asynchronous data stream. Examples include serial and parallel ports and modems. Applications access the resource through a service provider.

communications protocol—The rules that govern a conversation between two computers communicating via an asynchronous connection. The use of a communications protocol ensures error-free delivery of the data being communicated.

Compact Disc-Digital Audio (CD-DA)—An optical data storage format that provides for the storage of up to 73 minutes of high-quality digital-audio data on a compact disc. Also known as Red Book audio or music CD.

Compact Disc-Extended Architecture (CD-XA)—See Compact Disc-Read-Only Memory Extended Architecture (CD-ROM/XA).

Compact Disc File System (CDFS)—A file system that controls access to the contents of CD-ROM drivers.

Compact Disc-Read-Only Memory (CD-ROM)—A form of storage characterized by high capacity (roughly 600 megabytes) and the use of laser optics rather than magnetic means for reading data.

Compact Disc-Read-Only Memory Extended Architecture (CD-ROM/XA)—An extended CD-ROM format developed by Philips, Sony, and Microsoft. CD-ROM/XA format is consistent with the ISO 9660 (High Sierra) standard, with further specification of ADPCM (adaptive differential pulse code modulation) audio, images, and interleaved data.

Computer Browser Service—An Executive Service that identifies those NT computers that have resources available for use within a workgroup or domain.

computer name—A unique name that identifies a particular computer on the network. Microsoft networking uses NetBIOS names, which can have up to 15 characters but cannot contain spaces.

CONFIG.SYS—An ASCII text file that contains configuration commands. Used by MS-DOS, OS/2, and Windows NT 4.0 to load real-mode device drivers.

APP
A

Configuration Manager—One of three central components of a Plug and Play system (one for each of the three phases of configuration management). The Configuration Managers drive the process of locating devices, setting up the hardware tree, and allocating resources.

context menu—The menu that is displayed at the location of a set menu when you right-click. It is called the context menu because the contents of the menu depend on the context it is invoked in.

Control Panel—The primary Windows NT 4.0 configuration tool. Each option that you can change is represented by an icon in the Control Panel window.

controller—See domain controller.

conventional memory—The first 640KB of memory in your computer, used to run real-mode MS-DOS applications.

cooperative multitasking—A form of multitasking in which threads cooperate with each other by voluntarily giving up control of the processor. Contrast: preemptive multitasking.

CPU—See central processing unit.

crash—A serious failure of the software being used.

CTS—See clear-to-send.

cursor—A bitmap whose location on the screen is controlled by a pointing device, such as a mouse, pen, or trackball. See also bitmap.

DARPA—See Defense Advanced Research Projects Agency.

data frame—A structured packet into which data is placed by the Data Link layer.

datagram—A packet of information and delivery data that is routed on a network.

DDE—See Dynamic Data Exchange.

default—An operation or value that the system assumes, unless the user makes an explicit choice.

Defense Advanced Research Projects Agency (DARPA)—An agency of the U.S. Department of Defense that sponsored the development of the protocols that became the TCP/IP suite. DARPA was previously known as ARPA, the Advanced Research Project Agency, when ARPAnet was built.

desktop—The background of your screen, on which windows, icons, and dialog boxes appear.

destination directory—The directory to which you intend to copy or move one or more files.

device—A generic term for a computer component, such as a printer, serial port, or disk drive. A device frequently requires its own controlling software called a device driver.

device contention—The method that Windows NT 4.0 uses to allocate access to peripheral devices when multiple applications are attempting to use them.

device driver—A piece of software that translates requests from one form into another. Most commonly, drivers are used to provide a device-independent way to access hardware.

device ID—A unique ASCII string created by enumerators to identify a hardware device and used to cross-reference data about the device stored in the Registry.

device node—One of the data structures that make up the hardware tree; a device node is built by the Configuration Manager into memory at system startup. Device nodes contain information about a given device, such as the resources it is using.

DHCP—See Dynamic Host Configuration Protocol.

dialog box—The type of window that is displayed by Windows NT 4.0 when user input is needed. It usually contains one or more buttons, edit controls, radio buttons, and drop-down lists.

Dial-Up Networking—Formerly known as Remote Access Service (RAS), a service that provides remote access to networks. Dial-Up Networking allows a remote user to access a network. Once the user is connected, it is as if the remote computer is logically on the network; the user can do anything that he or she could do when physically connected to the network.

DIP switch—Short for Dual In-line Package switch. A switch used to configure hardware options, especially on adapter cards.

Direct Memory Access (DMA)—A technique used by hardware adapters to store and retrieve information from the computer's RAM without involving the computer's CPU.

directory—Part of a structure for organizing your files on a disk. A directory can contain files and other directories (called subdirectories).

Directory Replication Service—A service that provides a means of copying a directory and file structure from a source NT server to a target NT server or workstation.

disk caching—A method to improve performance of the file system. A section of memory is used as a temporary holding place for frequently accessed file data. Windows NT 4.0 dynamically allocates its disk cache.

disk operating system (DOS)—See MS-DOS.

DLL—See dynamic link library.

DMA—See Direct Memory Access.

DMA channel—A channel for DMA transfers that occur between a device and memory directly, without involving the CPU.

DNS—See Domain Name Service.

DNS name servers—The servers that hold the DNS name database and supply the IP address that matches a DNS name in response to a request from a DNS client. See also Domain Name Service.

dock—To insert a portable computer into a base unit. Cold docking means the computer must begin from a power-off state and restart before docking. Hot docking means the computer can be docked while running at full power.

APP
A

docking station—The base computer unit into which a user can insert a portable computer, to expand it to a desktop equivalent. Docking stations usually include drives, expansion slots, AC power, network and SCSI connections, and communication ports.

document—Whatever you work with in an application.

domain—For DNS, a group of workstations and servers that share a single group name. For Microsoft networking, a collection of computers that share a security context and account database stored on a Windows NT Server domain controller. Each domain has a unique name. See also Domain Name Service.

domain controller—The Windows NT Server computer that authenticates domain logons and maintains a copy of the security database for the domain.

Domain Name Service (DNS)—A static, hierarchical name service for TCP/IP hosts. Do not confuse DNS domains with Windows NT domains.

DOS—See Microsoft Disk Operating System.

DOS Protected Mode Interface (DPMI)—A technique used to allow MS-DOS–based applications to access extended memory.

dpi—Short for dots per inch. A measurement of the resolution of a monitor or printer.

DPMI—See DOS Protected Mode Interface.

drag and drop—To select one or more files, drag them to an application, and drop them there.

DRAM—See Dynamic Random Access Memory.

Dynamic Data Exchange (DDE)—A form of interprocess communication (IPC) implemented in the Microsoft Windows family of operating systems. DDE uses shared memory to exchange data. Most DDE functions have been superseded by OLE.

Dynamic Host Configuration Protocol (DHCP)—A protocol for automatic TCP/IP configuration that provides static and dynamic address allocation and management.

Dynamic Random Access Memory (DRAM)—A computer's main memory.

dynamic link library (DLL)—A set of file functions compiled, linked, and saved separately from the processes that use them. Functions in DLLs can be used by more than one running process. The operating system maps the DLLs into the process' address space when the process is starting up or while it is running. Dynamic link libraries are stored in files with the .DLL extension.

Eform—See electronic mail form.

EISA—See Extended Industry Standard Architecture.

electronic mail (email)—A message in an electronic mail system.

electronic mail form (Eform)—A programmed form used to send email in an electronic mail system.

electronic messaging system (EMS)—A system that allows users or applications to correspond using a store-and-forward system.

email—See electronic mail.

EMM—See Expanded Memory Manager.

EMS—See Expanded Memory Specification; Electronic Messaging System.

Encapsulated PostScript (EPS)—A file format used to represent graphics written in the PostScript page description language.

enumerator—A Plug and Play device driver that detects devices below its own device node, creates unique device IDs, and reports to the Configuration Manager during startup.

environment variable—A symbolic variable that represents some element of the operating system, such as a path, a filename, or other literal data. Typically used by batch files, environment variables are created with the SET command.

EPROM—See Erasable Programmable Read-Only Memory.

EPS—See Encapsulated PostScript.

EPS file—A file containing code written in the Encapsulated PostScript printer programming language. Often used to represent graphics for use by desktop publishing applications.

Erasable Programmable Read-Only Memory (EPROM)—A computer chip containing nonvolatile memory. It can be erased (for reprogramming) by exposure to an ultraviolet light.

event—An action or occurrence to which an application might respond, such as mouse clicks, key presses, mouse movements, or a system event. A system event is any significant occurrence that may require user notification or some other action by an application.

expanded memory—Memory that complies with the Lotus-Intel-Microsoft Expanded Memory specification. Used by MS-DOS–based spreadsheet applications.

Expanded Memory Manager (EMM)—The device driver that controls access to expanded memory.

Expanded Memory Specification (EMS)—The specification that controls and defines Expanded Memory. Also known as the Lotus-Intel-Microsoft (LIM) specification, after the three major companies that designed it.

Extended Industry Standard Architecture (EISA)—An enhancement to the bus architecture used on the IBM PC/AT, which allows the use of 32-bit devices in the same type of expansion slot used by an ISA adapter card. EISA slots and adapters were formerly common in server computers but have been mostly replaced with PCI slots.

extended memory—Memory that occupies physical addresses above the 1 megabyte mark.

APP
A

Extended Memory Manager (XMM)—The MS-DOS device driver that provides access to XMS memory.

Extended Memory Specification (XMS)—The specification for the application program interfaces that allow an application to access and use extended memory.

family name—The name of a given font family. Windows employs five family names: Decorative, Modern, Roman, Script, and Swiss. A sixth family name, Dontcare, specifies the default font. See also font family.

FAT—See file allocation table.

FAT file system—A file system based on a file allocation table. Windows NT 4.0 uses a 32-bit implementation called VFAT. See also file allocation table, virtual file allocation table.

FIFO—See First In, First Out.

file—A collection of information stored on a disk and accessible using a name.

file allocation table (FAT)—A table or list maintained by some operating systems to keep track of the status of various segments of disk space used for file storage. See also virtual file allocation table.

file attribute—A characteristic of a file that indicates whether the file is read-only, hidden, system, archived, a directory, or normal.

file sharing—The capability of a network computer to share files or directories on its local disks with remote computers.

file system—In an operating system, the overall structure in which files are named, stored, and organized.

file time—A 64-bit value representing the number of 100-nanosecond intervals that have elapsed since January 1, 1601.

File Transfer Program (FTP)—A utility defined by the TCP/IP protocol suite, used to transfer files between dissimilar systems.

File Transfer Protocol (FTP)—The standard method of transferring files using TCP/IP. FTP allows you to transfer files between dissimilar computers, with preservation of binary data and optional translation of text file formats.

First In, First Out (FIFO)—An expression used to describe a buffer, where data is retrieved from the buffer in the same order it went in.

floppy disk—A disk that can be inserted and removed from a disk drive.

focus—The area of a dialog box that receives input. The focus is indicated by highlighted text or a button enclosed in dotted lines.

folder—In Windows Explorer, a container object, that is, an object that can contain other objects. Examples include disk folders, the fonts folder, and the printers folder.

font—A collection of characters, each of which has a similar appearance. For example, the Arial font.

font family—A group of fonts that have similar characteristics.

font mapper—The routine within Windows that maps an application's request for a font with particular characteristics to the available font that best matches those characteristics.

frame—See data frame.

free space—Unused space on a hard disk.

friendly name—A human-readable name used to give an alternative to the often cryptic computer, port, and share names. For example, "Digital 1152 Printer In The Hall" as opposed to "HALLPRT."

FTP—See File Transfer Program, File Transfer Protocol.

gateway—A computer connected to multiple networks and capable of moving data between networks using different transport protocols.

GDI—See graphics device interface.

graphical user interface (GUI)—A computer system design in which the user interacts with the system using graphical symbols, tools, and events rather than text-based displays and commands, such as the normal Windows NT 4.0 user interface.

graphics device interface (GDI)—The subsystem that implements graphic drawing functions.

GUI—See graphical user interface.

handle—An interface (usually a small black square) added to an object to enable the user to move, size, reshape, or otherwise modify the object.

hardware branch—The hardware archive root key in the Registry, which is a superset of the memory-resident hardware tree. The name of this key is HKEY_LOCAL_MACHINE\HARDWARE.

hardware tree—A record in RAM of the current system configuration, based on the configuration information for all devices in the hardware branch of the Registry. The Hardware tree is created each time the computer is started or whenever a dynamic change occurs to the system configuration.

high memory area (HMA)—A 64KB memory block located just above the 1MB address in a Virtual DOS Machine (VDM). Originally made possible by a side effect of the 80286 processor design, the memory is usable when the A20 address line is turned on.

High Performance File System (HPFS)—A file system primarily used with OS/2 operating system version 1.2 or higher. It supports long filenames but does not provide security. Windows NT 4.0 does not support HPFS.

Hive—A discrete body of Registry information, usually stored in a single disk file.

HKEY_CLASSES_ROOT—The Registry tree that contains data relating to OLE. This key is a symbolic link to a subkey of HKEY_LOCAL_MACHINE\ SOFTWARE.

HKEY_CURRENT_USER—The Registry tree that contains the currently logged-in user's preferences, including desktop

APP
A

settings, application settings, and network connections. This key maps to a subkey of HKEY_USERS.

HKEY_LOCAL_MACHINE—The Registry tree that contains configuration settings that apply to the hardware and software on the computer.

HKEY_USERS—The Registry tree that contains the preferences for every user who ever logged on to this computer.

HMA—See high memory area.

home directory—A directory that is accessible to a particular user and contains that user's files and programs on a network server.

host—Any device that is attached to the internetwork and uses TCP/IP.

host ID—The portion of the IP address that identifies a computer within a particular network ID.

hostname—The name of an Internet host. It may or may not be the same as the computer name. For a client to access resources by hostname, that name must appear in the client's HOSTS file or be resolvable by a DNS server.

host table—The HOSTS and LMHOSTS files, which contain mappings of known IP addresses mapped to hostnames.

HOSTS file—A local text file in the same format as the 4.3 Berkeley Software Distribution (BSD) UNIX /etc/hosts file. This file maps hostnames to IP addresses. In Windows NT 4.0, this file is stored in the \WINNT directory.

hotkey—A keystroke used in place of a mouse click.

HPFS—See High Performance File System.

I/O address—One of the critical resources used in configuring devices. I/O addresses are used to communicate with devices. Also known as port.

I/O bus—The electrical connection between the CPU and the I/O devices. The following are different types of I/O buses: ISA, EISA, SCSI, VLB, and PCI.

I/O device—Any device in or attached to a computer that is designed to receive information from or provide information to the computer. For example, a printer is an output-only device, whereas a mouse is an input-only device. Other devices, such as modems, are both input and output devices, transferring data in both directions. Windows NT 4.0 must have a device driver installed in order to be able to use an I/O device.

ICMP—See Internet Control Message Protocol.

icon—A small bitmap (usually 16×16 pixels or 32×32 pixels) that is associated with an application, file type, or a concept.

IEEE—See Institute of Electrical and Electronic Engineers.

IETF—See Internet Engineering Task Force.

IFS—See installable file system.

IHV—See independent hardware vendor.

independent hardware vendor (IHV)—A manufacturer of computer hardware. Usually used to describe the makers of add-on devices rather than makers of computer systems.

Industry Standard Architecture (ISA)—The same design rules and constraints that the IBM PC/AT adhered to.

INF file—A file, usually provided by the manufacturer of a device, that provides the information that Windows NT 4.0 Setup needs to set up a device. INF files usually include a list of valid logical configurations for the device, the names of driver files associated with the device, and other information.

INI files—Initialization files used by Windows-based applications to store configuration information. Windows NT 4.0 incorporates INI files into its Registry when upgrading from previous versions of Windows.

installable file system (IFS)—A file system that can be installed into the operating system as needed rather than just at startup time. Windows NT 4.0 can support multiple installable file systems at one time, including the file allocation table (FAT) file system and NTFS, network redirectors, and the CD-ROM File System (CDFS).

instance—A particular occurrence of an object, such as a window, module, named pipe, or DDE session. Each instance has a unique handle that distinguishes it from other instances of the same type.

Institute of Electrical and Electronic Engineers (IEEE)—An organization that issues standards for electrical and electronic devices.

Integrated Services Digital Network (ISDN)—A digital communications method that permits connections of up to 128Kbps. ISDN requires a special adapter for your computer. An ISDN connection is available in most areas of the United States for a reasonable cost.

internal command—A command that is built into the COMMAND.COM file.

International Organization for Standardization (ISO)—The organization that produces many of the world's standards. Open Systems Interconnect (OSI) is only one of many areas standardized by the ISO.

International Telephone and Telegraph Consultative Committee (CCITT)—The international organization that creates and publishes telecommunications standards, including X.400. The initials CCITT actually stand for the real name of the organization, which is French.

Internet—The worldwide interconnected wide area network, based on the TCP/IP protocol suite.

Internet Control Message Protocol (ICMP)—A required protocol in the TCP/IP protocol suite. It allows two nodes on an IP network to share IP status and error information. ICMP is used by the Ping utility.

APP A

Internet Engineering Task Force (IETF)—A consortium that introduces procedures for new technology on the Internet. IETF specifications are released in documents called Requests for Comments (RFCs).

Internet group names—A name known by a DNS server that includes a list of the specific addresses of systems that have registered the name.

Internet Protocol (IP)—The Network layer protocol of TCP/IP, responsible for addressing and sending TCP packets over the network.

interprocess communications (IPC)—A set of mechanisms used by applications to communicate and share data.

interrupt—An event that disrupts normal processing by the CPU and results in the transfer of control to an interrupt handler. Both hardware devices and software can issue interrupts. Software executes an INT instruction, whereas hardware devices signal the CPU by using one of the interrupt request (IRQ) lines to the processor.

interrupt request level (IRQL)—An interrupt ranked by priority. Interrupts that have a priority lower than the processor's interrupt request level setting can be masked (ignored).

interrupt request line (IRQ)—A hardware line on the CPU that devices use to send signals to cause an interrupt. Normally, only one device is attached to any particular IRQ line.

IP—See Internet Protocol.

IP address—An address used to identify a node on a network and to specify routing information on an internetwork. Each node on the internetwork must be assigned a unique IP address, which is made up of the network ID, plus a unique host ID assigned by the network administrator. The subnet mask is used to separate an IP address into the host ID and network ID. In Windows NT 4.0, an IP address can be assigned manually or automatically using DHCP.

IP router—A system connected to multiple physical TCP/IP networks that can route or deliver IP packets between the networks. See also gateway.

IPC—See interprocess communications.

IPX/SPX—Internetworking Packet eXchange/Sequenced Packet eXchange. Transport protocols used in Novell NetWare networks. Windows NT 4.0 includes the Microsoft IPX/SPX compatible transport protocol (NWLINK).

IRQ—See interrupt request level.

IRQL—See interrupt request line.

ISA—See Industry Standard Architecture.

ISDN—See Integrated Services Digital Network.

ISO—See International Organization for Standardization.

ISO Development Environment (ISODE)—A research tool developed to study the upper layer of OSI. Academic and some commercial ISO products are based on this framework.

ISODE—See ISO Development Environment.

KB—Standard abbreviation for kilobyte; equals 1,024 bytes.

Kbps—Kilobits per second.

kernel—The Windows NT 4.0 core component responsible for implementing the basic operating system functions of Windows NT 4.0, including virtual memory management, thread scheduling, and file I/O services.

LAN—See local area network.

legacy—Hardware and device cards that don't conform to the Plug and Play standard.

link—A connection at the LLC layer that is uniquely defined by the adapter's address and the destination service access point (DSAP). Also, a connection between two objects, or a reference to an object that is linked to another.

list box—In a dialog box, a box that lists available choices. For example, a list of all files in a directory. If all the choices do not fit in the list box, a scrollbar is included for access.

LLC—See logical link control.

LMHOSTS file—A local text file that maps IP addresses to the computer names of Windows networking computers. In Windows NT 4.0, LMHOSTS is stored in the WINNT\system32\drivers\etc directory.

local area network (LAN)—A computer network confined to a single building or campus.

local printer—A printer that is directly connected to one of the ports on a computer, as opposed to a network printer.

localization—The process of adapting software for different countries, languages, or cultures.

logical drive—A division of an extended partition on a hard disk, accessed using a drive letter.

logical link control (LLC)—One of the two sublayers of the Data Link layer of the OSI reference model, as defined by the IEEE 802 standards.

login—The process by which a user is identified to the computer in a Novell NetWare network.

logon—The process by which a user is identified to the computer in a Microsoft network.

logon script—In Microsoft networking, a batch file that runs automatically when a user logs on to a Windows NT Server. Novell networking also uses logon scripts, but they are not batch files.

MAC—See media access control.

MAC address—The address for a device as it is identified at the media access control layer in the network architecture. MAC addresses are usually stored in ROM on the network adapter card and are unique.

mailslot—A form of interprocess communications used to carry messages from an application on one network node to another. Mailslots are one-way.

mailslot client—A process that writes a message to a mailslot.

mailslot server—A process that creates and owns a mailslot and can read messages from it. See also process.

management information base (MIB)—A set of objects used by SNMP to manage devices. MIB objects represent various types of information about a device.

mandatory user profile—A user environment profile that cannot be changed by the user. If the profile is unavailable, the user cannot log on to the NT Enterprise.

map—To translate one value into another.

MAPI—See Messaging Application Programming Interface.

mapped I/O or mapped file I/O—The file I/O that is performed by reading and writing to virtual memory that is backed by a file.

MB—Standard abbreviation for megabyte, or 1,024 kilobytes.

MDI—See multiple document interface.

media access control (MAC)—The lower of the two sublayers of the Data Link layer in the IEEE 802 network model.

Media Control Interface (MCI)—High-level control software that provides a device-independent interface to multimedia devices and media files. MCI includes a command-message interface and a command-string interface.

memory—A temporary storage area for information and applications.

memory object—A number of bytes allocated from the heap.

message—A structure or set of parameters used for communicating information or a request. Every event that happens in the system causes a message to be sent. Messages can be passed between the operating system and an application, different applications, threads within an application, and windows within an application.

message loop—A program loop that retrieves messages from a thread's message queue and dispatches them.

Messaging Application Program Interface (MAPI)—A set of calls used to add mail-enabled features to other Windows-based applications. One of the WOSA technologies.

metafile—A collection of structures that store a picture in a device-independent format. (The two metafile formats are the enhanced format and the Windows format.)

MIB—See management information base.

Microsoft Disk Operating System (MS-DOS)—The dominant operating system for personal computers from the introduction of the IBM Personal Computer until the introduction of Windows 95 and Windows NT 4.0.

MIDI—See Musical Instrument Digital Interface.

minidriver—The part of the device driver that is written by the hardware manufacturer; it provides device-specific functionality.

MS-DOS—See Microsoft Disk Operating System.

MS-DOS-based application—An application designed to run under MS-DOS. Windows NT 4.0 supports most MS-DOS–based applications except those that communicate directly to hardware devices.

multiple document interface (MDI)—A specification that defines the standard user interface for Windows-based applications. An MDI application enables the user to work with more than one document at the same time. Microsoft Word is an example of an MDI application. Each of the documents is displayed in a separate window inside the application's main window.

multitasking—The process by which an operating system creates the illusion that many tasks are executing simultaneously on a single processor. See also cooperative multitasking and preemptive multitasking.

multithreading—The ability of a process to have multiple, simultaneous paths of execution (threads).

Musical Instrument Digital Interface (MIDI)—A standard protocol for communication between musical instruments and computers.

name registration—The way a computer registers its unique name with a name server on the network, such as a WINS server.

name resolution—The process used on the network to determine the address of a computer by using its name.

named pipe—A one-way or two-way pipe used for communications between a server process and one or more client processes. A server process specifies a name when it creates one or more instances of a named pipe. Each instance of the pipe can be connected to a client. Microsoft SQL Server clients use named pipes to communicate with the SQL Server.

NBF transport protocol—NetBEUI frame protocol. A descendant of the NetBEUI protocol, which is a Transport layer protocol, not the programming interface NetBIOS.

NCB—See network control block.

NDIS—See network device interface specification.

NetBEUI transport—NetBIOS (Network Basic Input/Output System) Extended User Interface. A transport protocol designed for use on small subnets. It is not routable, but it is fast.

NetBIOS interface—A programming interface that allows I/O requests to be sent to and received from a remote computer. It hides networking hardware from applications.

NetBIOS over TCP/IP—The networking module that provides the functionality to support NetBIOS name registration and resolution across a TCP/IP network.

network—A group of computers and other devices that can interact by means of a shared communications link.

network adapter driver—Software that implements the lower layers of a network, providing a standard interface to the network card.

APP
A

network basic input/output system (NetBIOS)—A software interface for network communication. See also NetBIOS interface.

network control block (NCB)—A structured memory block used to communicate with the NetBIOS interface.

Network DDE DSDM (DDE share database manager) service—A service that manages shared DDE conversations. It is used by the Network DDE service.

Network DDE (Dynamic Data Exchange) service—A service that provides a network transport and security for DDE conversations. Network DDE is supported in Windows NT 4.0 for backward compatibility because most of its functions are superseded by OLE.

network device driver—Software that coordinates communication between the network adapter card and the computer's hardware and other software, controlling the physical function of the network adapter cards.

network device interface specification (NDIS)—In Windows networking, the interface for network adapter drivers. All transport drivers call the NDIS interface to access network adapter cards.

network directory—See shared directory.

Network File System (NFS)—A service for distributed computing systems that provides a distributed file system, eliminating the need for keeping multiple copies of files on separate computers. Usually used in connection with UNIX computers.

network ID—The portion of the IP address that identifies a group of computers and devices located on the same logical network. Separated from the Host ID using the subnet mask.

Network Information Service (NIS)—A service for distributed computing systems that provides a distributed database system for common configuration files.

network interface card (NIC)—An adapter card that connects a computer to a network.

network operating system (NOS)—The operating system used on network servers, such as Windows NT Server or Novell NetWare.

network provider—The Windows NT 4.0 component that allows Windows NT 4.0 to communicate with the network. Windows NT 4.0 includes providers for Microsoft networks and for Novell NetWare networks. Other network vendors may supply providers for their networks.

network transport—Either a particular layer of the OSI Reference Model between the Network layer and the Session layer, or the protocol used between this layer on two different computers on a network.

network-interface printers—Printers with built-in network cards, such as Hewlett-Packard laser printers equipped with Jet Direct cards. The advantage of network-interface printers is that they can be located anywhere on the network.

New Technology File System (NTFS)—The native file system used by Windows NT 4.0 that supplies file and directory security, sector sparing, compression, and other performance characteristics.

NIC—See network interface card.

NIS—See Network Information Service.

NOS—See network operating system.

NTFS—See Windows NT File System, New Technology File System.

object—A particular instance of a class. Most of the internal data structures in Windows NT 4.0 are objects.

Object Linking and Embedding (OLE)—The specification that details the implementation of Windows objects and the interprocess communication that supports them.

OCR—See Optical Character Recognition.

OEM—See original equipment manufacturer.

OLE—See Object Linking and Embedding.

Open Systems Interconnect (OSI)—The networking architecture reference model created by the ISO.

operating system (OS)—The software that provides an interface between a user or application and the computer hardware. Operating system services usually include memory and resource management, I/O services, and file handling. Examples include Windows NT 4.0, Windows NT, and UNIX.

Optical Character Recognition (OCR)—A technology that is used to generate editable text from a graphic image.

original equipment manufacturer (OEM)—Software that is sold by Microsoft to OEMs only includes the operating system versions that are preloaded on computers before they are sold.

OS—See operating system.

OSI—See Open Systems Interconnect.

PAB—See Personal Address Book.

packet—A transmission unit of fixed maximum size that consists of binary information representing data, addressing information, and error-correction information, created by the Data Link layer.

page—A unit of memory used by the system in managing memory. The size of a page is computer dependent (the Intel 486 computer, and therefore, Windows NT 4.0, uses 4KB pages).

page map—An internal data structure used by the system to keep track of the mapping between the pages in a process's virtual address space and the corresponding pages in physical memory.

paged pool—The portion of system memory that can be paged to disk.

paging file—A storage file (pagefile.sys) the system uses to hold pages of memory swapped out of RAM. Also known as a swap file.

parity—An error-checking procedure in which the number of 1s must always be the same (either even or odd) for each group of bits transmitted without error. Also used in the main RAM system of a computer to verify the validity of data contained in RAM.

**APP
A**

partition—A portion of a physical disk that functions as though it were a physically separate unit. See also system partition.

partition table—A table that contains entries showing the start and end point of each of the primary partitions on the disk. The partition table can hold four entries.

password—A unique string of characters that must be provided before a logon or an access is authorized. A password is a security measure used to restrict access to computer systems.

path—The location of a file or directory. The path describes the location in relation either to the root directory or the current directory—for example, C:\WINNT\System32. Also, a graphic object that represents one or more shapes.

PCI—See Peripheral Component Interconnect.

PCMCIA—See Personal Computer Memory Card International Association.

performance monitoring—The process of determining the system resources an application uses, such as processor time and memory. Done with the Windows NT 4.0 Performance Monitor.

Peripheral Component Interconnect (PCI)—The local bus being promoted as the successor to VL. This type of device is used in most Intel Pentium computers and in the Apple PowerPC Macintosh.

persistent connection—A network connection that is restored automatically when the user logs on. In Windows NT 4.0,

persistent connections are created by selecting the Reconnect at Logon check box.

Personal Address Book (PAB)—One of the information services provided with the Microsoft Exchange client included with Windows NT 4.0. It is used to store the names and email addresses of people you correspond with.

Personal Computer Memory Card International Association (PCMCIA)—The industry association of manufacturers of credit-card-sized adapter cards (PC cards).

PFF—See printer file format.

PIF—See program information file.

pixel—Short for picture element, a dot that represents the smallest graphic unit of measurement on a screen. The actual size of a pixel is screen dependent and varies according to the size of the screen and the resolution being used. Also known as pel.

platform—The hardware and software required for an application to run.

Plug and Play—A computer industry specification, intended to ease the process of configuring hardware.

Plug and Play BIOS—A BIOS with responsibility for configuring Plug and Play cards and system board devices during system power-up; it provides runtime configuration services for system board devices after startup.

p-node—A NetBIOS implementation that uses point-to-point communications with a name server to resolve names as IP addresses.

Point-to-Point Protocol (PPP)—The industry standard that is implemented in Dial-Up Networking. PPP is a line protocol used to connect to remote networking services, including Internet service providers. Prior to the introduction of PPP, another line protocol, SLIP, was used.

pointer—The arrow-shaped cursor on the screen that follows the movement of a mouse (or other pointing device) and indicates which area of the screen will be affected when the mouse button is pressed. The pointer may change shape during certain tasks.

port—The socket into which the cable for a peripheral device is connected. See also I/O address.

port ID—The method TCP and UDP use to specify which application running on the system is sending or receiving the data.

Postoffice—The message store used by Microsoft Mail to hold the mail messages. It exists only as a structure of directories on disk and does not contain any active components.

PostScript—A page-description language, developed by Adobe Systems, Inc., that offers flexible font capability and high-quality graphics. PostScript uses English-like commands to control page layout and to load and scale fonts.

PPP—See Point-to-Point Protocol.

preemptive multitasking—A multitasking technique that breaks up time into time-slices, during which the operating system

allows a particular program thread to run. The operating system can interrupt any running thread at any time. Preemptive multitasking usually results in the best use of CPU time and overall better perceived throughput. See also cooperative multitasking.

primary partition—A portion of a physical disk that can be marked for use by an operating system. Each physical disk can have up to four primary partitions (or up to three, if there is an extended partition). A primary partition cannot be subpartitioned.

print device—The actual hardware device that produces printed output.

print monitor—A component that keeps track of printers and print devices. It is responsible for transferring information from the print driver to the printing device, including any necessary flow control.

print provider—A software component that allows the client to print to a network printer. Windows NT 4.0 includes print providers for Microsoft networks and Novell networks.

printer driver—The component that translates GDI objects into printer commands.

printer fonts—Fonts that are built into your printer.

priority class—A process priority category (high, normal, or idle) used to determine the scheduling priorities of a process's threads. Each priority class has five levels. See also thread.

APP
A

private memory—Memory owned by a process and not accessible by other processes.

privileged instruction—A processor-privileged instruction that has access to system memory and the hardware. Privileged instructions can be executed only by Ring 0 components.

process—The virtual address space, code, data, and other operating system resources, such as files, pipes, and synchronization objects that make up an executing application. In addition to resources, a process contains at least one thread that executes the process's code.

profile—A set of data describing a particular configuration of a computer. This information can describe a user's preferences (user profile) or the hardware configuration. Profiles are usually stored in the Registry; for example, the key HKEY_USERS contains the profiles for the various users of the computer.

program file—A file that starts an application or program. A program file has an .EXE, .PIF, .COM, or .BAT filename extension.

program information file (PIF)—A file in which Windows NT 4.0 stores information about how to configure the VM for running MS-DOS applications.

Programmable Read-Only Memory (PROM)—A type of integrated circuit usually used to store a computer's BIOS. PROM chips, once programmed, can only be read from, not written to.

PROM—See Programmable Read-Only Memory.

properties—The dialogs that are used to configure a particular object in Windows NT 4.0.

protocol—A set of rules and conventions by which two computers pass messages across a network. Protocols are used between instances of a particular layer on each computer. Windows NT 4.0 includes NetBEUI, TCP/IP, and IPX/SPX-compatible protocols. See also communications protocol.

provider—The component that allows Windows NT 4.0 to communicate with the network. Windows NT 4.0 includes providers for Microsoft and Novell networks.

RAM—See random access memory.

random access memory (RAM)—A computer's main memory, where programs and data are stored while the program is running. Information stored in RAM is lost when the computer is turned off.

read-only—A device, document, or file to which changes are not permitted.

read-write—A device, document, or file to which changes can be made.

reboot—To restart a computer. To reboot a Windows NT 4.0 computer, click the Start button, choose Shutdown, and then choose Restart Your Computer.

redirector—The networking component that intercepts file I/O requests and translates them into network requests.

Redirectors (also called network clients) are implemented as installable file system drivers in Windows NT 4.0.

REG_BINARY—A data type for Registry value entries that designates binary data.

REG_DWORD—A data type for Registry value entries that designates data represented by a number that is 4 bytes long.

REG_SZ—A data type for Registry value entries that designates a data string that usually represents human readable text.

Registry—Windows NT 4.0's and Windows NT's binary system configuration database.

Registry Editor (REGEDT32.EXE)—A utility supplied with Windows NT 4.0 that allows the user to view and edit Registry keys and values.

Registry key—A Registry entry that can contain other Registry entries.

Remote Access Service (RAS)—An NT Executive Service that provides remote networking access to the NT Enterprise for telecommuters, remote users, system administrators, and home users. See also Dial-Up Networking.

remote administration—The process of administrating one computer from another computer across a network.

remote initiation program load (RIPL)—A technique that allows a workstation to boot by using an image file on a network server instead of a disk.

remote procedure call (RPC)—An industry-standard method of interprocess communication across a network. Used by many administration tools.

Requests for Comments (RFCs)—The official documents of the Internet Engineering Task Force that specify the details for protocols included in the TCP/IP family.

requirement—The conceptual design and functional description of a software product and any associated materials. Requirements describe the features, user interface, documentation, and other functionality the product will provide.

resources—Icons, cursors, menus, dialog boxes, bitmaps, fonts, keyboard-accelerator tables, message-table entries, string-table entries, version data, and user-defined data available for use in Windows. The resources used by an application are either part of the system or private resources stored in the application's program file. Also, part of a computer system that can be assigned to a running process, such as a disk drive or memory segment.

RFC—See Requests for Comments.

RID—See relative identifier.

RIP—See routing information protocol.

RIPL—See remote initiation program load.

ROM—See read-only memory.

root directory—See directory.

router—A computer with two or more network adapters, each attached to a different subnet. The router forwards packets on a subnet to the subnet that they are addressed to.

APP A

routing—The process of forwarding packets until they reach their destination.

routing information protocol (RIP)—A protocol that supports dynamic routing. Used between routers.

RPC—See remote procedure call.

RPC server—The program or computer that processes remote procedure calls from a client.

SAM database—The Registry database that contains the user and group account information, as well as user account policies. It is managed by the User Manager or User Manager for Domains utility.

screen buffer—A memory buffer that holds a representation of an MS-DOS VM's logical screen.

screen saver—Pictures or patterns that appear on your screen when your computer has not been used for a certain amount of time. Originally intended to protect the monitor from damage, modern screen savers are used mostly for their entertainment value.

scroll—To move through text or graphics (up, down, left, or right) to see parts of the file that cannot fit on the screen.

scroll arrow—An arrow on either end of a scrollbar that you use to scroll through the contents of the window or list box.

scrollbar—A bar that appears at the right or bottom edge of a window or list box whose contents are not completely visible. The scrollbar consists of two scroll arrows and a scroll box, which are used to scroll through the contents.

scroll box—In a scrollbar, a small box that shows where the information currently visible is, relative to the contents of the entire window.

SCSI—See Small Computer System Interface.

Security ID (SID)—The unique randomly generated alphanumeric identifier assigned by NT when a new user, group, trust, or other security object is created.

sequence number—A number used by a receiving node to properly order packets.

Serial Line Internet Protocol (SLIP)—The predecessor to PPP, a line protocol that supports TCP/IP over a modem connection. SLIP support is provided for NT 4.0. See also Point-to-Point Protocol.

server—A computer or application that provides shared resources to clients across a network. Resources include files and directories, printers, fax modems, and network database services. See also client.

server message block (SMB)—A block of data that contains a work request from a workstation to a server or that contains the response from the server to the workstation. SMBs are used for all network communications in a Microsoft network.

server service—An Executive Service that makes resources available to the workgroup or domain for file, print, and other RPC services.

service—A process that performs a specific system function and often provides an application programming interface (API) for other processes to call. Windows NT

4.0 services include Computer Browser, Server, and Workstation.

Session—A layer of the OSI reference model that performs name recognition and the functions needed to allow two applications to communicate over the network. Also, a communication channel established by the Session layer.

share—In Microsoft networking, the process of making resources, such as directories and printers, available for network users.

share name—The name by which a shared resource is accessed on the network.

shared directory—A directory that has been shared so that network users can connect to it.

shared memory—Memory that two or more processes can read from and write to.

shared network directory—See shared directory.

shared resource—Any device, data, or program that is used by more than one other device or program. Windows NT 4.0 can share directories and printers.

sharepoint—A shared network resource or the name that one is known by.

shell—The part of an operating system that the user interacts with. The Windows NT 4.0 shell is Windows Explorer.

shortcut key—A combination of keys that result in the execution of a program, or selection of an option, without going through a menu.

shutdown—The process of properly terminating all running programs, flushing caches, and preparing the system to be powered off.

signaled—One of the possible states of a mutex.

SIMM—See Single In-Line Memory Module.

Simple Mail Transfer Protocol (SMTP)—The Application layer protocol that supports messaging functions over the Internet.

Simple Network Management Protocol (SNMP)—A standard protocol for the management of network components. Windows NT 4.0 includes an SNMP agent.

Single In-Line Memory Module (SIMM)—One of the types of RAM chips.

SLIP—See Serial Line Internet Protocol.

Small Computer System Interface (SCSI)—A standard for connecting multiple devices to a computer system. SCSI devices are connected together in a daisy chain, which can have up to seven devices (plus a controller) on it. (It is pronounced "scuzzy.")

SMB—See server message block.

SMTP—See Simple Mail Transfer Protocol.

SNMP—See Simple Network Management Protocol.

socket—A channel used for incoming and outgoing data defined by the Windows Sockets API. Usually used with TCP/IP.

APP
A

socket services—The protected-mode VxD that manages PCMCIA sockets adapter hardware. It provides a protected-mode PCMCIA Socket Services 2.x interface for use by Card Services. A socket services driver is required for each socket adapter.

source directory—The directory in which files in a copy or move operation start out.

spooler—A scheduler for the printing process. It coordinates activity among other components of the print model and schedules all print jobs arriving at the print server.

static VxD—A VxD that is loaded at system startup.

string—A sequence of characters representing human-readable text.

subdirectory—A directory within a directory.

subkey—A Registry key contained within another Registry key. All Registry keys are subkeys except for the six top-level keys.

subnet—On the Internet, any lower network that is part of the logical network identified by the network ID.

subnet mask—A 32-bit value that is used to distinguish the network ID portion of the IP address from the host ID.

swap file—A special file on your hard disk that is used to hold memory pages that are swapped out of RAM. Also called a paging file.

syntax—The order in which you must type a command and the elements that follow the command.

system directory—The directory that contains the Windows DLLs and drivers. Usually c:\windows\system.

system disk—A disk that contains the files necessary to start an operating system.

system partition—The volume that contains the hardware-specific files needed to load Windows NT 4.0.

TAPI—See Telephony Application Program Interface.

TCP/IP transport—Transmission Control Protocol/Internet Protocol. The primary wide area network transport protocol used on the worldwide Internet, which is a worldwide internetwork of universities, research laboratories, military installations, organizations, and corporations. TCP/IP includes standards for how computers communicate and conventions for connecting networks and routing traffic, as well as specifications for utilities.

TCP—See Transmission Control Protocol.

TDI—See transport driver interface.

Telephony Application Program Interface (TAPI)—An API that enables applications to control modems and telephony equipment in a device-independent manner. TAPI routes application function calls to the appropriate "Service Provider" DLL for a modem.

telnet—The Application layer protocol that provides virtual terminal service on TCP/IP networks.

Terminate-and-Stay-Resident (TSR)—A technique, used by MS-DOS applications, that allows more than one program to be loaded at a time.

text file—A file containing only ASCII letters, numbers, and symbols, without any formatting information except for carriage returns/linefeeds.

thread—The basic entity to which the operating system allocates CPU time. A thread can execute any part of the application's code, including a part currently being executed by another thread (re-entrancy). Threads cannot own resources; instead, they use the resources of the process they belong to.

thread local storage—A storage method in which an index can be used by multiple threads of the same process to store and retrieve a different value for each thread. See also thread.

thunking—The transformation between 16-bit and 32-bit formats, which is carried out by a separate layer in the VDM.

timeout—If a device is not performing a task, the amount of time the computer should wait before detecting it as an error.

toolbar—A frame containing a series of shortcut buttons providing quick access to commands, usually located below the menu bar, although many applications provide "dockable" toolbars, which may be moved to different locations on the screen.

Transmission Control Protocol (TCP)— A connection-based protocol, responsible for breaking data into packets, which the IP protocol sends over the network. This protocol provides a reliable, sequenced communication stream for internetwork communication.

Transmission Control Protocol/Internet Protocol (TCP/IP)—The primary wide area network used on the worldwide Internet, which is a worldwide internetwork of universities, research laboratories, military installations, organizations, and corporations. TCP/IP includes standards for how computers communicate and conventions for connecting networks and routing traffic, as well as specifications for utilities.

transport driver interface (TDI)—The interface between the Session layer and the Network layer, used by network redirectors and servers to send network-bound requests to network transport drivers.

transport protocol—A protocol that defines how data should be presented to the next receiving layer in the networking model and packages the data accordingly. It passes data to the network adapter card driver through the NDIS interface, and to the redirector through the transport driver interface.

TrueType fonts—Fonts that are scaleable and sometimes generated as bitmaps or soft fonts, depending on the capabilities of your printer. TrueType fonts can be sized to any height, and they print exactly as they appear on the screen. They are stored as a collection of line and curve commands, together with a collection of hints that are used to adjust the shapes when the font is scaled.

APP
A

trust relationship—A security relationship between two domains in which the resource domain "trusts" the user of a trusted account domain to use its resources. Users and groups from a trusted domain can be given access permissions to resources in a trusting domain.

TSR—See Terminate-and-Stay-Resident.

UDP—See user datagram protocol.

UMB—Short for Upper Memory Block.

UNC—See universal naming convention.

Unimodem—The universal modem driver used by TAPI to communicate with modems. It uses modem description files to control its interaction with VCOMM.

uninterruptible power supply (UPS)—A battery operated power supply connected to a computer to keep the system running during a power failure.

universal naming convention (UNC)—Naming convention, including a server name and share name, used to give a unique name to files on a network. The format is as follows:

```
\\servername\sharename\path\filename
```

UPS—See uninterruptible power supply.

UPS service—A software component that monitors an uninterruptible power supply and shuts down the computer gracefully when line power has failed and the UPS battery is running down.

usability—A determination of how well users can accomplish tasks using a software product. Usability considers the characteristics of a product such as software, manuals, tutorials, help, and so on.

user account—All the information that identifies a user to Windows NT 4.0, including username and password, group membership, and rights and permissions.

user datagram protocol (UDP)—The transport protocol offering a connectionless-mode transport service in the Internet suite of protocols. See Transmission Control Protocol.

username—A unique name identifying a user account in Windows NT 4.0. Usernames must be unique and cannot be the same as another username, workgroup name, or domain name.

value entry—A parameter under a key or subkey in the Registry. A value entry has three components: name, type, and value. The value component can be a string, binary data, or a DWORD.

VCPI—Short for virtual control program interface.

VDM—See virtual DOS machine.

VFAT—See virtual file allocation table, file allocation table.

virtual DOS machine (VDM)—A virtual machine that provides a complete MS-DOS environment and a character-based window in which to run an MS-DOS–based application. Every MS-DOS application runs in its own VDM.

virtual file allocation table (VFAT)—See file allocation table.

virtual machine (VM)—An environment created by the operating system in memory. By using virtual machines, the application developer can write programs that behave as though they own the entire computer. This leaves the job of sorting out, for example, which application is receiving keyboard input at the moment, to Windows NT 4.0.

virtual memory—The technique by which Windows NT 4.0 uses hard disk space to increase the amount of memory available for running programs.

visual editing—The ability to edit an embedded object in place, without opening it into its own window. Implemented by OLE.

VL—Local bus standard for a bus that allows high-speed connections to peripherals, which preceded the PCI specification. Due to limitations in the specification, usually only used to connect video adapters into the system. Also known as VESA bus.

VM—See virtual machine.

volume—A partition that has been formatted for use by the file system.

VxD—Virtual device driver. The x represents the type of device; for example, a virtual device driver for a display is a VDD, and a virtual device driver for a printer is a VPD.

wildcard—A character that is used to represent one or more characters, such as in a file specification. The question mark (?) wildcard can be used to represent any single character, and the asterisk (*) wildcard can be used to represent any character or group of characters that might match that position in other filenames.

WIN32 API—The 32-bit application programming interface used to write 32-bit Windows based applications. It provides access to operating systems and other functions.

window handle—A 32-bit value that uniquely identifies a window to Windows NT 4.0.

window name—A text string that identifies a window for the user.

Windows Internet Name Service (WINS)—A name resolution service that resolves Windows networking computer names to IP addresses in a routed environment. A WINS server handles name registrations, queries, and releases.

Windows NT—The portable, secure, 32-bit preemptive-multitasking member of the Microsoft Windows operating system family. Windows NT Server provides centralized management and security, advanced fault tolerance, and additional connectivity. Windows NT Workstation provides operating system and networking functionality for computers without centralized management.

Windows NT File System (NTFS)—The native file system used by Windows NT. Windows NT 4.0 can use NTFS or FAT; as of version 4.0, it can detect, but not use, HPFS partitions.

WINS—See Windows Internet Name Service.

wizard—A Windows NT 4.0 tool that asks you questions and performs a system action according to your answers. For example, you can use the Add Printer Wizard to add new printer drivers or connect to an existing network printer.

workgroup—A collection of computers that are grouped for viewing purposes but do not share security information. Each workgroup is identified by a unique name. See also domain.

workstation service—The NT computer's redirector. It redirects requests for network resources to the appropriate protocol and network card for access to the server computer.

WYSIWYG—An acronym that stands for "What You See Is What You Get."

X.121—The addressing format used by X.25 base networks.

X.25—A connection-oriented network facility.

x86-based computer—A computer using a microprocessor equivalent to an Intel 80386 or higher chip. Only x86-based computers can run Windows NT 4.0.

X.400—An international messaging standard, used in electronic mail systems.

XModem/CRC—A communications protocol for transmitting binary files that uses a cyclic redundancy check (CRC) to detect any transmission errors. Both computers must be set to transmit and receive eight data bits per character.

XMS—See Extended Memory Specification.

Certification Process

In addition to using a resource such as this book, the following list of tasks explains what you need to do to proceed with the certification process.

Get Started

When you have decided to start the certification process, you should use the following list as a guideline to get started:

1. Visit Microsoft's Certification Web site (http://www.microsoft.com/mcp/).

2. Choose the certification you want to pursue and note the exams required to attain the certification.

3. Take the Networking Essentials Self Assessment Test located on the CD-ROM that accompanies this book to determine your competency level. For exams other than Networking Essentials, you can use the Assessment Exams located at http://www.microsoft.com/mcp/ to get a feel for the type of questions that appear on the exam.

Get Prepared

Getting started is one thing, but the actual preparation for taking the certification exam is a rather difficult process. The following guidelines will help you prepare for the exam:

1. Review the Chapter Notes booklet that accompanies this book.
2. Gain hands-on experience working with computer networks by completing the lab exercises in Appendix F.
3. Review the Exam Preparation Guide found on Microsoft's Web site at http://www.microsoft.com/mcp/.
4. Take the Mastery test found on the enclosed CD to check your progress.

Get Certified

Call Sylvan Prometric at 1-800-755-EXAM or VUE at 1-800-TEST-REG to schedule your exam at a location near you.

Get Benefits

Microsoft will send your certification kit approximately two to four weeks after passing the exam. This kit qualifies you to become a Microsoft Certified Professional.

Testing Tips

You've mastered the required tasks to take the exam. When you have reviewed the exam objectives and are confident that you have the skills specified in the exam objectives, you are ready to perform at the highest cognitive level. It's time to head for the testing center. This appendix covers some tips and tricks to remember.

Before the Test

- Wear comfortable clothing. You want to focus on the exam, not on a tight shirt collar or pinching pair of shoes.

- Leave cellular phones and pagers in your car; they are not allowed during tests.

- Allow plenty of travel time. Get to the testing center 10 or 15 minutes early. Many testing centers are quite busy and expect you to start your exam promptly. Allow yourself time to relax.

- If you've never been to the testing center before, make a trial run a few days before to make sure that you know the route to the center.

- Carry with you at least two forms of identification, including one photo ID (such as a driver's license or company security ID). You will have to show proper identification before you can take the exam.

Remember that the exams are closed-book. The use of laptop computers, notes, or other printed materials is not permitted during the exam session.

At the test center, you'll be asked to sign in. The test administrator will give you a Testing Center Regulations form that explains the rules that govern the examination. You will be asked to sign the form to indicate that you understand and will comply with the stipulations.

If you have any special needs, such as reconfiguring the mouse buttons for a left-handed user, you should inquire about them when you register for the exam with Sylvan Prometric. Special configurations are not possible at all sites, so you should not assume that you will be permitted to make any modifications to the equipment setup and configuration. Site administrators are *not* permitted to make modifications without prior instructions from Sylvan Prometric.

When the administrator shows you to your test computer, make sure of the following:

- The testing tool starts up and displays the correct exam. If a tutorial for using the instrument is available, you should be allowed time to take it.

- You have a supply of scratch paper for use during the exam. Some centers are now providing you with a wipe-off board and magic marker to use instead of paper. After the exam, the administrator will collect all scratch paper and notes made during the exam in order to ensure exam security.

- Some exams might include additional materials or exhibits. If any exhibits are required for your exam, the test administrator will provide you with them before you begin the exam and collect them at the completion of the exam.

- The administrator explains what to do when you complete the exam.

- You get answers to any and all of your questions or concerns before the exam begins.

As a Microsoft Certification examination candidate, you are entitled to the best support and environment possible for your exam. If you experience any problems on the day of the exam, inform the Sylvan Prometric test administrator immediately.

During the Test

On many of the Microsoft certification exams, the testing software enables you to move forward and backward through the items so that you can implement a strategic approach to the test.

1. Go through all the items, answering the easy questions first. Then go back and spend time on the harder ones. Microsoft guarantees that there are no trick questions. The correct answer is always among the list of choices.

2. Eliminate the obviously incorrect answer first to simplify your choices.

3. Answer all the questions. You aren't penalized for guessing.

4. Don't rush. Haste makes waste (or substitute the cliché of your choice).

However, the Networking Essentials exam now uses the *adaptive* format, where the next question you get depends upon whether you answer a question correctly or not. In this newer format, you can go back to review your questions, but you cannot change the answers. Now, you *must* answer questions. Choose the best possible answer, and guess if you have to.

After the Test

When you have completed an exam, the following happens:

- The testing tool gives you immediate, online notification of your pass or fail status, with the exception of beta exams. Because of the beta exam process, your exam results are mailed to you approximately six to eight weeks after the beta exam.

- The administrator gives you a printed Examination Score Report indicating your pass or fail status.

- Test scores are automatically forwarded to Microsoft within five working days after you take the test. If you pass the exam, you will receive written confirmation from Microsoft within two to four weeks.

If you don't pass a certification exam, do the following:

- Review your individual section scores, noting areas where your score must be improved. The section titles in your exam report generally correspond to specific groups of exam objectives.

- Review the exam information in this book, then get the latest Exam Preparation Guide, and focus on the topic areas that need strengthening. Visit Microsoft's Training & Certification Web site at `http://www.microsoft.com/train_cert/` to ensure that you have the most recent Exam Preparation Guide.

- Intensify your effort to get your real-world, hands-on experience and practice with computer networking.

- Try taking one or more of the approved training courses.

- Review the suggested readings listed in Appendix G, "Suggested Reading," or in the Exam Preparation Guide.

■ Take (or retake) the Networking Essentials Assessment Exam provided by Microsoft. You might also try using some of the exam preparation tools available, including sample tests.

■ Call Sylvan Prometric to register, pay for, and reschedule the exam.

Objectives Index

Planning

Objective	Subobjective	Page
Create unattended installation files		65-71
Plan strategies for sharing and securing resources		191, 197-199
Choose the appropriate file system to use in a given situation. File systems and situations include:		
	NTFS	51-52 205-209 221-225
	FAT	51-52 220

...continues

Managing Resources

...continues

Objective	Subobjective	Page
Use various configurations to install Windows NT Workstation as a TCP/IP client		315-322
Configure and install Dial-Up Networking in a given situation		329-335
Configure Microsoft Peer Web Services in a given situation		338-340

Running Applications

Objective	Subobjective	Page
Start applications on Intel and RISC platforms in various operating system environments		285-306
Start applications at various priorities		298-299

Monitoring and Optimization

Objective	Subobjective	Page
Monitor system performance by using various tools		358-361, 363-370

…continues

APP
D

...continued

Objective	Subobjective	Page
Identify and resolve a given performance problem		350-352, 358-361
Optimize system performance in various areas		352-358, 363-370

Troubleshooting

Objective	Subobjective	Page
Choose the appropriate course of action to take when the boot process fails		71-81, 370-372
Choose the appropriate course of action to take when a print job fails		277-279
Choose the appropriate course of action to take when the installation process fails		61-65

APP
D

Using the CD-ROM

The tests on this CD-ROM consist of performance-based questions. This means that rather than asking you what function an item would fulfill (knowledge-based question), you will be presented with a situation and asked for an answer that shows your capability of solving the problem.

Using the Self-Test Software

The program consists of three main test structures:

- *Non-Randomized Test.* This is useful when you first begin study and want to run through sections that you have read to make certain you understand them thoroughly before continuing on.

- *Adaptive Test.* This emulates an adaptive exam and randomly pulls questions from the database. You are asked 15 questions of varying difficulty. If you successfully answer a question, the next question you are asked is of higher difficulty because it tries to adapt to your skill level. If you miss a question, the next one asked is easier because it, again, tries to adapt to your skill level. This tool is useful for getting used to the adaptive format, but not for actual study because the number of questions presented is so low.

- *Random/Mastery Test.* This is the big one. This test is different from the two others in the sense that questions are pulled from all objective areas. You are asked 50 questions, and it simulates the exam situation. At the conclusion of the exam, you will get your overall score and the chance to view all wrong answers. You will also be able to print a report card featuring your test results.

All test questions are of the type currently in use by Microsoft on this exam. In some cases, that consists solely of the multiple-choice type questions offering four possible answers. In other cases, there will be exhibits, scenarios, and other question types.

Equipment Requirements

To run the self-test software, you must have at least the following equipment:

- IBM-compatible Pentium
- Microsoft Windows 95, 98, or NT 4.0 (Workstation or Server)
- 16MB of RAM
- 256-color display adapter, configured as 800×600 display or larger
- Double-speed CD-ROM drive
- Approximately 5MB free disk space

Running the Self-Test Software

Access the SETUP.EXE file, and the self-test software installs on your hard drive from the CD-ROM and runs directly from there. After you have followed the simple installation steps, you will find the software very intuitive and self-explanatory.

Lab Exercises

Before You Start

The best way to become familiar with the installation process is to install Windows NT Workstation 4.0 a few times and pay close attention to what is happening. In the later part of this book, you will need at least two computers running Windows NT Workstation 4.0 in order to understand the way Windows NT handles access security. If you have two computers available, you can gain extra experience by installing Windows NT on one using the Custom option and on the other using the Typical option.

This appendix includes a preparation checklist against which you should double-check your hardware configuration before beginning setup. Then follow the setup process as outlined in Chapter 2, "Understanding Microsoft Windows NT 4.0," and this appendix . As you proceed with installation, be sure to read each screen so that you can learn as much as you can about the process.

Preparation Checklist

1. Read all Windows NT documentation files.

2. Assess system requirements.

3. Assess hardware compatibility. Refer to the Hardware Compatibility List.

4. Assess necessary drivers and configuration data, including the following:

Video	Display type, adapter and chipset type
Network	Card type, IRQ, I/O address, DMA, connector, and so on

SCSI controller	Adapter and chipset type, IRQ, bus type
Sound/media	IRQ, I/O address, DMA
I/O ports	IRQ, I/O address, DMA
Modems	Port, IRQ, I/O address, modem type

5. Back up your current configuration and data files.

6. Determine what type of initial setup will be performed. If needed, make sure you have three blank formatted disks before running setup.

7. Determine where the installation files are located.

8. Determine on what partition Windows NT system files will be installed.

9. Determine what file system you will install.

10. Determine whether you will you create an emergency repair disk. If you will, you need to have one blank disk available before running setup.

11. Determine your installation CD key.

12. Determine the unique name of your computer.

13. Determine the name of the workgroup or domain that the computer joins.

14. Gather network connection data, such as IP addresses, IPX card numbers, and so on.

15. Determine the time zone in which the computer is located.

Recommended Computer Configuration

- At least two 486/66 or higher computers with 16MB RAM.

- A working network connection between these computers.

- If you are part of a larger network, try to have your computer isolated into its own network. If you cannot do this, be sure to inform your network administrator of what you intend to do so that you can both take all necessary precautions to preserve security on the network.

- A FAT-formatted C: drive primary partition.

- At least 300MB free space on the same or another drive.

- Two or more physical disk drives to demonstrate disk striping.

- A CD-ROM drive for installation.

- (Optional) Four blank formatted 3.5-inch disks—three for startup and one to use as an emergency repair disk.

- One printer, attached to either computer.

Exercise 1: Setting Up Your Computers for This Book's Labs

1. If you have your own installation CD-ROM and a compatible CD-ROM drive, run setup from the CD-ROM. If you are accessing the installation files over the network, you must make a connection to the installation directory first. Connect as you normally would on your network, or consult with your network administrator for appropriate access.

2. If you have four formatted blank 3.5-inch disks available (three for startup and one for emergency repair), run WINNT.EXE from the installation directory and follow the directions on the screen. If you choose not to create the startup disks, run WINNT /B.

    If you are installing Windows NT on a RISC-based system, be sure to create a minimum 2MB FAT partition and a large enough system partition for Windows NT before starting setup. Then, follow the guidelines outlined in the notes and sidebars of Chapter 2 relating to RISC installations.

3. Press Enter to install Windows NT.

4. If you have any additional storage devices other than what Windows NT detects, add them.

5. Verify that your basic hardware settings are correct, and press Enter.

6. Create a 250MB partition out of the free space during installation, format it as FAT, and install the Windows NT system partition there, in a directory called WINNT40.

7. Let Windows NT do an exhaustive scan of your disk drive, and then reboot the computer.

8. If this is your first installation, choose Custom. If this is your second, choose Typical. Read all screens as you go along. Explore all buttons. It is impossible to create an exercise for all possible permutations that you might encounter, so it is up to you to explore.

9. When prompted for the user and company names, use your own.

10. When prompted for a computer name use COMPUTER1 for the first installation, COMPUTER2 for the second, and so on for additional installations. You can, of course name the computers anything you like. Future labs will refer to these suggested names. Just remember to substitute your own. If you are part of a larger network, be sure that your computer names are unique.

11. Enter studynt as your password, in lowercase. Again, you can choose your own password—just don't forget it!

APP
F

12. If you get a message regarding the floating-point error, do not choose the workaround.

13. If you have a formatted disk handy, create an emergency repair disk. Remember that you can create it later if needed.

14. Look at all the optional component lists and sublists so that you understand your choices. Install as many additional options as you like. Install at least the recommended options that Windows NT displays. If you are low on disk space, deselect games and other non-essential accessories.

15. Let Windows NT detect your network card, or if you have an OEM driver disk, install your card from the disk.

16. Deselect TCP/IP and select NetBEUI as your protocol. Also keep the default network services and bindings settings.

17. Create a workgroup called STUDYGROUP. As before, you can call the workgroup anything you like, as long as you remember what you called it for future exercises, and as long as it does not conflict with any other workgroup on your network.

18. Enter the appropriate date and time zone values.

19. Select the appropriate settings for your monitor.

20. Complete the installation, and let Windows NT restart the system.

Exercise 2: Optional NTHQ Exercise

Follow the instructions in the "Troubleshooting" section of Chapter 2, and run the NTHQ utility to see how it works. Log and print a report.

Chapter 3 Lab Exercise

There is no better way to get acquainted with the Windows NT 4.0 interface than by practicing, trying out the new features, exploring all the object property sheets, and just having fun with it. The following is an exercise that uses all the most significant features of the interface. You will need one blank formatted disk to complete this exercise.

Exercise 1: Navigating the Interface—Taskbar, Explorer, Shortcuts, and Briefcase

1. Start Windows Help, and click the Contents tab.

2. From the topic list choose HOW TO, Change Windows Settings, and Change Taskbar Settings. Following the directions, make it so the taskbar does not display on top of all other windows.

3. Open My Computer. Select View, Options, and then choose the option that replaces previous windows.

4. Right-click the A: drive icon and drag it to the desktop. Choose Create Shortcut from the pop-up menu.

5. Open the C: drive icon. From the File menu choose New, and create a new folder called LAB2.

6. From the Start menu choose Programs, Accessories, and then start the WordPad program.

7. Create a file called MEMO.DOC with the following text:

```
This is the first draft of my memo.
```

8. From the File menu choose Save As. Use the browse feature to find the LAB2 directory, and save the MEMO.DOC file in it. Minimize WordPad.

9. Open Windows Explorer and select the LAB2 directory. Right-click the file and drag it to the Briefcase icon on the desktop. Choose Create Synch Copy from the pop-up menu.

10. Place the formatted blank disk in the A: drive.

11. Drag the Briefcase from the desktop to the A: drive shortcut icon.

12. Move your mouse to the bottom of the screen, until the taskbar appears. Select WordPad. Open the MEMO.DOC file in the Briefcase on the A: drive. Add the following text and save the file:

```
This is the second draft of my memo.
```

13. Open the A: drive shortcut icon and drag the Briefcase back to the desktop.

14. Open the Briefcase and choose Update from the Briefcase menu option. Notice the window that displays the documents that have changed, and the suggestion to update the older document.

15. Choose Update All. Close Briefcase.

16. Start WordPad and open the MEMO.DOC file from the LAB2 directory. Verify that the file has been updated.

17. Start the Find program. From the Advanced tab, search for all files on the C: drive containing the text first draft. In the results window, verify that both copies of the file appear.

APP
F

Chapter 4 Lab Exercises

The best way to review the applets in Control Panel is to spend time with each one, reviewing what each accomplishes. There is no better exercise that I can recommend. However, the following are several that you can safely try that involve the Registry.

Exercise 1: Using the Control Panel to Configure Windows NT

1. Use Control Panel to modify the wallpaper on your computer to LEAVES.BMP, and change your Wait mouse pointer to the animated cursor BANANA.ANI. Note that these changes take effect immediately.

2. Close Control Panel and open the Registry Editor (which you might find in Start\RUN\REGEDT32.EXE).

3. Click in the HKEY_CURRENT_USER subtree window to make it active.

4. Select View, Find Key, and search for cursors. When the Cursors key is found, close the Find dialog box and select the Cursors key. Notice that the Wait cursor parameter on the right side of the window shows that BANANA.ANI has been selected.

5. Change the Wait value from BANANA.ANI to HORSE.ANI by double-clicking the Wait value and typing HORSE.ANI (and the appropriate path).

6. Choose Edit\Add Value, and enter the value name APPSTARTING, with the data type REG_SZ, choose OK and enter the filename and path to DINOSAUR.ANI.

7. Use Find Key again to find the WALLPAPER key. Were you able to find it? Recall that wallpaper is a feature of the desktop. Search for desktop.

8. Select the DESKTOP key and view the right side of the window for entries related to wallpaper. You should find two: WALLPAPER and TILEWALLPAPER.

9. Modify the WALLPAPER entry (currently LEAVES.BMP) to WINNT40\FURRYD~1.BMP. (Check the path for this file before making the change. Hint: Use Find.)

10. Modify the TILEWALLPAPER entry to the value 1.

11. Close the Registry. When do these changes take effect? Log off and then log back on and see if the changes have taken effect. If they have not, shut down, restart, and look again.

Exercise 2: Using the Registry, Part 1

1. Open the Registry Editor.

2. Click in the HKEY_LOCAL_MACHINE subtree window to make it active.

3. Expand through the SOFTWARE hive to find the WINLOGON key: SOFTWARE\Microsoft\Windows NT\Current Version\Winlogon.

4. Double-click the parameter `Legal Notice Caption` on the right side of the window and enter the caption `Legal Notice`.

5. Double-click the parameter `Legal Notice Text` and enter `Unauthorized access will be punished!`.

6. Choose Edit, Add Value, and enter the value name `DontDisplayLastUserName`, with the data type `REG_SZ`, choose OK, and enter the value `1` for yes.

7. Close the Registry. When do these changes take effect? Log off and then log back on and see if the changes have taken effect. If they have not, shut down, restart, and look again.

Exercise 3: Using the Registry, Part 2

1. Open the Registry Editor and make the `HKEY_USERS` subtree window active.

2. Expand through the `.DEFAULT` key to find `DESKTOP: .DEFAULT\Control Panel\Desktop`.

3. Modify the `WALLPAPER` entry with the value `LEAVES.BMP` and the `TILEWALLPAPER` entry to `1`. This changes the default wallpaper that displays when you boot Windows NT.

4. Close the Registry. When do these changes take effect? Log off and then log back on and see if the changes have taken effect. If they have not, shut down, restart, and look again.

APP
F

Exercise 4: Using the System Policy Editor

If you have access to a Windows NT 4.0 Server (that is, domain controller), and have a valid user account that you can use to log on from your workstation, complete this exercise. You must be able to log on to that server from your workstation, have the System Policy Editor tool installed on your workstation, and have administrative rights to create system policies.

1. From your workstation, log in to the server as Administrator.

2. Start the System Policy Editor by choosing Start, Programs, Administrative Tools, System Policy Editor.

3. If an existing `NTCONFIG.POL` file exists in `WINNT40\SYSTEM32\REPL\IMPORT\SCRIPTS`, open it. Otherwise, select File, New Profile.

4. Choose Edit, Add User, and enter your valid user account.

5. Double-click the New User icon to display the policies.

6. Select Desktop, click the Wallpaper check box, and enter the path and filename to your favorite wallpaper in the lower part of the window (for example, `WINNT40\leaves.bmp`).

7. Select System, Restrictions, and check Disable Registry Editing Tools.

8. Choose Shell, Restrictions, and check Remove Run Command from Start menu and Don't Save Settings at Exit.

9. Close the policy and save it as NTCONFIG.POL in the WINNT40\SYSTEM32\REPL\IMPORT\ SCRIPTS subdirectory.

10. Log off and log back on as the user whose policy you modified. You should note the changes that have taken effect: The wallpaper should now be LEAVES, you should be unable to run REGEDT32, you should not have Run as a Start menu option, and any changes you make to the environment—such as colors and cursors—will not be saved.

11. Log back on as Administrator, and make further changes to experiment or delete the policy.

Chapter 5 Lab Exercises

The following exercises are most helpful if you have two computers available.

Exercise 1: Creating Users and Groups

Complete this exercise on both workstations if you have two.

1. Using Notepad, create the following logon script, called KITE.BAT, and save it in the WINNT40\SYSTEM32\REPL\IMPORT\SCRIPTS subdirectory:

```
@echo Welcome to the Kite Flyers network!
@echo off
Pause
```

2. Use User Manager to create the following user accounts on both workstations:

Username	Full Name	Description	Password
BrownC	Charles Brown	Chairperson	password
VanPeltL	Lucille VanPelt	Secretary General	password
BumsteadD	Dagwood Bumstead	Marketing Manager	password
Dilbert	Dilbert	MIS Manager	password

Require each user to change his or her password upon logon (check User Must Change Password at Next Logon). In the Profiles button for each, enter the KITE.BAT logon script you created in step 1, and enter the home directory c:\users\%USERNAME%, using the drive in which you installed Windows NT and that contains the USERS directory.

3. Create the following group accounts:

Group Name	Description	Members
Managers	Kite Flyers	BrownC
Management Team	Leaders	BumsteadD
		Dilbert
		VanPeltL
Marketing	Marketing Team	BumsteadD
MIS	MIS Team	Dilbert

4. Create the following template accounts.

Username	Full Name	Description	Password
SalesTemp	Sales Template	Sales Representative	stemplate
MarketingTemp	Marketing Template	Account Manager	mtemplate
MIStemp	MIS Template	System Analyst	itemplate

Require the user to change the password at the next logon. Choose the Groups button, remove the Users group for each, and add the corresponding group you created in step 3 (that is, Sales for SalesTemp, Marketing for MarketingTemp, MIS for MISTemp). Choose the Profile button for each, and enter in the login script you created (KITE.BAT) and the home directory c:\users\%USERNAME%, using the drive in which you installed Windows NT that contains the USERS directory (use Windows Explorer to confirm it).

APP F

5. Create the following accounts by copying the appropriate template you created in step 4:

Username	Full Name	Password
Sales		
FlagstonL	Lois Flagston	password
BumsteadB	Blondie Bumstead	password
Marketing		
Dogbert	Dogbert	password
MIS		
GatesB	William Gates	password
BaileyB	Beetle Bailey	password

Notice what elements of the template account are copied (description, password options, group, profile information) and which you need to fill in (username, full name, password).

6. Use Windows Explorer to confirm that the home directories for each account were created.

Exercise 2: Managing User Profiles, Part 1

Complete this exercise from Computer 1.

1. Log on as GatesB. Change the password as instructed. Modify your environment settings by changing the screen colors, adding a wallpaper, and creating a shortcut to Solitaire on the desktop.

2. Log off and log on again as Administrator.

3. Use Windows Explorer to find the WINNT40\PROFILES directory. Notice the new sub-directory structure for GatesB, with the file NTUSER.DAT in the GATESB subdirectory. Expand GATESB to find the Desktop subdirectory, and notice the shortcut to Solitaire there.

4. Find the WINNT40\PROFILES\Default User subdirectory. Expand it to display the Desktop subdirectory. Create a shortcut here for Solitaire (right-click and drag the Solitaire icon from WINNT40\SYSTEM32). Also, rename the NTUSER.DAT file in Default User to NTUSER.OLD and copy the NTUSER.DAT file from GATESB.

5. Create a new user called PAT, with no password and no password options selected.

6. Log on as PAT. Notice that the Solitaire shortcut and the environment settings became part of PAT's profile. This is true not only for each new user you create, but also for any previous user who has not yet logged on for the first time, and thus created his or her own profile.

7. Log back on as Administrator. Use Windows Explorer to delete the NTUSER.DAT file from WINNT40\PROFILES\Default User and rename NTUSER.OLD back to NTUSER.DAT.

Exercise 3: Managing User Profiles, Part 2

1. Use Windows Explorer to create a new directory called Profiles in the root directory of Computer 2. Right-click it and select Sharing, choose Shared As, and select OK. (If you do not have two computers installed, complete this exercise from the same computer and adjust the directions accordingly.)

2. On the first computer, start User Manager. Delete the account PAT. Create a new user account called MEG, with no password and no password options selected. Choose Profile, and in User Profile Path enter \\Computer2\profiles\ntuser.dat.

3. Start the System applet from the Control Panel and switch to the User Profiles tab. Note that there is an entry for Account Deleted, for the account PAT, which you deleted in step 2. Select this entry and choose Delete and Yes.

4. In the list, select the entry for GATESB and choose Copy To.

5. In the Copy Profile To text box enter \\computer2\profiles, or choose Browse to find the directory in Network Neighborhood. In Permitted to Use, select Change and choose MEG from the list (be sure to select Show Users). Choose OK and exit from System.

6. Log on as MEG. Notice that MEG received her profile from the second computer and that her environment settings match those of GATESB.

7. On the first computer, log off and log back in again as Administrator. Open the properties for MEG in User Manager and change the profile file reference from NTUSER.DAT to NTUSER.MAN.

8. Log in as MEG. Notice that you are unable to log in because you have referenced a mandatory profile that does not exist.

9. Log back in as Administrator. Delete the account MEG.

Chapter 6 Lab Exercises

The following exercises are most effective if you use two computers, and if you have one NTFS partition created on each computer. Also, to complete these exercises, you must have completed all exercises from Chapter 5.

Exercise 1: Converting a FAT to NTFS

If you do not currently have an NTFS partition, but have an existing FAT partition that you can convert to NTFS (other than the boot partition), use the following steps to convert it to NTFS:

1. Open a DOS prompt window.

2. At the prompt, type CONVERT D: /FS:NTFS, where D: represents the letter of the partition that you are converting.

3. Press Enter. If there are any files in use by Windows NT on that partition, such as the pagefile, you get a message to the effect that you must reboot for the conversion to take effect. Do so. Otherwise, Windows NT will convert the partition when you press Enter.

APP
F

Exercise 2: Creating an NTFS Partition

If you do not have a partition that you can convert, but do have at least 50MB of free disk space available, you can use Disk Administrator to create an NTFS partition. Follow these steps:

1. Start Disk Administrator. If this is the first time you are starting this utility, click OK to start the message.
2. Click the free disk space available in the graphic screen provided.
3. Choose Partition, Create.
4. Specify the total size of the partition and click OK. The partition should be at least 50MB, and can be no smaller than 10MB.
5. Choose Partition, Commit Changes Now.
6. Choose Tools, Format and NTFS.
7. When the format is complete, exit Disk Administrator.

Exercise 3: Using Shares, Part 1

1. Log on as Administrator.
2. Using Windows Explorer, create the following folders and files on both computers in the NTFS partition, and place a couple lines of text in each file (you don't need to get fancy now):

\TOOLS	DOOM.TXT	(Create new text file)
	BUDGET97.DOC	(Create new WordPad file)
\TOOLS\DATA	MEMO.DOC	WELCOME.TXT

3. Share TOOLS as TOOLS.
4. Remove Everyone from the ACL for the share and add the Managers group, with Change permission, and the Sales group, with Read permission.
5. Create a new user called SimpsonB on Computer 1. Add this user to the Sales group on Computer 1.
6. Log on as SimpsonB on Computer 1.
7. Using Network Neighborhood, access the TOOLS share on Computer 2. Can you access it? Windows NT should tell you that you do not have a valid account or password on Computer 2. Recall that in a workgroup environment, you must either create a valid account for every user that needs access to shared resources on a computer or be able to connect as a valid user.

8. Create the account SimpsonB on Computer 2, using the same password as on Computer 1. Make this account a member of the Sales group on Computer 2.

9. On Computer 1, access the TOOLS share again. Your access should now be successful because you have a valid account on Computer 2 that matches the username and password of the account on Computer 1. Disconnect from the share.

10. On Computer 2, change SimpsonB's password to something else.

11. On Computer 1, right-click Network Neighborhood, and choose Map Network Drive.

12. Choose the TOOLS share from the list displayed, or type the path \\Computer2\TOOLS.

13. In the Connect As box, enter SimpsonB, and click OK. Windows NT requests the password for SimpsonB on Computer 2. Enter it to gain access to the share. If you know the name and password of a valid user account on another computer, you can access the share on that computer.

Exercise 4: Using Shares, Part 2

1. On Computer 1, log on as BrownC.

2. Connect to the TOOLS share on Computer 2.

3. Open the file DOOM.TXT and make a change to the file and close it.

4. Log off, and log in as BumsteadB.

5. Connect to the TOOLS share on Computer 2.

6. Open the file DOOM.TXT and make a change to the file. Note that Windows NT does not let you save changes made to the file because BumsteadB is a member of the Sales group, which has been given Read access to the file. Do not close the file.

7. On Computer 2, make BumsteadB a member of the Managers group.

8. On Computer 1, try to access the file and save changes again. Note that you are not able to save your changes because BumsteadB's access token for the file still reflects the old group membership.

9. Close the file, and try to access it again and save changes. Disconnect from the share and reconnect, modify the file and save the changes. Note for yourself at which point after group membership changes that the change took effect.

Exercise 5: Using Hidden Shares

1. Share the DATA folder on Computer 2 as DATA$. Give only Managers Change permission to the share.

APP

F

2. Log on as BrownC on Computer 1.

3. Using Network Neighborhood, look for the DATA share in the list of shares for Computer 2. You should not see it because the $ makes it a hidden share.

4. Right-click Network Neighborhood, and choose Map Network Drive. In the path box type \\Computer2\DATA$ and choose OK. You should be able to access the share.

5. Modify the file MEMO.DOC and save your changes.

6. Disconnect from the share and log off.

Exercise 6: Exploring File and Folder Permissions, Part 1

1. Log on to both computers as Administrator and make the following changes:

   ■ Modify the NTFS permissions for the TOOLS folder. Remove Everyone and add Managers, with Read permission, and Administrators, with Full Control permission.

   ■ Modify the NTFS permissions for the DATA folder. Remove Everyone and add Sales, with Change permission, and MIS, with Add.

2. Log on to Computer 1 as BrownC.

3. Use Windows Explorer to expand the NTFS partition. Open the file BUDGET97.DOC in TOOLS and modify it.

4. Can you save your changes? Note that the NTFS permission for Managers is Read. Because BrownC is a member of Managers, he also gets Read access to the file and therefore cannot save changes.

5. Log off and log back on as Dilbert, a member of the MIS and Managers group.

6. Use Windows Explorer to access the DATA folder. Because MIS has only Add permission, you cannot access the DATA folder.

7. Use Notepad to create a document called DILBERT.TXT. Try to save it in the DATA folder. (Access denied.) Try to save it in the TOOLS folder. (You have only READ access, so you can't write a file to this folder.) Save it in the root directory of the NTFS partition.

8. Open a DOS prompt window. At the prompt, copy the file DILBERT.TXT from the root of the NTFS partition to the TOOLS\DATA directory. Note that you can do this because you have Add permission to the DATA folder.

9. Log off.

Exercise 7: Exploring File and Folder Permissions, Part 2

1. Log on as BrownC.

2. Access the TOOLS share on Computer 2.

3. Open the file DOOM.TXT and modify it.

4. Save your changes. Can you do it? Not this time. The share permission is Change for Managers, and the NTFS permission is Read for Managers. When accessing a resource through a share, the most restrictive of the permissions becomes the effective permissions. Thus, your effective permission is Read and you cannot save changes.

5. Log on as Administrator on Computer 2.

6. Change the NTFS permission for Managers on TOOLS to Full Control.

7. On Computer 1, reconnect to the share and try to modify and save the file again. This time you can because the effective permission is Change (the more restrictive of the share permission—Change—and the NTFS permission—Full Control).

8. As BrownC, create a new file called BrownC.TXT in the TOOLS directory on Computer 2.

9. Log off.

10. As Administrator on Computer 2, change the NTFS permission for managers on TOOLS to Change.

Exercise 8: Exploring File and Folder Permissions, Part 3

1. Log on as Dilbert on Computer 2.

2. Locate the TOOLS folder on Computer 2.

3. Locate the file BrownC.TXT and display its Security properties (right-click, and then choose Properties, Security).

4. Choose Ownership, and note that BrownC is the owner.

5. Can you take ownership of the file? No, because you have only Change permission.

6. Log off and log back on as Administrator.

7. Add Dilbert to the ACL for the file BrownC.TXT, with the NTFS Special Access Take Ownership permission.

8. Log on as Dilbert again, and try to take ownership of the file. This time you can because you have the permission to do so. Verify that Dilbert is now the owner of BrownC.TXT.

APP
F

Chapter 7 Lab Exercises

The following exercises are designed for computers that have two physical disk drives, and at least 100MB of free space outside an extended partition on one or more drives. If you have less free space, or if the free space includes an area of an extended partition, you need to modify the exercise according to your configuration.

Exercise 1: Using Disk Administrator

1. Start Disk Administrator.

2. Select an area of free space.

3. Choose Partition, Create, and create a new primary partition of 20MB.

4. Create another primary partition of 50MB.

5. Commit the changes.

6. Change the drive letter for the 50MB partition to X and the 20M partition to Y through Tools, Assign Drive Letter.

7. Format drive Y as FAT and drive X as NTFS.

8. Close Disk Administrator and save your changes.

Exercise 2: Using Compression

1. Start Windows Explorer.

2. Select drive Y and create a new folder called TRUMP.

3. Copy WINNT256.BMP from the WINNT40 directory into TRUMP.

4. Look at the properties sheet for the file. Is there a Security tab? Is there a Compress attribute on the General tab? (No! It's a FAT partition!)

5. Copy the folder and its file from drive Y to drive X.

6. Look at the file's properties sheet again. Is there a Security tab and a Compress attribute option? (Yes! It's an NTFS partition!)

7. Enable the Compress attribute for the file and choose Apply. What is its compressed size?

8. Close Windows Explorer.

9. Open a DOS Prompt window by choosing Start, Programs, DOS Prompt.

10. At the prompt, type CONVERT Y: /FS:NTFS, and press Enter. Windows NT converts the partition from FAT to NTFS. (If it tells you to restart, do so.)

11. Start Windows Explorer.

12. Select drive Y and look at the properties of the file in TRUMP. You should now see the Security tab and Compress attribute option because the partition is now NTFS.

Exercise 3: Using Volume Sets

1. Start Disk Administrator.

2. Select drive Y and delete it. Note the confirmation message.

3. Select that area of free space (20MB) and the remaining free space on the drive.

4. Choose Partition, Create Volume Set. Note the change in legend information, indicating the new volume set.

5. Commit your changes, assign it drive letter Y, and format the volume set as FAT.

6. Close Disk Administrator.

7. Start Windows Explorer and select drive Y. Can you tell that it is a volume set? (No! Not even through its properties!) Windows NT treats the volume set as a single drive.

8. Copy TRUMP from the X drive to the Y drive.

9. Close Windows Explorer and start Disk Administrator.

10. Select the second member of Y and choose Partition, Delete. Note the confirmation message, and go ahead with the delete. What did you delete? (The entire volume set.)

11. Close Disk Administrator and start Windows Explorer.

12. Confirm that drive Y is gone.

Exercise 4: Using Extended Volume Sets

1. Start Disk Administrator.

2. Select any FAT partition on your computer, as well as an area of free space on the same or another drive.

3. Choose Partition, Extend Volume Set from the menu. Can you do it? (No! You cannot extend FAT partitions!)

4. Select the NTFS partition drive X and an area of free space on the same drive or another drive.

5. Choose Partition, Extend Volume set. Can you do it? (Yes! You can extend NTFS partitions!) What else do you notice? (The extended set is automatically formatted as NTFS.)

6. Delete drive X. Notice that if you delete any member of the extended volume set, you delete the entire volume set.

Exercise 5: Using Stripe Sets

Creating stripe sets is possible only if you have at least two physical disks with free space on each.

1. Start Disk Administrator.
2. Select an area of free space on one disk and an area of free space on another. (If you have additional disks, select free space on these as well.)
3. Choose Partition, Create Stripe Set.
4. Create the largest stripe set that you are allowed.
5. Notice in Disk Administrator how the stripe set is evenly distributed across the free space on the disks.
6. Delete the stripe set.

Exercise 6: Using Backup and Restore

Backup and Restore work only if you have a working tape drive attached to your computer.

1. Use Disk Administrator to create a 50MB NTFS partition, as drive Z.
2. Use Windows Explorer to create a folder called BITMAPS in this drive, and copy the bitmap files from the WINNT40 directory to BITMAPS.
3. Insert a new tape in the tape backup device.
4. Start Backup by choosing Start, Programs, Administrative Tools, Backup.
5. Select the Z drive and check the check box in front of it to select all its contents. Double-click it to verify that the bitmap folder and all its files have been selected.
6. Choose BACKUP. Enter a tape name, select Verify Files, keep all other defaults, and proceed.
7. When the backup is complete, exit the utility.
8. Use Notepad to view the BACKUP.LOG file created in the WINNT40 directory.
9. Start Windows Explorer.
10. Select drive Z and delete the BITMAPS folder.
11. Start Backup. The existing tape is displayed in the window, with the backup set you created listed.
12. If you appended to an existing tape, select Operations, Catalog to find and load the backup set for the BITMAPS files and folder. Otherwise, double-click the backup set in the tapes window to load the catalog for the backup set.
13. Select all files from the backup set including the BITMAPS folder.

14. Choose Restore and keep all defaults. Be sure the restore path is pointing to drive Z.

15. After the restore completes, exit the utility.

16. Start Windows Explorer and verify that the files and folder have been restored.

Chapter 8 Lab Exercises

The following exercises requires that you have one printer attached to one of your computers and assumes that it is connected to Computer 1. Installing Windows 95 print drivers is also an option if you have the Windows 95 CD-ROM handy.

Exercise 1: Creating a Printer

Even if you have installed a printer already, complete this exercise on Computer 1. Pay close attention to the screens, messages, and available options. Refer to the chapter text to highlight and clarify screens.

1. Start the Add Printer Wizard by choosing My Computer, Printers, Add Printer.

2. Install the printer on your local computer, and choose My Computer.

3. Select the port that your print device is attached to.

4. Select the manufacturer and model of the print device connected to your computer.

5. Set this to be your print default.

6. Call the print device Managers Printer and share the printer as NTPRINT. If you have the Windows 95 source CD-ROM available, select Windows 95 from the list of additional print drivers to support.

7. Print a test page to verify that the configuration works.

8. If necessary, enter the appropriate path to the Windows NT source files to complete installation.

Exercise 2: Optional TCP/IP Exercise

If you have a network TCP/IP printer available that you can use and are allowed to manage, be sure to add the TCP/IP protocol to your computer and repeat Exercise 1. For step 3, choose Add Port and select local port. Enter the IP address of the network printer.

Exercise 3: Connecting to a Network Printer

1. On Computer 2, start the Add Printer Wizard.

2. This time, choose Network Printer Server to connect to the printer you just created on Computer 1.

3. From the Connect to Printer browse screen, expand through the Microsoft Windows Network entries to find the printer you created on Computer 1 called NTPRINT and select it,

or

Type in the UNC path to the printer, as follows:

```
\\COMPUTER1\NTPRINT
```

4. Make this the default printer on Computer 2.

5. Complete the installation. A network printer icon is displayed in the Printers folder.

6. Use Notepad to create and save a short text document called PRINT.TXT that contains simple text such as If you can read this, printing was successful..

7. Print PRINT.TXT to the network printer you just connected to. Was printing successful? (Yes.)

8. On Computer 1, open the NTPRINT print manager window and pause the shared printer.

9. Resubmit PRINT.TXT on Computer 2.

10. In the NTPRINT window, select the PRINT.TXT print job and explore the Document Properties. Schedule the job to print at the next half-hour.

11. Resume the printer and wait until the next half-hour to see your print job print.

Exercise 4: Managing Printer Properties

1. On Computer 1, open the NTPRINT properties sheet and select the Scheduling tab.

2. Set the priority to the highest setting (99).

3. On the Security tab choose Permissions.

4. Remove Everyone and add Managers, with Print permission.

5. Close NTPRINT properties.

6. Create another printer for the same print device on the same port. Call it Staff Printer and share it as STAFFPRT.

7. After it is created, open its properties sheet and select the Scheduling tab.

8. Set the priority to the lowest setting (1).

9. On the Security tab choose Permissions.

10. Remove Everyone and add MIS, with Print permission.

11. Close STAFFPRT properties.

12. Make Dilbert a member of the Power Users group on Computer 1.

13. Log on to Computer 1 as a Manager account, such as Dilbert.

14. Open both the NTPRINT and STAFFPRT windows. Pause NTPRINT and STAFFPRT.

15. Create a text document called TESTP1.TXT that contains the text This is a test print - 1, and print to NTPRINT. You should see this file queued in the NTPRINT window.

16. On Computer 2, log on as GatesB.

17. Connect to STAFFPRT and make it the default.

18. Create a text document called Staffp1.TXT, that contains the text This is a staff test print - 1, and print to STAFFPRT. You should see this file queued in the STAFF-PRT window on Computer 1.

19. Create two more documents on Computer 1 (TESTP2.TXT and TESTP3.TXT, with similar text) and on Computer 2 (Staffp2.TXT and Staffp3.TXT, with similar text) and print them to their respective printers. You will see them queued.

20. Resume STAFFPRT, and then NTPRINT. In what order did the print jobs print? Chances are that because STAFFPRT was resumed first, its low-priority Staffp1.TXT job was sent to the print device ahead of TESTP1.TXT. Nevertheless, before any other staff jobs print, the Managers' jobs will print first because their print queue associated with the same printer has a higher priority than do staff print jobs.

21. If your computer had a previous printer setup, restore it as your default now if you like.

APP
F

Chapter 9 Lab Exercises

Portions of the following exercises require that you have installed at least two 16-bit Windows 3.1 applications. These might be earlier versions of Microsoft Office, or even your favorite Windows games.

Exercise 1: Running DOS and Windows 16-bit Applications

1. Right-click the taskbar and start the Task Manager. Choose View, Select Columns, Base Priority. Resize the Task Manager window so that you can see the Base Priorities column.

2. Switch to Processes. Unless you started a Windows 16-bit application earlier, you should see no entries for NTVDM.

3. Choose Start, Run, and start the MS-DOS application EDIT.COM. This is the 16-bit MS-DOS editor and comes with Windows NT, in the WINN40\SYSTEM32 directory.

4. Switch back to Task Manager and notice the addition of a new NTVDM entry. Notice the amount of memory allocated for it and its priority.

5. Start one of your Windows 16-bit applications.

6. Switch back to Task Manager and notice a new NTVDM entry, with subentries for the application and WOWEXEC.EXE. Notice also its memory usage, CPU usage, and priority settings.

7. Start another Windows 16-bit application. Note the speed with which it loads. Because it is being loaded into an existing WOW NTVDM, it loads rather quickly.

8. Switch back to Task Manager and notice its subentry in the WOW NTVDM, as well as the memory and CPU changes.

9. Close the DOS application and both of the Windows 16-bit applications, and note the changes in Task Manager. The WOW NTVDM remains loaded in case a new Windows 16-bit application starts, but the closed application entries have been removed.

10. Leave Task Manager running.

Exercise 2: Running 16-bit Windows Applications in Their Own Memory Space

1. Start both of the Windows 16-bit applications.

2. Switch to Task Manager and notice the WOW NTVDM sub-entries. On the Performance tab, note the total physical RAM in use.

3. Close one of the Windows 16-bit applications, and notice the change in physical RAM.

4. Create a shortcut on your desktop for the Windows 16-bit application you closed. Right-click it and display its properties. On the Shortcut tab select Run in Separate Memory Space.

5. Start the Windows 16-bit application from its shortcut. Notice that it takes a little longer to load than in Exercise 1. This is because Windows NT must create a new WOW NTVDM for this application.

6. Switch back to Task Manager and confirm that a new WOW NTVDM has been created. Note its memory, CPU, and priority statistics.

7. Switch to the Task Manager Performance tab and note the total physical RAM in use. It is noticeably higher than when both applications ran in the same WOW NTVDM.

8. Close each Windows 16-bit application and monitor the decrease in physical RAM used. How many WOW NTVDM entries remain on the Processes tab? (One.)

Exercise 3: Managing Process Priorities

1. Start Pinball by choosing Start, Programs, Accessories, Games. If it is not available, load it through the Add Programs applet in Control Panel. (A quick way to activate a Pinball game and notice changes in this exercise is to run a demo game from the Game menu.)

2. Switch to Task Manager and find its entry. Notice that its priority is set to Normal.

3. Close Pinball. Open a DOS Command Prompt window.

4. Start Pinball with a low priority by typing

   ```
   START  /LOW  PINBALL
   ```

5. Switch to Task Manager and verify that Pinball is running with low priority. Pinball itself should appear to be running a bit sluggishly, though on fast Pentium systems the decrease in speed might not be noticeable.

6. On the Processes tab in Task Manager, right-click the Pinball entry and choose Set Priority. Change the priority to normal. Switch to the Performance tab and arrange Pinball so that you can see part of the Performance charts in the background. Notice that the charts continue to record data while you play Pinball.

7. Switch to Task Manager. On the Processes tab, right-click Pinball and change its priority to high. Switch to the Performance tab and arrange the screens as before. Notice that the chart ceases to record, or it records very slowly while you play Pinball in the foreground.

8. Close Pinball and Task Manager.

APP

F

Chapter 10 Lab Exercises

Exercise 1: Managing Network Properties

Complete this exercise from both Computer 1 and Computer 2.

1. Start the Network applet from Control Panel (or right-click Network Neighborhood and view its properties).

2. Select the Adapters tab to view your installed network adapter card.

3. Select the adapter card from the list and choose Properties. Note the properties of your adapter.

4. Close the adapter properties window and select the Bindings tab. Record the bindings for NetBEUI under NetBIOS, Workstation, and Server.

5. Select the Protocols tab and note that only NetBEUI is installed (unless you did something that I didn't tell you to do in another exercise).

6. Choose Add, and select TCP/IP from the network protocols list. Be sure to have the source CD-ROM available. When prompted, enter the drive and path to the source files.

7. After the protocol is installed, choose OK. Windows NT prompts you for TCP/IP protocol settings. For Computer 1, enter 121.132.4.1 with subnet mask 255.255.255.0, and for Computer 2, enter 121.132.4.2 with subnet mask 255.255.255.0. (If you are connected to your company network and are using TCP/IP, use your company's recommended IP address and subnet mask, if appropriate. If you have a DHCP server available, and can use it, configure the computers to obtain their IP addresses from the DHCP server.)

8. Restart Windows NT when prompted. After Windows NT reboots, open the Network applet again.

9. On the Bindings tab, note the additional bindings for TCP/IP. Record these and compare them against the NetBEUI bindings. Notice that both bindings are bound to the Workstation and Server service. This means that you can connect to network resources on any server by using NetBEUI or TCP/IP, and that your computer can service requests from any computer by using NetBEUI or TCP/IP.

10. At a command prompt, enter the command IPCONFIG. What information is displayed? (IP address, subnet mask, and default gateway.) Record the information.

11. Now enter the command IPCONFIG /ALL. What additional information is displayed? (Host, DNS, node and other Windows NT IP configuration parameters, and the description and physical address of the adapter card.) Record the adapter information.

12. At the command prompt, PING the other computer's address. For example, on Computer 1 type PING 121.132.4.1. You should receive four Reply from... messages, indicating that communication is established between the computers.

13. Through Windows Explorer, map a network drive to a resource on Computer 2. You should be successful. Disconnect the mapping.

14. In the Network applet on Computer 1, select the Protocols tab and remove NetBEUI. Restart Windows NT when prompted.

15. After Windows NT reboots, use Windows Explorer to map a drive to the same resource on Computer 2. You should be successful. Why? (Windows NT used

TCP/IP to establish the connection. Computer 2 has both NetBEUI and TCP/IP installed.) Disconnect the mapping.

16. In the Network applet on Computer 2, select the Protocols tab and display the properties for TCP/IP.

17. Change the subnet mask to `255.255.0.0`. Restart Windows NT when prompted.

18. When Computer 2 reboots, use Windows Explorer on Computer 1 to map a drive to the same resource on Computer 2. You should be unsuccessful this time. Why? (Even though both computers are using TCP/IP and are on the same subnet, they have different subnet masks and so are treated as though they are on different subnets. Therefore, they cannot communicate with each other.)

19. At a command prompt, try the `PING` command again. You should be unsuccessful, for the same reason as in step 18.

20. Change the subnet mask on Computer 2 back to `255.255.255.0`. After the computer reboots, verify that communications can be established between the computers. (Use `PING` and Windows Explorer.)

21. Reinstall NetBEUI on Computer 1. Restart Windows NT when prompted.

Exercise 2: Using Workstation Bindings

1. In the Network applet on Computer 1, select the Bindings tab and expand the Workstation bindings. Highlight Workstation in the list and choose Disable to disable its bindings. Choose OK, and restart Windows NT when prompted.

APP F

2. When Computer 1 reboots, you are likely to get a service message error. Use Event Viewer to note which service failed to start (Workstation), and what other services dependent on it also failed to start (Computer Browser, Messenger).

3. Use Network Neighborhood to locate Computer 2. Were you successful? (No, because the Workstation service is used to perform this network request, and its bindings have been disabled.)

4. Use Network Neighborhood to locate Computer 1. Were you successful? (Yes.) Connect to a shared folder on Computer 1 and copy a file to your desktop. Were you successful? Yes. Why? (The Server service on Computer 1 handles requests for resources from other computers. These bindings are still enabled, so Computer 1 can't browse the network, but it can still share its own resources. This tactic can be used to optimize bindings and improve network performance for Windows NT computers that only need to make their resources available to other computers, but not establish connections of their own.)

5. Reenable the Workstation bindings on Computer 1 and restart Windows NT when prompted.

Exercise 3: Using RAS

To complete this exercise, you must have either a null modem cable to connect to the COM1 port on both computers, or modems installed in both computers and a separate working phone line and number for each. Perform these steps on both computers.

1. Log on as Administrator.

2. Start the Network applet, and select the Services tab.

3. Choose Add, and select Remote Access Service from the list. Be sure to have the source files ready and provide Windows NT with the installation path when prompted.

4. The New Modem Wizard appears. If you are using a modem, let Windows NT detect it. Otherwise, choose to select it yourself, and select Dial-Up Networking Serial Cables Between 2 PCs. As you continue through the wizard, choose COM1, specify your country and area code, and finish the modem installation.

5. Next, you need to configure the COM port. In the RAS Setup dialog box, choose the COM port from the list and select Configure. On Computer 1 choose Dial Out Only and on Computer 2 select Dial Out and Receive Calls. Then choose OK.

6. Select the Network button and verify that all protocols are selected for both computers. For each protocol on Computer 2 under server settings, be sure that the Entire Network option is selected. For TCP/IP, select Use Static Address Pool and enter 121.132.4.100 and 121.132.4.110 as the beginning and ending addresses.

7. Choose OK and complete RAS installation. Choose No when asked if you want to enable NetBIOS Broadcast Propagation. Restart Windows NT when prompted.

8. After Windows NT reboots, start the Remote Access Admin program on Computer 2 (from the Administrative Tools folder).

9. Choose Users, Permissions, Grant All to grant permission to all users.

10. On Computer 1, start the Dial-Up Networking program from Accessories. Create a phonebook entry for Computer 2 (be creative). Leave the phone number blank if using a null modem cable, or the actual phone number if you are configured with modems and separate phone lines.

11. Disconnect Computer 1's network cable connection.

12. Connect the null modem cable to the COM1 port on both computers.

13. Restart Windows NT on Computer 1. When the logon box appears, select Logon using Dial-Up Networking. Select the phonebook entry you created for Computer 2 as your dial-up number, and choose Dial. If prompted for a password, enter the appropriate password for your account. RAS connects you to Computer 2.

14. Use Windows Explorer to connect to a resource on Computer 2. Were you successful? (Yes. You are connected using RAS.)

15. Note the connection statistics recorded in the Remote Access Admin utility on Computer 2.

16. Start the Dial-Up Networking program again, and choose Hang Up.

17. Remove RAS from both computers by starting the Network Applet, selecting Remote Access Service from the Services tab, and choosing Remove. Answer Yes to the warning message, and restart Windows NT when prompted.

18. Reconnect Computer 1 to the network and remove the null modem cable from both computers.

Exercise 4: Using NetWare Connectivity

Complete this exercise if you have access to a NetWare server. Create an account on your Windows NT Workstation that matches your account and password on the NetWare server. Make this account a member of the Administrators local group on your Windows NT workstation.

1. Start the Network applet on Computer 1. On the Protocols tab, select Add, and choose NWLink from the list. Be sure to have the source files available. On the Services tab select Add, and choose Client Services for NetWare from the list. Choose OK, and restart Windows NT when prompted.

2. When Windows NT restarts, log on using the Windows NT account you created to match the account on the NetWare server. You are prompted for a preferred NetWare server. Select the NetWare server that you have access to, and choose OK. You are logged in to the NetWare server.

3. Start the newly added CSNW applet in Control Panel. Review the options that are available. If your NetWare server is version 4.x, enter any NDS information that is appropriate.

4. From Windows Explorer, choose Tools, Map Network Drive. Notice the new entry for NetWare or Compatible Network. Expand this entry and find your server in the list.

5. Expand the server entry and select a directory that you have access to. Connect to it. If there is another server on which you have an account, select it from the list, choose a folder, and in the Connect As box, enter the logon ID for that NetWare server. CSNW completes the connection, probably asking for a password for that server.

6. Disconnect from both NetWare servers.

7. In the CSNW applet, set the preferred server to <NONE>.

APP
F

Exercise 5: Installing Peer Web Services

Complete this exercise from Computer 1

1. Log on as Administrator.

2. Start the Network applet, select the Services tab, choose Add, and select Peer Web Services from the list. Be sure to have the source files available.

3. Select all the options except ODBC drivers.

4. Accept all the other defaults, and complete the setup. Restart Windows NT when prompted.

5. When Windows NT reboots, check the Services applet to see what additional services have been installed. (FTP Publishing, Gopher Publishing, WWW Publishing Services.)

6. From Windows Explorer, check the Windows NT system file partition for the INETPUB folder. Share it as INETPUB. Find the WINNT40\SYSTEM32\INETSRV\IISADMIN folder and copy it to INETPUB.

7. Start Internet Explorer. Read the startup document. In the Address box enter \\COMPUTER1\INETPUB\WWWROOT\Default.htm. This displays one of the sample Web page documents that is installed. Browse through it, clicking the hypertext links to display other documents. Be careful because some of those links are designed to connect you directly to Microsoft's Web site on the Internet. If you do not have Internet access, don't select these. (Hint: As you place your mouse pointer over a link, its target is displayed in the status line at the bottom of the Internet Explorer window.)

8. Start Internet Explorer on Computer 2. In the Address window, enter \\COMPUTER1\INETPUB\WWWROOT\Default.htm. You are using Computer 1 as if it were an intranet publishing site for your workgroup.

9. From either computer, enter the address \\COMPUTER1\INETPUB\IISADMIN\HTMLDOCS\iisdocs.htm. This is the Installation and Planning Guide for Peer Web Services site. Happy surfing!

Chapter 11 Lab Exercises

Exercise 1: Optimizing Virtual Memory

This exercise assumes that you have at least two physical disk drives installed and formatted on your computer.

1. Start Windows NT Diagnostics, and determine how much RAM you have installed on your computer.

2. Start the System applet from Control Panel, and switch to the Performance Tab. Choose Virtual Memory.

3. Note the location, initial, and maximum sizes of the pagefile. Verify that the pagefile is 12 + physical RAM (on some computers this may be 11 + physical RAM because of the way BIOS reads memory addresses).

4. Change the pagefile size so that the initial and maximum values are half what they were.

5. Restart the computer. You might get a message that the pagefile is inadequately sized for the computer. If this is the case, Windows NT displays the virtual memory window. If it does not, open it again.

6. Change the pagefile size back to what it was. Restart the computer and verify that the error message (if any) has gone away.

7. Open the virtual memory window again and create a second pagefile on another disk. Make it the same size as the original page file. (If you can, continue with steps 8–10. Otherwise skip to step 11.)

8. Remove the original pagefile by selecting it and deleting its initial and maximum values, and choosing SET.

9. Restart Windows NT. The computer should start without a problem. Windows NT is using the new pagefile you created on the other disk drive.

10. Open the virtual memory window again and create the original pagefile again.

11. Restart Windows NT. The computer should start without a problem. Windows NT now has two pagefiles to use and writes to each concurrently if your computer's disk controller supports it.

12. Delete the second pagefile and leave only the original. Restart Windows NT.

APP
F

Exercise 2: Using Event Viewer to Troubleshoot

1. Use the Services applet in Control Panel to change the startup value for the Messenger Service to Manual.

2. Restart Windows NT. You should get the message `At least one service or driver failed to start..`

3. Start Event Viewer and look for the first Eventlog entry for the approximate time you restarted Windows NT. Look at the message for the first Stop error right above it. This entry tells you that the Messenger service failed to start.

4. Use Services in Control Panel to set the Messenger Service startup value back to Automatic, and restart the computer.

5. The error message should not now occur.

Exercise 3: Viewing Audit Events

1. If you haven't already, start User Manager. From Policy, Audit, enable auditing for successful and failed logons and logoffs.

2. Log on to the workstation as BrownC, using the wrong password.

3. Try again, using the correct password.

4. Log off and log back on as Administrator.

5. Start the Event Viewer and switch to the Security Log.

6. Locate, or filter, Logon/Logoff entries.

7. Find the entry for the incorrect password. (Hint: Look for the lock icon.) What information do you get? (Reason for the failure, the user account involved, and the workstation on which the logon attempt took place among other things.)

8. Review the entries for the successful logons.

9. Close Event Viewer.

Exercise 4: Using Performance Monitor

1. At a command prompt type DISKPERF -Y.

2. If your computer has more than 16MB RAM installed, modify the BOOT.INI file so that you boot with only 16MB of RAM: To the line under [Operating Systems] that contains the location of the NT 4.0 workstation system files add the switch /MAXMEM:16. (Remember that BOOT.INI is a read-only file.)

3. Shut down and restart Windows NT to enable the Performance Monitor disk objects and their counters.

4. Start Windows Explorer and Pinball.

5. Start the Performance Monitor from the Administrative Tools group, and add the desired objects and counters to a new chart.

6. Track the values of each of the counters you added to the chart, especially noting the working set values for Performance Monitor, Windows Explorer, and Pinball (about 2.2MB, 175KB, and 184KB, respectively). Note also the commit limit for the pagefile (which varies). (Hint: Press Ctrl+H to highlight each line graph.)

7. Switch to Explorer, and create a new folder called PERFMON. Switch to Pinball, and start the demo game.

8. Track the activity of the chart again, and note the average values for each of the counters in the chart. Note any significant changes. In particular you should have noticed a spike for %Processor Time for the processor and each of the three processes driven proportionately as each one performed its activity (creating the

folder, running the demo game, updating the chart with the new statistics). Notice the initial flurry in disk counter activity, and then how it settles after the actions were performed. Notice, too, the increased amount of memory required by Pinball and Performance Monitor to correspond with their activities. Multiply Pages/Sec and Avg. Disk sec/Transfer to obtain the percentage of disk I/O related to pagefile activity. It is well below Microsoft's suggested 10% threshold.

9. Switch to Windows Explorer. Copy the files from the WINNT40 directory into the PERFMON folder. While the copy is taking place, switch to the Performance Monitor and note the Pages/Sec and Avg. Disk sec/Transfer. These have all peaked at or near the top of the scale. Multiply the average value for each together to obtain a percentage. This should be just over 10% and indicates that for this activity, the percentage of disk I/O related to pagefile activity was greater than Microsoft's recommended 10%. If this was consistently above 10%, you might consider adding more RAM.

10. Open the BOOT.INI file and remove the /MAXMEM:16 switch. Restart Windows NT.

11. If you have more than 16MB RAM installed, repeat steps 4–9 and note the differences. (All disk values and processor times should be less, though they vary depending on the amount of additional RAM you have.)

12. Close Windows Explorer and Pinball.

APP
F

Exercise 5: Using Performance Monitor Logs

1. With Performance Monitor still running, select View from the menu, and then select LOG. Choose Add to Log, and add each of the following objects to the log: Logical Disk, Memory, Process, Processor. Then choose Done.

2. Select Options from the menu, and then choose LOG. Enter PERF1.LOG for the log name and save it in the PERFMON folder. Set the interval to 1 second, and choose Start Log.

3. Start Pinball, and run the demo. Start Windows Explorer, and create a new folder called PERFMON2. Copy everything from PERFMON into PERFMON2.

4. Switch to Performance Monitor. Wait another minute, and then select Options, LOG, and Stop Log. Save the log file.

5. Select File, New Chart to clear and reset the chart view for new values.

6. Select Options, Data From. Under Log File, find and select the PERF1.LOG file you just created. Choose OK.

7. Select Edit, Add to Chart. Note that the entries listed represent those you collected during the log process. Add the following objects and counters to the chart as you did before. This time, the chart represents static data collected from the log.

Object	Processor	Instance
Processor	%Processor Time	0
Process	%Processor Time	Perfmon, Explorer, Pinball
Process	Working Set	Perfmon, Explorer, Pinball
Memory	Commit Limit	N/A
Memory	Pages/Sec	N/A
Logical Disk	Avg. Disk sec/ Transfer	pagefile drive
Logical Disk	%Disk Time	pagefile drive

8. Note the average values for each during the log period.

9. Use Edit, Time Window to change the time range to show only the period of peak activity. Note how the average values change.

10. Close Performance Monitor.

11. Use Windows Explorer to delete the folders PERFMON and PERFMON2.

Suggested Reading

Titles from Que and Macmillan USA

Que Corporation and Macmillan USA offer a wide variety of technical books for all levels of users. The following are some recommended titles that can provide you with additional information on many of the exam topics and objectives.

Tip

To order any books from Que Corporation or other imprints of Macmillan USA, call 800-428-5331, visit Macmillan's Web site at **www.informit.com**, or check your local bookseller.

MCSE Fast Track: Windows NT Server 4

Author: Emmett Dulaney

ISBN: 1-56205-935-1

New Riders

MCSE Fast Track: Windows NT Server 4 Enterprise

Author: Emmett Dulaney

ISBN: 1-56205-940-8

New Riders

MCSE Fast Track: Windows NT Workstation 4

Author: Emmett Dulaney

ISBN: 1-56205-938-6

New Riders

MCSE Fast Track: Networking Essentials

Author: Emmett Dulaney

ISBN: 1-56205-939-4

New Riders

Windows NT 4.0 Installation and Configuration Handbook

Author: Jim Boyce

ISBN: 0-7897-0818-3

Que

Special Edition Using Windows NT Server 4.0

Author: Roger Jennings

ISBN: 0-7897-1388-8

Que

Special Edition Using Windows NT Workstation 4.0

Author: Paul Sanna

ISBN: 0-7897-0673-3

Que

Windows NT 4.0 User Manual

Author: Jim Boyce

ISBN 0-7897-1954-1

Que

Peter Norton's Complete Guide to Windows NT 4.0 Workstation, 1999 Edition

Author: Peter Norton

ISBN: 0-672-31373-1

Sams

Other Titles

Advanced Windows, 3rd Edition, by Jeffrey Richter (Microsoft Press; ISBN: 1-5723-1548-2)

Inside Windows NT Server 4.0, 2nd Edition, by Drew Heywood (New Riders Publishing; ISBN: 1-56205-860-6)

Mastering Windows NT Server 4, 6th Edition, by Mark Minasi (Sybex; ISBN: 0-7821-2445-3)

Microsoft Windows NT Network Administration Kit (Version 4.0) (Microsoft Press; ISBN: 1-57231-832-5)

Windows NT 4 Server Unleashed: Professional Reference Edition, by Jason Garms, et al (Sams Publishing; ISBN: 0-672-31002-3)

APP
G

FAT (File Allocation Table), 22, 220
  characteristics, 220-221
  NTFS comparison, 51
  partitions, 81-82, 222
  Windows 4.0 NT support, 22
FAT32 (Windows 95 file system), 220-221
Fault Tolerance (Windows NT Server 4.0), Disk Administrator, 235
FDISK, 82, 226
File Allocation Table. *See* FAT
File and Print Service (FPNW), 340
File Manager, 26
File menu (Explorer), 108
File System layer (networks), 309-310
file systems
  CDFS, 220
  CONVERT.EXE , 222
  FAT
    characteristics, 220-221
    FAT/NTFS partition conversion, 222
    NTFS comparison, 51
    uninstallation process, 81-82
    Windows 4.0 NT support, 22
  FAT32, 220-221
  HPFS, 52, 220
  NTFS, 22, 220
    characteristics, 221-222
    compression, 225-226
    FAT comparison, 51
    FAT/NTFS partition conversion, 222
    permissions, 205-210
    uninstallation process, 82-83
  Sector Sparing, 222
  selecting, 51
  supported, 220
  Transaction Tracking, 222
  Windows NT 4.0 support, 22
files. *See also* folders
  answer, 66-68
  Backup utility
    backups, 239-241
    restores, 241-243
  boot sector, troubleshooting, 79
  BOOT.INI, 73-75, 78
  characterization data (print drivers), 257

  compression, 225
    COMPACT.EXE utility, 226
    enabling, 225-226
    spool files, 258
  copying
    Setup Wizard, 60
    xcopy command (DOS), 66
  corrupted, 246
  deleting, 104
  executables, 46
  installation files, 45, 48
  log
    Application Log, 358
    duration, 360
    entry information, 359
    Error entry, 359
    Event Viewer, 358
    Failure Audit entry, 359
    filtering entries, 360
    Information entry, 359
    Performance Monitor, 365
    searching entries, 360
    Security Log, 358
    size, 360
    sorting entries, 360
    Success Audit entry, 359
    System Log, 358
    Warning entry, 359
  names
    8.3, 223
    long, 222-225
  NTDETECT.COM, troubleshooting, 79
  NTLDR, troubleshooting, 78
  NTOSKRNL.EXE, troubleshooting, 79
  ownership, 210
  pagefiles
    default size, 352
    moving, 353-354
    multiple, 356-357
    optimizing location, 353-354
    optimizing size, 354-356
    planning location, 353
    planning size, 352-353
    viewing size, 355
  permissions, 192, 205-206
    copying, 211
    editing, 209
    moving, 211
    NTFS, 205-210
    setting, 208-209
    share-level permissions comparison, 206
    standard, 208

  recovering, 104
  Registry, 80
  size, 22
  swap, 350
  synchronizing, 105-106
  uniqueness data files (UDFs), 68-69
Filter dialog box, 360
filtering log file entries, 360
Find command, accessing shared folders, 202-203
FIND KEY function, 141
Find utility
  Help program, 112-113
  Start menu, 100, 109-110
Finger utility (TCP/IP), 316
firewalls, 332
first-time installation, 46
floating-point modules (Setup Wizard), 56
floppy disks. *See* disks
folders. *See also* files
  Backup utility
    backups, 239-241
    restores, 241-243
  compression, 225-226
  corrupted, 246
  ownership, 210
  permissions, 192, 205-206
    copying files, 211
    editing, 209
    moving files, 211
    NTFS, 205-210
    setting, 208-209
    share-level permissions comparison, 206
    standard, 207
  Printer, 276
  PWS, 340
  shared, 197
    access, 198, 201-205
    adding permissions, 198
    Explorer, 204
    Find command, 202-203
    My Computer, 203-205
    Network Neighborhood, 201-202
    planning permissions, 200
    share-level permissions, 199
  spool (printing), 258
Fonts applet (Control Panel), 124
forcedos command, 295
format, Microsoft certification exams, 2

V

Exam Guide

The One Source for Comprehensive Solutions™

The one stop shop for serious users, *Exam Guide* offers readers a thorough understanding of software and technologies. Intermediate to advanced users get detailed coverage that is clearly presented and to the point.

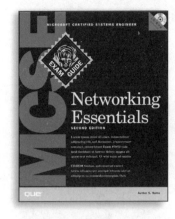

MCSE Networking
Essentials Exam
Guide, Second
Edition
0-7897-2265-8
Dan York
$39.99 US/
$57.95 CAN

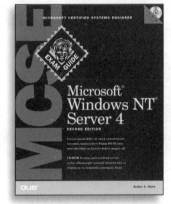

MCSE Microsoft
Windows NT
Server 4 Exam
Guide, Second
Edition
0-7897-2264-X
Emmett Dulaney
$39.99 US/
$57.95 CAN

MCSE Windows NT
Enterprise Server 4
Exam Guide,
Second Edition
0-7897-2263-1
Emmett Dulaney
$39.99 US/
$57.95 CAN

All prices are subject to change.

What's on the Disc

The companion CD-ROM contains Que's new TestPro test engine as well as MCSE Networking Essentials, Second Edition in Adobe PDF format.

Windows 95 Installation Instructions

1. Insert the CD-ROM disc into your CD-ROM drive.
2. From the Windows 95 desktop, double-click on the My Computer icon.
3. Double-click on the icon representing your CD-ROM drive.
4. Double-click on the icon titled START.EXE to run the installation program.

Note: If Windows 95 is installed on your computer, and you have the AutoPlay feature enabled, the START.EXE program starts automatically whenever you insert the disc into your CD-ROM drive.

Windows NT Installation Instructions

1. Insert the CD-ROM disc into your CD-ROM drive.
2. From File Manager or Program Manager, choose Run from the File menu.
3. Type `<drive>\START.EXE` and press Enter, where `<drive>` corresponds to the drive letter of your CD-ROM. For example, if your CD-ROM is drive D:, type `D:\START.EXE` and press Enter.

Technical Support from Macmillan

We can't help you with Windows or Macintosh problems or software from third parties, but we can assist you if a problem arises with the CD-ROM itself.

Email Support: Send email to `http://www.mcp.com/support`

Telephone: (317) 581-3833

Fax: (317) 581-4773

Mail: Macmillan USA
Attention: Support Department
201 West 103rd Street
Indianapolis, IN 46290-1093

Here's how to reach us on the Internet:

World Wide Web

`http://www.quecorp.com`